THE PLEBEIAN REPUBLIC

Cecilia Méndez

The Plebeian Republic

THE HUANTA REBELLION AND

THE MAKING OF THE PERUVIAN STATE,

1820–1850

Duke University Press   Durham and London

2005

© 2005 Duke University Press

All rights reserved

Printed in the United States of America

on acid-free paper ∞

Designed by C. H. Westmoreland

Typeset in Dante with Egyptienne display

by Keystone Typesetting, Inc.

Library of Congress Cataloging-in-

Publication Data appear on the last

printed page of this book.

FOR JOSÉ

AND SHAUNA

Contents

Illustrations

Under the title of general, . . . [Huachaca] has not only established himself as a justice of the peace and governor, but he has moreover set himself up as the supreme chief of the *republiqueta* of Iquicha. And since the government itself seems to have tolerated and confirmed the different titles that the *señorones* of Iquicha have arrogated themselves and presents them with this and that other gift, the attorney refrains from opening process, for he does not know for certain what set of laws [i.e., *fuero*] protects Don Antonio Huachaca. Therefore, should you deem it convenient, you may direct this dossier to the illustrious prefecture, in order for it confirm, in written fashion, the titles, honors, prerogatives and immunities that the government has bestowed upon the titled General Huachaca, and so it be public.

—ATTORNEY VALDIVIA to the Minister of the Superior
Court of Justice of Arequipa and *Juez de Letras*.
Ayacucho, February 16, 1838

There was widespread disgust and aversion among the old aristocrats toward the turn of events in the republican experiment.

—JORGE BASADRE, *Historia de la República del Perú*, 1983

Acknowledgments

In Peru in the eighties, violent death became a routine event as Sendero Luminoso's insurgency acquired greater proportions. During the early stages of the war, however, other than experiencing frequent power outages, we *Limeños* did not feel much affected. The death toll then was worst in the south-central departments of the highlands, most prominently in Ayacucho. It was during these early years of the war, in the early to mid-eighties, that I completed my university education in Lima and became a historian. But it was not until I moved to Ayacucho between 1986 and 1987 that the reality of the violence began to have a major impact on my work—this book attests to what extent.

On my subsequent trips to the highlands of Huanta in the early to late nineties I continued to nurture the dialogue between past and present that I have sought deliberately to keep alive during the lengthy process of writing this book. Present-day Huanta's war-torn agrarian landscape has informed my representation of Huanta's nineteenth-century rural landscape. My conversations with villagers and communal authorities, and the simple observation of the geography and facts of life in the *punas,* the highest ecological niche where humans settle in the Andes, rendered meaningful often difficult and decontextualized archival data.

Although the events this book deals with are not directly connected to Peru's recent wave of violence, my motivations were. Writing about a nineteenth-century uprising in Ayacucho was probably my way of coming to terms with a present which I did not feel prepared to deal with in more direct ways—or could not otherwise grasp as rationally. To say it more optimistically (and "professionally"), as a historian I felt driven to dig up the past in search of answers to the present. Be that as it may, the feelings of fear and confusion that prompted me to write about Ayacucho in the first place did not dissipate after I had left the scene of the war to become established in purportedly safer places, and for this reason bringing this book to completion felt at times beyond my strength. Luckily, I have counted on the support of many people, and thus my list of acknowledgments, though necessarily incomplete, is lengthy.

I should like to thank in the first place my friends and colleagues in Ayacucho, Delia Martínez, Jaime Urrutia, Denise Pozzi-Escot, Alicia Echecopar, Juan Granda, Enrique Gonzales Carré, and Teresa Carrasco, with whom I shared not only my very first concerns about the history of Huanta back in 1986–87, but a very important stage in my life as well. The same goes for my students at the Universidad Nacional de San Cristóbal de Huamanga. More directly related to this research, I wish to thank Víctor Solier for his effective research assistance in the Archivo de Huamanga and Mauro Vega and Marcela Llosa for the same in the archives of Lima. I am most grateful to Jeffrey Gamarra and Luli Abarca, who were always ready to shelter me during the worst moments of my trips to Ayacucho, and to José Coronel for being such a generous colleague and hospitable host. The Centro de Investigación y Promoción para el Desarrollo y la Paz en Ayacucho (IPAZ), directed by Jeffrey Gamarra, provided the necessary environment and logistics for two trips to the Huanta communities in 1994 and 1997, respectively. Renée Palomino of the Asociación Yactan Chicta Qatari Chisu generously volunteered to be my guide and interpreter during a crucial trip to Uchuraccay and other puna communities in 1998. On that same trip, fate led me to Ms. Julia viuda de Argumedo, who generously shared delicate information about the times of violence and about life in Chacabamba. The *comuneros* (community peasants), authorities, and *ronderos* (peasant patrollers) of Cunya, Uchuraccay, Chaca, Ccarhauhurán, Secce, Iquicha, and Huaychao patiently endured all my intrusions. I am also grateful to Leoncio Cárdenas and Arturo Tineo for allowing me to work in their archives in Huanta and Huamanga, respectively, and to Ponciano del Pino for sharing his knowledge about the location of documents in Huanta. Philip Bennett provided me with a transcript that became crucial in the early stage of my investigation, and Delia Martinez helped translate the Quechan segments in it.

At the State University of New York at Stony Brook, where the first drafts of this book were written, I wish to thank my professors Brooke Larson and Barbara Weinstein for their exemplary dedication to their students, their critical advice, constant support, and lasting faith in my work. Larson's seminars, in particular, provided solid theoretical foundations from which I still profit, as well as priceless advice in the "art" of writing grant proposals. Weinstein's classes exposed me to the most vital North American scholarship on Latin America. Also at Stony Brook, Gary Marker and Fred Weinstein introduced me to a non–Latin American literature that proved to be crucial. In New York City, Deborah Poole's anthropologically informed advice was eye-opening. From among my friends at Stony Brook I wish to thank in particular Eleonora Falco, Isabel Soveral, Iván Almeida, Eduardo Prado, Ariel de la Fuenta, María Cecilía Cangiano, Silvana Palermo, and Sergio Serulnikov for many significant moments.

In Lima, where I learned the historian's craft and where part of me still lives, a stimulating group of friends and colleagues made my research a truly unpredictable intellectual adventure and a real pleasure. I thank, in particular, Betford Betalleluz, Juan Carlos Estenssoro, Susana Aldana, Gabriela Ramos, Alfredo Tapia, Cecilia Monteagudo, Jesús Cosmalón, Ricardo Portocarrero, Natalia Majluf, and Beatriz Garland. Pedro Guíbovich and Luis Eduardo Wuffarden proved helpful with their erudition at different moments, and Víctor Peralta and Marta Irurozqui made me feel at home everywhere. Jaime Antezana introduced me to the Iquichanos in Huachipa. Maruja Martínez (no longer with us) opened the doors of SUR, Casa de Estudios de Socialismo, where I presented several advances of this research. Carlos Iván Degregori, Carlos Contreras, and Cecilia Blondet did as much at the Instituto de Estudios Peruanos. Nicanor Domínguez created the earliest versions of the maps that appear in this book, which were subsequently digitalized by Óscar Multiservicios Gráficos in Lima, and then painstakingly redrawn by Natalie Hanemann, who produced the final digital versions. Luis Paredes generously provided me with rare maps that shed valuable information on Iquicha.

This project benefited from several grants which provided financial aid for both the research and writing stages. Support was forthcoming from the Social Science Research Council of New York, The Wenner-Gren Foundation for Anthropological Research, The Harry Frank Guggenheim Foundation, the Mildred and Herbert Weisinger Dissertation Fellowship, and the Beca de Hispanistas Extranjeros granted by the Ministry of Foreign Affairs of Spain, thanks to which I was able to expand my research in the Archivo de Indias in Sevilla and in the libraries of Madrid in the spring of 1994. The hospitality of Fermín del Pino in Madrid and that of Raúl Navarro in Sevilla was especially encouraging on that occasion as was the friendship of Eduardo Flores Clair.

Another important stage in the production of this book took place at Yale University, thanks to a postdoctoral fellowship provided by the Program in Agrarian Studies. My special thanks to James Scott, the program director, for his painstaking comments on an early draft of this book; to Larry Lohmann, Tom Abercrombie, Enrique Mayer, and Bill Christian for stimulating discussions; and to Kay Mansfield for being so welcoming. While I was at Yale the manuscript also profited from long-distance comments by Orin Starn and John Lynch.

Most of the early chapters of this book were originally drafted in Spanish and then translated into English by Renzo Llorente. I subsequently rewrote the entire manuscript in English, in which process I was assisted by several graduate students from the University of California in Santa Barbara: Alistair Hatting and Hugo Hernández provided stylistic and copyediting help on early versions; David Torres-Rouff and Steven Pent did as much in the close-to-final and final versions, respectively. A sketchy Spanish version of chapter 6 was published as "Pactos sin tributo: caudillos y campesinos en el nacimiento de la república," in Rossana Barragán et al., *El Siglo xix en Bolivia y América Latina* (La Paz: IFEA, 1997). Chapter 6 also includes material that appeared in "The Power of Naming, or the Construction of Ethnic and National Identities in Peru: Myth, History and the Iquichanos," *Past and Present*, 171, May 2001: 127–60.

This book reached completion at the University of California in Santa Barbara, where I have been teaching since 1997. The University provided additional funds for new trips to Ayacucho and teaching release time that was crucial for the completion of this project. I was also lucky to count on the supportive environment provided by my colleagues in the History Department, Alice O'Connor, Mary Furner, Erika Rappaport, Stephan Miescher, John Lee, Adrienne Edgar, Hilary Bernstein, David Rock, Sarah Cline, Frank Dutra, and Gabriela Soto Laveaga, among many others. Also while in Santa Barbara, I profited from long-distance comments by, and fruitful intellectual exchange with, Karen Spalding (who eventually disclosed her identity as one of Duke's "anonymous readers") and David Cahill. My "long-distance" friends Brett Troyan and Carmen McEvoy added their quota of hope to my work on more than one critical occasion, for which I am very grateful. Valerie Millholland, at Duke University Press, has been an editor nonpareil, always keeping the faith I myself lacked in my capacity to meet deadlines. Steven Pent displayed his usual thoroughness in preparing an index that surpassed my expectations both in detail and conceptual depth.

Without the unconditional support of my parents, siblings, and extended family in Peru this project would have been more difficult to pursue. I am very grateful to them. This book is dedicated to my brother José Méndez and to my psychoanalyst, Shauna Kloomok, whose affection and intellectual companionship have helped me grow in ways I would have never foreseen, rendering the final stage of production of this book, if not easier, by all means more meaningful. Last but not least, at the very moment when the copy-edited version of the manuscript reached my hands for revision, I met James McKernan, whose company, affection, and unmatched culinary talents brought unexpected joy to my life, for which I am deeply thankful.

1

Introduction

In January 1983, as the insurgency unleashed by the Communist Party of Peru-SL, best known as Sendero Luminoso (Shining Path), entered its third year, eight Peruvian journalists set out from the city of Ayacucho on their way to Huaychao, a peasant village in the province of Huanta, in the Andean department of Ayacucho. Their purpose was to investigate the murders of a group of alleged Senderistas that a sector of the press attributed to the military. Five of the journalists had come from Lima for the journey, and three others from Ayacucho joined the Limeños on the way. They never arrived at their destination. Not long after their departure, the press reported the discovery of their lifeless bodies in the vicinity of Uchuraccay, another village in Huanta. The corpses, which were buried, bore signs of a horrifying death. The case passed into history as the "massacre of Uchuraccay" and became one of the most controversial, emblematic, and talked-about murders in an internal war that ultimately claimed nearly seventy thousand Peruvians lives.

Although prior to the Uchuraccay massacre nearly two hundred people had been killed in the violence unleashed by Sendero since 1980, none of those killings received nearly as much media attention as the journalists' deaths. While in previous cases low-ranking policemen (*guardias civiles*) and mostly illiterate, Quechua-speaking peasants were the victims, on this occasion they were men of letters. Painful as it is to admit, adversity had to touch the urban, educated sector directly for the media and the government to pay more attention to a war that had already hit the rural populations of the south-central highlands of Peru harshly.

The case became politically charged when some of the media, especially those on the left, held the military responsible for the journalists' murders.[1] Controversy grew, moreover, because the massacre and, perhaps more force-fully, the ensuing trial of the Uchuraccay *comuneros* (community peasants) gave rise to debates about the (unresolved) nature of Peruvian identity, with not a few commentators evoking images of the Spanish conquest. The trial of the comuneros, held in Lima, pitted monolingual (or barely bilingual) Quechua-speaking villagers against Spanish-speaking magistrates, requiring the presence of interpreters; the villagers remained for the most part silent or refused to collaborate with the magistrates. More than any truth regarding the deaths of the journalists, the hearings of Uchuraccay laid bare another truth: the extent to which ethnic and linguistic markers still defined the place of the powerful in Peruvian society at the very moment social analysts were envisaging a new era of "modernity" and democratization.[2]

Then President Fernando Belaúnde appointed a commission presided over by novelist Mario Vargas Llosa to investigate the events (henceforth the Vargas Llosa Commission). The commission, which included, in addition to Vargas Llosa, two anthropologists, a linguist, a psychoanalyst, and a lawyer, arrived at the conclusion that the villagers of Uchuraccay killed the journalists because they mistook them for Sendero Luminoso guerrillas—and that they did so following the military's own advice that the villagers should defend themselves against the *terroristas*.[3] This hypothesis was endorsed by the comuneros themselves, and its credibility lay in the fact that Uchuraccay did have a history of confrontations with Sendero.[4] Still, the general tendency was to exonerate the peasants from responsibility by appealing to the classic stereotype that emphasizes peasants' "naiveté," in consonance with the image the villagers themselves chose to present.[5] Few could accept (without resorting to other stereotypes that associate peasants with savagery and brutality) the idea that the peasants, if they indeed killed the journalists, might have had their own reasons, which they chose not to reveal.[6]

The ensuing hearings in Lima found some military officers indirectly responsible for the crime, but in the end none were convicted. Three Uchuraccayan villagers were found guilty of the massacre and condemned to various prison sentences, but they never disclosed any further evidence, and one of them eventually died in jail, a victim of tuberculosis.[7] The press continued to speculate, and, in the end, each Peruvian was left to compile her own version of the events.

As I finished writing this book, and in the climate of dialogue created by the Truth and Reconciliation Commission (TRC), the Uchuraccay villagers had acknowledged that they killed the journalists. But they were far from endorsing the "cultural" arguments provided in the Vargas Llosa Commission's report on Uchuraccay (i.e., the *Informe* [1983]), which stressed the comuneros' allegedly innate violent predisposition, resulting, in turn, from the "secular isolation" in which, the commission believed, the peasants had lived since "pre-Hispanic times."[8] Instead, the villagers pointed to current matters. They explained that most villagers in Uchuraccay were indeed convinced that the journalists were Senderistas, partly because they identified the guide who came with the journalists himself as a Senderista, eventually killing him too. They added that when the journalists arrived, the villagers were in high alert against Sendero, which had in recent months, even weeks, killed many people in Uchuraccay and the neighboring communities who refused to abide by the dictates of the Maoist group. Of particular note were the cruel deaths suffered by communal authorities, whom the Senderistas killed sometimes by dyna-miting their bodies in "public executions" (*ajusticiamientos públicos*). The vil-lagers, in a word, had begun taking justice into their own hands, applying severe sanctions, including death, against those suspected of Senderismo with-in and without their community; in this, they were joined by other villages in the Huanta highlands that refused, like them, to give in to the dictates of Sendero. The Uchuraccayan comuneros who accounted for these facts apolo-gized in the name of their community in the context of the *audiencias públicas*, or "public hearings," staged by the TRC. At the same time, however, they have denounced, emphatically for the first time, that in the months following the journalists' massacre their community was victim of severe retaliation by Sendero Luminoso as well as by military aggression. Between April and De-cember 1983, 135 Uchuraccayinos lost their lives. Most fell victim to Sendero. Others were killed by the military. Among the former were reportedly all the villagers who took part in the journalists' murder. A list with the 135 names was made public by the TRC, giving the national community, which until then had likened the "tragedy of Ucchuraccay" with the deaths of eight men of the press, much to reflect upon.[9]

At the time of the killing of the journalists I was completing my studies in Lima, and like many other Peruvians, I was disturbed by those events. My unease resurfaced with particular intensity some years later, as I took a teach-ing position at the National University of San Cristóbal de Huamanga, in the city of Ayacucho. During my tenure there I began an inquiry into the history of the peasants of Uchuraccay and other high-altitude communities in Huanta, an inquiry that has resulted in the present book.

From local monographs to archives, I set myself in search of references to the "Iquichanos," the name which the Vargas Llosa Commission, following

(above) The old
town-casa hacienda
of Uchuraccay as
seen from an incline
where the new
town lies.
(right) Villagers
assembling in the new
town of Uchuraccay.
Modern houses in
the background were
built under a special
program sponsored
by the Alberto
Fujimori government
in the late nineties.
*Both photographs by the
author, ca. 1998.*

ethnographies and histories of Huanta, used to designate the high-altitude peasant communities of Huanta, including Uchuraccay. Colonial ethnographic sources make no mention at all of the Iquichanos. References to them started appearing only during the republican period starting in the 1820s. These sources, especially those originating in the late nineteenth century, portrayed the Iquichanos as descendants of the so-called Chanka Confederation and attributed to them a warlike tradition of opposition to the Incas. They also emphasized the Iquichanos' "hostility toward outsiders" and unwillingness to submit to the laws of the state.

I later learned, however, that such conceptualizations, which were echoed in the Vargas Llosa *Informe*, did not reflect an actual knowledge of the pre-Hispanic or colonial history of Huanta. Rather, they were construed with a more recent episode in mind: the rebellion that Huanta peasants (thereafter called Iquichanos), in alliance with a group of Spanish officers and merchants, mestizo hacendados (estate owners), and priests, launched against the nascent Republic, between 1825 and 1828.[10] The rebels, acting in the name of King Fernando VII, aimed to restore colonial rule. Their supreme leader was Antonio Abad Huachaca, an illiterate muleteer from the *punas* (high-altitude lands) of Huanta who was said to have held the position of General of the Royal Army. As my research progressed, I found myself immersed in the work of reconstructing the history of this rebellion and its aftermath, which constitute the subject of this book.

One of the details which initially drew my attention to the monarchist rebellion of Huanta was the similarity between the opinions of contemporaries toward the royalist peasants in 1825–28 and those of the press in relation to the murder of the journalists in Uchuraccay in 1983: basically, the same resistance to accepting that villagers had acted of their own volition. If in 1983 the peasants were persuaded by the military, in 1826 they were duped by the Spanish. Moreover, historians who attempted to explain peasant participation in the monarchist uprising limited themselves to reproducing the interpretations made by contemporary observers. Juan José del Pino, a local historian to whom we otherwise owe a careful compilation of sources about peasant rebellions in Huanta, endorsed the theory of "deception" and peasant naïveté: "These attacks took place because of the deceptions of a group of Spaniards in Ayacucho, who took advantage of the ingenuousness of the indigenous, and made them believe in the arrival of a Spanish squadron on the coasts along with the return of the chiefs defeated on the 9th of December."[11]

The "weak spot" in the interpretation of the Huanta rebellion, however, went beyond the confines of local history. "National" historians themselves had not advanced much farther than local historians in their understanding of peasant attitudes in Independence and post-Independence conflicts. As Juan José del Pino was writing the paragraph quoted above in Huanta, Lima historian José Agustín de la Puente y Candamo developed the idea that Independence grew out of the development of a collective consciousness in which distinct social sectors came together under the leadership of the creoles (Americans of Spanish descent).[12] The creoles were at the top, indians, mestizos, blacks, and *castas* (people of mixed racial backgrounds) were at the bottom, all asserting their will to belong to Peru. National identity was less a problem to be explored than a truth to be preached. Consequently, it seemed sufficient to look into the doctrines and well-meaning intentions of certain illustrious creoles in search of the right heroes. De la Puente's became the dominant interpretation of Independence in the 1960s. Within this scheme, an inquiry into "royalist indians" was not to be expected.

Not long after the publication of the second edition of de la Puente's book in 1970, another interpretation gained momentum. It shared de la Puente's idea that Independence had internal roots but highlighted indian and mestizo rather than creole leadership and sought to emphasize popular participation in general.[13] This interpretation was favored by the left-leaning military regime that ruled Peru under the presidency of General Juan Velasco Alvarado between 1968 and 1975. Velasco's government was characterized by a nationalist, anti-imperialist rhetoric and pro-peasant policies—and by its rewriting of Peruvian history. Velasco made Túpac Amaru II, the indigenous leader of the major anti-Spanish rebellion in colonial Spanish America (which took place in Cuzco in 1780–81), the government's official icon. This was a gesture without precedent because of the violent nature of the Túpac Amaru rebellion and because of the fact that, in addition to killing Spaniards, it also attacked creoles. Hence, the figure of Túpac Amaru historically elicited discomfort among the creole elites of Peru, who banned him from historical records for more than a century. By the mid–twentieth century Túpac Amaru's persona was gaining increasing official acceptance as his image as a bloodthirsty indian rebel was "rehabilitated" by historiography, although no previous Peruvian president had gone as far as Velasco in elevating Túpac Amaru to the standing of national hero and foremost symbol of Independence.[14]

Despite their obvious differences, creole and Velasquista / *indigenista* interpretations of Independence converged in conceiving of it as a process of "national liberation." As a sample of its conciliatory spirit, the military, on the occasion of the celebration of the 150th anniversary of the proclamation of Independence, erected a monument in a public park in Lima, and renamed it Parque de los Próceres ("Park of the Illustrious men [of Independance]"). The monument featured large statues of "precursors" of Independence from different ethnic backgrounds, including the (historically proscribed) effigy of Túpac Amaru.[15]

Challenging these two official nationalisms, a third interpretation of Independence emerged at the beginning of the 1970s. It was strongly influenced by Marxism and dependency theory and came to the fore in a polemical article by historians Heraclio Bonilla and Karen Spalding, published in 1972. The authors claimed that Independence was not—and could not have been—the result of a process of development of collective consciousness, as the official historiography claimed.[16] In the first place, the creoles were never convinced of the need for Independence. Their future and prestige were tightly connected to those of the Crown, and in this respect they differed from the creole elites of Río de la Plata and Nueva Granada; in addition, Peruvian creoles feared the implied risks of a mobilization of the indigenous population, who during prior rebellions in 1780–81, 1812, and 1814–15 had become radicalized beyond the creole elite's expectations. In the second place, asserted Bonilla and Spalding, indians themselves could not have been active agents in the process of Independence because they had not yet recovered from the wave of repression that followed the defeat of Túpac Amaru in 1781. The defeat of Túpac Amaru, the argument went, aggravated the "ethnic fissures" and fragmentation that generally divided peasant and popular sectors.[17] Finally, peasants were not likely to form alliances with creoles, whom they distrusted as much as, if not more than, Spaniards.

For Bonilla and Spalding, an elite that lacked nationalist convictions, and popular classes that neither identified with them nor offered viable alternatives, were unlikely to have been protagonists in an Independence scenario that was "conceded more than conquered." Rather, it was "brought from without" by the inevitable collapse of the Spanish Empire and the emergence of Great Britain as a new imperial power eager to promote and assist the process of emancipation of the Spanish colonies overseas. Only because they were coerced did "indians, blacks and mestizos" fight "equally in the ranks of the patriot and royal armies."[18]

Bonilla's and Spalding's core arguments were far from new. The idea that Independence came to Peru "from without" was widespread by the mid-nineteenth century and the early part of the twentieth century.[19] When de la Puente articulated his thesis of Independence "from within," it was precisely to counter a long-established historiographical trend that in many variations stressed the opposite. On the other hand, Bonilla's and Spalding's interpretation of Independence echoed (though not explicitly so) that of José Carlos Mariátegui, the celebrated early-twentieth-century Peruvian Marxist thinker. Advancing a hypothesis that was to become central to dependency theory, Mariátegui criticized the "alienation" and lack of nationalism among Peruvian elites, stressing the role of Great Britain in the consummation of Spanish American Independence and upholding the idea that Independence brought neither social transformation nor economic change.[20] A similar criticism of the upper classes had been made earlier by historian José de la Riva Agüero, himself an offspring of the creole nobility he condemned.[21]

Despite their differences, both nationalist and Marxist historians converged in assigning peasants a passive role. For the nationalists, peasants were the unquestioning followers of an illustrious vanguard; for the Marxists, they were "cannon fodder" or at best spectators. If in the first case their role was to support and assent, in the second their indifference was to be attributed to their lack of understanding of the conflict: "The indian masses could not, were not able to, clearly differentiate between an autonomous government of creoles and a colonial government dependent of the metropolis."[22]

The Marxist-*dependentista* interpretation of Independence was not without its merits. In seeking to understand this process in terms of class, it exposed the theory of "national unity" as a myth; in questioning the depth of the changes brought about by Independence, it served as a reminder of the tasks of "nation building" that lay ahead. But it oversimplified at least two other questions: the participation of the "popular sectors," which were seen as an unconscious and manipulated mass; and the implications of the political changes that did occur in the wake of Independence. The first issue had been partially taken up by the interpretations that assessed the popular sectors' patriotism, which flourished in the seventies, although, to be sure, critical, nonpatriotic approaches to popular participation in Independence are still scarce.[23] The second question was addressed by a historiography that focused on trade policies and economic nationalism in the caudillo era.[24] None of these currents addressed the problem posed by the royalist peasants. Interestingly, it took anthropologists to do so.[25]

In 1983, the French anthropologist Patrick Husson completed a study in which he compared the Huanta uprising of 1825–28 with another rebellion that had also occurred in Huanta toward the end of the nineteenth century.[26] According to Husson, the Independence wars and subsequent political decisions by the new republican government affected regional rhythms of production and commerce, particularly in Huanta, provoking discontent among the different sectors involved in these activities. This discontent found expression in a monarchist rebellion. Husson's economic interpretation provided valuable information and insights that have inspired and guided my own investigation. Unfortunately, Husson diminished the value of his findings when explaining peasant participation. Forcing the logic of his evidence, Husson defended the Marxist theory of "manipulation."[27] Later on in his work, however, Husson insisted on a specific logic with respect to the attitudes of the peasants. He concluded that Huanta peasants rebelled on account of their "natural" resistance to the changes brought about by the new order: "More than the fall of the empire, or more than the weight of a new fiscal burden, the peasant uprising was . . . a peasant reaction to a social change that brought uncertainty."[28] Or more forcefully still: "It seems that the peasantry, because of its structural position in the society that encompasses and defines it, can only feel horror at changes it had never imagined and had rarely been suggested for it, even when those changes came with the best intentions."[29]

Husson's assessment that Huanta villagers were reacting against "social change" brought about by Independence is a bit puzzling given that earlier in his book he had endorsed the Marxist-dependentista interpretation, according to which Independence brought about no change. The unresolved contradiction constitutes, nonetheless, a powerful example of structural Marxism's and modernization theory's limitations to grapple with the reality of Latin America. In keeping with these theoretical and political dictates, Husson's analysis becomes fatalistic: the peasantry is a class destined to perish under the weight of capitalist modernity and thus adopts a defensive position before it, which is inevitably violent: "The only means available for the peasantry to make their complaints heard against the irremediable injustice that it endured was and continues to be violence."[30] Interestingly but not at all surprisingly—given that both Marxists and liberals share the same "modernizing" principles—this conclusion mirrored the one that, from a very different political angle, Vargas Llosa reached in his quest for "cultural" reasons with which to make sense of the journalists' murders: "It is unquestionable that this atavistic attitude explains, in part as well, the Iquichan decision to combat Sendero Luminoso, and to do so with *rude and fierce methods, which are the only ones they have at their disposal since time immemorial.*"[31]

In brief, the Huanta rebellions did little more than demonstrate what was already known: that peasants are exploited beings who resist change and are doomed to react to injustice with violence.[32]

Against studies that portrayed peasants as victims, a literature emerged in Peru during the seventies that highlighted peasants' role as "champions." Significantly, it concentrated on the twentieth century. The so-called literature of peasant "struggles" or "movements" arose alongside that of "labor movements" in the field of sociology. Actually, this model did not so much oppose as complement that which defined peasants as victims—both converging in defining peasants, first and foremost, as exploited beings. The difference was that while in Marxist and modernization-theory paradigms peasant destiny was forlorn, in the *movimientista* perspectives it was heroic: peasant acts were endowed with a revolutionary and vindicatory character. The victims became heroes. The tendency was selectively to extract certain rebellious peasant acts from their contexts in order to fit them into a politically defined sequence of events. This led to the proliferation of texts that were more chronicles than histories of peasant rebellions.[33] It was a good example of what E. P. Thompson referred to as the "spasmodic" vision of history: detached from the everyday, historical subjects existed and were defined precisely in terms of their moments of "explosion."

Some time would pass before other researchers—some of whom, interestingly enough, were also initiated in the field of sociology (and not far chronologically and generationally from the movimientista boom)—transcended these rigid and linear models, applying a more respectable dose of history and professionalism. In 1981 Nelson Manrique published *Las guerrillas indígenas en la guerra con Chile.*[34] Manrique's central preoccupation was to apply an appropriate logic to the participation of the peasants of the Central Sierra in the War of the Pacific (better known in Peru as the War with Chile, 1879–83). His study emerged in response to interpretations of Independence such as those discussed above that overlooked peasants' capacity to perceive the national dimension of the conflicts and consequently opt for a nationalist position.[35] Based on extensive archival research, Manrique's work overcame the structuralist rigidity of studies that assigned peasants fixed roles and always predictable positions. It also encouraged understanding of peasant assimilation of national conflicts through their cultural expressions, including dances, music, and oral traditions. Perhaps Manrique's major accomplishment was to give further legitimacy to what (given the absence of empiricism in which Peruvian historiography debated the "national question") was most necessary: sensitivity to the primary sources, archival research, and sufficient sense to discard the idea of a peasantry cut off from its mental faculties and either eternally manipulated or perpetually heroic. The key was the regional focus. The national conflict transcended abstractions when observed in a regional context. Peasants' alignment with national parties (whether nationalist or not) were understood like those of any other group, namely, in terms of their ties, relations, alliances, and conflicts with other local and regional sectors, including officials, landowners, and other peasants. As a work that included a theoretical proposition and a political preoccupation, *Las guerrillas indígenas en la guerra con Chile* was a true milestone and provoked one of the few genuinely significant debates about the "national question" in contemporary Peruvian historiography. Not long after, historians in North America followed suit.[36]

As the nineteenth century was "rediscovered" by historians—and seduced anthropologists—other studies appeared, which, although they did not necessarily touch on the issue of the peasants' role in national conflicts, still managed to situate them as active participants in the nineteenth-century state, previously the exclusive domain of oligarchs and military caudillos. From the 1980s on, peasants were defined less and less as "indians" and began to be taken into account in analyses of local power, in their role as tribute payers, in their participation in markets, in their capacity as litigants, and as creators of new meanings for a legal terminology emanating from the early republican elites. Despite their differences, most of these studies sought to break away from heroic expectations as well as from the image of a passive and defenseless peasantry.[37] Whether or not this scholarship succeeded in achieving these goals remains debatable. Idealization of peasant and "indian" political goals (or rather what scholars render as such) remains widespread in academia.

Nonetheless, the constructions of peasants as inherently passive or irremediably violent have, at any rate, receded.

My own book may be situated within these most recent historiographical coordinates. It springs as well, however, and perhaps more decisively so, from my own attempts at gauging the political weight of rural Andean society in the shaping of the national state in Peru. This problem, largely marginal to Peru's mainstream political history, became, however, difficult to relegate ever since Sendero Luminoso put Ayacucho at the center of national attention in 1980. As the Sendero insurgency escalated to become "the greatest insurrection in Peruvian history,"[38] it became increasingly clear to me the extent to which historians, and not just the government, had forsaken this region.

Researchers attracted to the study of Andean rebellions have, in fact, generally privileged regions such as Cuzco and Peru's "Andean South," which bred the major anticolonial uprisings of the late colonial period. What happened in Ayacucho (called Huamanga in the colonial period) remained largely unknown. But this historiographical void only gave more impetus to my decision to investigate the history of Huanta and, more specifically, of Uchuraccay.

The dearth of studies dealing with the political history of Ayacucho is, in fact, striking considering the role that this Andean department has played in Peru's republican history. One of the poorest departments of Peru, and largely marginal to the nation's economy, Ayacucho has nonetheless played a central role in its politics. In addition to incubating Sendero Luminoso, Ayacucho furnished the site for the battle that ensured Peruvian and Spanish South American independence in 1824 and at the same time became the last royalist stronghold. As such, Ayacucho gave birth to the only peasant uprising in the first four decades of republican life in Peru, the monarchist uprising of Huanta in 1825–28.

This book constitutes the first in-depth reconstruction and analysis of this uprising. Its aim is, however, less to trace a history of "resistance" than of relationships—asymmetrical, more or less violent, convenient or inevitable—between the emerging republican state and a rural society of the south-central Peruvian Andes. Huanta's highland inhabitants, at first reluctant to submit to the Republic, would eventually adapt to it and become, moreover, indispensable allies of a faction of "nation builders." Thus, my study, while seeking to shed light on Peru's troubled present, hopes to demonstrate as well that Peru, though conspicuously absent from the most comprehensive studies of cau-

dillismo and rural society's input in the process of "state making" in Latin America, was by no means impervious to the process of "ruralization of power" that Tulio Halperín once suggested engulfed Spanish America following Independence.[39]

The men and women who supported the Huanta uprising were, for the most part, native speakers of Quechua, but rarely used this language in written communication, even in the few cases of Huantans who were literate. My sources are, consequently, all in Spanish. As usual, government agents have left more paper trails than the common people we are most concerned with. My analysis builds largely on these official records, including trial proceedings, notary records, wills, customs records, military and prefectural records, newspaper articles, tributary rolls, and many others. But it draws as well from documents produced by the various leaders and participants in the Huanta rebellion, including war dispatches, manifestoes, and letters exchanged between them as well as documents generated by guerrilla commanders and other actors in the civil wars of the 1830s and petitions that peasant communities addressed to the state up through the 1840s. These records, more often than not, "leak" Quechua terms, syntax, and phonology, and these elements, when compounded with features of the Spanish language, calligraphy, and quality of paper where originals are available, provide useful hints to their possible authorship and context of production. Unfortunately, much of the specificity of the language will not be apparent in the English translation of the citations. Yet, to the extent that the sources have allowed, I have illustrated every aspect of this rural society that may further the comprehension of its political expressions as they became apparent at the moment of the outbreak of the monarchist rebellion. I have followed this rural world's incorporation into the power structures of the early republican state up to the 1840s. My goal has been to trace the story of a political event as much as to account for a political process: Peru's transition from imperial to republican rule, as experienced by a high-altitude rural society which is usually considered to have been "historically isolated."

The province of Huanta is located at the northernmost edge of the current department of Ayacucho, midway between the cities of Cuzco and Lima and at the crossroads of the trade routes that linked Buenos Aires and Lima during the colonial period. San Pedro de Huanta (as the town was called originally), today Huanta city, the province capital, lies in a temperate, narrow valley, the most fertile in the province, some 2,620 meters (8,596 feet) above sea level and 25 kilometers (16 miles) north of Ayacucho city, capital of the department of the same name. Both the department and the city of Ayacucho were called Huamanga during the colonial period, but the province of Huamanga, of which Ayacucho is also the capital, kept its colonial name. For this reason, the name "Huamanga" has prevailed, and Ayacucho city's inhabitants still commonly refer to their city as Huamanga, a usage I myself adopt wherever pertinent.

The province of Huanta displays almost as much ecological variety as one can find elsewhere in the Andes of Peru. Its towns, villages, and hamlets are spread along narrow valleys and ravines that range from 1,000 to 4,000 meters (3,281 to 13,124 feet) above sea level and enjoy a variety of ecologies and microclimates. The most densely populated ecological niches in Huanta include *quechua* (from 2,300 to 3,200 meters, or 7,546 to 10,499 feet, above sea level) and *suni* (3,200 to approximately 3,900 meters, or 10,499 to approximately 12,795 feet, above sea level). The Razuhuilca peak crowns the landscape at an elevation of nearly 5,000 meters (16,404 feet) above sea level. The quechuas are good lands for growing vegetables and maize, while the sunis are best suited for potato and other Andean tubers like *oca* and *olluco*, in addition to broad beans and barley (the latter introduced by the Spanish). In the lower edges of the suni vegetables are also cultivated. Above the suni is the *puna*, 3,900 to 4,800 meters (12,795 to 15,748 feet) above sea level. These are the highest lands in which humans are settled, and their poor soil, subject to intense erosion, is the least suitable for agriculture. Still, *ichu*, a wild, dry plant commonly used as fodder and for roof making, among other domestic uses, grows abundantly here, and villagers farm a variety of potatoes in small plots scattered about the steep slopes that dominate the landscape. On the other side of the Andean cordillera, to the north and east of Huanta city, lies the *ceja de selva* (literally, the "eyebrow of the jungle"), also called *montaña* or *selva alta* (upper jungle). In this sloped, forestlike ecological niche usually between 500 and 2,300 meters (1,640 to 7,546 feet) coca has traditionally been cultivated. These lands also produce sugarcane and a variety of tropical-like fruits, including avocados and bananas.[40] Montañas enjoy a rather humid atmosphere and increasingly warm temperatures as one descends to the rivers Apurímac and Mantaro. These rivers mark the border of the province while demarcating the frontier with the *selva baja* ("lower jungle"), best known plainly as *selva*. To the north lies the

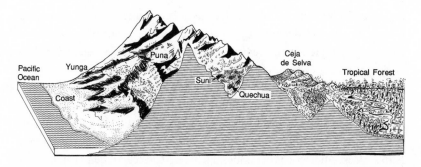

Ecological niches of the Peruvian Andes. Reproduced with permission from Richard Burger, *Chavín and the Origins of Andean Civilization*. London: Thames and Hudson, 1995.

selva of Junín, to the east the selva of Cuzco. West of Huanta is the Andean department of Huancavelica, a mining region. (See maps 1, 2, and 5.)

In all of these ecological niches, except for the selva, the monarchist rebels established encampments and headquarters. But the most important hideouts were situated in the highest elevations, in the sunis and punas. Uchuraccay, then a hacienda 4,000 meters (13,123 feet) above sea level, was the most unassailable of them. Within its borders lay the so-called fort of Luis Pampa, the rebels' main headquarters.

In spite of the ecological diversity of the area, the various niches of Huanta have a common feature: a markedly rugged and jagged topography. This is especially true of the punas. The jagged quality of the terrain and its numerous rocky, cavelike structures lend these punas a strategically defensive value, which when coupled with their strategic location explains why the zone, unfriendly to the casual traveler, would attract those plotting rebellions or seeking refuge.[41] The punas of Huanta, in fact, bridge the lower valleys, where the largest towns of the province are located, with the eastern and northern selvas used by the monarchist rebels as critical hideouts, and where some detachments of Sendero Luminoso still operate.

The province of Huanta is smaller today than it was in the late colonial and early republican periods. At that time it embraced the current provinces of Huanta and La Mar and the northern portions of the province of Huamanga, covering an area roughly the size of Puerto Rico.[42] This larger Huanta constitutes the core setting of our study. As Ayacucho's northernmost province, Huanta forms part of a region of the Peruvian Andes commonly referred to as the "south-central sierra"—not quite the south, and not yet the center, but historically connected to both by trade and culture. The northern stretches of Huanta are, in fact, at the center of Peru, and its southern area marks the beginning of Peru's southern Andes. "Central sierra" and "southern sierra" are historically as well as geographically defined regions. The central sierra contains important urban centers of relatively recent development, that is, late colonial or republican, such as the trading city of Huancayo and the mining center of Cerro de Pasco, whereas the southern sierra is home to some of Peru's oldest Andean colonial cities, including Cuzco, Arequipa, and (if one stretches the south a bit toward the center) Huamanga itself. The southern sierra was likewise the core economic region of the viceroyalty of Peru, which up to the eighteenth century comprised all of Spanish South America. Concentrated in the south, in fact, were the richest silver ores and mining cities, Potosí in Upper Peru (present-day Bolivia) being foremost among them. Many of Huamanga city's first Spanish settlers, the *encomenderos*, also owned mines in neighboring Huancavelica, especially mercury mines, mercury being a vital ingredient in the processing of silver. Huamanga was indeed the breadbasket for this mining area—its temperate weather made it the favorite place of residence for the region's wealthy mine-owning encomenderos.[43]

In the wake of the Independence wars, the central sierra started to thrive by virtue of the recovery of Cerro de Pasco's silver ore, but the fate of the southern sierra looked less promising.[44] Thus, Huanta's traditional ties to the central sierra became ever more prominent during this period. Huancayo city, located in the center of the ample Mantaro Valley (also known as "Lima's granary") was the largest settlement in the central sierra and remains so even today. Its rise as a thriving commercial center paralleled the advent of the Republic. Huanta has long been tied to Huancayo by trade and perhaps shares, economically speaking, more traits with this city than with its closest neighbor, Huamanga. Like Huancayo, Huanta lacks the seignorial architectural beauty for which Huamanga is renowned, and, also like Huanta, it served as a breadbasket for the neighboring areas. Huanta's fertile valleys and montañas supplied foodstuffs to Huamanga and its hinterland from early colonial times.[45]

For most of the colonial period, Huanta had been a predominantly indian town, the head of the *doctrina* (ecclesiastical district) of the same name, and head as well of the *corregimiento* (indian tax province) of Sángaro (or Azángaro). Although by the late eighteenth century the town remained largely indigenous, it began to experience some important demographic changes,

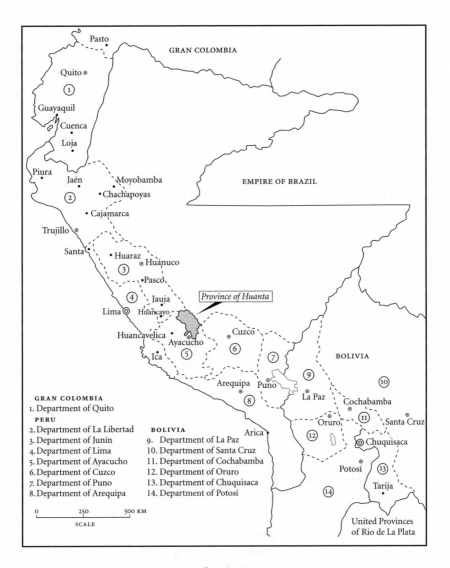

GRAN COLOMBIA

Pasto

Quito ◎

①

Guayaquil

Cuenca

Loja

Piura

Jaén

Moyobamba

②

•Chachapoyas

• Cajamarca

Trujillo ◎

Santa

• Huaraz

③ ◎ Huánuco

•Pasco

④ •Jauja

Lima ◎ Huancayo

Huancavelica

Ayacucho

⑤

Ica

EMPIRE OF BRAZIL

Province of Huanta

Cuzco

⑥

⑦

Arequipa

⑧

Puno

⑨

La Paz

BOLIVIA

⑩

Cochabamba

Oruro

⑪

Santa Cruz

⑫

Arica

◎ Chuquisaca

Potosí

⑬

Tarija

⑭

United Provinces
of Rio de La Plata

GRAN COLOMBIA
1. Department of Quito
PERU
2. Department of La Libertad
3. Department of Junín
4. Department of Lima
5. Department of Ayacucho
6. Department of Cuzco
7. Department of Puno
8. Department of Arequipa

BOLIVIA
9. Department of La Paz
10. Department of Santa Cruz
11. Department of Cochabamba
12. Department of Oruro
13. Department of Chuquisaca
14. Department of Potosí

0   250   500 KM

SCALE

MAP I. Peru in 1827.

marked by the growth of the nonindigenous populations, including Spanish and especially mestizos. These changes were partly a consequence of a series of decrees issued by the Bourbon state to boost the economy and foment the colonization of Peru's ceja de selva. The decrees were launched within the framework of a sweeping program of political and administrative reforms known as the Bourbon Reforms, which aimed at making Spain's overseas colonies more profitable and efficiently administered; they also encouraged migration of Spaniards from the Peninsula to the Americas. Although it is hard to tell how many Spaniards arrived in Huanta province as a result of these migratory waves, the evidence indicates that their numbers increased exponentially during the last two decades of colonial rule. A source from 1819 estimated that 14,000 *españoles* lived in Huanta at that time, undoubtedly a highly inflated figure but suggestive of a considerable increase from the 219 españoles (less than the 1 percent of the population!) recorded in the census for the province of Huanta of 1795.[46] The word *español* as used here should be taken with caution. At the time, it did not necessarily denote, as it does today, birthplace or nationality but rather Spanish ancestry or "culture" or even status; hence many individuals identified as españoles were, in fact, American-born creoles and mestizos. Nevertheless, the increase in the nonindigenous population in the closing stages of the colonial period is evident.

The Spaniards arriving in the early nineteenth century established themselves in Huanta and Luricocha, the most fertile valleys of the province, and acquired lands in the montañas. Some of these new residents were officers in the Royal Army, others were merchants with links in Huamanga, Lima, and Cádiz, and still others were both. Very few went to live in the high-altitude hamlets, where Quechua speakers had come to predominate ever since the first Spanish encomenderos took over the richest lands in the lower valleys, pushing native peoples to increasingly higher elevations.

The census of 1795 includes other pieces of information that, in the absence of analogous evidence for the time of the monarchist rebellion, allow us to picture two other salient features of Huanta's demographic landscape at the end of colonial rule. First, Huanta, with its 27,337 inhabitants, was the most populous province in the intendancy of Huamanga (followed by Huamanga with 25,970). Second, Huanta was the province with the largest number of mestizos: 10,080, or 36 percent of the total population. Its indian population, according to the same census, was close to 17,000, or approximately 62 percent of the total, second only to the province of Huamanga where indians made up 78 percent of the population.[47]

There are no records of the indian population of Huanta as of the 1820s. But the indian tributary roll of 1801 registers 2,582 male individuals, which, assuming a six-member family per tribute-paying individual and considering that some villagers might have escaped registration, allows one to estimate an indian population in the range of 16,000 to 18,000, mostly grouped in villages. This number is consistent with the almost 17,000 indians given for the same province by the census quoted above. It is this segment of the population that contributed the bulk of the *montoneros* (irregular army combatants) for the monarchist rebellion.

In the republican period, a source from 1834 gives 12,000 inhabitants for the *villa* (city) of Huanta alone, that is, the parish of Huanta, including the four *ayllus* or *parcialidades* that comprised it. This figure increases to 36,000 with the inclusion of the districts of Ccarhuahurán, Ayahuanco, and Acón, also belonging to Huanta province.[48]

To what extent, then, is the history of Huanta an isolated case? Or, more broadly, to what degree is the history of northern Ayacucho "exceptional"? Most historical studies do not address this question directly but invariably single out three events that highlight the region's symbolic importance and strategic location. All three belong to Ayacucho's distant past, and the first is related to Ayacucho city's founding by the Spanish. The Spaniards founded the city of Huamanga in 1539, so the story goes, to secure a Spanish settlement as a gateway to the eastern jungles of Vilcabamba, where the Incas had been offering stiff resistance to the Spanish invasion ever since the rebellion of 1536 led by Manco Inca, which had attempted but failed to retake Cuzco from Spanish hands; his followers were to remain up in arms in their Vilcabamba refuge for decades. Huamanga was thus called San Juan de la Frontera de Huamanga ("Saint John of the Frontier of Huamanga") and over time became, indeed, a borderland, a Spanish city at the gateway to the still-unconquered selva. But it demarcated not a boundary between Spanish and indian settlements as much as one between "conquered" and "unconquered" indians (then referred to as "infidels"), for on both sides of the supposed frontier the natives constituted the overwhelming majority of the population. This was true even in Huanta, the most mestizo of Huamanga's seven provinces.[49] The story of

Huamanga's Spanish founding matters, however, in that it looms large in Huamanguinos' representation of their capital city and is usually recalled with pride by local historians, who are fond of boasting of the city's Spanishness or, better, of the ancientness of its Spanish past, particularly when compared to Huanta's. Architecture more than demography no doubt speaks in their favor, for while Ayacucho city is renowned for its thirty-three plus Spanish churches and monasteries dating back to the early colonial years, Huanta city has not a single Spanish structure (of which I am aware) from that era.

The second historical event highlighted by Huamanga historians also relates to the Spanish conquest. Local histories record that the department of Ayacucho furnished the stage of the Battle of Chupas (1542), in which the armies of the Spanish king's emissary, Vaca de Castro, defeated the Spanish rebel conquistador Almagro *"el Mozo,"* thereby securing the Catholic monarchs' hold over the land of the Incas that the rebel conquistadores were struggling to keep for themselves. This royal triumph, which has likewise been recalled with pride by chroniclers of the region, including the celebrated late sixteenth- and early seventeenth-century native writer Guamán Poma de Ayala, was also integrated into the city's name. Thus, in addition to being a "frontier" city, Huamanga became a city symbolizing royal victory, "the very noble and loyal San Juan de la Frontera y Victoria de Huamanga."[50]

The third memorable "epic" experience goes back to Ayacucho's pre-Hispanic past and is shrouded in legend. It is the history of the region's resistance to being conquered by the Incas, which the Incas' own narratives aggrandized in order to glorify their final subjugation of the region's populations, the so-called Chankas. Although the facts surrounding these events are in dispute and the very existence of the Chanka Confederation is a subject of controversy, evidence of tension is apparent. Bearing witness to this are the pre-Inca high-altitude fortified buildings that archaeologists identify as "Chanka," and, most importantly, the proliferation of *mitma* populations in the Pampas river basin, between the Ayacucho and the Apurímac departments, which historians trace back to Inca times. The mitmas were "ethnic colonies" of sorts, made up of entire communities that were forced to leave their native lands and resettle in those that the Incas considered strategically important or potentially rebellious. Mitma colonization was the Incas' nonmilitary means of securing control over the territories they conquered. Although mitma colonies could be found almost anywhere within the realm of the Incas at the time of the Spanish invasion, historians have been particularly intrigued by the profusion of such settlements in Huamanga's Pampas river basin.[51]

Reading these three fragments of evidence of Ayacucho's distant past in light of its most recent history, as outlined at the beginning of this introduction, the temptation to argue for the region's "uniqueness" or particularly violent and conflictive history is great. Nevertheless, having wrestled with the question of Ayacucho's "exceptionality" for a long time, I will not argue for it here. Ayacucho—or, more precisely, northern Ayacucho, where Huanta is located—may not be so much an "exception" as a place where problems afflicting the national society of Peru simply take on sharper contours or more extreme expression. Closely observed, it is the area's strategic location at the crossroads of economically and politically neuralgic zones in South America that accounts for most of the difference, having rendered it a decisive stage for battles of great symbolic importance. Other than that, one can see more commonalities than differences between northern Ayacucho and the rest of Andean Peru.

Take, for instance, the geography. Huanta's rough topography, its narrow valleys and steep, hardly arable lands are a distinctive feature of the Peruvian Andean landscape, which harbors the highest and most rugged section of the Andean cordillera. The boundary that northern Ayacucho shares with the selva is shared as well by most of Peru's other Andean departments. Moreover, the coexistence of two cities as historically different as Huanta and Huamanga, separated by a mere twenty-five kilometers (sixteen miles), makes this region a privileged laboratory in which to observe Peru's social contrasts and its historical trends generally, with Huanta representing a rather mestizo and market-oriented society and Huamanga embodying the paradigm of the early colonial, seignorial city.

Second, consider Ayacucho's most recent political developments. Thought of initially as an isolated "Andean" phenomenon, Sendero Luminoso's insurgency, born in the Ayacucho countryside, escalated to become the most devastating insurrection in Peru's history—probably the only one to have affected all of the nation's populated territories.[52] That is, the conditions that led to the rise of Sendero in Ayacucho in 1980 were soon replicated nationwide.

Likewise, and closer to our subject matter, if Ayacucho became "the last bastion" of the royalists in Peru, Peru was the last bastion of the royalists in Spanish America. Thus, if Huanta was exceptional at this historical moment it was not precisely on account of its royalism or even its "monarchism" but because in this region alone conditions were ripe for waging war under such banners.

Finally, I shall argue that the makeup of the peasant communities' leadership in the Huanta uprising may reflect a reality akin to the rest of rural Peru of the time, more so than the widely studied indian leadership of the great anticolonial rebellions of the "Andean South," of which Cuzco was the foremost political center. Since this idea constitutes a crucial aspect of my overall interpretation of the Huanta rebellion it deserves further explanation.

Unlike the well-known indian leaders of the great Cuzco uprisings—from Túpac Amaru to Pumacahua—native leaders of the Huanta rebellion, the so-called Iquichanos, were inconspicuous, barely literate, and humbly born men from the highest punas. They lacked noble indian lineages, spoke little Spanish and no Latin. None of them, moreover, would claim, or pretend to claim, the status of "ethnic chief," or *kuraka*, or the rights over a *kurakazgo*.[53] And the reason I say they may represent Andean Peru's indian or peasant leadership better than the noble rebels of Cuzco is that late colonial Peru was a society in which noble indians may have retained social prestige but were inexorably losing political power; this trend was exacerbated by the repressive measures following the defeat of the Túpac Amaru uprising. The diminishing power of the kurakas and the concomitant waning of the indian-nobility-based political leadership in Peru was a late colonial trend that crystallized under the Republic. And this trend seems to have been especially evident in Ayacucho, perhaps even developing earlier there.

The title of this book, "Plebeian Republic," aims to capture this process. It also aims to call attention to the role of plebeian rural actors in the play of politics in the early republican state. The recomposition of the authority system in Andean society after the demise of the kurakas has been traditionally a topic dealt with by late–colonial period specialists, but it has not been discussed in the context of early republican caudillo politics. Nevertheless, my study suggests that native Andean peasant leaders played an active role in the play of politics of the early republican state. This role, therefore, merits investigation.

The historian Jorge Basadre once claimed that the Republic politically empowered social sectors which, on account of their racial features or plebeian origins, would not have been able to attain high office under the ethnically stratified colonial society. Basadre was referring to the dark-skinned mestizo caudillos who became presidents of the Republic, who never became wealthy but instead died in poverty.[54] He had less to say about what was happening at the bottom of the political system. But it is precisely here that my study of Huanta offers useful referents. What I am suggesting is that the "plebeianization of politics" Basadre alludes to was not just about the highest caudillos but occurred also at the very bottom of the political system. In fact, it began earlier there. The caudillo state, which made warfare a way of life and rewarded military skill with political office, opened new avenues of social ascent for plebeian sectors, that is, those who, like the peasant leaders of Huanta, were not able to claim noble lineages of either Spanish or Inca origin.

Historians who have followed the demise of the kurakas have suggested that their functions were taken up by mestizo (and *criollo*) authorities and by the *varayoqs*, indian mayors, or *alcaldes vara*, who, unlike the kurakas, ruled over just one community / village and whose position was rotative rather than lineage-based.[55] My research supports this idea. But it uncovers yet another type of indian / peasant chieftainship: that whose authority was rooted neither in their nobility (as was that of the kurakas) nor in community rights (as was that of the varayoqs), but rather in war. And although this new leadership's powers may resemble at times those of colonial kurakas and at other times those of varayoqs, they do not really conform to either pattern. Neither can these characters be classified as *mistis* (the mestizo authorities and hacendados reviled by twentieth-century indigenista fiction writers and usually portrayed as exploiters of the indians) for they did not always master the literary skills associated with the condition of misti, though they were, like mistis, brokers of sorts. These new chiefs partook of indian / peasant community culture and accomplished important economic functions in the peasant communities' life, especially at the level of circulation of goods. They were muleteers, petty hacendados, and even cattle rustlers. Their economic functions were the basis of their political power and ascendancy over the peasantry. But it was war that ultimately legitimized and enhanced this power. For it was the state that ultimately legitimized war.[56]

These types of petty caudillos, simultaneously montoneros and local authorities, reigned in the heights of Huanta, and notably in Uchuraccay, within a time period that I call the Plebeian Republic (1821–50). And these very same commanded the montoneras that fought the Republic "in the king's name" in the wake of the Independence wars. I will attempt to show that any belligerency that the peasant leadership of the monarchist uprising may have displayed in the context of rebellion was not so much suppressed as rechanneled in the interests of republican politicians, and, ultimately, to serve the state. Inasmuch as the demands of the state and of caudillos striving for state power upon the rural populations presupposed the military mobilization of the peasantry in the form of guerrillas, there is every reason to suppose that a similar type of chieftainship might have emerged in other Andean regions of Peru.

As can be surmised from the discussion above, this book is about more than a "monarchist rebellion." But inasmuch as it is fundamentally about this rebellion, some further clarifications must yet be made. When I have described to friends and colleagues the subject matter of my investigation, I have been met with a common reaction. Upon learning two of the most salient features of the 1825–28 Huanta rebellion—that is, that it challenged the Republic and that it called for the return of the rule of the Spanish king—not a few of them have pictured it as a "backward-looking" or "traditionally oriented" movement, reminiscent of the French Vendée rebellion (1793), the war waged by the most traditional sectors of the French society affected by the liberal and anticlerical measures of the French Revolution. Perhaps this interpretation is viable if the Huanta uprising is viewed superficially or on the basis of its proclamations alone, but it is, however, problematic in that it obscures some of the rebellion's most significant political features. Such an interpretation also risks distorting the historical context in which the rebellion originated. Likening the Huanta rebellion to a Vendée-like war assumes, first of all, that the Republic in Peru was the outcome of a liberal revolution. Such an assessment itself is controversial given that Peru has been widely regarded as the "reluctant republic" in the context of the Spanish American struggles for Independence. But secondly, and more importantly, the comparison may not apply here because the Huantinos themselves were not, in fact, waging this war in defense of "tradition" or in the hope of restoring the "old regime."

Far from being a beleaguered nobility, a landed elite, or a priesthood stripped of long-held privileges, the promoters of this uprising were either newcomers or social upstarts, this being valid not only for the local but also for the European members of the alliance. Huanta itself, as already mentioned, was a province of rather late Spanish colonization. The rights and privileges that the Huanta rebels claimed were recent and specifically defined rather than "traditionally held" or "ancestral." Most importantly, although the defense of absolute monarchy was indeed quite explicit in the leaflets and proclamations that called for rebellion, this idea, along with the rumors that announced the imminent landing of troops sent by the king, was more entrenched among the Spanish members of the alliance than among the local Huanta populations. It was held particularly by former officers of the defeated king's regiments who found refuge in Huanta after the Ayacucho battle. None of this negates the presence of doctrinaire monarchists among the Huanta as well. But let us not forget that doctrinaire monarchists and Spanish royalists could be found throughout Peru, especially in the urban centers of early Spanish influence, including Lima.

My contention in this book, therefore, is that for most local leaders of the Huanta uprising, monarchism represented an instrumental more than an ideological option. That is, the king's name was invoked as a symbol of prestige and a source of legitimacy, but monarchy as a political system was not necessarily espoused by the local people. Consequently, monarchism as an ideology did not ultimately take hold in Huanta. It didn't take hold in Peru either, for that matter, as it did in Mexico, where Itúrbide and Maximilian were crowned emperors, and Ecuador, which experienced the monarchist projects of the caudillo Flores.[57] But even in these two cases, monarchism was short lived, and in the case of Ecuador, abortive. Broadly speaking, monarchies did not make a comeback in America as they did in Europe once the republics were proclaimed.

Ultimately, and paradoxical as it may sound, Huanta province's subsequent political trajectory tended toward liberalism. In the civil wars of the 1830s and also later during the political confrontations of the 1850s, the Huanta montoneros aligned themselves with caudillos who were identified with liberal programs, leaders like Luis José de Orbegoso and Andrés de Santa Cruz. Later in the century, Huanta peasants adopted a nationalist stance, joining Andrés Avelino Cáceres's campaign of resistance to the Chileans in the central sierra. Early in the twentieth century, Huanta became the seedbed of anarchist reformers and a cradle of nearly all the liberal-minded intellectuals of Ayacucho.[58] With this in mind, it would be misleading to brand the province's historical trajectory as "conservative," let alone conceive of its peasantry as having lived "isolated" since pre-Hispanic times, as the official interpretation of the journalists' murders in Uchuraccay in 1983 assumed, citing the Huanta monarchist rebellion precisely as "proof" of the alleged aloofness.[59]

The "cultural" arguments in the Uchuraccay *Informe*, particularly in the main Vargas Llosa report and the anthropological appendixes by Juan M.

Luricocha, the second most important town in the Huanta valley and capital of the district of the same name at the time of the monarchist rebellion. In the early nineteenth century, owners of coca plantations settled here and in Huanta (a fifteen-minute drive away). *Photograph by author, ca. 1997.*

Ossio and Fernando Fuenzalida, have been widely contested, and I will not claim originality in disputing them once again. But this book might not have been written had I not been convinced that similar arguments continue to be widespread (and not limited to the peasants of Uchuraccay) inside and outside Peru, within and beyond academia.

Overview

Chapter 2, "The Republic's First Peasant Uprising," presents the events which are central to the rest of the book. It follows the Huanta uprising from its inception in 1825 to its defeat in 1828, through its aftermath into the 1830s. Each of the following interpretative chapters scrutinizes a different aspect, or aspects, of the uprising. In doing so, the core narrative of chapter 2 is expanded, synchronic details are exposed, and historiographical interpretations are brought to light.

Chapter 3, "Royalism in the Crisis of Independence," captures the "moment" and precipitating factors of the uprising; it furnishes the short-term explanations at regional and national as well as political and economic levels; it answers such questions as why a monarchist uprising was triggered in this region at this particular juncture.

Chapter 4, "Words and Images: The People and the King," contextualizes the discourse that the rebel caudillos, both Spaniards and natives, made explicit. It introduces and analyzes the ideological propaganda in their leaflets and proclamations and hypothesizes about the roots of their professed adherence to the king.

Chapter 5, "The World of the Peasants: Landscapes and Networks," sets the geographical scope of the rebellion; it describes the types of settlements comprising it and where the bulk of the restorationist army originated. It also gives a sense of the social background of the main protagonists, including peasants and muleteers, hacendados and merchants, and establishes the socioeconomic ties that linked the sectors engaged in the rebellion. This chapter is also crucial in that it uncovers a telling silence: the contemporary town of Iquicha, which supposedly gave name to the so-called Iquichano rebellion, is absent from all colonial tributary, ethnographic, and cartographic sources consulted and therefore does not form part of the setting. For the "Iquichanos"—if a name can create, or help create, an identity—began their existence as such only after, and as a result of, the monarchist uprising.

Chapter 6, "Government in Uchuraccay," returns to the question of the causality of the rebellion posed in chapter 2, but from a perspective beyond the circumstances that explain the outbreak: the reasons that made it possible to prolong and maintain it. In other words, it explores the social bases of the rebellion. These are found in the rebel caudillos' ability to handle the problems and meet the needs of the local people through actions which theoretically should have been carried out by the state: redistribution of surpluses through appropriation of tithes, administration of justice, and "social control," among others. The rebel caudillos did not accomplish these tasks through random deeds but rather in an institutional fashion, through an organization which I call the Government in Uchuraccay, named after the rebels' main headquarters. This chapter is relevant not only in that it adds one more causal explanation to the uprising, but also in that it tries to decipher its meaning by decoding chiefly nonverbalized and nonarticulated messages: the meaning of the Uchuraccay government hierarchies; the tenor of the rebels' appoint-

ments; the manner in which the rebels adopted colonial and republican bureaucratic terminology and the implications of this adoption; the extent of
rebel officers' powers. This chapter makes clear that besides waging a war, the
rebels were, in their own way, creating government. The quality of the sources
used in this chapter provides a unique opportunity to trace the workings of
both the late colonial and the early republican state at the local level and in a
rural setting.

Chapter 7, "The Plebeian Republic," expands the narrative of the first chapter's final section. It follows the fate of the defeated rebels from 1828 to ca. 1850
and shows how they ended up not only accommodating but taking an active
part in the new Republic they had initially so utterly rejected. It analyzes this
process at both military and civil levels. Unlike the Spanish instigators of the
monarchist rebellion, who ended up exiled or in prison, the native chieftains of
Huanta were either pardoned or eluded capture. They remained politically
active and formed guerrilla armies that aligned with President Orbegoso in the
civil war of 1834 and with Santa Cruz in the Peruvian-Bolivian Confederation
of 1836–39. In gratitude for their services, these governments publicly honored the peasants and compensated their leaders with appointments in the
local state bureaucracy. Antonio Huachaca, for example, became a justice of
the peace. This recognition was ephemeral. But their exploits and political
ventures—some real, some exaggerated, some invented—produced enough
memories among Huantinos and state officials alike to allow for the creation
of a new identity—that of the "Iquichanos"—a new village, and a new district,
Iquicha, which twentieth-century indigenista writers and academicians would
ironically conceive of as being "ancestral."

There was never anything stable or permanent about the Iquichano identity
in the nineteenth century, nor is there now. And I would be surprised if
someone in Huanta who is not native to the village of Iquicha were to identify
himself or herself as Iquichano or Iquichana, particularly considering that the
district of Iquicha, at the time of this writing, no longer exists. Ever since the
term *Iquichano* began "making history" in 1826, the Iquichanos, conceived of
either as a union of ayllus or as an "ethnic group" in Huanta, have been an
entity more real in the minds of those using the label to designate Huanta
villagers and their caudillos than in the villagers' perception of themselves;
peasants continue identifying most commonly with their individual villages.
For this reason, I have tried not to be as expansive as my sources in the usage of
the terms *Iquicha* and *Iquichanos* and have adopted, wherever possible, more

precise forms of identification instead. Nevertheless, this has not always been possible, or convenient, as I later realized, if the perspective of government authorities, which in turn peasants used as a point of reference for their own forms of self-identification, was to be conveyed. Hence, I have resolved that dropping the term altogether would risk downplaying the intricacies of the story that makes the Huanta rebellion so compelling a historical event in the first place. Mental constructions really do matter because they lead humans to carry out precisely the kinds of things that we, in turn, group under the label of "making history." And history is what government officials, the peasants of Huanta, and their montonero leaders made in claiming or disclaiming, boasting of or repudiating, denouncing or embracing Iquicha and the Iquichanos.

2

The Republic's First Peasant Uprising

It was the end of the year 1824 and a new life was beginning for the newly proclaimed republics of South America. The victory of the patriotic forces over the royalist armies on December 9 on the fields of Quinua, in Ayacucho, marked the end of three centuries of Spanish domination in Peru and the New World. The Ayacucho victory represented the culmination of Simón Bolívar's emancipationist dreams and, not without reason, carried him to the peak of his glory.

Hundreds of Spaniards were returning to the Peninsula, while the more established chose to remain in America. Meanwhile, Bolívar the Liberator was engaged in a triumphant victory tour through towns, hamlets, and villages, where the residents lavished upon him every sort of honor. After his journey to Arequipa, Bolívar entered Cuzco, where, following a tremendous reception, he was crowned with a garland made of gold, a gift from the area's merchants.[1] Lima, too, was undergoing the "Bolivarian frenzy," and there was no want of poets to sing the praises of the Liberator.[2]

Entrusted by Congress with dictatorial powers over the government of Peru, Bolívar issued his first decrees. Abolition of the *kurakazgos* and nobility titles, prohibition, once again, of unpaid indian labor, and decrees bearing on the sale of communal lands aimed to transform the ex-colony into a modern nation. Peruvians had to transform themselves from subjects to citizens. This was a change still far from being realized in Europe itself; such was Bolívar's dream.

Realizing these dreams and furthering the projects he had envisioned would not be easy, however. The end of Spanish rule in Peru had been too abrupt not to leave many disaffected. Peru had been the viceroyalty which, after New Spain (today Mexico), had attracted the greatest concentration of Spanish power. Its capital, Lima, was the strategic center from which military expeditions set out to vanquish the revolutionary movements that flared up in various parts of the Peruvian viceroyalty and neighboring Spanish domains during the last decades of European rule. These campaigns had been financed by Lima's most affluent merchants who remained loyal to the Crown to the very end. These elites did not necessarily share Bolívar's political projects, notwithstanding their obsequious gestures and flattery and outward show of acceptance. A similar attitude characterized Cuzco's elites. A few months before "crowning" Bolívar, the inhabitants of the Incas' ancient capital had given refuge to José de la Serna, the last viceroy of Peru.

Peru now had to recuperate from the disastrous effects of the war. Four years of military campaigns had left the country in ruins, and the patriotic enthusiasm of many would not be long in vanishing amidst the war's rubble. With the enemy defeated, internal dissent was forthcoming, and Bolívar's newly inaugurated government soon found itself confronting numerous sources of opposition. One was the national Congress, in which representatives' personal ambitions mingled with an emergent nationalism that frowned upon the presidency-for-life envisioned by Bolívar. Meanwhile, to the south, some leaders advocated "microfederalist" projects while a separatist spirit seemed to be sprouting with particular vigor in Arequipa. The discontent made itself felt in the military as well, owing to the supposedly preferential treatment received by the Colombian forces still stationed in Peru. Disgruntled and ill-paid, Peruvian soldiers initiated a wave of mutinies in 1826 that shook the barracks of Lima, Ica, and Camaná along the coast and of Huancayo in the sierra. It was said that some servicemen were conspiring with groups of civilians to wrest command from Bolívar.[3]

A third source of discontent was felt among the remnants of the royalist army. Far from capitulating, the last remaining royalist officers in Lima barricaded themselves in the Real Felipe fortress of Callao, where they continued, under the command of José Ramón Rodil, to offer tenacious resistance to the government of Bolívar. This strategic position enabled them to control Peru's most important port, the gateway to the city of Lima. Through their mouthpiece newspaper, *El Depositario*, they inveighed relentlessly against the Liberator,[4] and, skeptical of the decisive character of the Ayacucho victory, they circulated all sorts of news items announcing an imminent landing of Spanish troops who would take charge of restoring the throne of Fernando VII in the Kingdom of Peru.[5] With their hopes set on this possibility, other royalists were also conspiring in various parts of Peruvian territory. Meanwhile, General Pedro de Olañeta directed monarchist resistance in Upper Peru (Bolivia).

Some groups of *capitulados* (members of the royalist army defeated in the

Simón Bolívar, as rendered by José Gil de Castro. Reproduced with permission from the Museo Nacional de Arqueología, Antropología e Historia del Perú, Lima. *Photograph by Daniel Giannoni.*

battle of Ayacucho) settled in the department of Ica. In June 1825, the authorities arrested forty-six of them for "the crime of failing to report to the Government, despite numerous edicts with which they were summoned." During the same period, an equal number of local civilians were detained. The local authorities accused them of conspiring with the *godos* (pejorative for Spaniard) against the government.[6] Yet the most significant group of capitulados found refuge in the province of Huanta, only a few kilometers from the Ayacucho battlefield where they had been defeated.[7] Unlike their counterparts in Ica, they found relatively favorable conditions for the pursuit of their conspiratorial projects. The rugged, mountainous northern Ayacucho landscape made for an ideal refuge. But perhaps more decisively, they were favored by complicity, active and passive, of an avowedly proroyalist population. The same year General José de San Martín proclaimed independence in Lima, Viceroy La Serna honored Huanta with the title of "Loyal and Invincible Villa of Huanta," in virtue of services rendered to the Crown, a distinction the town's inhabitants took great pride in.[8] Thus, it was to be this very province, encompassing the northernmost area of the department of Ayacucho, that would give rise to the largest upheaval facing Bolívar's recently inaugurated government and the Republic at large for decades to come.

The epicenter of the disturbance was located in the "punas of Iquicha," also called the Ccarhuahurán punas, names designating a region of the province of Huanta populated chiefly by peasant communities settled among hacienda territories. Of these haciendas, Uchuraccay, also known as "Luis Pampa," stood out as the rebel's most important headquarters, at nearly four thousand meters above sea level. For reasons I shall mention in due course, the inhabitants of this area had also maintained their loyalty to the king until the very end. The same republican army that had proven victorious at Ayacucho would once again have to enlist its forces to combat not merely a handful of Spanish capitulados, but also an army of peasants who had now joined with them, and who, paradoxically enough, formed part of that overwhelming majority of Peruvians for whose benefit the republicans professed to govern: the "indians."

The Rebellion

Americans: . . . here you have the extraordinary miracle that, in the
small Niche of these Punas, but a few men, with neither discipline nor
arms, but only Stones and sticks, have several times defeated those
who called themselves invincible, leaving us the field covered with
arms and cadavers. With such prodigious marvels, you have nothing
to fear. To arms Brave Americans, a Heretical Enemy wishes to tyrannize Religion and the Hereditary Throne of Fernando.

— "Proclama," Francisco Garay

News of the "insubordination" of the peasants from the "towns of Ccarhuahurán" and the "punas of Huanta and Luricocha" reached the city of Ayacucho as early as March 1825. The peasants evidently had blocked the roads
and were refusing to recognize the authorities identified with the government of Bolívar. The prefecture dispatched a battalion that subdued the rebels in fifteen days. Yet in the course of the following months new unrest
shook these towns. New battalions were dispatched to the punas; this time
they had less luck. Favored by a daunting topography and years of experience
in military campaigns, the peasants skillfully resisted the troops, some twelve
hundred men whose horses, succumbing to the difficult terrain and the scar-
city of water and other provisions, died on the steep roads leading to the
hamlets. Strategically posted among the summits, the villagers turned away
their pursuers with boulders. It was December 1825. The War of the Punas
had begun.[9]

In the following weeks the rebels sacked the haciendas of landlords accused
of lending support to the troops of the *Patria*. Under the command of their
alcaldes (indigenous mayors), villagers from Huaychao and Cunya stormed the
Choquepunco hacienda, the property of the intendant Jorge Aguilar y Vílchez,
and carried off several hundred head of cattle and dozens of beasts of burden.[10]
That same month, some three hundred peasants from the village of Aranhuay
under the command of the Ayacuchan hacendado Marcelo Castro and the
Spaniard Miguel Fariña seized the town's governor, who had displayed "adherence to the cause of independence," reportedly killing him and one of his
sons. In January of the following year, the prefect Juan Pardo de Zela led a new
"punitive expedition" to the punas, and by the beginning of April informed the

minister of war that these areas had been pacified.[11] He was mistaken. For "as a result of these military movements," the tithe collector Pablo López Gerí noted, "the indians dug in their heels,"[12] and their "insubordination," far from abating, assumed greater proportions, spreading toward places like Tambo, a few kilometers to the east of Huanta city, by way of the *selva*. Encircled by spectacular mountains offering vistas in virtually every direction, Tambo was a strategic location and a much sought-after military outpost, alternating as center of rebel operations and republican headquarters. In May 1826 the governor of Tambo informed the prefect that the "peacekeeping troops" had beheaded fifty rebels and shot many others.[13]

Beyond the plundering and violence that characterized the confrontations between the peasants and the army, the most salient feature of the rebellion was the control the rebels exerted throughout 1826, 1827, and into 1828 over the surpluses produced in the zone's most important agricultural units. This included the tithes corresponding to the haciendas of the punas with their production of potatoes, broad beans, and livestock, and, more significantly— because of their profitability—the more than 230 coca haciendas situated in the gorges of Acón and Choimacota, northeast of Huanta, and in the warm valleys along the rim of the forest surrounding the Huanta punas to the north, east, and southeast.[14] Operating out of their "headquarters" and "town councils" the rebels named their own authorities, among them "subdelegates" and "tithe collectors," who played a key role in the expropriation of the tithes. All leaders answered to the uncontested authority of Antonio Abad Huachaca, a muleteer presumably born in the Uchuraccay hacienda, who was said to have received the rank of general from Viceroy La Serna himself. Huachaca asserted his rank in his appointments of tithe collectors and in his various edicts and proclamations, issued always "in His Majesty's service" and "in defense of the law."[15] Wielding the authority conferred upon them by Huachaca, the insurgent tithe collectors proceeded to lay claim to the tithe due at each harvest from the hacendados.[16] The tithe had been a colonial-era ecclesiastical tax levied on agricultural landowners, who were to surrender one-tenth of their production to a tithe collector, who in turn was answerable to a Board of Tithes. In the initial decades of the Republic the tithe remained in force, the prefect taking the place of the intendant as head of the Board of Tithes. Yet in the province of Huanta there was little the authorities could do to prevent the appropriation of these surpluses by the rebels. Tomás López Gerí, at the time a tithe collector for Huanta, reported the following to the Board of Tithes:

Since the auction [of January 31, 1826] not one *arroba* [approximately twenty-five pounds] of coca has been received, let alone the least produce from the towns of Ccarhuahurán and the punas, for the revolution of these indígenas soon increased so much it obstructed altogether communication with the towns and the montañas. Two infantry battalions and two cavalry squadrons have made expeditions to these spots of insurrection, and after a long stay during most of the past year, the indians, though they remain peaceful, are not paying the tithes, and have instead appropriated it, even those the montaña produces in coca, where they have confiscated, from their authority, some haciendas.[17]

Pablo López Gerí, likewise a tithe collector, corroborated the testimony of his son Tomás, adding that the indians, "delighted with their impunity, have gone as far as selling the tithes of the whole Province, to the point of introducing their collectors in the center of Huanta itself, whose district falls within my jurisdiction."[18] The aggrieved tithe collector also reported that "the height of the rebels' brazenness is to extend their jurisdiction to places in which the republic's troops are present," and he went on to say that "the intrusive new tithe collectors in the center of Huanta threaten me continually and . . . have attempted to take me, tied up, from Huanta to Huachaca's location."[19]

Tomás and Pablo López Gerí were not exaggerating. Documents recording the appointments of subdelegates and tithe collectors (or mayors) bearing Huachaca's signature, correspondence between the rebels, and depositions taken from numerous witnesses, all attest to the rebels' capacity to impose their authority in the region. Among the tithe collectors appointed by Huachaca were Spaniards, such as José Pérez del Valle, local people whom we could call "mestizos," such as Huachaca's own secretary general Rafael de Castro, and *indígenas* (republican term for *indio*) like the muleteer Manuel Leandro. When Leandro was captured, he had in his possession a list of names of more than 170 hacendados from the *montañas* who were liable to the rebels in connection with the tithes owed from 1826.[20] Huachaca's orders authorizing Valle to collect the tithes were likewise strict, "so that none of the individuals and hacendados expressed in the deed will hinder him [Valle] in the collection of this payment, so privileged as it is for the aid of the most worthy troops of the King, may God save him, for which I beg and entrust all civil and military authorities ["ministros de bara siviles y militares"] they give them [*sic*] all necessary assistance."[21] With the product of the tithes—the most valuable of which consisted of coca leaf—the rebels paid their troops, manufactured weapons, and acquired provisions; in short, they completely financed the rebellion, for coca had a high market value and was commonly used for barter, as well as in lieu of cash.

In the meantime, Bolívar, alarmed by the news reaching the capital, sent another military detachment to Ayacucho in July 1826, this time under the command of the Council of State's own president, General Andrés de Santa Cruz. Arriving in Ayacucho, Santa Cruz announced a general amnesty in the hope that "the stubbornness of those indígenas would end."[22] He initiated negotiations with one of the rebel caudillos, Pascual Arancibia, a hacendado from Luricocha and a man of great influence among the villagers.[23] As a result of the negotiations some rebels laid down their arms. Within a few weeks the newspaper El Peruano announced that the towns of Huanta had been pacified and that their inhabitants had become reconciled "wholeheartedly with the new institutions."[24] Shortly thereafter, Bolívar took it upon himself to "honor with expressions of appreciation" Prefect Pardo de Zela and other officials "for their actions against the rebels of the puna."[25]

Once again a brief, if only apparent, calm reigned in Huanta. Neither the amnesty nor the honors extended by Bolívar, however, were sufficient to contain the mounting insurrection, which was looming larger every day. By November 1826, the same Pardo de Zela, without concealing his alarm, informed the minister of finance that the inhabitants of the villa of Huanta were being instigated by "the daring of those in the punas" and that furthermore they had planned "to imitate them and follow their example by disobeying superior orders," refusing to pay a quota that the government had levied on them.[26] Meanwhile, many Huanta conspirators, emboldened by the incessant rumors of the arrival of the king's troops from Spain and by the growing climate of political instability, grew more ambitious in their intentions.

Thus over the course of 1826, Huachaca, together with Tadeo Choque and Arancibia—collectively referred to as the generals—and in concert with other hacendados, Spanish capitulados, ex-officers of the Royal Army, merchants, and a sector of the local clergy, prepared to carry out their boldest actions yet. They contrived a vast plan to do nothing less than reconquer the Kingdom of Peru for Fernando VII![27] If Huachaca stood as supreme caudillo of the movement and at the same time its most important indigenous chief, Nicolás Soregui, a French-Basque ex-officer of the Royal Army who at the time of the rebellion was a merchant in Huamanga, stood as the most prominent European leader. Encouraged by rumors "of the impending landing of 22,000 French and Spanish forces at the port of Callao" under the flags of Spain and the Holy Alliance, they mobilized supporters and disseminated propaganda not only in Huanta, but also throughout the neighboring towns of Huamanga and the most distant ones of Jauja, Huancayo, Huancavelica, Andahuaylas, and Cerro de Pasco. The Huanta rebels were also joined by groups of capitulados conspiring in Ica and in Lima.[28] Communiqués signed by Huachaca and other caudillos issued strict orders that "all scattered soldiers and capitulados be organized."[29]

Eighteen twenty-seven was a year of intense mobilization among the capitulados and their allies along the heights of Huanta. The rebels established headquarters in the village of Secce and in the haciendas Paraíso, Choimacota, Cancaíllo, and Uchuraccay as well as command posts and encampments elsewhere (see maps 5 and 6). They prepared armaments, recruited troops, and mobilized their montoneros. Community peasants were recruited by summoning their mayors, or *alcaldes de indios*, and those of the haciendas were enlisted through their foremen, the *mayordomos* (administrators), or the hacendados themselves. The haciendas of the Spaniards Juan Cantón from the montañas, Salvador Pérez from Luricocha, and the Ruiz family from Tambo served as refuges for the rebels; documents and armaments were hidden there and fighters were recruited. Although these hacendados evidently took part of their own volition, others were forced to cooperate with the drastic laws laid down by the insurgents. Those who refused ran the risk of losing their livestock or property and ultimately, as Huachaca himself threatened, "of being executed."[30]

While the rebels equipped themselves the government was undergoing important changes. Bolívar had left Peru in September 1826, and Marshall José de La Mar now assumed the presidency. Domingo Tristán, a veteran officer who had fought for many years on behalf of the king before distinguishing himself in the patriotic army, replaced Juan Pardo de Zela as prefect of Ayacucho. The Congress kept abreast of the upheavals taking place and continued, along with the executive, the policy of amnesty and punitive expeditions that the previous administration had pursued. In October 1827, President La Mar extended a new pardon "to the inhabitants of the Huanta punas" in which he promised to exempt from payment of tributes and military draft those towns that would lay down their arms.[31] At the same time various priests were commissioned to exhort the peasants and their leaders to surrender.[32]

These measures in effect convinced some of the insurgents to lay down their arms, but the most committed ones remained defiant.[33] Shortly before the promulgation of La Mar's pardon, Soregui, Choque, the priest Francisco Pacheco, the priest Manuel Navarro, Arancibia, and José Ruiz, among others, swore an oath in the town of Aranhuay not to surrender.[34] Faithful to that oath, and convinced that the king's generals were on their way, they began preparations for what would be their two most daring actions: the capture of the town of Huanta on November 12, 1827, and the siege of the city of Ayacucho a few days later.

In October and November 1827 news that "Spanish generals were nearing" reached Huanta from Lima and Huancayo, prompting the rebels to invade Huanta: "It was publicly known," said the soldier Juan Ramos, "that Tadeo Choque had sent one Rodríguez to Lima and this man had arrived with communiqués . . . as a result of which all the leaders gathered and spread the news that the Royal Army was near . . . and decided to march on Huanta."[35] Another witness was more explicit: "Rodriguez came [to the punas] with proclamations and papers that, he claimed, a general of the Spanish troops who was in Huaura [near Lima] had given him. Armed with this news, all the leaders and Zoregui gathered and immediately tried to invade Huanta."[36] Authentic or apocryphal, such proclamations had a tremendous impact. The leaders circulated them "and then resolved upon a general uprising in the towns of those punas," to which, some said, "Soregui gave the whole impetus."[37]

At dawn on November 12, the montoneros, led by their commanders and generals, invaded Huanta. They seized the military barracks and set it afire after overwhelming some 170 soldiers, 12 of whom died, and many more were wounded as a result of the conflagration. The soldiers who managed to flee took refuge in the church and subsequently escaped to Ayacucho. The encounters resulted in dozens of casualties on both sides. The montoneros would stay on a few days in Huanta. Protected by the fear or complicity of the population, they secured some prisoners in the house of Doña Teresa Arbizu, a woman slightly over forty who was a relative of several rebel leaders. Among the prisoners was the hacendado and ex-provisional intendant of Huanta, José Jorge Aguilar y Vílchez. A few days later the rebels proceeded to Mollepata, where they planned the attack on Ayacucho.[38] This time their good fortune ran out.

The seventeen-day interval between the capture of Huanta and the planned attack on Ayacucho allowed the rebels to raise reinforcements, but it also afforded government forces the time they needed to gain the upper hand. The prefect of Ayacucho justified his military mobilization to the minister of war: "The arrogance with which the Iquichanos have behaved since the seizure of Huanta and their most recent operations and raids in the neighboring towns, addressing proclamations to even the most distant hamlets of the Department, made clear their intention of attacking the capital [Ayacucho], thus I did not hesitate for a moment to prepare myself for its defense."[39]

The prefect's intuitions proved to be correct, as did his plan for taking the rebels by surprise. While the insurgents were readying themselves for the attack on Ayacucho, Prefect Tristán mobilized, in addition to his regular forces, groups of peasants from the neighboring province of Tayacaja and the district of San Miguel, northeast and southwest, respectively, of the area of unrest. The key role in the repression of the Huanta rebels would, however, be reserved for the Morochucos, a designation given to the inhabitants of Pampa Cangallo, an extensive plain in Cangallo province, south of Huamanga (see maps 2 and 3). Tristán, in short, cleverly envisioned surrounding the Huanta rebels from every possible angle. The Morochucos, renowned as skilled horsemen, had already served on the republican side during the wars of Independence and as a result had suffered reprisals from the royalist troops, including the burning of their towns. Tristán, who commanded bands of Morochucos during those conflicts, not only offered them the opportunity to exact compensation for these wrongs, but also exhorted them, once again, to prove their patriotism:

> Inhabitants of Cangallo: The same general under whose orders you so heroically served in the year of '22 has been appointed by the worthy and virtuous president of the Republic prefect of this department. . . . Noble Morochucos: founders of Perú's liberty, your General Prefect calls on you to arm yourselves so that we can finish off these perverted Peruvians. . . . I would like, my dear compatriots, for you to earn this glory before our veteran troops come and wrest victory from your hands. . . . Chiara, November 15, 1827. Domingo Tristán.[40]

The prefect would succeed in his mission. Eight days after the capture of Huanta, a Morochuco army led by Tristán marched through the main square of Ayacucho. The shrewd prefect thereby hoped to raise the town's spirits in preparation for the anticipated invasion of the Iquichanos.[41] Yet the military preparations did not deter Tristán from continuing to negotiate his enemies' surrender by peaceful means, for which he employed all of the astuteness at his disposal. On November 22 he addressed a letter to the "Chiefs of the Iquichanos," who were then occupying Huanta; enclosed were new guarantees of pardon issued by President La Mar. The prefect once again urged them to surrender: "Ask, decide what it is that you wish to have explained, and I shall come forth as guarantor that nothing proper is denied to you." The response was a defiant declaration of war: "We request only, and our weapons demand, that this plaza be left to us, and to this end a surrender can take place which will be honorable for you, and firm without for that reason lacking propriety, but if it is not to be so, we shall not delay in setting our armies upon it and seize it by fire and sword, on the dagger of our honor. . . . The experience of the events which have occurred in our punas will afford you unequivocal proof of the valor of the troops which we proudly command in the name of the king."[42]

The tone of defiance reflected not only the self-assurance accrued as a result of the inroads made by the rebels, but above all the relative ease with which they had taken possession of Huanta, the most important city of the department after Ayacucho. The insurgents' leaders seemed neither to fear nor to expect the defeat that was to follow.

On November 29 approximately fifteen hundred montoneros descended from the hills to attack Ayacucho and were overpowered in short order by Tristán's forces, strategically positioned along the city's outskirts. The largest skirmish took place in Pampa del Arco,[43] although what transpired at the site could hardly be construed as a battle, if the figures provided by Tristán himself are true: 290 dead on the rebel side, with only 1 Morochuco death on the government side. The numbers suggest rather the orchestration of an extensive massacre. Of the survivors, 130 were taken prisoner, while the rest fled to the punas,[44] among them the most important leaders, including Soregui, Huachaca, and the priests Navarro and Pacheco along with other Spanish and Huantino leaders. It would not be easy to track them down. After seven months of repressive campaigns that included renewed clashes in the punas as well as the ransacking and burning of towns implicated in the revolt and at the cost of hundreds of lives, republican troops managed to capture the last rebels, who after crossing the punas had found refuge in the Acón and Choimacota *montañas*, on the banks of the Apurímac river. Huachaca, however, succeeded in evading this last expeditionary force and would elude subsequent attempts to capture him. A few years later he could be seen walking about the streets of Huanta, unpunished and under escort.

The defeat at Pampa del Arco was the most severe blow to the insurgent cause since the start of the hostilities. Three hundred men died that day cheering the king, not far from another battlefield where merely three years earlier many others had given their lives for the Republic. Yet this war—let us call it of "reconquest"—scarcely differed from previous confrontations in terms of those suffering the worst fate. The almost three hundred cadavers left on the battlefield, which grieved Tristán, or so he claimed, were those of peasants from village communities and laborers and farmhands from the haciendas. These were "anonymous" dead, and so, perhaps, the leaders who remained in safekeeping did not feel altogether defeated. They harbored a secret hope of reversing their dramatic setback, despite having perhaps become convinced, in the aftermath of the defeat, that the Spanish generals in whom they had placed their hopes would never come to their aid. Still armed and sustained by tithes collected in areas under their control, they continued to encourage war against the Patria. They appointed authorities and mobilized resources and personnel in an attempt to persuade wavering elements on the government side to join their ranks. Surprisingly, given the unfavorable circumstances, they convinced some to do so. In January 1828, not long after the massacre at Pampa del Arco, twelve soldiers from one of the Ayacucho companies passed over "perfidiously"—as Tristán would later remark—to the Iquichanos.[45] Whether genuinely persuaded or enticed by the financial rewards the rebels were offering to those willing to serve in their ranks, these soldiers joined others who had entered the insurgents' army before the latest attacks.[46] The desertions proved disastrous to the government at such a critical juncture. Desperately lacking in regular troops, the government increased the number of recruits being drawn from surrounding towns such as Acobamba, a move which ultimately turned out to be counterproductive. Shortly after the desertion of the twelve soldiers, Tristán commissioned one Captain De los Ríos to draft twenty-five men from Acobamba. The abuses committed by De los Ríos in the course of carrying out these orders were vehemently denounced by the town's governor: "Not one man remained, but only women weeping together, with neither sons nor husbands. . . . An excess such as this was never suffered even in the past, under the government of the Spanish tyrant."[47] Similar cases were denounced by the governor of the district of San

Miguel, Nicolás López, who complained to the prefect about the abuses and excesses committed by troops under Commander José Gabriel Quintanilla.[48]

These incidents were tinder for inflamed political speeches delivered by undaunted militant leaders, who from the beginning of the movement demanded "that the *señores militares* depart." The abuses, moreover, ensured that the rebels' propaganda would continue to attract an audience despite their having cast lots with a seemingly lost cause. In towns farther removed from Huanta, support for the rebellion remained intact. In January 1828, citizens of Huancavelica allegedly revolted "because of a desire to receive all the Spaniards and Capitulados"—as an optimistic Francisco Garay reported to Nicolás Soregui—precipitating the flight of the town's intendant to Huamanga.[49] However, neither Huancavelica nor Andahuaylas, where many capitulados had settled, was to be the final refuge of the remaining insurgents. They would always return to their headquarters at Uchuraccay, where it had all started. This was indeed an "impregnable land," as noted and bemoaned time and again by the authorities, a place from which the rebels could slip away (as indeed they did) into the montañas or even downstream toward the selva.

From their headquarters in the punas, Antonio Huachaca, José Pérez del Valle, Nicolás Soregui, and the priests Manuel Navarro and Francisco Pacheco kept track of enemy movements and prepared to pursue their war to the bitter end. This was not true of Arancibia, Choque, and the soldier de la Barreda, all of whom, sensing imminent defeat, had opportunely (or opportunistically) changed sides.[50]

During January and February 1828, Huachaca and Soregui continued issuing orders for the collection of tithes and appointing new officials and military leaders. It is important to take note of one of the documents issued by Huachaca at this time, a special decoration he bestowed on Soregui, for it sheds light both on the hierarchy of the rebellion and on the expectations of its supreme caudillo. Convinced, or perhaps seeking to convince himself, that his authority and prestige remained intact after the serious setback at Pampa del Arco, Huachaca honored Soregui with the title Brigadier in the King's Name:

> Don José Antonio Abad Huachaca[,] General in Chief of the Royal Armies of Peru. Aware of the merits and services of the distinguished Colonel Don Nicolás Soregui[,] his conduct and the interest that this worthy leader has taken in the formation of the line troops and what he has achieved in redeem-

ing the bulk of the confidence that I have placed in him[,] I have seen fit to reward [him], heeding the powers that I have been granted in the name of the King and the communities and divisions[,] I have come to grant him distinction for his merits and I promote him to the rank of Brigadier in the name of the King and until the resolution of His Majesty [arrives, he] shall be recognized as such commissioned Brigadier who shall be obeyed and respected as such[,] rendering him all the honors and privileges that correspond to him. Issued in San Luis. Signed by me on 20 February, 1828, José Antonio Abad Huachaca, José Giron, General Secretary.[51]

That same day, Huachaca ordered Soregui to send him "the traitor Pascual Arancibia," "under arrest and well guarded."[52]

But the bestowal of honors and issuance of fresh orders would be of no avail to the Uchuraccay caudillo. The "traitor" Arancibia was now secure among the government's top men. And despite the attachment of new volunteers to their ranks following the defeat at Pampa del Arco, the outlook for the insurgents became bleaker with each passing day. The rank of brigadier at this stage of the conflict would no doubt have elicited derision, as opposed to respect, from the enemy side, and perhaps even among the rebels themselves, given their growing sense of discouragement and skepticism. Not only were some of his closest collaborators crossing over to enemy lines, but even those peasant communities whom Huachaca boasted of representing had begun to surrender. They simply were no longer willing to sacrifice themselves.

By March 1828 groups of *comuneros* (community peasants) from Ranra and Chacabamba were turning themselves in to Commander Quintanilla in Tambo. Encouraged by these desertions, other peasants transmitted the following message to their caudillo: "That since he [Huachaca] had abandoned them and left them without recourse while those others had now turned themselves in, they too were going to turn themselves over and therefore expect no reprisal."[53] It was during this same period that Huachaca fled with Soregui, Valle, and another caudillo, Mariano Méndez, to the town of Osno (near Tambo), escaping the persecution of Quintanilla's troops. Arriving there they sacked the church and caused other disturbances.[54] However, on March 20, the same day the priest Francisco Pacheco, the treasurer and agent in charge of providing arms to the insurgents, was announcing to his comrades, from Aranhuay, that "the troops of the pilfering Patria" had been defeated on the outskirts of Lima, Commander Quintanilla triumphantly informed his superiors of the death of sixty-six peasants following military incursions into the surroundings of Uchuraccay.[55] The site had been the rebels' most important stronghold, and Quintanilla's successful raid showed not only the decisiveness of republican victory but also perhaps a degree of violence that had not been observed since the massacre at Pampa del Arco.

On March 19, 1828, Quintanilla's troops surprised the residents of Uchuraccay in their homes, "at daybreak, killing many," as Ylairio Taype, a villager who survived the massacre, would later explain.[56] Among the dead was Prudencio Huachaca, brother of the general. Quintanilla's attack on the unarmed settlers was driven back by an armed rebel contingency, just as the commander had begun to retreat. It was in the course of this counterattack that the majority of the peasants were killed—some forty in all, according to Quintanilla. Twenty-four peasants, both men and women, were taken prisoner, while the rest "fled utterly terrified to the hills and others hid in their ravines and precipices, abandoning women, children, and their few belongings, and those who could escape put their cows and horses out of danger by throwing boulders."[57] Thus, the most important insurgent redoubt was left in ruin. "The great palace of General Huachaca, the fort of Luis Pampa, all of Ninaquiro, and all the rebels' homes, each and every one has been burned."[58]

A few weeks after these events, the authorities captured the wife and two children of Huachaca in the hacienda Chaca, on the outskirts of Huanta (see figures on pages 46 and 124). The same day, the head of José Pérez del Valle, who had been gravely wounded in the confrontation at Uchuraccay, was sent to Prefect Tristán.[59] Pérez del Valle had been a Spanish capitulado. Appointed as tithe collector by Huachaca, he had consistently proven himself to be one of the most loyal followers of the Uchuraccay caudillo. Undoubtedly, his head was a valuable trophy, over which the government gloated, and a shocking and daunting sign for other rebel caudillos.

Following on these military defeats, which had been sufficiently dramatic in and of themselves, came acts of ritual submission on the part of the peasantry. On May 12, several communities laid down their arms in Tambo, and under the guidance of their mayors and by order of Quintanilla proceeded to the town square to take an oath of allegiance to the constitution. "In the carrying out of my commission," wrote a proud Quintanilla to Prefect Tristán, "I have made them understand through positive acts the lofty aims of sovereignty; they have recognized the error in which the Spanish had encased them. In short, my General, as a witness to the repentance of these wretches I inform

Old church in Chaca, today a pueblo and at the time of the monarchist rebellion a hacienda. Huachaca's wife and two children were reportedly captured in Chaca during the raids that followed the rebels' failed assault in Ayacucho in November 1827. *Photograph by author, ca. 1994.*

Tambo, a town coveted by both sides in the monarchist rebellion because of its strategic placement. The mountains in the background face the selva. Peasants from various communities surrendered their weapons to the government and swore an oath to the constitution here in 1828. *Photograph by author, ca. 1997.*

you that they have handed over their firearms, their spears, mostly made of *chonta* [a palm tree], and a partial box of bullets; and that the mayors and community members of those punas have accompanied me to this plaza, where I have made them swear an oath to the Constitution."[60]

The last rebel leaders were captured in the montañas of Acón, on the banks of the Apurímac, between the end of May and the first weeks of June. "These montañas are now devoid of a single well-organized disturber of the peace, their respective governors and mayors [constituted by] men of integrity and patriotism," boasted Commander Quintanilla.[61] It was June 12, 1828, and the restorationist dream had come to an end after more than three years of bloody confrontations, hundreds of deaths, devastated towns, and lost harvests. Soregui, Garay, Juan Fernández, and other Spaniards and Huantinos were condemned to various prison sentences and (in the case of the Europeans) exile. Other Huanta leaders, however, such as the prominent Arancibia and Choque, were granted pardons by the state, having surrendered in a timely manner, and were set free after a brief interrogation. The priest Pacheco was excommunicated, while "indians," to whom no responsibility was attributed, were assigned to "serve the Patria" as recruits.[62] The government of Marshal La Mar could now boast of having put down the most tenacious rebellion that the newborn republican state had so far confronted since the wars of Independence.

Contrary to all expectations, calm did not prevail in the punas, however. Neither General Huachaca nor his lieutenants Mariano Méndez and Manuel Ynga were ever subdued. In May 1828, in the midst of a repressive campaign and with several successes under his belt, Subprefect Francisco Vidal boasted, "I am certain that not fifteen days will pass before we have the pleasure of seeing Guachaca delivered by the same indians who turned themselves over to us."[63] He was mistaken. Two years later Prefect Juan Antonio Gonzales reported helplessly to Vidal's successor, "I have just learned for certain that Guachaca and Méndez not only allow themselves to be seen in the Carhuaurán punas, but one or both of them come down weekly to Guanta, and remain there for a number of days, on account of which one perceives a degree of haughtiness among the indigenous highlanders."[64]

Three years later, on July 24, 1833, the author of those lines was victimized by a new insurrection.[65] This time, however, the uprising was not the work of peasants. The rebels were a group of officers from a mutinied Ayacucho garrison who, calling themselves The Avengers of the Law Division, killed

Colonel Juan Antonio Gonzales, prefect of the department, and Colonel Mariano Guillén, commander of the garrison, for "trying to force presidential elections" in favor of the continuity of Agustín Gamarra.[66] The dissidents caused some disturbance in Ayacucho and then continued on into Huanta. Three weeks later, President Gamarra and his troops entered Ayacucho, and on August 15, 1833, a fierce battle took place on Pultunchara hill, on the outskirts of Huanta, where the rebels were finally subdued by government forces; several of them were eventually executed.[67]

The Ayacucho military uprising of 1833 was but one of seventeen rebellions and conspiracies that Gamarra had to confront during his four-year term as president (1829–33)—this alone foreshadows the degree of political instability that was to ravage Peru in years to come. Ironically, the Huanta peasants, who had no stake in the conflict, were drawn into it by the very same officer who had raided their towns with such great determination not many years before in the name of "order": Commander—now Lieutenant Colonel—José Gabriel Quintanilla. Quintanilla was, in fact, a co-conspirator with the mutinous officers of 1833 and had, according to some sources, managed to escape retribution by Gamarra's troops by concealing himself in the so-called Iquichano territory that he knew so well—most likely taking advantage of his acquaintance with and position of power vis-à-vis the former monarchist montoneros.[68] Yet, regardless of the stratagem Quintanilla and other officers may have resorted to in order to evade capture, most Huanta highland villagers did not take well to receiving seditious officers into their communities—one historian has gone so far as to say even that the peasants were instrumental in the officers' defeat at Pultunchara.[69]

Huanta's were not the only rural communities to be forced into a conflict in which initially they had no stake. The so-called Morochucos of Cangallo province in Ayacucho, who, it will be recalled, had fought against the Spanish during the Independence wars and subsequently had been mobilized to fight in the monarchist rebellion, were being called in to fight once again. Through the prompting of the Gamarra government they were assigned now to the most challenging of tasks: the repression of the Ayacucho rebel officers. As historian Nemesio Vargas points out, "It was actually the indians of Iquicha and the Morochucos who finished off the revolutionaries."[70] If our sources are accurate, then, both "Morochucos" and "Iquichanos" this time fought side by side to help the government put down a military insurrection! Surprisingly, this was not to be the only time it would happen.

A few months later, with the memory of the mutiny of 1833 and the entrance of President Gamarra's heavily armed troops into Ayacucho city still fresh in the minds of Ayacuchanos, another political upheaval shook the Republic. Ex-president Marshall Agustín Gamarra himself was the culprit this time. On January 2, 1834, he orchestrated a coup to oust his successor, General Luis José Orbegoso, who had been elected president by the National Convention on December 21, 1833. But the coup failed to attract supporters in Lima, forcing Gamarra to wage war against Orbegoso from the highlands.

Orbegoso's government in turn made preparations for its defense. In command of his armies were some of the most prominent veterans of the Independence wars, including generals Guillermo Miller and Mariano Necochea as well as the ex-prefect of Ayacucho and mastermind of the monarchist uprising's final repressive campaigns, General Domingo Tristán. Orbegoso began by deploying his forces in strategic locations to repel the advances of Gamarra's armies, including the sierra of Lima (Lunahuaná and Yauyos), the central sierra (Huancayo, Locllapampa, and Huancavelica), and Ica, to the south of Lima (see map 2). From these positions the Orbegosista generals set into motion all of their resourcefulness in order to win over the rural populations, just as they had done (with some success) during the Independence wars. Early in April 1834, writing from Lunahuaná, General Tristán reported an initial success, as more than four hundred guerrillas were joining the army in that area, mobilized by the authorities of the towns of Víñac (in the sierra of Lima) and Chupamarca (in Huancavelica).[71]

The sierra of Lima was thus being won over to Orbegoso's side, but there still remained the south. At the same time, Gamarra's forces, now in full retreat, planned to reach Gamarra's stronghold in Cuzco, by way of Ayacucho. The Orbegosistas' push to secure Ayacucho was therefore of primary importance, and they would spare no effort to attain their objective. In effect, the Orbegoso generals, knowing that the Huantinos had proven in the past to be efficient fighters (though not on the same side), reasoned that should they win them over to the government camp this time around, Gamarra would suffer a serious blow in Ayacucho. Being experienced proselytizers, they wasted no time in enticing them with "the rewards and distinctions" reserved by the state for those who would offer "eminent services" to the Patria. Orbegoso and his officers, including Tristán himself, wrote deferential pleas to the caudillos Choque and Huachaca, whom they had so derided not long before. They addressed them now as "brave Iquichanos" and, professing admiration for their courage, summoned them to "save the nation" from the hands of the "tyrant."[72] In this context, Gamarra and his right-hand man, General Pedro Bermúdez, were "the enemies of the nation," as General Miller wrote to Antonio Huachaca; and they "had broken the laws," "making a revolution that has caused tremendous damage to the Patria," according to President Orbegoso's letter to Choque.[73] Huachaca and Choque accepted the deal, and by the end of April 1834 Gamarrista armies were defeated in Ayacucho. By early May the civil war had (temporarily) ended in favor of Orbegoso, who returned to Lima a popularly acclaimed hero.

Unlike the case of the Ayacucho military mutiny of 1833, in which the Huanta peasants were drawn into a conflict they initially had no stake in, their involvement in the Gamarra–Orbegoso civil war had more complex motivations. In other words, the peasants' choice to heed Orbegoso's call to resist Gamarra was as conscious as their decision to fight against the Republic in the king's name had been years before. The prestige inherent in acting on behalf of "the state" and "its laws," the spoils to be gleaned from joining the battle, and, most importantly, their own local grievances against the unpopular Gamarrista regional political authorities, among other reasons to be explored in depth in chapter 7, all go a long way in explaining the peasants' attitude.[74] Yet in responding to the government's call, Huanta montonero chiefs and their peasant followers were not merely obeying orders from above; they were, in fact, making these struggles their own. At any rate, this is what the tithe collector Manuel Santa Cruz de la Vega, among other eyewitnesses, conveyed when he announced that by March and April of 1834—precisely the same months during which peasants were forming guerrilla bands in support of President Orbegoso—"indians" had appropriated the collection of tithes with nobody resisting their actions, just as they had during the monarchist uprising. As on the latter occasion, too, the peasant leaders assumed this time the rank of "general" and claimed to be acting "to defend the laws"; this time, however, the prevailing laws were no longer those of the king, but rather those of the "state" and the "nation." In the tithe collector's own words, "The tithe was in the main collected by those self-appointed 'general': Huachaca, Mendes, Choque and Huamán, saying that the tithe belonged to the state, that since they defended the nation they had the right to take advantage of all of its resources in order to uphold and defend the laws."[75]

Considering that President Orbegoso had called on the peasants to arm themselves in defense of "the state," the "nation," and "its laws" and that the state, moreover, had authorized the collection of tithes to be used on behalf of the montoneras, as we will observe better later,[76] then the peasants' behavior cannot be deemed mere acts of defiance or resistance. Logically, it ought to be considered as well an outright claim to citizenship.

The war of the punas had come to an end. The defeat of the restorationist project meant the breakdown of the Spanish–indigenous alliances that had made the rebellion possible in the first place; but this defeat did not entail the subjugation of the indigenous populations that were at the source of these alliances. Yet their attitude could hardly be identified as one of mere "resistance." While it is true that their appropriation of tithes and subsequent refusal to pay tribute were actions that challenged state authority, it is no less certain that these stances were not only supported but eventually encouraged —or condoned—by the state itself. Fragile as it seemed, the early republican state could not rely on the army alone to assume the defense of the state; it needed the support of rural communities and so encouraged the formation of irregular troops, such as guerrillas, and made use of the montoneras for that very purpose. In so doing, statesmen of the early republic were entrusting civilian rural masses with tasks of state building just as surely as they prolonged the state of warfare inherited from the campaigns for Independence. It mattered little whether peasants at that time had fought for or against the Patria. What was at stake beginning in 1824 was the survival of a sovereign state.

Thus the peasants and muleteers of Huanta, renouncing their restorationist undertakings, came to be involved in a series of pacts with the republican state they had initially so utterly rejected and with its caudillos. And thus these seemingly insignificant towns of the high sierra began to play a major, albeit unsuspected and largely ignored, role in the history of the Republic of Peru.

3

Royalism in the Crisis of Independence

> Fifteen or twenty individuals employed in Peru are with us; all the oth-
> ers have stayed in the enemy's ranks, not so much for being godos but
> rather out of desperation. For, given that here one has seen not miracles
> but disasters, few believe in our wonders. They are almost right.
>
> —Simón Bolívar to Santander, May 1824

Rumors of a possible landing of royalist troops at the port of Callao significantly influenced the mindset of the Huanta rebels, driving them to radical
actions like the capturing of Huanta city and an attempt to invade Ayacucho.
Rumors seldom take hold in relatively stable social situations, but they flourish
under conditions of social instability and political crisis, like those that existed
in Peru in 1826. Not only did the circumstances make the rumors possible, but
above all they made them credible. Such rumors circulated in Peru even before
the crisis precipitated by Bolívar's departure in 1826; they can be traced back to
San Martín's proclamation of Independence of July 28, 1821. Notwithstanding
the euphoria and excitement that accompanied this celebration, the proclamation was hardly more than a rhetorical exercise; it was an auspicious beginning
or a milestone in a long campaign waged in the face of resistance.

Though driven out of Lima, royalist forces continued to control strategic
locations throughout Peruvian territory during and after 1821. The campaign
to defeat them would be long and drawn out, and the uncertainty as to
whether the project could be achieved remained great for years to come. Who
would govern? How would the political change affect peoples' lives? Was
independence truly possible? From the moment San Martín delegated his
power to the first Peruvian National Congress in September 1822 and set off in
the direction of Valparaíso, Peruvians became entangled in a series of factional
struggles that ceased only (and but momentarily) with the arrival of Bolívar a
year later. Conflicts arose between Congress and the military, within the
military, and within the Congress itself. In February 1823 an army insurrection

dissolved the governing junta and required the Congress to accept Colonel José de la Riva Agüero as head of state. Besieged by the military, in what some consider to be the first coup d'état in the history of Peru, the Congress made Riva Agüero the first Peruvian president.[1] But he did not hold office for long. Four months later Spanish troops occupied Lima. The Congress, having taken refuge in Callao, voted to depose Riva Agüero and delegated supreme military command in Peru to the Colombian General Antonio José de Sucre, whom they expected to quell the Spanish military threat while paving the way for Bolívar's arrival. Riva Agüero, however, refused to yield his command and instead dissolved the Congress, appointing a ten-man "senate" which he thought might enable him to cling to the presidency from his base in the city of Trujillo. In the meantime, the Spanish had evacuated Lima, while the Congress, reinstalled in the capital, named Marquis Bernardo de Torre Tagle as president of Peru. Hence, when Bolívar arrived he found two presidents: Riva Agüero in Trujillo and Torre Tagle in Lima.[2]

Thus, in the span of one year following the proclamation of Independence, Peru had been ruled by one so-called protector (General San Martín), one governing junta, two presidents, and at least three military commanders, while its capital was raided by Spanish troops for more than a month. It was in this atmosphere fraught with expectation and uncertainty that one day in May 1822, with San Martín still in the government, a seemingly banal incident occurred, perhaps even routine for the guardians of public order of the time; but the episode turns out to be extremely significant for us. Luis Moreno, a young soldier from Lima who had recently crossed over to the patriot side, was arrested in the streets of Lima on charges of carrying a scrap of paper with the following "seditious contents":

> No wheat comes from Chile
> No silver comes from Pasco
> Poverty has reached its limit
> And they're saying "Viva la Patria."[3]

The paper sufficed for Moreno to have to stand trial on charges of conspiracy. Asked on what grounds he founded his suspicions of Moreno, Juan Prieto, one of the witnesses at the trial, and likewise a soldier, answered that he

> thought of him [Moreno] as very patriotic because together they went over to
> the army of liberation; but the following fact changed him. It was about a

month ago, and without a doubt on the Sunday of Quasimodo, that the declarant encountered said Moreno in Santa Rosa de las Monjas in the company of José Prieto and . . . Pedreros, and after greeting one another, Moreno asked: what is new? And the declarant replied: I don't know anything; as you are in the Palace, you will have more news than I, and Moreno answered that there was one great piece of news: The *Spanish* [godos] *are approaching with more than 20,000 men* and in that case [i.e., of their arrival] a friend and I have an agreement to go to Huahura because we must protect Number One. He who is explaining this was astonished to hear that from a Patriot, and responded, Goodness gracious! So many people? Yes, he replied: Don't you see that they *have the people of Cuzco, Areguipa, and all of those provinces on the side of the King's government and that* [he] has only this city and its inhabitants who are discontented? At which point the declarant told him [Moreno] to go ahead and support the King, and left.[4]

The veracity of this testimony was corroborated by another witness, José Prieto, who confirmed that what his son Juan had said about Moreno was true, "except for the capital's residents being discontented, for what he [Moreno] said was that the indians were very variable and that the Godos seduced them with promises or with threats."[5]

Lost in the anonymity of its protagonists, the arrest and trial of Luis Moreno are nevertheless of great significance for us insofar as they contain crucial elements for understanding what I call "the crisis of Independence." The incident reveals, first of all, the skepticism of the citizenry with respect to the patriots' triumph. Second, it discloses the principal causes of this skepticism: on the one hand, the shortages and paralyzation of production; on the other, the conviction that the Spanish still controlled the most important cities of the sierra: "Cuzco, Arequipa and all of those provinces" siding with the king, while Lima remained discontented or irresolute. Third, the incident is significant because of the political evolution of the accused, Luis Moreno, and that of the witness, Juan Prieto. Both men, soldiers in the patriots' army, had belonged to the royalist army until only a short while before. Their change of parties was akin to that of most officers who became prefects and presidents of the Republic as well as to that of other distinguished creole intellectuals who are today reckoned, ironically, the "precursors" of Peruvian emancipation.

The elements of this testimony thus serve to profile with striking clarity and economy a state of crisis, and so long as one remains unaware of the critical

dimensions of that situation it is next to impossible to comprehend the enduring hopes that inspired restorationist rumors and the Huanta rebellion. The
crisis of Independence (1820–26) is the subject of this chapter. I first discuss the
crisis in its national manifestations, focusing attention on Lima-Callao and the
south-central sierra. Subsequently, I examine the specific ways in which the
crisis affected the province of Huanta. Whereas the national focus privileges
political and military aspects, my treatment of the crisis in Huanta will highlight economic aspects. All of these factors, however, are so closely interrelated
that such boundaries cannot be regarded as sharply defined: political and
military factors were as much at play in Huanta as economic factors were at
the national level. If, however, I have opted to present the problem in this
fashion, it is because, in gauging the crisis, I take into account perceptions
rather than abstract parameters. Therefore, although the political crisis may
have been perceptible throughout virtually the entire territory of the viceroyalty, it took on especially dramatic overtones in Huanta upon colliding with
an economic catastrophe, or such at least was the perception and experience
of those who would have to cope with the crisis.

The Nation, A Political Crisis

Lima, the Aristocracy, and the Caudillos: The Abrupt Change

Peru has now been in revolution for nine months, and its capital has
found itself in the most horrific anarchy for more than four, the authority that governed on behalf of the king having been deposed.
         —*El Depositario*, June 28, 1821

The Patria has only this city and its inhabitants are discontented.
         —Luis Moreno, Lima, May 1822

When Bolívar arrived in Peru in September 1823 and assumed the post vacated
by San Martín, the Republic was, as noted earlier, ruled by two presidents,
Torre Tagle in Lima, and Riva Agüero in Trujillo. In February 1824 the Congress, having ousted President Torre Tagle under accusation of plotting with
the Spaniards, handed Bolívar dictatorial powers "at the same time as it was
decreeing its own recess until summoned by the Liberator."[6] Although the
accusations against Torre Tagle were not'proven, Bolívar ordered his arrest

and, with Riva Agüero already out of the picture, proceeded to appoint the Rioplatense General Mariano Necochea as military and political chief of Lima. Necochea, however, abandoned the capital shortly afterward, leaving it completely leaderless (Bolívar being at his headquarters in Pativilca). As Jorge Basadre has written, "The soldiery having gone over to the royalist side, the montoneros and gangs of criminals devoted themselves to looting and murder in Lima, while the inhabitants prayed for the arrival of some organized troops, whoever they might be."[7] The troops arrived, to be sure, but they were Spanish troops, dispatched from the sierra, where the king's defenders had stationed their forces. "General Juan Antonio Monet, the new Spanish governor of Lima, published an edict promising its peaceful citizens that he would completely forget the past with respect to their conduct and opinions."[8] It was February 1824, and the Spanish had recovered—albeit for one final moment only, as it turned out—the capital city of what had once been their largest colony in America. Three years after the proclamation of Independence, history seemed to be moving in reverse—and rumors turning into prophecies.

This "posthumous" capture of Lima by royalist troops is probably absent from most Peruvians' historical memory of the events surrounding Independence. And yet, it is precisely this sort of action—exemplifying the patriots' difficulty in retaining control even of the very capital of the Republic—that enables one to understand the fact that, whether out of fear or hope, the shadow of an imminent return of the Spanish persisted. The mutual distrust between a significant portion of the Peruvian ruling elite and Bolívar became a major source of political instability and seriously undermined the ability of the partisans of Independence to quell Spanish military threats.

One of the most vivid cases of Peruvian antipathy toward Bolívar was that of President Riva Agüero himself. An exceptional character among Peru's early republican military caudillos, Riva Agüero, unlike most of them, had never fought on the king's side but had been involved instead, as early as 1809, in revolutionary conspiracies.[9] Moreover, he had never been a colonel in the army, having served in this capacity only in militias; not until Congress proclaimed him president did he obtain the rank of army colonel and the honorific title of grand marshall. And yet, for Riva Agüero, the Liberator was so loathsome that he thought "it was preferable to join the Spaniards than to submit to Bolívar."[10] Similar sentiments were echoed by his successor to the presidency, Marquis Torre Tagle, the moment he learned that Bolívar had ordered his arrest on suspicion that he too had entered into agreements with the Spaniards.[11] The alternative to Bolivarian rule that Riva Agüero had in mind and which he had apparently begun negotiating with Viceroy La Serna, did not differ much from the plans that San Martín had envisioned for an independent Peru two years earlier: the establishment of a constitutional monarchy ruled by a Spanish prince. San Martín's project failed for lack of support, but at that time it was seen neither as "betrayal" nor as "anathema." Yet, under Bolívar, conditions were different. Bolívar's military prestige in South America was rivaled only by that of San Martín, as was his resolve to wage war to the death against the Spaniards, having done so already in his native Venezuela (then a part of the territory known as Gran Colombia or simply "Colombia"). Bolívar left little room for middle-ground positions. Had Riva Agüero's parallel "negotiations" with La Serna succeeded, they would have proved fatal to the continental liberation project that Bolívar had foreseen, insofar as the Spanish still controlled key Peruvian cities.[12] Furthermore, the animosity between Peru's upper class and Bolívar would continue to be volatile, surviving the Battle of Ayacucho and resurfacing once Bolívar had left Peru for his native Caracas; ultimately, it would ignite Peru's war with Colombia in 1829.

Given this scenario, it is not surprising that the return of Spanish rule came to be considered a desirable option among the populace, who were feeling alienated by such a prolonged state of anarchy and unruliness and by a seemingly mindless war. They, we may assume, desired stability, a stability that many associated with the distant figure of the king. For those higher up on the social scale, however, there was more at stake than stability. Historically, their bonds with Spain had proven strong—and they would cling to those bonds even at the expense of political stability, as the cases of Riva Agüero and Torre Tagle pathetically illustrate. The creole elite of Lima owed their power, prestige, and sources of livelihood precisely to their ties to (or membership in) the colonial bureaucracy. Both the nobility and the high-ranking military owed their titles, awards, and honors to the Crown, which the vast majority of them relinquished only after the arrival of San Martín. The fact that the first two Peruvian presidents, Riva Agüero and Torre Tagle, belonged to prominent families of the creole nobility of Lima explains in part why, despite having favored independence, they did not conceive of the Spanish as their natural enemies, particularly when confronted with Bolívar's dominant personality and limitless political ambitions, which they saw as no less of a threat.

Baptized Ciudad de los Reyes (City of Kings), Lima was the most important political and administrative center of the Spanish Empire in South America. Its most affluent merchants historically had benefited from Spain's decision to grant the city monopoly over trade in the South Pacific. Faithful to their longtime protectors, the merchants of Lima, associated through the Tribunal del Consulado (Lima's merchant guild), became the chief financiers of the wars against revolutionary movements that broke out in various regions of South America following Napoleon's invasion of Spain in 1808, and were to remain loyal to the very end. The tribunal's commitment to the royalist cause led it to offer rewards "to the bodies and individuals of the army or navy that distinguish themselves in some way against the patriots."[13]

Not all corporations and creole elites in Lima were to prove that subservient, however. The *cabildo* (city council), in particular, underwent a process of liberal reforms propelled and inspired by the Cádiz Constitution of 1812 and by the democratic revolution that Spain itself was then experiencing. The changes brought into its ranks professionals, artisans, and even nobles, such as the famed Conde de la Vega del Ren, who were critical of the regime. Newly elected liberal councilmen advocated, among other things, educational reform in Lima while fustigating the vices of the colonial system, particularly Viceroy Abascal's unabashed despotism and commitment to absolutism. The cabildo's liberal reign, however, proved to be ephemeral, for in 1814, with Fernando VII back in power, the Crown abolished both the Cádiz constitution and the liberal reforms enacted in all Spanish domains, giving an overjoyed Abascal a free hand to expel all liberals from the cabildo and arrange for a reinstatement of absolutism. The Limeño liberal current thus began to die out politically, along with its short-lived mouthpiece *El Peruano Liberal*.[14] Thereafter, as long as Spain's rule in Peru persisted, Lima's political liberalism would be relegated to a powerless minority position.

Other provincial capitals in what is today Peruvian national territory experienced similar processes during the same critical juncture, and in some places, for example, Tacna, Huánuco, and Cuzco, liberal mobilization developed into violent insurrection. All of these rebellions were defeated, the case of Cuzco being perhaps the most dramatic. Between 1814 and 1815, Mateo García Pumacahua, an interim president of Cuzco's Audiencia (high court), joined Vicente and José Angulo, creoles from Cuzco and ex-officers in the Royal Army, to lead a widespread insurrection that no doubt evoked reminiscences of the Túpac Amaru rebellion. Unlike most other rebel leaders that historians tend to associate with Independence (and to some extent unlike

Túpac Amaru himself), the Angulo brothers openly sought to break with the Crown.[15] The severe suppression of this movement ended up consolidating absolutist rule in what hitherto had been a center of major anticolonial rebellions. As Basadre once reflected, Cuzco was thus transformed from rebel epicenter to royalist bastion.[16]

Paradoxically, it was the military and civilian members of the creole elite who had either remained loyal to, or uncritical of, the regime—when not actively participating in the repression of revolutionary movements such as the aforementioned—those that played the leading role in the foundation of the Republic. In fact, most of Peru's "founding fathers" and early republican caudillos follow this pattern. Attentive more to opportunity than to ideology, they swiftly converted to separatism not long after San Martín's triumphant entry into Peruvian territory at the head of the Army of the Andes. Indeed, most of the members of the creole elite who took part in the Independence struggles had decided to join the revolution shortly before the proclamation of Independence by San Martín on July 28, 1821; it was usually a question of months, at most a year. Hipólito Unanue, deemed to be one of Peru's "founding fathers" and a "precursor of emancipation" in official historiography, strove to demonstrate his fidelity to Spain, in the name of the city of Arequipa, as late as 1819.[17] The marquis de Torre Tagle, who would become president of Peru, had received the rank of lieutenant colonel and commander from Viceroy Abascal and was, moreover, a member of the Distinguished Volunteers of the Spanish Concord in Peru. José de la Mar, a distinguished military man and likewise president during the first years of the Republic (precisely when the Huanta rebellion was triggered) had been a member of Viceroy Pezuela's Advisory War Junta.[18] General Domingo Tristán, prefect of Ayacucho on successive occasions (and an implacable persecutor of Huanta's monarchists—see chapter 2), had been, like Torre Tagle and La Mar, a distinguished officer in the Royal Army. An illustrious member of Peru's creole nobility, Tristán had acquired his most valuable military experience fighting in and for Spain. His notable performance in battle against rebel forces in La Paz during 1809 earned then-colonel Tristán the intendancy of Arequipa, his hometown. It was not until September 1821 that Tristán finally joined San Martín's liberation army as it was occupying Lima.[19] Something similar occurred with generals Andrés de Santa Cruz and Agustín Gamarra, natives of La Paz and Cuzco, respectively, whose lesser share of European blood did not prevent them from serving in the king's armies along with the "white" generals of aristocratic lineage. Both of them would pass over to the patriotic army as late as 1820,[20] and both would become presidents of the Republic.

With most of Peru's military, aristocrats, and intellectuals recently converted to the independence cause, and with most of the major merchants undecided or as yet loyalist, one ought not be surprised at the sense of uncertainty pervading Peru in the year intervening between San Martín's proclamation of Independence and the arrival of Bolívar, nor at the magnitude of the political crisis. The Peruvian elite had been capable of undergoing an abrupt change in attitude, faction, uniform, or party, as indeed it did. Erasing ties based on affiliation, way of life, tradition, and political expectations proved more difficult. Given the reliance of many of them on the state and Church treasuries, the stakes were particularly high in making a political decision for or against Spain, since not just their political fate but their very survival as a class would be decided. "Until total victory was won," wrote historian Timothy Anna, "how could they risk everything on an untimely or early declaration of support for one side or the other? . . . Since the most ancient bonds of history tied them with the Spanish cause, how could they be certain Independence was the solution to their grievances?"[21]

The Real Felipe

Ships will soon arrive, our troops will come. — *El Depositario*, April 7, 1825

Tradition, culture, power, and economic interests thus sustained a skeptical or proroyalist attitude among Lima's great merchants and aristocrats. Yet, apart from the position of its elites, a strategic consideration reinforced Lima's status as a privileged site of Spanish power in America. In Lima's port city of Callao stood the Real Felipe fortress. Built during the height of Spanish imperial expansion, this stone-walled, fortified castle was Spain's primary military bulwark on the Pacific. Following the capitulation of Ayacucho, the Spanish military, still garrisoned at the Real Felipe, refused to concede defeat and under the command of José Ramón Rodil remained reluctant to surrender for as long as thirteen months after the patriot victory at Ayacucho. In effect, the Real Felipe established itself as the last holdout for loyalists of the king on the Pacific coast, the center of conspiracies, and a seedbed of monarchical ideas and restorationist rumors. The newspapers *El Depositario, El Triunfo del Callao*, and *El Desengaño* were printed within its walls, some as late as 1825. Rich in invective, these publications sought to discredit Bolívar, "that Goddamned son of a bitch,"[22] and erode the credibility garnered by the republicans after the victory of Ayacucho. *El Depositario* was the most radical and incendiary of all the royalist newspapers. Its refusal to accept the inexorable collapse of the Spanish Empire in America led it to adopt a restorationist-absolutist stance, in tandem with the royalist invectives fomenting insurrection in Huanta.[23] The conjunction of the two was no coincidence. Spaniards on both ends kept in contact, a key link being the captain of the Royal Army Sebastián Riera, transferred to Callao in 1824.[24] Riera had arrived in Ayacucho by way of Ica, with plans of stirring up a great insurrection and to join the Huanta rebels. According to Juan Heredia, who shared a prison cell with him in Ayacucho, "He had really come from Lima, by way of Ica, with that aim, and his intention was none other than to raise 200 men there, capture Huanta and that city. . . . On several occasions he proposed . . . fleeing from the jail in order to go to Iquicha, saying that there he could gather 200, that he would capture Huanta and Ayacucho, beheading the inhabitants of the latter because they were evil, and that after this had happened, Lima and Ica, where he had many friends, would then revolt."[25]

Riera was not able to carry out his plans because the prefect of Ayacucho, finding his behavior suspect, ordered him transferred to Lima just as he was preparing to escape from jail.[26] Nevertheless, he succeeded in creating a climate of expectation and alarm in Ayacucho by disseminating news of conspiratorial movements in other areas and by raising the specter of the imminent arrival in Lima of spies sent by the Holy Alliance. Fact or fiction, the rebels in Huanta hoped this news to be certain, and even published a proclamation in the montaña of Acón and the Paraíso hacienda "on the coming of Riera and his imprisonment."[27] Juan Ramos, a Lima-born lieutenant in the republican army who deserted to join the rebels of Huanta, provided still more extensive testimony about the news disseminated by Riera. He disclosed the scope of the conspirators' network, the extent of their ambitions, and, most amazingly, General Augustín Gamarra's (would-be president of Peru) keen awareness of and possible complicity in such machinations:

> Six spies from the Holy Alliance, who had come on a French ship, had met with all of the capitulados then in the capital, and tried to make a revolution in the following way: by inciting Huancavelica, Ica, Aymaraes, and Cerro de Pasco to rebellion; and they were relying on a capitulado colonel whom General Gamarra brought over to his side, and who was in Cuzco at the head of a squadron that he had promised to lead into Aymaraes and stir up this province with other capitulados, among them an infantry official who had been an

adjutant in the Spanish forces, and whom said señor Gamarra, not wanting to take sides, demoted to private, and who a few days later was, through a trade-off, made an officer; and as a result of this meeting which Riera attended they offered him the Castillo del Sol, promised to wipe away the blemish and support the revolution in Iquicha, and to work in conjunction with the others, and as, indeed, all was granted to, he left by the route of Ica for Quicamachay, where he was taken prisoner; and *in Ica the capituldos had gathered to act in accordance with Riera,* but he [Riera] did not mention their names, *because their main hopes lay in the expedition coming from Spain, but they wanted to have the merit of rousing Peru in advance.* They had sent communiqués to a jailer of don Pedro de Abadía in Cerro de Pasco and others, passing on the news of the number of troops who were making their way from the Península to the coast, and the generals who were coming; that Rodil had been given the title of Marquis of Callao, and Moyano that of Brigadier General, and Rivero was coming at the head of a regiment. *They were sure that their efforts would succeed because all of the capitulados were in agreement with the many residents of the towns of Huanta, Huancayo, and Huamanga.*[28]

According to this testimony, all of the localities sympathetic to or in contact with the Lima conspirators, with the exception of Ica, were situated in Peru's central and southern sierra; these included Cerro de Pasco, Huancayo, Huancavelica, Huanta, Huamanga, Aimaraes (in Apurímac), and Cuzco (see maps 1 and 2). The reason that conspirators concentrated in these areas is fairly obvious: it was in the central and southern sierra that the battles of Junín and Ayacucho, that is, the two final, decisive battles for Peruvian Independence, were fought. Many officers and soldiers who had fought in those battles and managed to elude capture were still wandering about the region, and it was them— *"los dispersos"* ("the scattered ones" of the Royal Army)—who the conspirators in Huanta and the Real Felipe sought to recruit. But there were yet other reasons for the monarchists to place their restorationist hopes in the sierra.

The Sierra, Royalist Bastion

Don't you see that they have the people of Cuzco, Arequipa, and all of those provinces on the side of the King's government?
—Luis Moreno, Lima, May 1822

They cried most enthusiastically, "long live the king!"
—Eugenio Garzón, Izcuchaca, November 22, 1824

When in 1820 General San Martín's Army of the Andes reached Peruvian territory after a successful campaign in Chile, the royalist army withdrew from the capital to the central and southern sierra, where they regrouped and set about planning their resistance. The king's generals continued to recruit followers in the region, especially among the peasants. Thus, it was in the sierra where Bolívar would engage the main royalist commanders upon his arrival in Peru in September 1823. General Loriga was stationed in Jauja, Canterác in Huancayo, and Viceroy La Serna in Cuzco.[29] The reception that city officials gave them was far from hostile, especially in Cuzco, where La Serna had moved with his vice regal court in response to an invitation from the city's Audiencia to leave behind "the obscure town of Huancayo" in favor of "the Court of the Incas."[30] The hispanophile attitude (or, perhaps, lofty ambitions) of the former Inca capital's elites led its cabildo to request, as late as May 1824, that the Crown formally declare Cuzco the capital of Peru.[31] Also in the south, Arequipa "had earned a royalist reputation for itself and remained loyal until the very last minute."[32] Such illustrious Arequipeños as Domingo Tristán and Hipólito Unanue were ardent defenders of the king until shortly before San Martín's arrival, as previously mentioned. Tristán's loyalty was evident on the battlefield; that of Unanue in his writings and duties as a member of the Arequipa city council. In 1818, responding to a request submitted by Unanue himself, King Fernando VII issued a royal decree granting the city the title of *Excelencia entera en cuerpo* and authorizing the use of uniforms "to individuals of its city council as long as they remain members thereof . . . in consideration of their constant fidelity and extraordinary services" to the king.[33] The loyalty of other affluent Arequipan creoles proved to be even more long-lasting, as in the case of Pío Tristán, a high officer in the Royal Army. Pío Tristán's commitment to the prolongation of Spanish rule led him to assume the post of viceroy of Peru following La Serna's capture on the Ayacucho battlefield. Only when the official dispatch of the Spanish capitulation in Ayacucho arrived in Arequipa did Tristán resign and assume the position of "interim viceroy," which he held for only six days before deciding to abide by the laws of the Republic.[34]

In Huamanga and its capital, "the most noble and loyal city of San Juan de la Frontera y Victoria de Huamanga," the situation was not very different. Although separatist rumors and anti-Spanish leaflets had circulated in Huamanga under the cover of the La Paz insurrection in 1809 and above all during the tumultuous year of 1812, they scarcely posed a threat to the royalists, who at most ended up migrating to the neighboring town of Huanta.[35] When Huamanga's

Independence was proclaimed in 1821—"with the greatest sumptuousness," according to Prefect Pardo de Zela—patriotic fervor seemed to have been suddenly reborn. This was at any rate the way the prefect reported the event to the minister of war: "I no longer have even the slightest doubt about the interest that inspires them [Huamanga's inhabitants] to uphold the Independence that all of the citizens have proclaimed."[36] Nevertheless, two years later not a trace of the initial patriotic fervor remained, at least not among the intellectual elite of the city. *La Aurora Astral*, the first newspaper to appear in Ayacucho, printed each of the speeches that celebrated a Spanish victory at Moquegua in October 1823. One of these orations, that of José Joaquín Larriva, closed with an overtly loyalist benediction: "I unceasingly beseech heaven to extend the duration of a reign which we have reason to expect will wholly reestablish the beloved tranquility."[37]

Such was the prevailing spirit in the most important cities of Peru's south-central sierra during the months leading up to the Battle of Ayacucho. But the loyalist vocation (or propensity for it) so clearly manifest in the speeches and proclamations of the enlightened figures of those cities had its corollary in the countryside. The officers in command of the United Liberation Army reported on the hostility or indifference of a large part of the population. Only a few weeks before the Battle of Ayacucho, the prefect of Ayacucho, Juan Antonio Gonzales, reported as follows to General Santa Cruz from the town of Izcuchaca (Huancavelica):

> The enemy had occupied the city of Huamanga on the day of the seventeenth and . . . the intendants of Huanta and Angaraes, from whom news was expected, had migrated. There were no officials to commission in order to obtain some knowledge of the enemy, nor any person among the inhabitants of Huancavelica, for although I called on several, all refused, because they did not want to become involved. I had no soldiers other than my two assistants and six montoneros of Commander Fresco, so it was not possible to make them respect my orders. Nor could I obtain any news because there was no one to report them to me, since there were only two officials, and on the eighteenth I sent them to the most interesting places so that they could get some news, but they did not return. There was no longer anything that I could do in Huancavelica because all resources had been withheld from me, for there was not a single person who wanted to get involved. . . . Yesterday afternoon I left for the town of Huando, and on the way I found out that the indians had revolted.[38]

The following day, November 22, Eugenio Garzón continued the report in another letter to Santa Cruz. He recounted how a group of officers and civilians accompanying the prefect "had been surprised at dawn, overpowered and looted by indians of Huando [Huancavelica] where they had slept[;] they [the indians] had been completely persuaded by the Spaniards."[39] Garzón went on to describe how the hostilities continued unrelentingly as he ordered the destruction of a bridge in the strategic location of Izcuchaca: "They continued to pursue us constantly for more than twenty-five blocks. General, I assure your lordship that from Huancavelica to here the entire country has risen against us, and they are angry, too. . . . They cried most enthusiastically, 'Long live the King,' their armament is ordinary, and we know that they are saving it in order to wage war against us, for they did not fire a single shot against the Spaniards in their retreat."[40]

In Huanta the population had been in revolt against the occupying patriot army since November 16, according to Antonio José de Sucre, Bolívar's most trusted general and head of military operations in Ayacucho: "Its inhabitants and those of the entire district have obstructed us in every way," wrote Sucre. "They have killed our sick, taken the charges that were destined for the army, stolen the equipment . . . and most recently introduced a montonera of two thousand men to serve the Spaniards."[41] Marshall Guillermo Miller, another high-ranking patriot general, would recall in more disdainful terms the hostility of Huanta's villagers: "The heights which tower above the town of Quinua were occupied by indians of this sort, who had the audacity to come within a half mile of the patriots' encampment, and take several head of livestock from a group of Dragoons."[42] His testimony was echoed by that of a young officer who, as part of the Pichincha battalion, was later sent to pacify the punas of Huanta: José Rufino Echenique, would-be president of Peru.[43] In Huanta and Huando the hostilities against the patriots continued incessantly after the Battle of Ayacucho. On December 12, 1824, the peasants of Huando reportedly assassinated Commander Medina, Sucre's emissary, who was headed for Lima to deliver a report on the patriot victory at Quinua to Bolívar, intercepting the report in the process.[44]

Over and above the guerrilla opposition, proroyalist sentiment in the towns located along the Jauja-Huancavelica-Huanta route was also felt among unarmed civilians. Shortly after the Battle of Ayacucho, residents of Acomayo turned against a neighbor with the intention of relieving him of some papers allegedly giving evidence of their royalist militancy.[45] In Huancayo, Jauja, and

Huaribamba (province of Tayacaja, Huancavelica), loyalty to the king was preached from the pulpit (see maps 4 and 5).[46] And in Huancavelica the same spirit had taken root among merchants and the more prosperous sectors of the capital, although for reasons that, as was true of the Huantinos also (as we shall later see), were not disconnected from their economic interests.[47]

If, as the testimonies suggest, a spirit of loyalty was so deeply entrenched in various towns of the central sierra, it follows that this inclination would hardly be eradicated by two patriot victories in battle. These were victories that, without deprecating the contributions made by the townspeople of Huaychao, Acosvinchos, Quinua, San Miguel, Pampa Cangallo, Vilcashuamán, Parinacochas, and Lucanas to the cause of Independence—to mention only the most committed patriotic towns in Ayacucho—could not have been attained without the participation of the armies of the Gran Colombia (modern Ecuador, Venezuela, Panama, and Colombia), who made up the bulk of the United Liberation Army. It is beyond the scope of this book to analyze the rationale behind the support for the Patria shown by these Ayacuchan towns, all of which were, interestingly, located south of Huanta. But admittedly, the topic deserves attention, especially in the case of the Morochucos of the province of Cangallo, who to this day maintain a strong sense of pride in their ancestors' contribution to the patriot cause.[48] Unlike most urban intellectual elites, the Morochucos had a long and very consistent history of support for Independence. When revolution broke out in La Paz in 1809, they joined the insurgents that marched on Arequipa and were defeated by the city's loyalists. The then staunchly loyalist Hipólito Unanue boasted of this victory, which the king rewarded by bestowing special honors to the city council of Arequipa of which he was a member.[49] Subsequently, in 1814, the Cangallinos joined the rebellion of Cuzco, and in the early 1820s sided with the army of San Martín. It is worth noting, as well, that while the Ayacuchan towns that supported the patriots were located either south or east of Ayacucho city (in today's provinces of Huamanga, Cangallo, Lucanas, and part of La Mar), the northern edge of the department (today's province of Huanta and the northern portion of La Mar) remained royalist (see maps 3, 4, and 5). Not coincidentally, the Battle of Ayacucho took place on a plain allegedly named Ayacucho, on the outskirts of the town of Quinua. Located squarely between these two sharply demarcated political fields, the site was only fifteen kilometers north of the city of Huamanga, which Bolívar rebaptized Ayacucho after the battle.

Despite the dozens—and possibly hundreds—of books dedicated to glorify-

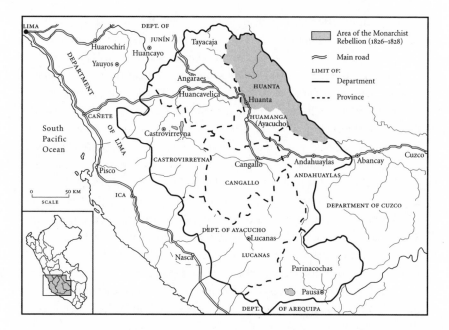

MAP 2. Area of the monarchist rebellion.

ing this famous battle, we, in fact, know little about the social and ethnic composition of the troops that clashed on the battlefield. What we know for sure is that there were more Peruvians in the defeated King's Army than in Sucre's victorious United Liberation Army; that, given its numbers, the latter suffered relatively few causalities (308); and that only a minority of its fighters were Peruvian—1,500 out of 5,800, while 4,000 were Gran Colombian and the remaining 300 from various other places (including some officers from Río de La Plata and Great Britain).[50] Conversely, among the more than 9,000 men that made up the Spanish army there were only 500 Europeans, the rest coming from Peru (some 6,000) and Upper Peru (approximately 3,000).[51] The Spanish general Gerónimo Valdés noted the irony: "The enemies were like foreigners, finding themselves 600 and some even 1,500 leagues away from home" (Valdés was probably thinking, in addition to the Americans, of the several British officers fighting with the patriots). "Thus Bolívar's army looked more like the Spanish Army than that of the Viceroy in whose ranks one could count no more than 500 Europeans, from soldier to chief, the rest being prisoners from previous battles or recruits from the country."[52] Valdés stressed the latter in his attempt to convince the king that the main reason for the defeat (and thus for the loss of Peru) was the troops' lack of willingness to fight: as drafted natives, they were more eager to desert and had even begun rebelling against their officers. Valdés wrote convincingly. At the same time, however, it is important to keep in mind that there was nothing unusual about the army of the king being constituted mainly of Andean-born soldiers. Since the mid–eighteenth century the Crown had encouraged the formation of mulatto, mestizo, and indian militias—the latter usually commanded by their own kurakas to combat the indigenous rebellions that became endemic in Peru's southern sierra during the second half of the century.[53] That this strategy of "divide and rule" proved so effective is attested to by the fact that a Royal Army so constituted had been militarily successful for decades. The Spanish army that crushed the Túpac Amaru rebellion had been, like its opponent, a mostly indian army, as was the army that would defeat Pumacahua's rebellion decades later.[54] To be sure, much had changed during the four decades between the rebellion of Túpac Amaru and the Battle of Ayacucho: in the long run, one must consider the waning of kuraka authority, so central to the recruitment and mobilization of indians; and in the short term the dramatic and demoralizing setback suffered by the Royal Army at Junín accounts for the state of virtual disarray of the Spanish army at the Battle of Ayacucho. Nevertheless, the military defeat in itself reveals little about the actual political strife in Ayacucho in the months preceding and following the battle. In other words, what needs to be explained is not so much why the Spanish lost the battle (in this, most historians would probably agree with Valdés), but rather why the patriots' military victory was not complemented by a political victory in the region where the battle took place.

Let us first consider what political issues were at stake at the national level. The fact that Peruvians owed the victory of Ayacucho—that is, their most decisive battle of the struggle for independence—to a largely Gran Colombian army loomed large in the politics of the new Republic. Bolívar's purported preferential treatment of the Colombian army stationed in Peru upon his assumption of power alienated a discontented and ill-paid Peruvian military, who would, in July 1826, initiate a wave of mutinies that compromised the stability of the Liberator's regime. Two months later, Bolívar would leave Peru in frustration, heading for Colombia.[55] The rebellion of two squadrons of the Junín Húsares battalion in Huancayo is, on the other hand, a highly poignant and pertinent episode in this story because they had evidently established some degree of coordination with none other than the rebels of Huanta, with whom they were united in their opposition to Bolívar.[56] If contact did in fact take place (and the presence of some deserters from these squadrons among the Iquichano armies suggests it did) it would mean that anti-Colombian (that is to say, anti-Bolivarian) nationalism proved more persistent than anti-Spanish nationalism. This state of affairs, which brings to mind Riva Agüero's predicament years earlier, could only embolden the plans of the rebels in Huanta.

At the local level, the presence of well-organized militias (as opposed to the drafted soldiers and war prisoners to which Valdés referred) fighting alongside the Spanish and effectively disrupting patriot movements along the Huancavelica-Huanta trade routes—which the testimonies quoted above so vividly describe—suggests the existence of complex alliances favoring the Spanish among these populations, even after the Battle of Ayacucho.

Following the trail of proroyalist activities and restorationist rumors, one arrives at a connection that is not all ideological. In Huancayo, Huancavelica, Huanta, and Andahuaylas, where rumors, pamphlets, and lampoons announcing the return of the Spanish and decrying the Patria were endemic, defense of the king was not the only aim—more immediate and specific interests were defended as well. Indeed, the rumors and pamphlets traveled the very routes along which the coca produced in Huanta was marketed.[57] Some of the most prominent leaders of the Huanta rebellion were indeed coca traders and hacendados from the coca-growing montañas of Huanta; other participants, including priests, ex-soldiers from the Spanish army, and peasants from the montañas and highland communities, worked as administrators, employees, farmhands, and peons on these haciendas. This introduces the economic problem confronting Huanta and the first level of analysis for understanding the rationale behind the alliances that lent the rebellion its viability.

An Economic Crisis: The Region

Corporeal eyes suffice and are more than enough to sense the extreme misery of this city, and of the surroundings that form the province of Huamanga.—Unos Vecinos, 1825

The countryside, though crowned with trophies, is devoid of corn-
fields . . . and . . . the parishioners . . . crushed by other burdens, and as a
result of the misfortunes attached to the war are so many wretched
beggars. — Curas de Huamanga, 1827

"Independence in Peru, in the immediate aftermath, was more of a disaster for
the national economy than for that of other countries," wrote Jorge Basadre.[58]
Levies, war quotas, the pillage of haciendas, and forced recruitment funneled
human and material resources into the war machine, visiting ruin on indus-
tries and productive enterprises that were not necessarily thriving to begin
with. In Huamanga, small-scale mining, large-scale muleteering, and *obrajes*
(textile mills) had begun to decline with the waning of mining centers in
Huancavelica and Potosí under Spanish administration and with the impact of
the Bourbon reforms, which discouraged local manufacturing. What remained of these three activities when the Independence wars shook the region
could not have been considerable.[59] In a sense, if the war affected the economy
of the region as a whole, it is likely to have inflicted the most dramatic losses
on the most flourishing sectors of the economy, which in northern Huamanga
meant the production and marketing of coca.

The most intensive coca cultivation was in the montañas of Huanta province, whence the leaves were then transported to the town of Huanta for retail
sale in the primary market of Huancayo, 130 kilometers to the north. Other
important markets were Huancavelica, 80 kilometers to the west, and Andahuaylas, 115 kilometers southeast of Huanta.[60] According to a group of Huanta
hacendados writing in 1819, "The profitable business of coca . . . is the principal
source of [the town's] subsistence."[61] Indeed, by the late eighteenth century,
coca had become Huanta's most important trade commodity, also providing
the bulk of the province's tithe revenues by the time the Independence wars
hit the region.[62] Unlike other crops in Huamanga, such as sugarcane and
wheat, that were hard hit by the reorganization of agricultural markets over
the course of the eighteenth century, coca remained stable[63] and even showed
signs of growth in the first two decades of the nineteenth century.

Coca was farmed in haciendas that varied greatly in size, and their ownership was rather loosely regulated. The lands in which these haciendas were established were called *tierros realengas* (regal lands) because Spanish authorities
assumed them to be royal property insofar as no owners had officially claimed
them. Coca haciendas became established in the montañas of Huanta in the

early colonial period and grew considerably over the years as population increased and new settlers were driven into the area. In 1802 the intendant and *visitador* (official inspector) of Huamanga, Demetrio O'Higgins, informed the minister of the Indies, "On the borders of the districts of Anco and Guanta there are more than seven hundred coca haciendas established by Spaniards and indians in tierras realengas, with no title or purchase from His Majesty other than the fact that each has appropriated lands in accordance with his wishes."[64] Loyal to his mission of increasing the Crown's revenues, O'Higgins embarked on a process of land settlements, or *composición de tierras*, whereby hacendados were required to formalize the ownership of the lands they culti-vated by purchasing land titles from the Crown. Between 1800 and 1802, in response to these measures, about two hundred requests for land settlement were made in the Buena Lerma and Choimacota gorges alone. All were coca haciendas (see map 4).[65]

O'Higgins's attempts to rationalize the ownership of coca plantations in the montañas, however, met with serious opposition from some hacendados who refused to enter into land agreements. In most cases it was the officials, called subdelegates, themselves who sought to frustrate the agreements, in order to uphold privileges they had derived from the arbitrary appropriation of lands. This was not a little ironic because subdelegates were charged with assisting intendants in preserving order and administering justice in the provinces under their jurisdiction.[66] The most notorious case of opposition to land settlements was that of the controversial subdelegate of Huanta, Bernardino Estébanez de Cevallos, who as late as 1809 was fighting to impede land settlement payments that many hacendados owed the Crown.[67] Although many landowners man-aged to legalize their properties, the irregularities persisted, especially among hacendados linked to the subdelegate's cliques. In the end, not only was Estébanez not punished, but his appeals to the Crown were favorably resolved. By a royal warrant (*real cedula*) of May 1816, and in response to demands made by a group of Huanta hacendados, King Fernando VII granted an "exemption from taxes for ten years to the discoverers and developers of the lands in said montañas to whom the subdelegates and authorities are to lend assistance in accordance with the law."[68] The power struggle that for years had pitted the inspector-intendant against the subdelegate-hacendados in Huanta thus ended with the indisputable victory of the latter. Ironically, the subdelegate-hacenda-dos won the battle against control by the Crown (O'Higgins) thanks to the Crown itself![69] In this context, the subdelegate-hacendados, in defending the

king, were in effect defending their own private interests. Moreover, if in fact
the royal warrant of 1816 was to be applied as stipulated, it could potentially
benefit more than just the relatively well-to-do hacendados or Spanish settlers,
for it granted special benefits to indians also, who, according to the warrant,
"should be preferred first [in the allocation of lands], other circumstances being
equal."[70] In light of this, loyalty to the king on the part of those who, regardless
of social scale or ethnicity, had benefited from such measures in the years
leading up to Independence becomes more intelligible.

The patriots' war was turning out to be the worst possible scourge for
hacendados, montaña settlers, and (by extension) coca merchants, who had received such special favors from the Crown. The war of Independence worked
to their detriment not just because its quotas and appropriation of livestock
and beasts of burden affected the hitherto flourishing coca trade: it was ultimately detrimental to them because the patriots emerged the victors. And just
as the patriots, once in power, exempted from tax payments those towns that
had collaborated with their armies, so they also severely taxed those who,
like the inhabitants of the province of Huanta, had antagonized them. The
most drastic measure in this respect was taken by General Sucre, who six days
after the Battle of Ayacucho levied a fine of 50,000 pesos against the town
of Huanta, as a reprisal for its inhabitants' hostility toward patriot troops.[71]
The same decree exempted the peasants of the towns of Quinua, Acosvinchos,
and Guaychao, from the province of Huamanga, from paying tribute for six
months "because they treated us very well and their residents gave the army
all that they had."[72] Republican reprisals against the Huantinos extended even
to the ecclesiastical sector. In February 1825, Sucre levied a fine of 20,000 pesos
on "the godo priests of the bishopric of Guamanga . . . since these priests were
the ones who incited the Indians to steal equipment and kill the sick men [of
the patriot army]."[73]

It was not easy, however, for Huantinos to pay the fine. In August 1825, Intendant Mariano Maldonado reported "insurmountable difficulties" in carrying out the collection "because of the misery reigning in this province . . . as a
result of the total decline of the province's only business: that of coca."[74] Of the
50,000 pesos demanded, he had succeeded in collecting barely 412. Later,
however, the most well-to-do royalists began to hand over quotas in exchange
for their freedom. Such was the case of Francisco Ruiz, who paid 400 pesos,
and Juan Cantón, a Spanish hacendado who was required to pay 10,000 of the

50,000 pesos that had been assessed to Huanta! According to his own statement, Cantón managed to raise only 5,000, promising to cover the remaining
debt with his holdings and haciendas. This brought about his release from jail.
Not surprisingly, once freed, he became the most ardently involved hacendado
in the restorationist war and probably the wealthiest as well.[75]

The measure adopted by Sucre was thus the last straw for a population
whose spirits were already quite dampened by the triumph of the Patria. Yet,
one additional factor threatened still more harm to Huanta's already stricken
coca economy, one in which political decisions had no part. The Huantinos
were on the point of losing to Huánuco's producers their monopoly over the
provision of coca leaves to Huancayo, their most important market up to this
time.[76] Huánuco's coca production was quite likely increasing as a consequence of the demand generated by the mining centers at Cerro de Pasco to
the north, which had made a quick recovery after Independence.[77]

Thus, while the imminent loss of markets for Huanta's coca was not directly
attributable to the victory of the Patria, in the minds of those who were
affected by the loss the Patria and misfortune arrived together. The same
voices that hailed the king cursed "the vile patriots . . . these base men, thieves
who think of nothing but robbing us with taxes."[78] Antonio Huachaca complained bitterly to the prefect of Ayacucho,

> Away with these soldiers [señores militares] who are . . . stealing, raping
> married women and maidens, violating even temples, in addition to the
> bosses [mandones], like the Intendant [who] wants to destroy us with taxes [con-
> tribuciones] and tributes, without taking into account that we are very low
> because gentleman Vílchez and other lasones [Lazones, i.e., members of the
> Lazón family] seek only to humiliate us without allowing us to have access to our
> trade, the coca haciendas being lost. . . . Seeing all of this, you must determine
> that our trade be left alone, that we be allowed freely to carry on our trade.[79]

Hence, the crisis of the coca trade was aggravated by the military presence
and the new taxes ordered by Sucre. Furthermore, since the fine of 50,000
pesos was to be collected from all of the town residents, the priests having to
fulfill their own quota of 20,000, the royalist outcry had a broad social basis
working in its favor: "In Huanta, with the exception of a few visible persons,
all of the people fomented revolution and made war."[80] Or, as one dismayed

lawyer put it at the time of the capture of Huanta, "Since November 13 [1827] the indians have been in Huanta, where nearly the entire population is involved with them."[81]

For their part, the hacendados of the district of Acón, most of whom were residents of Huanta, had formed a "council of hacendados" and were periodically meeting to hail Fernando VII, thereby nourishing their hopes of defeating the new regime with the help of troops supposedly to be sent by Spain and the Holy Alliance.[82]

In response to the pressures to which they were subjected, populations in several districts of Huanta stopped paying their tributes. The collection of taxes from *indígenas* and *castas* (people of mixed blood) had practically come to a standstill as well in many towns within the *doctrinas* of Luricocha, Tambo, and San Miguel, and even within Huanta city itself, whose inhabitants "in imitation of those of Luricocha refuse payment."[83]

This was the manner in which the Huantinos experienced the crisis of Independence. In many ways, the rebellion of Huanta was the result of an alliance between a sector of hacendados, peasants, muleteers, priests, and coca merchants in response to the plunder and exactions they all suffered—albeit to varying degrees—with the arrival of the Patria. The shortages arising from the war and the abuses committed by the military stationed in their town for over two months undoubtedly helped to broaden the social base of the rebellion. And it is precisely these factors which, along with Huanta's proximity to the Ayacucho battlefield—which meant in all probability the easy availability of arms and potential combatants—enable one partially to understand why, despite the presence of royalist sympathizers and conspirators and a climate of discontent in so many other regions of Peru, in Huanta alone the flame of insurrection ignited.

As crucial as these factors are, however, they constitute but a point of departure for reaching an understanding of the reasons behind the rebellion. The deeper, that is to say, the less immediate, reasons will be explored in the remaining chapters.

4

Words and Images:
The People and the King

[Micaela Bastidas] acknowledges that she has been imprisoned because her husband [Túpac Amaru] killed the Corregidor. Asked whether her imprisonment is not due to another reason, she answered no. Summoned as to why she declares not to have been imprisoned for other reasons when it is public knowledge that she rose up in arms together with her husband[,] she replied: that it was not against the King or the Crown.—Confession of Micaela Bastidas, Cuzco, April 22, 1781[1]

What did the rebels of Huanta say, openly, with words? What did they say by means other than words? What were they trying to convey through all they "said" either way? These are questions whose answers amount to what Michel Foucault has called discourse.[2] The inquiry into nonverbal components of the rebels' discourse is a very important aspect of our interpretation of the Huanta rebellion, but one for which I reserve a separate chapter. This particular chapter discusses the discourse that the rebels did make explicit and that was intended as "ideological" propaganda. What sort of conceptual framework or system of beliefs, if any, animated the rebels' actions or unified them beyond momentary impulses and transcending the economic interests dealt with above? Can one find in the Huanta rebels' discourse an ideology, in Geertzian terms, "a . . . symbolic framework in terms of which to formulate, think about, and react to political problems?"[3] Was there any specific tradition behind the monarchist option in Huanta? These are questions to be addressed in the present chapter. But first, some methodological remarks are in order.

Our analysis begins with a scrutiny of the documents that were meant for ideological propaganda. It can be argued that the Huanta rebellion is not suited to, say, the kind of ideological analysis that Christopher Hill carried out for the 1640–60 English revolution, based chiefly on documents. The English revolution was, as Hill himself put it, a "revolution of the paper," in which popular ideas could be traced through a wide array of printed media.[4] Nothing like that happened in the early nineteenth century in Huamanga, where an overwhelming majority were illiterate and the production of documents was the domain of a few.

Yet late colonial Peru did have a written culture, and so did Huamanga.[5] Hence, documents that disseminate ideological propaganda constitute a necessary point of departure in this analysis, especially since illiterate people could be involved in their production and diffusion. Not only were texts often dictated by illiterate leaders to secretaries, but also illiterate people endowed documents with meaning. This was possible because in an illiterate world the document was an object in and of itself. As something only a few could decipher, the document was not always fully understood, but it was deeply respected, and so its dissemination usually had an impact. A document could animate debates and rumors theoretically derived from, but many times in spite of, its own text.[6] Or, as we saw in previous chapters, proclamations purportedly signed by the king of Spain raised rebel spirits and were vital in sparking action, despite their dubious origin and authenticity.

A second way of understanding the ideology of the Huanta uprising is by focusing on the cultural practices with which the images evoked in the documents can be associated. The proclamations and lampoons that animated rebel propaganda generally resorted to symbols, images, and values that formed part of a culture, at least a culture as expressed in official ceremonies and rituals. A connection between the monarchist ideological sermon and the cultural practices linked to it is therefore fundamental. It was, I believe, only through these practices that an ideology could find full expression in an illiterate world.

In the third place, allegiance to the king should be understood as well within the framework of the historical legacy of the Túpac Amaru II rebellion of 1780–81 (otherwise known as "the Great Rebellion") along with the iconographic battles that it entailed. This aspect is particularly important for assessing allegiance to the king among Andean populations. For, following Túpac Amaru's defeat, the colonial administration reasserted with special zeal the image of the king as a means to counteract the image of the Inca and its subversive potential among Andean populations.

This chapter thus explores the ideology of the monarchist uprising in this threefold dimension: as ideological propaganda, as cultural practices and political rituals, and as enduring influence of the Great Rebellion upon Andean people's adherence to the Spanish king. It is accordingly divided into three parts: the first one delves into the documents themselves, their content, their authors, their process of production and, when applicable, their diffusion; the second focuses chiefly on political rituals that projected the image of the king at their center; the third furnishes the historical background for an understanding of what may be called "indigenous royalism."

Lampoons, Proclamations, and Letters: Authors and Ideas

Very few of the propaganda-oriented and ideologically explicit documents produced by the rebels of Huanta have survived. For purposes of analysis we shall organize them into three sets. The first "set" consists of a single document, a *pasquín* (or lampoon leaflet), containing several compositions, which was posted in the central square of the town of Andahuaylas (125 kilometers, or about 78 miles, southeast of Huanta city, in today's department of Apurímac) in November 1827. The second set is made up of two proclamations attributed to the former Spanish officer Francisco Garay. The third group comprises two letters that the Huanta leaders addressed to the republican authorities and their emissaries during the height of the uprising. All three sources are handwritten and converge on one central theme: the defense of the absolutist monarchy, embodied in Fernando VII, and of the Catholic religion.

The Lampoon (Pasquín)

At dawn on November 28, 1827, a few hours after the town's intendant had left for Ayacucho with reinforcements to engage the announced rebel attack on that city, an anonymous lampoon entitled "Viva el Rey!" (Long live the king!) was posted on the door of Anselmo Beingolea's home, located on a corner of Andahuaylas's central square. Celedonio Páez, a neighbor of Beingolea's, alerted him about it, whereupon Beingolea reported the incident to the surrogate intendant, Joaquín Lino, and not long after, the lampoon was removed by order of the authorities.[7]

The leaflet consisted of four compositions in verse form (one of them an acrostic) and one prose composition arranged in the center of the sheet.

Unlike the prose piece, the verses were written in virtually flawless Spanish; they were also technically sophisticated and markedly doctrinaire in tone. The verses' political critique was focused on the theme of the oppression of conscience. They mocked the principle of liberty that the patriots used as their slogan. To censor religion was to oppress the conscience, they claimed; what, then, was their professed liberty? One of the poems read,

> ¡Oh Patria tan deceada!
> Dime ¿cual es la livértad?
> De la conciencia és fatal
> por Dios siempre reprobada
> . . .
> questión de nombre y novedad
> han facinado en verdad
> siendo así que el despotismo
> con el rigor son el mismo
> dime ¿quál es la libertad?
>
> Abatida la religion
> por Catesismo Palmira
> a todo el mundo admira,
> al crisitiano su perdicion:
> y a la tierra la proscripcion
> no es conforme ala piedad
> ni conservar la sociedad
> de nuestra Patria Amados,
> ni que estemos separados
> de la Conciencia es fatal[8]

The final stanza shrewdly combined political and ethical judgments on religion. The Patria's new civil codes could not favor humankind as much as "good deeds" could:

> Las potestades terrenas
> Sibiles no favoresen
> A los mortales que fallesen
> sí, solo las buenas obras
> en el recto Juicio apenas:

luego es bana y para nada
esta Patria escudada
con la tirania y opresion
sin piedad ni religion
por Dios siempre ripiorada [*sic*][9]

Furthermore, the Patria—understood as both the republican government and its armies—was accused of violating laws and *fueros* (Church and military rights and privileges) and inciting the subjects of Peru to an upheaval that brought only misfortune and distress:

¡OH PATRIA!
Infame peste, estrago de la vida
trope peso de honrrados pensamientos
pecho de pedernales abarientos
boca de bestia fiera mal herida:
fueros y Leyes quiebras fementida
montañas rompes, pielagos vientos,
ni embotas tus hidropicos alientos
con tanta sangre humana mal vertida

The lampoon's verses strongly advocated the Spanish monarch's right over Spain's possessions overseas. Spain and her possessions should not be separated because this would constitute an outrage against the nation, conceived of as the unified monarchy. The disruption of this order had wrought tremendous havoc, as the poem "¡Oh Patria!" went on to describe:

tu armaste contra el Padre mas piadoso
del hijo vil la mano aleve
quien las lagrimas del hermano con rapiña beve
como tantalo, o carive rapas furrioso[10]

In this poem the Spanish nation is represented as a family: the monarch, depicted as a merciful father ("el padre más piadoso"), and his two sons, Peru and Spain. The Patria, on the other hand, is the personification of evil, inciting one brother—the bad one—Peru, to fight against the other, Spain. Peru, who is seduced by the Patria, finally turns into a bloodthirsty savage ("como tantalo, o carive rapas furrioso") and voraciously drinks the tears of his victimized brother, Spain ("las lagrimas del hermano con rapiña beve"). Thus, in addition to its disrespect for God and religion, the Patria is condemned for "stealing" Peru from the Spanish monarchy, to whom it legitimately belongs. The images forcefully suggest a nationalist sentiment in the imperialistic sense.[11] These ideas become even sharper in the acrostic "Fernando Impere" (May Fernando reign), which was also part of the leaflet:

Viva Yquicha que	F elizmente
un mortal golpe	E a la vil Patria a dado
volviendo a recobra	R lo que usurpado
al Peru le havia con traicio	N indignamente
El leal Yquicha haga	A larde eternamente
de la gloriosa acció	N que nos alibrado [sic]
del barbaro poder	D e ese malvado
que el titulo se di	O de omnipotente
E por que mas se	I rrite el monstruo fiero
y hacerse ver quien	M alamente espera
Apropiarse del	P erú altanero
nuestro grito se	E leve hasta la esfera
diciendo con ardo	R siempre guerrero
el Congresillo y President	E muera, muera[12]

Beyond its obvious imperialistic overtones, the nationalism expressed in these verses may well have appealed to a broader audience than the outraged supporters of the Spanish throne, chiefly because of its strong anti-Bolivarian stance. In fact, the verses of the acrostic, though very openly pro-Spanish, blended well with Peruvians' own anti-Bolivarian nationalism, which was so widespread in those years. The acrostic astutely, though not necessarily accurately, attributed Bolívar's departure from Peru (in June 1826) to the onset of the Huanta monarchist uprising. Bolívar's retreat from Peru was therefore celebrated as a rebel triumph, one of which they boasted openly ("El leal Yquicha haga alarde eternamente / de la gloriosa acción que nos ha librado / del barbaro poder de ese malvado / que el titulo se dio de onmipotente").

The shortest poem in the lampoon, entitled "Voz Preventiva" (Preventive Alert), raised the nationalist issue again, resorting this time to a rather traditional Spanish theme:

Voz Preventiva
Alerta Patriotitas Alerta
San Quintín con nombre de Yquicha
por vuestra negra desdicha
ya lo teneis muy a la puerta[13]

San Quintín, the site of the sixteenth-century battle in which the Spanish army led by Philip II defeated the French,[14] elicited strong nationalist sentiments, again in an imperialistic sense. The imperial power of Spain, which had defeated the French then, took on new life through the Iquichano rebels, this time to reverse the patriot victory at Ayacucho.

Who wrote these verses? Following the removal of the lampoon, a suspect was brought to trial: Matías Guerrero, a thirty-year-old Ayacuchan tutor and resident of Andahuaylas. Guerrero was suspected not so much on the grounds of his ideological affiliation as for his skill in writing poetry. A number of witnesses were cross-examined at Guerrero's trial, among them Anselmo Beingolea, the man on whose door the lampoon had been posted. Beingolea declared that Guerrero had written some verses on the occasion of the oath of Independence, though these were favorable to the patriots.[15] A former classmate testified in a similar vein, remarking that Guerrero "knew how to compose verses" but added, "I did not see him showing off any [on this occasion]."[16] Guerrero himself denied having composed any lines whatsoever, admitting only that in 1825, on the occasion of the oath of the Constitution in Andahuaylas, he copied some quatrains that a priest had given him, this being probably the reason people believed he composed verses.[17] In the end, he was sentenced to several months in jail, where he continued to uphold his innocence; eventually he was released. The authorship of the verses remained a mystery.

According to the magistrate who issued the verdict, the authors of the lampoon had to have been outsiders, for "neither the said Guerrero nor any other person in the province is competent in the seductive meter that was employed in the lampoon."[18] Consequently, he blamed two unidentified muleteers, who had been seen staring at the lampoon very early the morning it was posted, for being its bearers from somewhere out of town. He concluded "that the two strangers [forasteros] on horseback who had been up very early reading the lampoon and who immediately after had passed on to the house of the witness Don Anselmo Beingolea asking for sugar, are the emissaries who bring from one spot to another these kinds of lampoons that disrupt peace and order."[19] However, he was not able to prove his assertion, and the muleteers were never seen again in town.

Our own judgment could hardly improve on that of the magistrate. Though Guerrero may well have been a skilled poet and may even have been acquainted with some of the Huanta caudillos, none of this evidence in and of itself makes him guilty.[20] What nonetheless appears more likely is that whoever was the author of the verses in the lampoon may not have been the author of the prose piece embedded in the composition. The poems' style, language, and content differ from those of the prose piece sufficiently enough to allow for the possibility that at least two minds were involved in producing the leaflet's compositions. The magistrate's opinion that the author of the verses was probably an "outsider" cannot be ruled out. A virtually perfect Spanish, containing no trace of Quechua syntax, grammar, and phonetics, in addition to a manifest familiarity with Spanish nationalist themes, leads one to believe that the verses' author was, indeed, either a Spaniard with strong ties to the Peninsula or a non-Spaniard acquainted with Spanish history and traditions, but whose Spanish remained unaltered by the Quechua-infused Spanish of the local people.

Reinforcing this hypothesis is the fact that the poetic language, style, and themes are akin to those employed in proroyalist newspapers and leaflets issued until about 1826 by Spanish officers at the Real Felipe fortress in Callao. Such writings contained the same defense of monarchical principles and the Catholic religion, the same hatred of Bolívar, the same contempt for the Congress, and many of the same epithets.[21] This evidence ought not to be all that surprising, for as noted in previous chapters, Huanta rebels had been in contact with promonarchist conspirators in Callao and in Lima. Furthermore, it can still be argued that, were it not for the explicit allusions to "Yquicha," the lampoon could just as well have been identified as standard proroyalist propaganda—with the added restorationist ingredient. Ironically, it is precisely the allusion to Iquicha that suggests, rather than denies, a foreign author, as it would have been foreigners, not local people, who first adopted and spread the appellatives Iquicha and Iquichano beyond the confines of Huanta.[22] Thus, the magistrate may not have been far from the truth when he ascribed a possible foreign authorship to the verses.

The same cannot be said of the prose piece in the middle of the document. Written in rather hasty and faulty Spanish, the piece displays some traits which lead one to believe that a local person was either its author or copyist. A slight interjection of Quechua phonetics insinuates itself in such words as "mesericordia," "meserias," and "quitud"; Quechua syntax was perhaps also influencing errors of agreement, as in the phrase "sus hijitos se muera de hambre," although the possibility that this construction reflected a phonetic influence from the Peninsula cannot be ruled out.[23] Judging by the protocol used to address local and peasant authorities, we may surmise that the author was acquainted with local peasant problems and complaints. The piece very well could have been improvised hastily and in situ. All this stands in stark contrast to the verses, which in spite of their rather spurious allusions to "Yquicha" were more prone to introduce Spanish themes and traditions. Moreover, in contrast to the verses, the prose piece broached social issues. For instance, it blamed the Patria for present misfortunes, pointing out the taxes and losses brought about by the Independence wars. It also charged the Patria on ethical / religious grounds with being indifferent to the teachings of the gospels, and particularly to the gospels' identification with the poor. The prose made a melodramatic appeal to the consciousness of local *patriota* authorities:

> Sirs: It is not an [incendiary?] lampoon, but a truthful and certain discourse; for God enjoins us to dress the naked, feed the hungry and have compassion for our fellow human beings. Have you observed these *things* [i.e., commands]? Rather, with impious heart you have devoured the innocents' Hearts [illegible] and deprived them of their wretched little hides and tattered blankets . . . and the rest of the Patriot mayors and governors: if you have any little compassion left it would be so that you take their lives once and for all, so that they don't see their little children suffer, and their women deprived of men and seventy thousand miseries. Or else leave them undisturbed in their sad ranches, at peace and quiet so that they may go and look for the moneys to pay the unjust taxes that matter little if their children dies [*sic*] of starvation, for they would be comforted to see that they alone would suffer your fury, wrath and voraciousness and . . .[24]

That two styles (call one "Peninsular" and the other "local") were present in the same document suggests the existence of agreements between peoples of different social backgrounds and possibly different ethnic origins—an issue we shall explore in more depth later. The agreements become clearer in a second set of sources: two rebel proclamations confiscated by the authorities.

Proclamations

The first proclamation is a formal call to arms entitled "Proclama" and is signed by the Spaniard Francisco Garay; it is divided into two sections, each of which begins with the summons "Americanos."[25] The second proclamation is a general exhortation to the populace of Huancavelica to resist the Patria and bears the signature "the Yquichano Lover of the King."

The vindication of the monarchy as embodied in Fernando VII and of the Catholic religion appears juxtaposed in both proclamations with an open rejection of the Patria and the ever-vile patriotas. Both proclamations draw attention to the most pressing problems facing the regions' populations, such as forced contributions and other losses caused by the patriotas' war. The first section in the "Proclama" speaks in particular of the suffering of all who have lost loved ones in the war, especially widows and their children, and even of the rape of married women in front of their husbands:

> [Americans]: Tell me you, who so anxiously wished to rest in the arms of Freedom, what have you gained by it? I cannot understand. Let the wretched publish it—those who watering the soil with tears of blood do not have enough to support their families because of the heavy tributes that over-whelm them. Let the streets and plazas throughout Peru, watered with the innocent blood of your parents, say it. Speak out, unfortunate widows who clamor with their children on their backs for their Parents. And finally, speak out, married women who were raped in front of their husbands.[26]

The criticism of the Patria in this passage has no doubt more of an ethical than ideological bent, yet it established a political agenda. A more direct call to political and military action is suggested in the following section, in which the accomplishments of those involved in the struggle are given prominence, motivating a general call to arms:

> Americans: [. . .] Be sure that I speak to you in the language of truth, and to prove it here you have the extraordinary miracle that, in the Small Niche of these Punas, but a few men, with neither discipline nor arms, but only Stones and sticks, have several times defeated those who called themselves invincible, leaving us the field covered with arms and cadavers. With such prodigious marvels, you have nothing to fear. To arms Brave Americans, a Heretical

Enemy wishes to tyrannize Religion and the Hereditary Throne of Fernando. The Lord of the Armies tells us to war, to war, the fields of Mars invite you to a glorious Fight that you should not hesitate [to undertake]. Francisco Garay.[27]

At his trial later, the *capitulado* and former lieutenant of the Spanish Royal Army Francisco Garay, originally from Cádiz, age thirty-two when captured, admitted that he had written the proclamation but denied being its author. Instead he argued "that he had copied it from the one made by Don Antonio García, who lived in Viracochán[;] that he [García] had sent it to him [Garay] . . . and that he [Garay] had transcribed it for fun."[28] Therefore, although Garay claimed that the proclamation had never circulated, it is possible to surmise, assuming he was telling the truth, that other copies might have.

The second proclamation, also attributed to Garay, was addressed to the "communities of the towns of the villa of Huancabelica" and bore the signature "The Yquichano Lover of the King." It conveyed the same central elements of the first: the endorsement of the absolutist monarch and the Catholic religion, with the resultant censure of the "infamous" Patria, which is to be blamed for the current unrest. But perhaps because the proclamation was meant to be disseminated in an area affected by, though not central to, the uprising, its tone tended to be more triumphalist. After highlighting the Huanta rebels' early victories, it called upon Huancavelicans to follow their example by diverting their attention to a most favorable turn of events: the loyalist takeover of the Real Felipe fortress and the imminent arrival of "Spanish Generals" from the Peninsula:

To the communities of the towns of the villa of Huancabelica:
Beloved Brothers: We have already let you know that not only have we not turned ourselves in to the infamous government of the Patria, but also it has not occurred to us even to do so. And we beg you to believe them not, even when some evil men tell you [to]. Now we ask you what you think? Are you pleased with being slaves of the vile Patriots, those base men and thieves who think of nothing else but rob us with taxes[;] can it be possible that we only work for them while our dear wives and our tender children starve and we see them naked? We do not think so lowly of you, let alone do we think that you have hearts of beasts: learn from us who without any hope of support from our troops have freed ourselves from the yoke of tyranny, today that our

champions and invincible sirs Loriga, Rodil Ricafor and Morales are on our coasts will they not raise the cry of Long live the King and Death to the Patria and its satellites: arm yourselves brothers of valor, have a place free from this vile cast of insurgents, [give] all your fidelity to our beloved King Fernando[;] that brothers is what we expect of your deeply entrenched Royalism, and that raising the cry of Long live the King shall we wait for our Spanish Generals and may we have the glory of giving him these places, that we have defended with a portion of our blood, so we expect from [your] love for Religion and the best of kings: the Yquichano Lover of the King.[29]

As in the case of the first proclamation, Garay admitted to copying the document but denied authorship. He claimed instead that "it was Huachaca who made [me] write it in the town of Ayhuanco [sic], dictated by the deceased Mariano Belarde and one Escurra from the towns of Tayacaja," (Belarde and Escurra were secretaries of Huachaca).[30] Although Garay claimed that this proclamation, like the first one, did not circulate, what he did say concerning its authorship indicates that other copies probably did. Hence, one may infer that its ideas, as in the first case, could have been disseminated by other means.

Whether or not Garay was truthful about his noninvolvement in the proclamation's authorship is hard to prove. But his own background makes him suspect. Francisco Garay arrived in Peru in 1817 as an officer in charge of the printing press of the Royal Army. The year is important because King Fernando VII was at the time Spain's autocratic monarch, having abolished the liberal Constitution of 1812, which was drafted in Cádiz while he was still a prisoner of the French. In accordance with his profession, Garay would have been trained in the crafts of reading and writing, but, most importantly, he would have been familiar with the language of political propaganda used by the partisans of absolutism and Fernando VII. Furthermore, following on the trail of many other capitulados after the Battle of Ayacucho, Garay took refuge in the *montañas* of Huanta, where he became *mayordomo* (administrator) of haciendas belonging to friar Eduardo de la Piedra (himself an old sympathizer of the royalist cause); he engaged as well in the coca trade.[31] Once established here, he did not wait long to join the monarchist rebels. Huachaca reportedly named him *teniente coronel* and *mayor comandante*. His former training as spokesman for the Royal Army, compounded with his new position as coca merchant—which required great mobility—made Garay well suited to the task of writing and distributing proclamations. Thus his arguments denying authorship in the proclamations likely were exculpatory, particularly since the signature on one of them, "The Yquichano Lover of the King," was not of the sort generally used by the Huantino caudillos.

But beyond the understandable fact that Garay would have wanted to beat the charges brought against him, he may not have been equivocating in attributing a kind of collective authorship to the proclamations. Written by hand, proclamations were copied and recopied, undergoing any number of changes in a fashion similar to the instructions and orders issued by rebel commanders. Such documents were normally drafted by one person but could be reformulated by copyists. One should keep in mind as well that, at the time, those who conceived the ideas were not necessarily those who knew how to write them (or who were willing to do so). Generally, one person wrote another person's ideas, just as one person would sign for another. Illiterate leaders could have as many signatures as they had secretaries; and secretaries' signatures were, in turn, "borrowed." As Gregorio Guijas, a Spanish former officer who took refuge and settled with Garay in the hacienda Marcarí after the Battle of Ayacucho, said at trial, while denying having signed a document that bore his signature: "There in the punas any one who wanted to assume another person's signature, signed [the documents]."[32] He added that he in fact "had once signed for Huachaca I don't know what paper, in the absence of Belarde, who was a secretary of Huachaca, and at Huachaca's own request."[33] This testimony corresponded with that of another witness, José Girón, himself secretary of Huachaca, who claimed that "said caudillo [Huachaca] made use of the first among those who knew how to write to carry out his writings."[34] Secretaries, in turn, were not merely copyists; they also could reformulate instructions issued by rebel commanders, as Belarde once did with instructions issued by the Spanish hacendado Juan Cantón.[35] Thus, even if Francisco Garay gave final form to the two proclamations, the ideas conveyed in them may not have been exclusively of his own production. Perhaps the input of local people should be considered.

The Letters

In contrast to the lampoon and the proclamations, which were addressed to common people, the two letters composed by Huanta leaders to be analyzed in what follows were directed to republican authorities and their mediators. Both were written in 1827, at the height of military hostilities in Huanta, as part of the negotiations between the government and the rebels. Notwithstanding their different contexts and addressees, the ideological content of the letters bears a striking resemblance to that of the lampoons and proclamations.

The first letter was signed by General Tadeo Choque, Mariano José Belarde (a secretary of Huachaca), and the Spaniards Gregorio Guijas and Francisco Garay. It was written in Cancaíllo, rebel headquarters and hacienda of Choque, and was addressed to the "religious of the enemy army," who had been commissioned by the government as mediators between the state and the Huanta insurgents.[36] Perhaps because it was directed to a group of clerics, the letter was especially poignant on the subject of religion. The signatories branded the patriotas "a party of Masons who try to get rid at once of our Holy Religion and the hereditary throne of Fernando." In addition, the letter, which was written prior to the Huanta takeover of November 1827, made clear the rebels' willingness to wage war to the end to defend their principles, while scolding the religious emissaries for having taken the wrong side: "You should be the first ones," wrote the authors, "to raise the battle cry and the weaponry to defend the rights we have known since we were born." They backed up these principles with an ethical maxim: "He who stands for God is a man of good." Like the lampoon and proclamations discussed above, the letter sought to justify the rebellion by decrying the disasters brought about by the patriotas' war: "In every town, small and large, everyone is upset and curses the unfortunate hour in which the insurrection set foot in these lands, and proof of it is that fourteen years ago everybody lived in peace and nobody lacked anything, the means of subsistence [residing] in each one's house."[37] The signatories ended their letter with a bold, indignant statement which underscored once again their Catholic convictions: "We do not want any ambassadors," they said to the priests, "and if you dare to set foot in our lands you will be taken, with an escort, to the banks of the Marañón, to conquer infidels, for it is them to whom you shall devote your energies, and not us, who are C.A.R [Catholic, Apostolic, and Roman]."[38] The authors' reassertion of their Catholic militancy by emphasizing their difference from the "infidels" of the jungles of Marañón (also called *salvajes* or *chunchos*) is especially noteworthy because the Huanta rebels, particularly those branded "indian" by the authorities (among whom was Choque, a signer of this letter), were highly sensitive to being deemed "savages" themselves. The highest republican authorities, in effect, commonly alluded to them as "beasts" and "drunkard indians" in an attempt to delegitimize any moral and political authority they claimed to have.[39] In this context, then, the Huanta rebels' defense of religion was more than the blind defense of a doctrine or dogma; it was also a means of reasserting their human condition—their condition as moral and religious beings, which the Republic constantly called into question.

Let us now look at the second letter, addressed to Prefect Domingo Tristán by the three general montoneros, Choque, Pascual Arancibia, and Antonio Huachaca, among others, while they were occupying Huanta city in November 1827. It is a unique document, not only because of its unabashed tone, but chiefly for being the only extant document relevant to the uprising that carries the signature of all three of the main Huantino "generals." The letter was a response to one addressed to them by Prefect Tristán demanding their capitulation. The generals adopted the tone of one who speaks from a position of advantage or superiority. In addition to restating the argument that they struggled "to uphold the religion and the rights of a Sovereign," they accused Prefect Tristán and his "henchmen" of being "usurpers of the religion, the crown, its interests, and our native soil [patrio suelo]." Echoing the arguments of the lampoon and proclamations, they went on to blame the Patria for the current distress, mocking the slogan of liberty with which the patriots identified themselves.[40] Lastly, they protested the fact that Tristán employed priests as mediators, "for the ministries of the Sanctuary should limit themselves to exert the functions of their ministry, that is, dedicate themselves to the Divine cult, but not . . . employ themselves in matters of War, for this is only military competence, that [sic] comes to agreements with Army to Army parleys."[41] This was certainly a curious theory of the separation of powers, coming as it did from militant monarchists who themselves incorporated priests into their own militias.

More than a contradiction, however, the statement veiled a complaint. For in scolding Tristán for having sent religious instead of civilian or military envoys to negotiate with them, generals Choque, Huachaca, and Arancibia were not so much denying the idea that priests should participate in politics as they were reproaching the prefect for not comprehending (or perhaps not recognizing) the political nature of their rebelliousness. That is (they may have thought), the prefect was forgetting that if he was a general they too were generals and deserved to be treated accordingly. Therefore, in rejecting the religious envoys sent to them by Prefect Tristán, the montonero leaders were actually demanding to be treated as political enemies, not as the "infidels" of the Marañón, who, in contrast to them, needed religious assistance—or so the montoneros claimed.

On several occasions the Huantan generals had expressed the political nature of their intentions and their openness to entering political agreements; for example, when they withdrew to the punas following the failed siege of Ayacucho, "from the heights of their mountains" they demanded the negotiation of treaties.[42] Or when, not long afterward, Huachaca demanded of Commander Quintanilla that he accept two prisoners in exchange for Huachaca's wife, at that time a prisoner of the Republic, adding the challenge, "if you want this to be a political war." "Otherwise," Huachaca threatened, "we will commit the most hideous atrocities that not even the beasts would dare commit."[43]

The question of whether the signatories to the two letters were also their authors is not as pertinent here as it was with the lampoon and the proclamations. For, unlike them, the letters were not anonymous, and their authors' identity was not called into question. However, in spite of their different contexts and at least one different author, the letters tend to agree with the lampoon and the proclamations in their pro-Catholic and monarchist stance as well as in the urgency of the restorationist undertaking.

To what extent were the rebel caudillos' professed beliefs sincere or serious? To what degree were their avowals on behalf of Catholicism and the king merely a rhetorical recourse to advance other, more worldly interests? The answer, I think, varies according to the individuals involved.

Not long after having sworn their oath not to surrender, Tadeo Choque, Pascual Arancibia, and Juan Ramos joined the ranks of the Patria they had so utterly repudiated. In contrast, Nicolás Soregui, the priest Francisco Pacheco, and Huachaca himself remained loyal to their restorationist faith until the very last. This was true of some of their followers, too, including Huachaca's secretary Mariano Méndez, who, lying moribund in Tambo, sent word that he "died in the name of God and the King."[44] Pacheco showed a similar commitment. Commander Quintanilla recalled, "Until the very day he fell to my party in those rough mountains, [Pacheco] remained hopeful about the success of his folly, as did his companions."[45]

Quintanilla was not mistaken. Francisco Pacheco, the Mercedarian priest who took on the roles of weapons provider and accountant in the rebel army, was indeed one of the most loyal defenders of the banner of Fernando VII and the Catholic religion. "Patria ladrona" (thieving Patria) and "chusma de los Patriotas" (the patriot riffraff) were expressions of his authorship, and he openly supported the king in his sermons. Yet more than his words, it is Pacheco's deeds that attest to his commitment to the rebellion and its supreme caudillo. In fact, Pacheco stands out for his closeness to Huachaca, whom he respectfully referred to as "the general" (which not every priest in Huanta did). On one occasion Pacheco wrote Huachaca to warn him of the "treason that our own friends want to do to us," while calling on him to talk about certain issues "for the best service of God and the king."[46] Pacheco was the most vocal of the religious who undertook an active role in the uprising, constantly encouraging the rebel leaders and reminding them that the cause for which they were fighting was a just one. Huachaca in turn relied on Pacheco for advice and priestly services. Having arrived one day at the headquarters of Uchuraccay, the Mercedarian priest was not able to return to Secce as he intended because, as he wrote to Soregui, "the General [Huachaca] insisted that [I] stay to give the Holy Oil to his son, for which purpose you will do me the good of sending me the ornaments."[47] Notable for what it tells about Pacheco's commitment to his priestly duties, this piece of evidence also attests to Huachaca's own concern with the observance of the Catholic liturgy. On other occasions Huachaca had been friendly with the priests who stood by his side, either encouraging them to preach to his troops or taking their counsel in making decisions.[48]

Interpreting the Ideology: The Place of Religion

Why was the Huanta rebels' sermonizing so concerned with the defense of Catholicism? The question begs to be asked because the answer is far from obvious. Indeed, if most patriots had anything in common with the Spaniards against whom they fought it was religion. After Independence, as Basadre has rightly pointed out, in religious matters, as in others, "there was in the main a continuity of the Spanish *ethos*, even if Spanish *imperium* was acrimoniously rejected."[49] In the earliest Peruvian legislation the Constitution held a status equal to that of the Catholic religion.[50] The Constitution of 1823, the first in independent Peru and a markedly liberal one, invoked in its preamble "the name of God, by whose power all societies are instituted and whose wisdom inspires all legislators to justice."[51] It declared as well "that any nonreligious Peruvian was not worthy of the name Peruvian." The Congress suppressed writings against religion, legislated against Freemasonry, and prescribed the minutiae of rituals to be followed in religious ceremonies at which the presence of state officials was required.[52]

By the same token, the 1823 Congress provided that in the course of the Independence war rogations were to be made in all churches, and in September of that year, it proclaimed the Virgin of Mercedes Patronness of the national militias. The Congress of 1828, in turn, made Saint Joseph the Patron Saint of the Republic.[53] The Constitution of 1826 spoke "on behalf of God," and that of 1827 "took the name of 'God Almighty, Father Son and Holy Spirit, Supreme Author and Legislator of Society.' "[54]

Given such obvious openness toward Catholicism by early republican legislators, both conservative and liberal, the Huanta restorationists' ranting against atheist and heretic patriots seems out of place. But it was not. Even though the religious devotion or Spanish *ethos*, as Basadre rightly points out, remained intact during the early republican years, the republican state concurrently issued measures that hit the Church hard, particularly under Bolívar. Evidently, it was in reaction to these measures that the restorationist outcry was heard.

Decrees prohibiting men under thirty and women under twenty-five from taking religious vows were issued as early as 1821 and reissued in 1825. That same year clerics who were expelled from the country for having been against Independence were prohibited by the Congress from receiving monetary compensation. By 1823 the Congress had ordered that novitiate houses be closed, a measure ratified in 1825 and 1826. Anti-Church measures like these became especially severe during the Bolívar administration (1823–26), when not a few convents were closed and their goods and interests confiscated by the state. These included the convent of Ocopa, overseen by Franciscan Missionaries: by Bolívar's decree of November 1, 1824, it was closed and made into a public school.[55] Located in the Andes of Junín, at the core of the central Peruvian *ceja de selva*, Ocopa's missionary influence reached the Huanta selvas, montañas, and highlands, where Franciscans had founded several *doctrinas* during the late eighteenth century.[56] According to the Franciscan historian Dionisio Ortiz, the Independence wars hit these friars' missions in the selva so severely that many were forced to emigrate to Spain or take refugee in Cuzco.[57] Other forms of state intervention in the Church included reduction of the number of canonries, *dignidades* (ecclesiastical benefits for high-ranking Church officers, or the officers themselves), and prebends in the cathedrals as well as intervention in the administration of conventual incomes, for example, by allowing prefects to nominate their own officials.[58]

How these decrees, which were meant to weaken the Church's position nationwide, affected the material bases of the Church in Ayacucho and Huanta in particular is not clear. The fine imposed by Sucre on the Huamanga clergy in 1825 must certainly have affected the local church, yet one ought to keep in mind that this measure was part of the government's fiscal "punishment" of the province, not an anticlerical measure per se.[59] It can be argued as well that, insofar as its missionary influence had reached the selva of Huanta, the closing of the Ocopa convent in 1824 was the most severe blow to the Church's missionary efforts in the region. Yet even if this were true, Huanta itself may not have perceived its impact, as Franciscan missionaries had abandoned the province more than a decade before the enforcement of the measure that closed their convent.[60] Significantly in this regard, while one finds Mercedarians, Franciscan Capuchins, and lay clergy in the ranks of the monarchist rebellion, no actual member of the Franciscan Missionary order appears to have been involved.

On the other hand, the anticlerical decrees were clearly meant to hit the material bases of the Church and probably had a noticeable impact (for better or for worse) on the Church's relationship with its parishioners. The priests could have, for instance, increased the amount or number of the parish members' duties so as to compensate for their own losses. Or conversely, upon seeing their spiritual or churchly benefits endangered, parishioners may well have made common cause with their priests, as happened, for example, in the Vendée rebellion, which reacted to the anticlerical measures of the French revolution.[61] Yet no sources attest to such a reaction—a silence that would be less surprising were it not for the overwhelmingly Catholic disposition of the region's population.[62]

Thus it appears that if the religious elements in the restorationist discourse were not reacting against the material impact of early republican anticlerical measures, they must certainly have been reacting against their imminent implementation and the threat they represented. The poignancy of the phrases attacking the republicans as heretics and atheists in both lampoons and proclamations evidently was aimed at instilling fear in an overwhelmingly Catholic population, a sentiment that could be channeled toward the rebels' own political ambitions. Along the same lines, the insurgents created a scenario in which the patriots were condemned for their lack of respect to the temples, which they sacked to fund the "damned insurrection," or so the Huanta rebels claimed. Yet, as other evidence indicates, this is a charge that could well be laid at the feet of the accusers themselves.[63]

Hence, it is safe to surmise, at least while the material effects of the anticlerical decrees in Huanta remain uncertain, that the engine driving the use of religious elements in restorationist preaching was highly ideological. The influence of European absolutism, which advocated the divine right of monarchs and the legitimacy of the Catholic Church's political power, is unquestionable. Born out of a reaction to agnostic liberalism stemming from the French Revolution, this philosophy reached its peak in the course of the first two decades of the nineteenth century, in response to both Napoleonic expansionism and the outbreak of the Spanish American revolutions. One of its clearest expressions was the famous antirevolutionary front known as the Holy Alliance, which, among other things, harbored the hope of reconquering for the dismembered European monarchies their lost American colonies. Indeed, both the leaflets encouraging the Huanta uprising and the rumors that circulated in several regions of the former Peruvian viceroyalty not long after the proclamation of Independence were permeated with this ideology.[64]

In regard to the second ingredient of the restorationist propaganda—that of the vindication of the monarchical system and the king's person—the arguments appear more understandable. For while the Catholic religion, which the lampoons, letters, and proclamations so vigorously defended, may not have been seriously endangered, this was obviously not the case with the king, the personification of the monarchy that had just collapsed.

Interpreting the Ideology: The Image of the King

The Palace of San Clout will be shaken from its foundation by the incomparable fidelity of these remote provinces, which an immense ocean sets apart from the Metropolis, and which are in turn separated one from another by distances that are unknown in the kingdoms of Europe. They all proclaim in unison, Our king is Fernando: the crown and the primogeniture are hereditary.[65] —"Expresión Leal Y Afectuosa del Ayuntamiento de Lima"

The large ocean that separates Spain from America was not a hindrance to the circulation and assimilation of ideological sermons promoting the Spanish Empire in the colonies. Sermons, rites, feasts, and royal edicts guaranteed the continuity of imperial rule since the early colonial period. Sermons delivered on the occasion of the king's birthday, coronation, or death were far more than mere reproductions of the original Spanish versions. They were addressed to a specific audience and adapted to local traditions so as to achieve a more enduring effect.[66]

Sermons and ceremonies, in conjunction with a corpus of laws, were crucial in shaping people's images of the power and magnanimity of the king. Although the declaration of loyalty to the king became something of a bureaucratic formula throughout the colonial period, it did not cease to have a practical impact on peoples' lives. Native Andeans, in particular, were expected constantly to reassert their fidelity to the Spanish emperors in all their legal demands, notably when seeking recognition of their position as *kuraka*, or noble indian status. Andean commoners were likewise privy to a policy of special rights and "privileges." This policy was expressed in laws and provisions and materialized in institutions such as the Protector de Indios. Native Andeans assimilated and utilized these laws and institutions to the extent that they could benefit from them—their petitions commonly show a keen awareness of their "protected" status. Issues of this sort have been underscored in recent research, and we need not delve into details here.[67]

Less known is the extent to which the relationship between the king and the people was charged by latter with emotional content. Did the image of a protector and benevolent king transcend the public realm to invest meaning in peoples' daily lives and expectations? Possibly, as some of the testimonies cited above suggest. Yet sources that could answer the question definitively do not abound. The few we have at our disposal are official and stem not from the people they were directed at but from parties in charge of arousing an emotional response in them. Nonetheless, they illustrate the means by which the magnanimity of the king was represented and possibly received.

The issuance of royal decrees granting amnesty was one of those means. For instance, in Huamanga during the last years of colonial rule a royal warrant (*real cédula*) issued by Fernando VII himself circulated on the occasion of his wedding with the infanta of Portugal in 1817 (only a few years after he had recovered the throne of Spain and was ruling as absolute monarch). This *real cédula* offered pardon not only to common culprits but also, significantly, to those "tried or not tried, present and absent, for the crime of insurrection committed before the publication of this pardon."[68] While the tradition of royal pardons sought to assure the internalization of the king as a benevolent figure, in this particular case it accomplished a very specific political goal: to quell dissent in the colonies by bestowing benevolence upon those who had defied his power through insurrection.

A more visual means of reasserting the king's power was through official rituals. The years 1808–14 were particularly eventful in this respect. With Spain kingless, its monarch a captive of the French, and the Peninsula invaded by Napoleon's troops, the drive to reassert the king's image and authority in the colonies became more urgent. The routing of Fernando VII by Napoleon in May 1808 and the resulting destitution of the king had a twofold effect on the political life of the Spanish Empire. On the one hand, it created a problem of legitimacy for Spanish administrators, paving the way for the colonies' push for independence; on the other hand, it engendered spontaneous public outbursts of loyalty to the king, not only in the colonies but in the Peninsula as well. This loyalty was expressed through oath ceremonies carried out in various cities shortly after Fernando VII was brought low. Promoted and choreographed chiefly by public officials, the ceremonies left room nonetheless for popular spontaneity. Multitudes showed up in the squares where the ceremonies took place to express their allegiance to the monarch.[69]

The portrait of the king played a prominent role in the ceremonies. "Central to every oath ceremony, the portrait of the king now acquired a new, more spontaneous and affective tonality."[70] On the basis of a newspaper article, historian François-Xavier Guerra describes the oath ceremony to Fernando VII that took place in Mexico City on July 30, 1808:

> After the viceroy ordered the portrait [of the king] to be placed on the central balcony of the palace so it could be exposed to the crowd's veneration, "he asked the people to display it triumphantly around the city's streets," which was done in the midst of overflowing enthusiasm. The city adorns itself with tapestries "and the acclaimed sovereign's portrait is exhibited in the most visible places." Later on, "at 4 o'clock in the afternoon, all the people . . . numbering eighteen to twenty thousand persons of all classes, showed up carrying a banner with the sovereign's portrait under a canopy. Many carried the same portrait, made of paper, on their hats."[71]

"The royal portrait comes out of its habitual ceremonial place by being re-produced by the thousands," points out Guerra, "as a sign of personal ad-herence to the monarch, as if the attempt were to compensate for his physical absence by the multiplication of his image."[72] Basing himself on the same testimony, Guerra likewise draws attention to "the personal character of the link between each vassal and the King," claiming that it was precisely this bond that explains the "difficulties that the partisans of independence subse-quently had in America in giving free reign to total Independence, that is, openly to reject the king. The obligatory deference to the king, even among the most devoted partisans of Independence—what has been called 'the mas-querade of Fernando'—finds here one if its essential sources."[73]

Ceremonies expressing allegiance to the king, similar to the one Guerra described for Mexico, took place in Peru—in Lima and Huamanga, among other cities.[74] Significantly, the ceremony took place first in Huamanga on October 2, 1808, and later in Lima, on October 13, 1808. A vivid description of the proclamation of Fernando VII in Huamanga, which underscores the popu-lar demonstrations of fidelity to the king, is provided by the sermon delivered on that occasion by Fray Calixto Cárdenas y Berrocal.[75] The portrait of the king played a central role in the ceremony, just as it did in Mexico City. Note how the author praises the loyalist spirit of the local people and their emo-tional involvement in the act:

When the chief of the Department carried the precious portrait of our be-loved Fernando in his hands, from the Intendancy to the chapter's room, you all accompanied such a circumspect audience repeating the acclamations and vivas to pour out your tender affection; but at the same time you shed, through streets and squares, the tears and sentiment that testified to your just sorrow. Was there, that day or the following, any resident of whichever condition and sex able to repeat the tender name of Fernando without crying out of anger, without dearly clamoring to heaven? Was there man or woman, big or small, who did not break out in rage and curses against the impious abuser of his magnanimous royal confidence? Was there in the city any tem-ple or Monastery where the prayers and sacrifices were not offered on behalf of his life, and his prompt restitution to the throne?[76]

In contrast to sermons delivered on other occasions, which concentrated on praising the virtues of the king, those delivered at Fernando VII's proclamation (at least in Huamanga) exalted the fidelity of the people. In so doing, they sought to reassert it. The sermon praised the material efforts made by the poor in expressing their allegiance to the king, almost as if an attempt were being made to prick the conscience of the rich, in a tone of affected emotionaliy: "As a second proof of their discrete love for our King Fernando, the poor generously offered, in place of the blood that the distance spared them, any possible contribution toward the just and saintly enterprise of freeing him from captivity and avenging the outrageous offenses he was object of."[77]

The emotional attachment of the poor to the king's persona was featured again, particularly in the response of the women, "those poor little ones from the lowest plebs, who crying out of tenderness offered their pitiful donations which they had acquired with the miserable spinning of their hands." Notice also how, in this same paragraph, the author suggests a similar devotion to the monarch stemming from all social strata:

> You received, Sr. Governor, these small but precious offerings [the women's] in the name of the Monarch with the sensitivity that they deserve for being accompanied by love's most tender affection. Oh! If our good Sovereign had only seen them, he would have appreciated them more than all the wealth of the earth. He would have doubtlessly accepted them, as the immortal testimony of the fine love that he enjoys from all the residents of Huamanga without exception. All of them, Ecclesiastics or Lay, noble or plebeian, Military and country laborers; small and great; men and women; all of them like Raquel who despite not having met his relative Tobías, embracing him kissed him and cried out of love. So do we Americans, without knowing the August Sovereign, embrace him in spirit, consecrating him these offerings, accompanied always with the tender tears of our loving heart.[78]

A few years after the fidelity oath ceremony in 1808, the image of the king again assumed a prominent role in public ceremonies at Huamanga. The occasion this time was the proclamation of the Constitution of 1812, when the king was represented by a bust. In contrast to the ceremonies of 1808 proclaiming loyalty to the king, which in some respects resembled a funeral, the oath swearing to the 1812 Constitution was performed in a festive setting. The book of the Constitution was, physically and symbolically, at the center of the celebrations, but the bust of the king played no less momentous a role. In Angaraes, for example, it was placed in the street facing the chapter house, where for three days following the oath of the Constitution, it was "solemnized" with music and dances by the "native indians," according to the description of the town's subdelegate:

> For three days the bells pealed and there was public general lighting; the lack of firearms did not allow for salvos, but they were replaced by skyrockets and many other demonstrations of merriment made by the joyful neighborhood, and in the one-room town council building where the bust of our much adored King Sr. Fernando VII was placed with the utmost brilliance in front of the street . . . all the residents came to solemnize it and the constitution for three consecutive nights with soirées, music, *baile*, and rejoicing of dances by the native indians.[79]

The participation of all social strata was encouraged in the swearing ritual itself, albeit in a more organized and symbolic manner than had been done in the oath of fidelity to Fernando. In the town of Angaraes, representatives of the Church, the military, the indians, and "distinguished *vecinos*" (townspeople) escorted the book of the Constitution, each carrying one corner. They were followed by a group of militiamen in a ceremony both martial and religious: "Placed on a richly adorned crimson damask pillow, the book of the constitution was carried with utmost splendor and tidiness by its corners, with bows made of the richest ribbon, by an ecclesiastic, a captain, a mayor of indians, and a mayor of the distinguished vecinos; it was escorted by a squad made up of more than forty men playing drum and fife, including one sublieutenant."[80] Similar celebrations, claimed the same witness, took place in the parishes of Lircay and Julcamarca "with as much pomp and solemnity." According to other testimonies, the constitutional oath was sworn, probably using very similar rituals, in at least 135 towns of the Intendancy of Huamanga.[81]

Was the link between the king and his vassals as personal and emotional as the sources describe? The answer remains to be seen because the sources cited are pieces of ideological propaganda in and of themselves and thus should be taken with a grain of salt. But the fact that the constitutional oath was sworn in 135 towns of the Intendancy of Huamanga, accompanied by rituals in which the king was symbolically present and the people's participation was evident, is itself remarkable given that in these overwhelmingly rural towns only a small percentage of the population was literate. At any rate, this was precisely what the juntas, the assemblies ruling Spain in the absence of the king, intended. The central junta in Cádiz, where the Constitution of 1812 was drafted, was committed to spreading it to as many people in the Spanish domains as possible, including those who did not speak Spanish, as the existence of bilingual Quechua / Spanish proclamations publicizing the Constitution attests.[82] To judge from other sources, the junta evidently succeeded. The diffusion of the Constitution in Peru exceeded any estimates made in the Peninsula, or so Viceroy Abascal of Peru reported to his superiors in November 1812. He had ordered the reprinting of 4,000 additional copies of the Constitution because the ones he had received "were insufficient to be circulated in the provinces under my command."[83]

But beyond the Constitution's physical multiplication and the rituals that accompanied its proclamation, its mostly liberal ideas also spread to many rural towns, sparking debate.[84] The messages of the Constitution of 1812 in all likelihood reached rural Huanta. In fact, some trace Antonio Huachaca's initiation into politics to his struggle against abuses committed by authorities in the collection of indian tribute during 1813—that is, barely a year after the promulgation of the 1812 Constitution in Huamanga.[85] Huachaca's early struggles are likely to have been inspired by the Constitution, which, among other measures, abolished indian tribute and forbade unpaid labor by indians. King Fernando VII himself was not fond of the Constitution—in fact, the first thing he did when he recovered the throne of Spain in 1814 was to abolish it.[86] Yet Huachaca, like many others no doubt—regardless of whether they participated in the monarchist uprising later on—seems not to have been too uncomfortable supporting an absolutist king while embracing clauses of a liberal Constitution; at least so long as he could derive benefits from both positions.

In short, between 1808 and 1820, the people in Huanta, like in most of Peru, were exposed to political rituals that demanded loyalty and submission to the king and also to political tools such as the Constitution of 1812 that allowed them to shape the form and limits of their loyalty and submission. Yet, as decisive as the events in Europe are to understanding plebeian political options and choices in America, they are no more so than America's internal political legacies. After the defeat of the Great Rebellion, Andean populations were subjected to policies that aimed at strengthening the image of the king as a counterweight to the possibility of Inca-inspired projects or revolts. This brings us to the third and last point of my analysis in this chapter: the historical background of indigenous royalism.

King Fernando VII, by José Gil de Castro, ca. 1812. Reproduced with permission from the Museo Nacional de Arqueología, Antropología e Historia del Perú, Lima. *Photograph by Daniel Giannoni.*

Royalism as Hispanism and
the Legacy of the Túpac Amaru Defeat

If royalism is understood as both the conscious and deliberate advocacy of monarchy and the recognition of the supreme political authority of the king, then royalist indians were present from the very first moments of colonial rule. From the moment of conquest, various Andean nations sided with the Spaniards in order to vent the resentments and animosities they felt toward the rulers of Cuzco. Indeed, when the Europeans invaded the Inca Empire, the Incas, though powerful, had not yet consolidated their rule over their many vassal nations. Anti-Inca tensions thus evolved into pro-Spanish sympathies, facilitating the implementation of the Spanish policy of divide and conquer.[87] After the conquest much of this anti-Incan attitude persisted among regional native lords, the kurakas, who during the eighteenth century were most commonly called caciques. Not incidentally, as Teresa Gisbert has pointed out, "the regional caciques [those from outside Cuzco] were the most resolute collaborators with the Spanish Crown."[88]

Yet for most of the colonial period, royalism, or at least the pledge of loyalty to the king, had not implied a renunciation of native sources of prestige and power, especially those of Incan origin, which came to be recognized and legitimized by the Spaniards. Inca dress, music, and symbols were not only protected but even adopted by the Spaniards themselves as a strategy of domination and "social control" beginning in the sixteenth century.[89] Marriages between elite Spaniards and noble Inca women occurred since the sixteenth century. Colonial policy sought, in addition, to protect kuraka privileges, since kurakas fulfilled two crucial tasks on behalf of the Crown: they collected indian tribute and mobilized native populations for draft labor, or *mita*. As key intermediaries between Spanish administrators and Andean commoners, the kurakas' social prestige and political legitimacy were nourished by both native and European sources. Kurakas were exempt from indian tribute and were granted "privileges" reserved for Europeans, such as riding horses and carrying swords; many wore European garments, were fluent in both Spanish and Latin, which they learned in exclusive kuraka schools, and lived in houses that "emulated those of their conquistadors."[90] None of this contradicted their drive to preserve, at the same time, their native sources of prestige, as is shown in their dress, paintings, and heraldry.[91] Inca titles of nobility became so prestigious in colonial society that the main provincial kurakas, forfeiting old animosities, sought to establish blood alliances with members of royal Inca descent groups, or *panaqas*, in order to enhance their status. Native Andean regional elites sought, in particular, to prove their links with the line of Inca Huayna Capac, for it was tacitly recognized by the Spaniards.[92] Native elites usually embellished their claim to Inca nobility or their right to a *kurakazgo* with a declaration of fidelity to the king, citing as proof long-standing alliances of their ancestors with the king on the battlefield. This, for instance, was the case with Don Fernando Ataurimachi, a "noble indian" of Sángaro (the pre-Hispanic name for the province of Huanta), who in the 1640s sought to prove his noble status by claiming that his forebears, "direct descendants of [the Inca] Huayna Cápac," had come to Huamanga to fight on behalf of "His Majesty" in the rebellions of Francisco Hernández Girón and the Incas of Vilcabamba in the mid–sixteenth century.[93] The need to reconcile Spanish and Andean sources of prestige was typical of native Andeans claiming noble status throughout the colonial period. This "fervently desired harmonisation and reconciliation of Incaic and Hispanic elites" expressed, according to the historian David Cahill, a "wish for a reconciliation of the colonial condition."[94]

The situation was to be drastically altered following the Great Rebellion (1780–81), whose most illustrious leader, the Cuzco cacique José Gabriel Condorcanqui, otherwise known as Túpac Amaru II, claimed descent from Felipe Túpac Amaru Inca, or Túpac Amaru I, the renegade Inca executed by order of Viceroy Toledo in 1572. The Great Rebellion turned out to be the most widespread and violent insurrection ever confronted by the Spaniards in America before the outbreak of the wars of Independence; it encompassed territories within present-day Peru, Bolivia, and Argentina. The repression that followed the defeat of the Great Rebellion brought not only the gradual extinction of the Inca nobility and the kurakazgos (and in the immediate aftermath, their delegitimization) but also regulations prohibiting native Andeans from partaking in any cultural expression, whether dance, music, clothing, painting, or theater, that might serve to revive or preserve the Inca past. The sentence passed on Túpac Amaru decreed that all paintings depicting Incas "be indefectibly erased," and if painted on walls of houses, churches, monasteries, or hospitals they were to be replaced by images of the current king and "our other Catholic sovereigns." Teaching of Spanish was to be promoted and the adoption of Spanish-style dress established among native Andeans. Indians were forbidden to identify themselves as Incas in signing their names.[95] Henceforth, it would be the creoles themselves who would assume the task of recreating Inca traditions, symbols, and historical representations—yet these manifestations, as Juan Carlos Estenssoro suggests, would be "strongly stylized by the official rhetoric," thus neutralizing "the political content of the cultural elements of indian origin."[96] Thus, the only legitimate symbols of prestige for native Andeans wishing to enhance their social and political status would be those emanating from the Spanish Crown. These measures must have strengthened the position of those who, like the Huantinos, had espoused the royalist cause during the Great Rebellion and forced many others to pledge their loyalty to the king. Ironically, while Spanish-descent creoles eventually turned to Incaism, native Andeans, either by choice or constraint, increasingly sought to enhance their social and political status by resorting exclusively to European sources of prestige.

In the final decades of colonial rule, Inca lineages amounted to very little in terms of social status and political power, while cultural expressions associated with native Andean populations, notably the Quechua language, came to be severely ostracized. The fading of indians from the high strata of Cuzco society, owing either to impoverishment or incorporation into the criollo strata, was evident during this period, according to the linguist César Itier. He goes on to say that "[Quechua] . . . receded from several spheres of communication as all those striving to disassociate themselves from an indianness that had become a stigma of inferior cultural and social status avoided expressing themselves in this language."[97] Although Quechua was subsequently used in patriotic poems and speeches by creoles and national caudillos, "the social, cultural, and ideological context prevailing during the last decades of Bourbon rule and the early Republic had become adverse to Quechua as an instrument of communication."[98] Thus, the *lengua general,* as Quechua was referred to in the earlier colonial period, having been extensively spoken and used artistically not just by the indian but also by the creole elites of Cuzco, increasingly "became an archeological object: 'the language of the Inca Empire.' "[99]

It seems rather simplistic to attribute the downgrading of key symbols of indian identity solely to the repression that followed the Túpac Amaru rebellion. Even before the rebellion, the Bourbon project had envisaged the political and cultural annihilation of the native nobility and kurakas, if not explicitly then de facto, by implementing rules that restricted their social reproduction. One such measure was the closure of schools for caciques, chiefly controlled by the Jesuits. Nevertheless, there is no question that the Great Rebellion hardened this position.[100]

This process, however, could not have happened overnight. The existence of an institutionally organized and economically prosperous group of Inca nobles who participated in the public life of Cuzco years after the Great Rebellion attests to the fact that Cuzco's native nobility had proven to be resilient; the same can be said of the provincial kurakas.[101] Nevertheless, their political power was to become irreversibly eroded, and their extinction as a political class was just a matter of time. Ultimately, kurakas would relinquish to criollo and Spanish authorities the functions and privileges that had distinguished them from Andean commoners—foremost among their functions was the collection of indian tribute and, among their privileges, exemption from paying it.[102] Bolivar's decree in 1825 abolishing kurakazgos and nobility titles made official a fait accompli, at least, in most of the territory corresponding to present-day Peru.

At any rate, the ability of kurakas and noble indians to withstand the repressive measures that followed the Túpac Amaru rebellion seems to have been directly proportional to the degree of opposition they had shown to the rebel cacique. Andean commoners who fought for Túpac Amaru also paid a high price for their choice. Suspicion of sympathy for Túpac Amaru became more than a political stigma; it even hindered native Andeans in their litigations before the courts.[103] Thus, if a declaration of loyalty to the Crown had always been a useful resource in legal battles, in the wake of the Great Rebellion it became an imperative of survival.

In order to ensure the success of the repressive measures, the Crown implemented a policy of prebends. Loyalist kurakas and soldiers were to be rewarded with money, lands, military promotions, and titles. The case of repaid royalism par excellence was that of Mateo García Pumacahua, cacique of Chincheros (Cuzco), who as recompense for his military services in the struggle against Túpac Amaru was promoted to the rank of colonel of militias. Later, in 1809, as a reward for his collaboration in defeating the Upper Peru insurrection, he was made colonel of the Royal Army, and in 1811 brigadier. His impeccable loyalist career was crowned by his nomination as "Governor and acting President of the Audiencia of Cuzco."[104] Other famous loyalist caciques who were rewarded include Diego Chuquiguanca, cacique of Azángaro (Puno), whose son José was granted a life pension of eight hundred pesos, and

Don Pedro Sahuaraura y Bustinza, cacique of Quispicanchis (Cuzco), whose death in battle fighting Túpac Amaru was recognized through honors and awards to his children. Characteristically, to strengthen their claims, Sahuaraura y Bustinza's children argued that the family's loyalty to the Crown dated back to the sixteenth century. Manuel Chuquinya, cacique of Copacabana (in present-day Bolivia), who also worked on behalf of the royalists, received a reward and a life pension of five hundred pesos for his services.[105] A number of other petitions by loyalist noble indians and caciques reached the Council of Indies in Seville.[106]

Probably on account of the kurakas' fervent zeal in proving their royalist commitment, in 1790 the Crown issued a new set of decrees providing that, in addition to their prebends, loyalist kurakas be allowed to retain their hereditary privileges and titles, which had been curtailed by the more radical provisions of 1782 and 1783 and by the sentence passed on Túpac Amaru in 1781. The 1790 provisions extended these "benefits" to kurakas from the provinces that did not take part in the Great Rebellion. Wrote the king,

> I have come to declare it fair and well deserved that the rebel Caciques, their children and descendants, and their accomplices and aspirants be completely deprived of the cacicazgos, but not so those Caciques and the children of those Caciques who proved loyal and resisted the rebels, for they are worthy of reward, and should they be deprived of their cacicazgos they may retract themselves from serving [the Crown] on other occasions. Neither should the deprivation of cacicazgos be applied to the Caciques who are so by blood right and by the authority of the laws in the provinces that did not take part in the unrests, for in addition to depriving them of a right they have acquired, one recognizes their fidelity in not having followed the example of the others and having kept due subordination. Aranjuez, May 9, 1790. Me, the King.[107]

An analogous policy of rewards for loyalty was implemented in the aftermath of the Cuzco uprising in 1814–15, which was led by Vicente and José Angulo, creoles from Cuzco, and Mateo García Pumacahua, who not long before had been a most conspicuous royalist cacique, as already noted. Soldiers and officers of the Army of Upper Peru who volunteered to fight against this rebellion were promoted and rewarded with lands according to their rank.[108]

How did the populations of Huanta province align themselves in these conflicts? There is some evidence that they formed part of the armies that crushed the Túpac Amaru uprising, but proof of their participation in defeating the Cuzco uprising of 1814–15 is more detailed and abundant. Significantly, though, and unlike other regions, in Huanta no single self-defined indian (noble or not) seems to have commanded battalions of indians in either conflict; the battalions were instead led by criollo and mestizo hacendados and priests. This does not mean that Huanta lacked noble indians altogether. As late as 1793, Gabriel Leandro, cacique of the *ayllus* Mitma and Cocha, of Huanta's capital, managed to achieve legal recognition of his cacicazgo, which he partially inherited from his father, Bernardo Sulca Ynga, who claimed nobility and who had been a "Sarjento Mayor del batallon de Naturales de esta Provincia" and "Cacique principal governador del ayllo Mitma," that is, a "sergeant major in the indian battalion of Huanta province" and a "Principal cacique and governor of the ayllu Mitma."[109] Similarly, around 1789 Don Bartholomé Marmolejo, "Kuraka of the town of Guamangilla of the Ayllu Chinchaysuio in the Partido of Guanta," was litigating against a marquis on behalf of the *común de indios* (community indians) of his ayllu about some irrigation rights.[110] Yet, regardless of how active these and other kurakas of Huanta may have been in representing their communities before the tribunals or in achieving legal recognition of their titles, their political role was nearly imperceptible, if not invisible, in the critical politico-military confrontations of 1780–81 and 1814–15. According to the records kept in the Archive of Indies in Seville, the Regiment of Infantry of Huanta that participated in the anti–Túpac Amaru armies was led by captains Domingo del Valle and Venancio Navarro, sublieutenants Pedro Lazón and Josef Lazón (the latter two, members of a well-to-do creole hacendado family in Huanta), Agustín Valladolid and Remigio Quintanilla. Another individual, Tomás Zifuentes, colonel of militias who commanded two hundred men from Huanta province against Túpac Amaru, was a criollo who claimed Spanish noble blood.[111] Some of these criollo family names—most prominently the Lazóns and in particular Tadeo Lazón—appear again among the commanders of the armies that mobilized peasants to crush the 1814–15 Cuzco uprising, which had expanded to Ayacucho. Others included the priests Pedro Tello and Manuel Navaro (the latter would later join the Huanta monarchist uprising).[112] Accordingly, whereas the available evidence corroborates Huanta's loyalist role in both the 1780 and 1814 uprisings, it reveals little about the justification for the title of general of the Royal Armies which Antonio Huachaca, the Quechua-speaking supreme commander of the Huanta monarchist uprising, would come to flaunt. Yet I suspect it is precisely this "silence" that ought to be considered in explaining Huachaca's and Huantino communities' particular "brand" of royalism.

First, to my knowledge, no indian, not even one of noble birth, ever claimed to have held the rank of general of the Royal Army. The highest military ranks ever claimed by an indigenous person under Spanish rule were those of brigadier and colonel of the Royal Army, both held by Pumacahua, the devoted loyalist Cuzco kuraka turned rebel whom we mentioned above. Second, the archives reveal no record of any legal attempt whatsoever on Huachaca's part to gain recognition as such, a situation that contrasts with the numerous indian petitions for legal recognition of prebends, military ranks, and nobility titles in other Andean regions—examples of which I have provided above. This is not to say that General Huachaca and his companions invented the story about their ranks. Huantino historians suggest, for instance, that Huachaca may have held in principle a military appointment, courtesy of Viceroy La Serna, issued perhaps as late as the Battle of Ayacucho (1824). La Serna allegedly made Huachaca a general to reward him for the services he rendered the Crown during the battles against the Cuzco rebels in 1815. In effect, during Huanta's conflicts with Cuzco rebel armies in September and October 1814 and into January 1815, Huachaca was reportedly commander of guerrillas under the orders of Colonel of Militias Pedro José Lazón, and, according to the same source, Viceroy La Serna allegedly "promoted him to the high rank of *General de Brigada*, [precisely] in recognition of his efficient services rendered to the Spanish government [in such battles.]"[113]

If one accepts this possibility, then it is easier to explain the absence of proof for Huachaca's appointment as general. In 1824, unlike 1780 and 1815, the royalist chiefs responsible for all appointments and promotions were vanquished and thus unable to enforce them or even leave written records of them. This very absence of documentary proof—not only for the historian but for the protagonists in this history—is perhaps what makes the zeal with which Huachaca sought to reassert his rank and status as general more comprehensible; it also suggests the prestige of the king. In effect, it was precisely the difficulty (or perhaps impossibility) of confirming such a high rank through legal means that strengthened the need to reassert it through verbal and written discourse as well as military action.

To reinforce this hypothesis, let us consider, in addition, the Huanta caudillos' plebeian roots. The rank of general constituted virtually the only designation of social and political prestige for these Quechua-speaking, puna-dwelling muleteers and petty hacendados, and this would have been especially true of Huachaca, who was illiterate. None of them ever claimed cacique status or noble descent. Unlike their Huanta forebears in the sixteenth and seventeenth centuries and unlike many other elite members of native Andean society in the aftermath of the Great Rebellion, Huachaca and the other Huantan royalist generals were unable (or unwilling) to trace their royalism back to a glorious past or noble ancestry; instead, they clung to the rank and power they claimed to have received rather recently from the king. These titles, though perhaps symbolic, were their single source of political prestige, but precisely because their legitimacy was dubious it had to be constantly reasserted.

As for the people who formed the lowest ranks, that is, the bulk of the Huantino peasants, their background seems to parallel the general fate of post–Túpac Amaru rural Andean society. The sentence passed on Túpac Amaru as well as other decrees and instructions regarding indians' political life issued in the aftermath of the rebellion provided that indians who were fluent in Spanish should be "preferred over the rest—other qualifications being equal."[114] The new stipulations endowed Spanish officials, mainly subdelegates, with the right and obligation of supervising the indian communities' political life, including the election of their representatives, and of controlling their resources, including the collection of indian tribute, which in the past had been the prerogative of the kurakas.[115] In practice, however, subdelegates and their aides were not just Spanish but often creoles or mestizos who, significantly, along with the subdelegates, began calling themselves "caciques." After Túpac Amaru, then, Spanish and mestizo "caciques" proliferated. What this meant, semantically, is that the term *cacique* progressively lost its ethnic connotation and began to designate, more often than not, the officer in charge of collecting indian tribute, that is, the subdelegate and his collaborators, regardless of their ethnicity. Thus, the post of *cacique gobernador* (the "ethnic" cacique, who usually inherited his position) gave way to *cacique recaudador*, the one who collected the tribute.[116]

These developments ran parallel to a policy of reasserting the image of the king while delegitimizing that of the Inca. Yet in some regions, such as Huanta, which in addition to remaining loyalist never seemed to have felt very close to the Incas, and where the prestige of the native nobility seemed to have been declining many years before the Great Rebellion—possibly as early as the seventeenth century[117]—the process of post–Túpac Amaru royalist hispanicizing indoctrination may have been more fluid and more compatible with their own history. The fact that no ethnic caciques—who despite their ambivalences could work as guarantors of local and regional "ethnic" continuity and pride— led Huantino peasants either in the convulsions of 1780–81 and 1814–15 or in the 1826 monarchist uprising itself helps one understand why the powerful image of the king could have worked as the single, albeit momentary, unifying figure among these peoples.

5

The World of the Peasants: Landscapes and Networks

Whereas the sea offers me a diluted landscape, mountains impress me as being a concentrated world. They are so literally, since their pleats and folds provide a relatively greater surface area over a given distance. Also, the potentialities of this denser universe are less quickly exhausted; the changeable climate prevailing there and the differences caused by altitude, exposure and the nature of the soil encourage clear-cut contrasts between the various slopes and levels, as well as between the seasons. Unlike so many people, I was never depressed when staying in a narrow valley, the sides of which were so close that they seemed like walls, above which only a fragment of the sky was visible, to be traversed by the sun in the space of a few hours.

—Claude Lévi-Strauss, *Tristes Tropiques*, 1955

The bulk of the restorationist army consisted of peasants from the high-altitude communities of Huanta and, to a lesser extent, of hacienda laborers. It is to these people, their towns and territories, and their relationship with such groups as muleteers and hacendados that I shall refer in the present chapter. The first section of the chapter maps the territory of the rebellion, its settlements and populations, and the latter's presence in the monarchist rebellion. A second section introduces some of the key characters of the rebellion and discusses the social and economic relationships that linked community peasants with noncommunity peasants, muleteers, hacendados, and other inhabitants of the region. Because the mapping of peoples and places is not a neutral process but is determined rather by value judgments one makes about the things to be classified and the names given to them, I should first like to discuss my choices of terminology for this chapter. I use the term *community* to refer to towns or villages (that is, pueblos) organized in *ayllus* or to the ayllus themselves. Ayllu is a form of social organization and extended kinship peculiar to the Andes, around which community life is structured, from farming to religious practices. Ayllus constitute as well one of the most resilient Andean social formations of pre-Hispanic origin. They certainly have evolved over time, although knowledge about how they operated in the early nineteenth century is far from plentiful. The historiography for this period has portrayed them as social units with access to corporate land.[1] Nevertheless, the evidence for Huanta suggests that ayllus also continued reproducing themselves within haciendas, even after having forfeited their lands to them.

For most of the colonial period, ayllu membership was also a fiscal category indicating indian tribute-liability. The practice of imposing an indian tribute upon members of the ayllus, established by the Spanish in the sixteenth century, persisted with some changes into the first decades of the Republic. At this time it was reclassified as a head tax and renamed *contribución de indígenas* until its formal abolition in 1854.[2] Nevertheless, not every individual paying indian tribute was necessarily attached to an ayllu or settled in a town or village. In Huanta, for instance, during the late colonial period, indian tribute payers could also be registered in haciendas or *estancias* (cattle ranches); many others were landless—approximately 47 percent of the indian tribute-paying population, according to figures from 1801[3]—and probably worked on rented lands. For this reason, the widespread idea that during the nineteenth century indian tribute was a guarantee that the state would respect and protect peasants' communal lands, as appears to have been the case in northern Potosí, cannot, and should not, be taken for granted elsewhere in the Andes.[4]

In the *repartimiento* (tax district) of Huanta, most pueblos had two ayllus, a few had only one, and others had none at all, according to the tributary rolls of 1801, the only ones available for the early nineteenth century. Of the twenty-seven settlements registered as pueblos in 1801, twenty are listed with their respective ayllus, while seven appear with no ayllu; of these twenty, sixteen have two ayllus and four have one.[5] Certainly, these official records do not necessarily reflect all living realities. For instance, the 1801 tribute roll mentions no ayllu in connection with the town of Huanta, but other pieces of evidence suggest that an ayllu named Cocha was still part of the town as late as 1804.[6] The other ayllu historically associated with the town of Huanta was the ayllu Mitma. By 1793 the ayllus Cocha and Mitma were under the authority of a single *kuraka*, but in the tribute rolls prior to 1801 only the ayllu Cocha is mentioned in association with the town of Huanta, while the ayllu Mitma is listed as a separate tributary unit.[7]

The quality of information recorded in the tributary rolls, moreover, depended on a number of factors, including the degree of meticulousness of the record keepers, who (regrettably for historians) were generally devoid of the ethnographic interest that characterized their sixteenth-century counterparts. They limited themselves to registering only the data that were strictly "fiscally relevant" (one may add that the realm of the fiscally relevant had itself shrunk in relation to the early colonial period). On the other hand, some ayllus may have indeed escaped official inspection or not yet constituted themselves as fiscally accountable units at the time of the *empadronamiento*, that is, the process of registering population in the *padrones tributarios*, or tributary rolls. Whatever the case, what seems clear in Huanta, and is consistent with information gathered for other regions, is that ayllus were constantly metamorphosing, splitting themselves into smaller units, splitting apart from the towns and jurisdictions they belonged to in order to form separate hamlets or villages; melting into other constituencies or becoming "neighborhoods" within larger towns.[8] Indeed, the term *ayllu*, as it appears in geographical dictionaries and official sources of the republican nineteenth century, usually had no ethnographic connotation and was increasingly used as a synonym for *parcialidad*, that is, a neighborhood or settlement within or on the outskirts of a town, or for a hamlet (*caserío*) or an *anexo*, that is, a hamlet subject to a larger town's jurisdiction.[9]

Whether these territorial units corresponded to ayllus in the anthropological sense defined above is hard to tell. But in any case, judging from the number of peasant communal authorities active in Huanta, it seems accurate to say that ayllus were indeed living social entities, not the mere territorial units that appear in nineteenth-century geographic and demographic sources.

Not all the individuals paying the indian tribute were permanent residents of the settlements where they were registered on the tributary rolls. Settlement patterns in the Andes have traditionally been very fluid, allowing people to take advantage of the ecological diversity of their surroundings. Villagers spent long hours, sometimes days, commuting to lands they farmed in a diversity of ecological niches, and once there they might remain for hours, days, or months, according to season or need. The haciendas in Huanta shared some of the features of the communities, since their lands too commonly embraced a variety of ecological niches.[10] In addition, one finds entire ayllus established in estancias and haciendas.

The villagers and hacienda laborers of Huanta highlands for the most part spoke only Quechua and did not know how to read or write. Their contemporaries who wished to disassociate themselves from them called them "indians." I use this term to refer to them solely when my purpose is to emphasize their "ethnic" and fiscal condition (ayllu membership and tribute-liability) or linguistic (Quechua-speaking) status. Otherwise, I shall refer to them simply as peasants or villagers. I favor this approach because at the time of the events recorded here the word *indian* had begun to undergo semantic transformations that we would be unable to convey were we to use the word as a neutral "ethnic" category whose meaning is taken for granted. It was not. The term *indian* had by this time already acquired pronounced pejorative connotations. During most of the colonial period the status of "noble indian" and kuraka afforded a segment of the native society privileges, social status, and the power to rule over other indians, but in the early Republic indian identity was strongly stigmatized, thus losing its appeal as a vehicle for upward mobility. As we saw in the preceding chapter, this change started taking place during the last decades of colonial rule, in the wake of the Túpac Amaru rebellion, when the Spanish gradually abolished indian nobility and kurakazgos, measures which the Republic consolidated with Bolívar's decree of 1825. Thus, the word *indian* became increasingly associated with the Quechua-speaking and poor, a rural dweller at the very bottom of the social hierarchy. To call someone an indian was to assume his or her inferiority, his or her subcitizen status, which may have been one of the reasons General San Martín decreed in 1821, shortly after proclaiming the independence of Peru, that indians were henceforth to be called "Peruvians."[11]

The linguistic repercussions of this decree were felt, as far as I have been able to determine, chiefly in the sphere of official documentation: prefect communiqués, war reports, and also in the patriotic poetry of the time. Paradoxically, the decree, which was meant to achieve, at least symbolically, the "integration" of indians into the nation, ended up reinforcing the exclusionary notions it sought to attack. Indeed, *Peruvian* became a substitute for *indian*, a name given to indians *alone*, rather than a name given *also* to indians. The change in terminology did not imply a change in meaning and hence it was soon discarded.[12]

This failed attempt to "Peruvianize" indians is nonetheless telling, for it shows that although the term *indian* was used in colloquial speech, there existed at this time an awareness that this word, so identified with colonial rule, conflicted with the very idea of a "free nation." This might also explain why republican legislators subsequently adopted the term *indígena* for indian, a change that proved more successful and was to persist throughout most of the twentieth century.[13]

For Peruvians today, however, both *indian* and *indígena* remain highly derogatory terms, notwithstanding a recent and largely successful worldwide political trend vindicating "indigenous" identity(ies). And although my preference for *peasant* may not be the perfect choice, in Peru *peasant* in its Spanish equivalent, *campesino*, has a much more positive resonance than *indian*. At any rate, poor Andean rural workers in this country identify much more readily with the term *campesino* for purposes of political organization than with the pejorative *indian*, which still evokes notions of poverty, "ignorance," and wretchedness, while *campesino* conveys instead the idea of a rural worker who is politically aware and worthy of respect. The change has become more apparent since General Juan Velasco's agrarian reform law of 1969 transformed "indigenous communities" into "peasant communities," thus establishing another important (yet to date little studied) linguistic threshold in the history of relations between peasants and the national state.[14]

In Huanta during the early Republic, the authorities and hacendados who did not consider themselves indians used *indian* or *indígena* for landless hacienda laborers (who preferred to identify themselves as *labradores*) or community peasants as well as for leaders like Tadeo Choque, who was likewise a hacendado, and Huachaca, who was a muleteer. In a similar vein, Huachaca's foes (some of whom were themselves referred to as indians) branded him an indian, in an obviously derogatory tone. Those who backed the revolt, on the other hand, never referred to Huachaca or Choque as indians—they used titles like *Señor* or *don* or *General* or *Señor General*—nor did they apply this category to themselves except when they knew they could benefit from legal advantages accruing from this status, as in the colonial period. However, whereas during the colonial era the category "indian" was legally established, during the Republic this legality became ambiguous. And it could hardly have been otherwise.

The birth of the Republic entailed the adoption of new constitutions and the issuance of a decree which, in making indians Peruvians, sought to reclaim not merely the indians but language itself from colonial stigma; even so, in the realm of jurisprudence the *Leyes de Indias* (Laws of the Indies), instituted for ethnically divided societies, remained in force for several decades after Independence, as did ethnically based taxes. In effect, perhaps the only unambiguous aspect of the early Republic's legal definition of the indian was his status as tributary. Thus the advent of the Republic came to problematize a category which, for all its complexities, had fit more or less comfortably within the colony's classificatory and legislative system. Our language cannot afford to be indifferent to this problematization. Therefore I shall use, as I have been thus far, the term *indian* when it is a matter of emphasizing the ethnic, linguistic, or legal (fiscal) status of its bearer, as noted above—especially when dealing with the republican period; yet I may borrow the term more freely from the sources when dealing with the colonial era. It should be clear, however, that whenever I am dealing with the colonial period (at least, during that part of it in which an indian nobility and kurakas survived) the equation peasant=indian (or indian= poor) cannot, and should not, be taken for granted.

When it comes to the experience of the peasants who participated in the monarchist uprising, the record is largely silent. Very few of them have allowed us to hear their voices. Their declarations in the tribunals are brief; in most cases they appear in the capacity of witnesses and are heard through interpreters. They were required not so much to speak about themselves as to confirm or supplement information provided by or relating to other witnesses or persons under accusation. This was so because in accordance with the paternalist mentality of the time, peasants (being "indians") were thought of as childlike beings—that is, beings not wholly accountable for their actions— and thus deserved the indulgences to which their "inferior" or "needy" condition entitled them. Accordingly, the penalties meted out to them, such as "serving the *Patria*" as recruits, were more edifying than punitive.

For reasons that are understandable, a majority of peasants denied their involvement in the rebellion, and their declarations to this effect are understandably more extensive. The peasants of the village of Ayahuanco, for example, declared before the prefect that their "sufferings were caused by a treacherous Huachaca and his allies," while insisting that they were "by no means accomplices in this action [the monarchist rebellion], but rather lovers of, and partial to, the sacred and merciful Patria."[15] The statement is striking, considering that Ayahuanco was clearly implicated in the rebellion. Nevertheless, within the context in which it was formulated, Ayahuanquino testimony made perfect sense. The villagers happened to have been victimized by the theft of their livestock at the hands of a hacendado who collaborated with Huachaca. The peasants' avowed repudiation of Huachaca and adherence to the Patria may have been rather a ploy to convince the prefect to assist them in recovering livestock lost at the hands of a monarchist. If, however, these sentiments were genuine, then we may have to consider the possibility that the community was drawn into the rebellion against its will.

The cases in which peasants openly expressed their support for the restorationist cause are less telling, perhaps because they virtually always reach us by indirect routes. Hence, one witness, while at a party in the town of Tircos, "heard that everyone was saying that it was necessary to tie up the priest [Navarro] and take him to Huachaca, since he was against them and was a double-dealing patriot."[16] At this same event, another witness "heard it said . . . that in Tircos they had thrown stones at the priest because he told them to give up fighting."[17] Similar intimidation was felt by the hacendado Pedro Calienes from Aranhuay, according to subsequent testimony: "Here the indians told don Pedro Calienes that they were going to kill him because he wanted to go to Guamanga . . . deserting his hacienda, for he had communicated with the Patria."[18]

Harangues on behalf of the king and Huachaca were also made public by villagers of San Cristóbal in Huancavelica: "They have even insulted the government in the streets and plazas, cheering señor Huachaca," reported one authority.[19] There were others like Jacinto Coica, an "indígena" of Cuenca (present-day Ecuador) but a longtime resident of Huanta, who "openly stated that Huachaca was not harming anyone and that he was having only the patriots executed, and that not only did he not do the royalists any harm, but he was awarding them the insurgents' possessions as well."[20] This testimony allows one to begin to perceive the motives behind peasant involvement in the rebellion. I shall return to this question later. First, it is necessary to clarify who the peasants were and where they came from.

The Territory and Its Populations

The territory shaken by the rebellion corresponded to the repartimiento of Huanta, whose towns and haciendas were distributed in four *doctrinas*, or ecclesiastical districts: Huanta, Luricocha, Ccarhuahurán, and Tambo, corresponding to today's provinces of Huanta and La Mar. With the exception of

Huanta and Luricocha (2,621, and 2,550 meters—or 8,599 and 8,366 feet—in altitude, respectively), most of the towns in the repartimiento of Huanta were between 3,000 and 4,100 meters (9,843 and 13,451 feet) above sea level. Huanta's most populous area thus encompassed at least three different ecological niches: *quechua*, *suni*, and *puna*.[21] In addition to these highlands, or sierra, were the *montaña* territories—or *selva alta* (upper jungle), also called *ceja de selva* (mountainous rim of the jungle), ranging from 500 to 2,300 meters (1,640 to 7,546 feet) above sea level and located along the Mantaro river to the north and the Apurímac to the east.[22] The rivers demarcate the frontier zone from the *selva baja* (or lower jungle, commonly called simply *selva*) while establishing the boundaries of Huanta province. Unlike the highlands, where peasant communities were preponderant, in the montañas, the coca-growing region par excellence, haciendas predominated. Yet it was in the sunis and punas, both above 3,000 meters (9,843 feet) in altitude, that the most important headquarters were located (see maps 2, 3, 5, and 6).

The area in revolt stretched from the town of Huanta to the montaña of Viscatán in the north, a distance of some seventy-five kilometers; from this point it spread to the northeast as far as the montañas of Acón and Tamboconga, passing through the Choimacota gorge, some fifty to sixty kilometers from Huanta. The rebellion extended from the town of Huanta eastward as far as the town of Osno, passing through Tambo, some thirty-five kilometers from Huanta; and toward the southeast to the montañas of Chungui, passing through Anco, roughly seventy kilometers from Huanta as the crow flies. Toward the west and northwest the rebellion advanced as far as the present department of Huancavelica, including the towns of Izcuchaca, Huando, and San Cristóbal, nearly a hundred kilometers from Huanta, but also affecting the towns of Caja and Acobamba on the road to Huancayo, the largest city in the central sierra, with which Huanta has been traditionally linked through commerce.[23] These distances, however, insofar as they correspond to straight lines, that is, aerial kilometers, can only be relative. In a topography in which gorges at an elevation of 1,500 meters (4,921 feet) above sea level often reach 4,000 meters (13,123 feet) in altitude, roads are steep and winding, making walking distances several times longer than they appear on the map (see maps 5 and 6).

The rebellion did not extend southward; it stopped at the boundary of the present-day provinces of Huanta and Huamanga. South of this border, the towns of Quinua, Acosvinchos, and Huaychao, located in the modern province of Huamanga,[24] as well as some of the towns in the eastern district of San

Miguel (Coscosa, Chilcas, and San Miguel itself), which at the time of the rebellion formed part of Huanta province (and today belong to the province of La Mar), joined with the Republic's troops to defeat the monarchist insurrection. These towns were joined by others from farther south, whose inhabitants, the so-called Morochucos of Pampa Cangallo, contributed much to the defeat of the rebellion. All of these towns had likewise actively participated on the patriot side during the wars of Independence (see map 3).[25]

The repartimiento of Huanta was the most populous of the four tax districts that made up the *partido* (province) of the same name in the late eighteenth century and early years of the nineteenth, and Huanta province was itself the most populous of the intendancy of Huamanga. In 1782, the repartimiento of Huanta totaled 1,362 tributaries, whereas those of Tambillo, Quinua, and Caviñas together amounted to a mere 791. In 1787, the tribute-paying population of the repartimiento of Huanta had risen to 1,710, while in Tambillo, Quinua, and Caviñas the number was 1,039. In 1796, the figures were 2,404 for the repartimiento of Huanta and 1,595 for the other three, while in 1801, they were 2,582 and 1,811, respectively.[26]

Insofar as the repartimiento of Huanta was the one comprising the greatest number of tributaries in the province, it also had the greatest number of pueblos and the fewest haciendas. Of the 33 localities on Huanta's tributary rolls, only 9 were haciendas in 1782, that is, 27.2 percent, as opposed to 72.8 percent corresponding to pueblos, estancias, and unclassified areas. In 1801, the number of registered settlements was 59, of which only 15, or 25.4 percent, were haciendas, while 74.6 percent represented pueblos and estancias (27 pueblos and 17 estancias). In other repartimientos the situation was the reverse. By 1782 the proportion of haciendas in the repartimiento of Quinua equaled 80 percent, in Tambillo 71 percent, and in Caviñas 61 percent. In 1801 the proportion of haciendas in the repartimiento of Quinua held steady at 80 percent, while it rose to 76.4 percent in Tambillo but fell to 53.4 percent in Caviñas. Thus, revealingly—and this might be one of the most significant conclusions to be drawn from the figures—whereas in the royalist region (the repartimiento of Huanta) the predominant pattern of settlement was the village, in the patriotic quarter, which coincided with the repartimientos of Quinua and Tambillo, haciendas predominated. These figures, of course, take into consideration only those populations subject to indian tribute as of 1801, which concentrated heavily in the highlands; indian tribute rolls leave virtually the whole montaña zone uncharted (see maps 3 and 4).

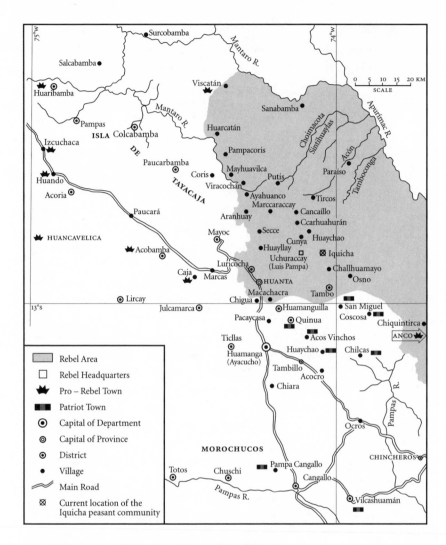

Map key:

- Rebel Area
- ☐ Rebel Headquarters
- Pro – Rebel Town
- Patriot Town
- ◉ Capital of Department
- ◎ Capital of Province
- ⊙ District
- • Village
- Main Road
- ⊠ Current location of the Iquicha peasant community

Place labels (as shown on map):

Surcobamba, Salcabamba, Mantaro R., Viscatán, Sanabamba, Huaribamba, Pampas, Mantaro R., Huarcatán, ISLA Colcabamba, Izcuchaca, Pampacoris, Choimacota, Sintihuaylas, Acón, Apurímac R., Paucarbamba, Mayhuavilca, Coris, Putis, Paraiso, DE, Huando, Viracochán, Acoria, TAYACAJA, Ayahuanco, Tircos, Tamboconga, Marccaraccay, Cancaíllo, Paucará, Aranhuay, Ccarhuahurán, Mayoc, Secce, Huaychao, HUANCAVELICA, Cunya, Acobamba, Huayllay, Iquicha, Uchuraccay (Luis Pampa), Challhuamayo, Caja, Marcas, Luricocha, Osno, HUANTA, Macachacra, Tambo, Lircay, Chigua, Julcamarca, Huamanguilla, San Miguel, Pacaycasa, Coscosa, Chiquintirca, Ticllas, Quinua, ANCO, Acos Vinchos, Huamanga (Ayacucho), Huaychao, Chilcas, Tambillo, Acocro, Chiara, Pampas R., Ocros, MOROCHUCOS, CHINCHEROS, Totos, Chuschi, Pampa Cangallo, Cangallo, Pampas R., Vilcashuamán

MAP 3. Patriot and royalist towns.

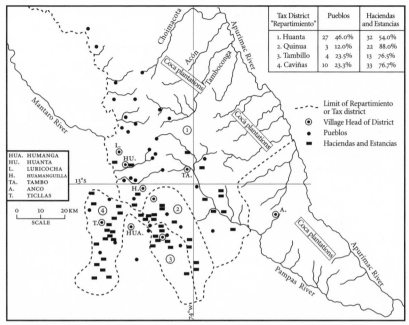

Tax District "Repartimiento"	Pueblos		Haciendas and Estancias	
1. Huanta	27	46.0%	32	54.0%
2. Quinua	3	12.0%	22	88.0%
3. Tambillo	4	23.5%	13	76.5%
4. Caviñas	10	23.3%	33	76.7%

Limit of Repartimiento or Tax district
⊙ Village Head of District
• Pueblos
■ Haciendas and Estancias

HUA. HUMANGA
HU. HUANTA
L. LURICOCHA
H. HUAMANGUILLA
TA. TAMBO
A. ANCO
T. TICLLAS

NOTES: Tribute rolls have no data for coca plantations area. Not all the places listed in tribute rolls have been located in modern maps. Haciendas and estancias are grouped together. Disaggregating, in the repartimiento of Huanta there were 17 estancias and 15 haciendas. Three of these estancias and two of these haciendas contained ayllus, one per settlement.

MAP 4. Haciendas and pueblos in Huanta.
Based on AGN, Tributos, Huanta, leg. 5, cuad. 19, 1801.

Despite applying to a period prior to the rebellion, these figures give a sense of what the settlement patterns and demographic landscape of the repartimiento of Huanta may have been at the time the rebellion broke out. Keeping in mind that behind each tribute-paying person there was a family, and that by the time of our most recent tributary roll (1801) the number of tributaries in the repartimiento of Huanta was 2,582 individuals, one may surmise a population of around 13,000 to 15,400 (assuming families of 5 to 6 members) tribute-paying indians and their families in 1801. Analogous data are not available for 1825, at the outbreak of rebellion, but a later source estimates that the *villa* of Huanta alone was home to 12,000 inhabitants in 1834.[27]

The tributary records cannot possibly register every single settlement—some of them may not yet have existed as tributary units at the time of our most recent tributary roll, while others probably escaped official inspection.

Pueblos not registered in the available tributary rolls but accounted for in the facts of the rebellion include Mama and Mayhuavilca, the latter located in the vicinity of the towns of Pampacoris and Huarcatán, the site of saltpeter mines and deposits of other minerals used by the rebels in making gunpowder and armaments. There were more than two dozen high-altitude towns and villages in Huanta at the time of the rebellion, not including their anexos, the estancias, and the haciendas.

These communities were surrounded by haciendas and sometimes formed a part them. There were at least two types of hacienda: those which did not contain tribute-paying populations and those which did, whether accounted for individually or grouped in ayllus. Notable among the haciendas that included ayllus at the time of the monarchist uprising were Ranra and Chacabamba, near Tambo; Lucre, the hacienda belonging to the Spaniard Salvador Pérez; Marcarí, a property belonging to Magdalena Pons and Pedro Calienes;[28] and Chaca and Guancayoc. Significantly, some of these haciendas, for example, Chacabamba and Guancayoc, were classified as estancias, or, like Chaca, as pueblos in the tributary rolls of the first years of the nineteenth century, that is, more than two decades before the rebellion. Interpreting the change in nomenclature is difficult, for no clear pattern emerges from the rolls to enable one to differentiate estancias from haciendas. An estancia could have more or fewer tribute payers than a hacienda and both could include tributaries with and without lands. In the Latin American context, the most widespread translation of *estancia* is "cattle ranch," or a property dedicated to cattle raising. However, in early nineteenth-century Peru a more common term for that kind of settlement was *hato*, meaning literally a livestock hacienda. One also finds that in nineteenth-century republican sources estancia is used interchangeably with *caseríos* or *aldeas* (hamlets or small villages subject to a larger town's jurisdiction), some of which had a well-established tribute-paying tradition and were organized in ayllus. Hence, I have, according to context and timing, translated *estancia* as either "cattle ranch" or "hamlet."[29]

As murky as the taxonomy gets at this point, at least two important ideas may be drawn from the available evidence on estancias and haciendas. First, unlike estancias, haciendas usually had clearly identifiable owners. The idea of individual, "private ownership" should thus be associated more with the hacienda than with estancias. In this part of the Andes, then, there were estancias but not *estancieros* (that is, owners of large cattle-raising properties like those in the Argentinean pampas). Second, the growth of haciendas at the expense of ayllu lands seems to be an ongoing process in this period, as the example of

Chaca, Chacabamba, Guancayoc and other pueblos or estancias that later became haciendas suggests; on the other hand, the slow but steady increase of landless tribute payers (*tributarios sin tierras*) from 39.4 percent in 1782 to 46.8 percent in 1801 may also be considered a manifestation of that process.[30] Analogous data for the early republican period are not available, but what seems clear—and must be kept in mind—is that the loss of community land to the haciendas by no means implied the dissolution of peasants' communal organization.

In effect, ayllus and ex-pueblos that fell within haciendas continued to govern themselves through their *alcaldes de indios* (indian mayors), also called *alcaldes vara* or *ministros de vara* (staff-holding officials), and took part in the restorationist rebellion alongside the communities that were not part of any hacienda. As a whole, peasants from the high-altitude communities composed two-thirds of the army that prepared to storm Ayacucho in November 1827, that is, if we take the figure of 1,500 provided by a participant in the events to be an accurate estimate—local accounts gathered in the aftermath of the events give much higher numbers, ranging from 3,000 to 4,000.[31] Joining the community peasants were hacienda laborers from the highlands and montañas, muleteers, hacendados and merchants who resided in the villa of Huanta, some thirty Spanish capitulados, a few deserters from the republican army, and a handful of priests.

Peasant mobilization in the communities was carried out by the alcaldes de indios, authorities that the Spanish established in the *reducciones*, or towns where the Spaniards resettled native Andeans beginning in the 1570s.[32] Alcaldes acted as communal authorities, and their importance increased as that of the kurakas declined. Unlike the traditional kurakas, who inherited their position, indian mayors and aldermen (*regidores*) undertook one-year terms. In the early Republic they were most commonly called alcaldes indígenas, or "indigenous mayors," and, from the mid–nineteenth century, *varayoqs*.[33] At the time of the monarchist rebellion and in subsequent years, indian mayors enjoyed a formidable legitimacy and representative authority; they represented the community in all of its legal transactions and claims and were responsible for rectifying irregularities or abuses which might affect the community. Their duty was, in the words of an indigenous mayor himself, to "protect morality and public order [and] make decisions in lesser matters"; their testimony could carry more weight than that of an ordinary villager.[34] The representative authority of the indigenous mayors was such that it found expression even in language:

The casa-hacienda of Chaca. The pueblo of Chaca became a hacienda in the early nineteenth century and it is now a pueblo again (bottom figure). The four towers surrounding the casa-hacienda were built recently by the villagers to protect the town from incursions by the Shining Path. *Photograph by author, ca. 1994.*

The town of Chaca. *Photograph by author, ca. 1999.*

Fernando Pariona, justice of the peace of Chaca, holding the staff he inherited from his grandfather, who was alcalde-vara. *Photograph by author, ca. 1999.*

on more than one occasion the terms *alcalde* and *indio* were treated inter-changeably.[35] It is surely for this reason that *montonero* leaders always appear concerned with legitimizing their authority before the communities and their alcaldes. Huachaca himself declared that his powers (*facultades*) came not only from the king but also from "the communities and divisions."[36] He also instructed "the civilian and military *vara*-officials" (that is, staff-officials) to ensure that his orders were followed.[37]

The various references here are significant. Huachaca was referring to two types of authorities: civilian authorities ("civilian vara-officials"), who gov-erned the communities, and military authorities ("military vara-officials"), probably the commanders who ruled the "divisions," or military forces. Whereas the "civilian *vara*-officials" presumably were guided by a dynamic peculiar to the community, the "divisions" and the "military *vara*-officials" were the corps and authorities, respectively, of an army headed by Huachaca as supreme commander. He himself held the power for appointing war leaders, and this prerogative may have created tensions among the alcaldes. Perhaps for this reason, the rebellion's military *caudillos* sought to legitimize their authority by appealing to the vote of the communities. The available data regarding the dynamics or frequency of the voting are not very precise, but clearly it did take place. For instance, the caudillo Choque charged the Spaniard Francisco Garay with urging communities to ratify Choque's authority as "captain" and "Chief of Staff" ("*Estado Mayor*" [*sic*]) and that of Garay as "commander," "by direct vote of the community."[38] The influence of the rebellion's military caudillos in community affairs went beyond the election of war leaders to include the election of civilian authorities, though in such cases the military commanders seem to have shown more respect for the communities' choices. In another letter to Garay, Choque wrote, "Don Melchor Porras must be alcalde mayor, for if the community chooses him to be in its royal service, he should not fail to construct roads and bridges, and tolerate neither thieves, nor those living in sin, nor adulterers."[39]

Perhaps the rebellion's main military commanders did not always succeed in having the communities legitimize their military authority through communal vote or in imposing the alcaldes of their choice. At any rate, however, evidence showing that Huachaca and the French-Basque Nicolás Soregui made both civilian and military appointments is much more abundant than voting records. Among the hundreds of documents related to the rebellion that I have reviewed, I have found only one that mentions a town council (*cabildo*) in the election of a civilian authority. The undated document names Manuel Leandro as "governor and subdelegate of Acón" and is signed by "I the designated commander of the Illustrious Town Council of Yquicha = I the commander *Dn.* Pedro Figueroa. I the Mayor *Dn.* Mariano Peres. Councilmen [*Cabildantes*]=."[40] How representative this town council of Iquicha was is hard to tell, given the absence of analogous information for the period. Yet, judging from the presence of military authorities, it seems that it was not a very conventional cabildo.[41] Note how two of the "councilmen" define themselves as "commanders," one of them explicitly attributing to himself the title "designated commander." Undoubtedly, this so-called "town council" was more military than civilian and perhaps more exclusive than representative, too. The authority which the "Yquicha Town Council" granted Leandro as governor and subdelegate of Acón was corroborated by an edict issued by Huachaca from his headquarters in Luis Pampa on April 17, 1827.[42] We do not know whether this edict preceded or followed Leandro's appointment by the "Yquicha Town Council." Whatever the case, the important point is that Leandro, a landless coca grower and muleteer in the montañas who identified himself as an "indian" in legal petitions, seemed to represent neither a specific community nor a group of them, but rather the military leaders who had appointed him.

In the final analysis, one could conclude that for the duration of the war civilian authorities were subordinated to military leaders and that, once the rebellion was suppressed, community authorities would recover the power they wielded in times of peace. Yet these punas hardly experienced any lasting peace. Following the defeat of the monarchist uprising, the province's inhabitants were engulfed in a series of civil wars that ravaged the highlands throughout the early republican era. During these conflicts, Huachaca and other montonero leaders continued to play key political and military roles, as we shall observe in detail later, and thus possibly continued wielding some influence over the political life of the communities. Yet their concern in legitimizing their authority before the communities and the references to communal voting are significant—and to a large degree understandable, for as we shall observe later, these military leaders were not precisely "outsiders" but part of the world of economic, social, and labor relations within which the communities operated. In fact, references to communal voting, though limited, suggest instances of communal government with which the military chiefs of the uprising could not fail to reckon. At the same time, the apparent ease with which the Huanta rebel military leaders and their Spanish allies influenced both the voting and direct appointment of civilian and military authorities in the course of the rebellion suggests the subordinated position and vulnerability that these institutions of communal government assumed. Moreover, the fact that mayors, governors, and other officials appointed by Huachaca exercised authority over territories that incorporated several towns and haciendas—whereas the traditional indian mayors governed only within one town—put the latter in an implicitly subordinate position to the former.

The ambiguity of the powers and interchangeability of duties of civilian authorities appointed by the rebellion's commanders are likewise significant. Despite the fact that Leandro was designated "subdelegate" and functioned as a tithe collector, among other things, he was also called "mayor." It is not difficult to sense that what lies behind this—deliberate or coincidental—ambivalence is the concentration of responsibilities in one individual; that is to say, the concentration of power.

The communities, then, were unquestionably strong in numbers; they were more populous in the repartimiento of Huanta than in any of the other repartimientos comprising the partido of the same name. Moreover, they made up the great mass of montoneros. And yet their direct representatives, the alcaldes de indios, were never among the highest in command during the war. The high commands were reserved for muleteers, merchants, and hacendados appointed by Huachaca. In like fashion, though the community peasants were masters of the geography in the core area of the uprising, they did not control the war. Consider the following: of the eight locations that fulfilled the function of headquarters or command posts during the rebellion, three were villages while five were haciendas. More than mere figures, distribution of military outposts reveals a truth that subtly creeps into the silences of the documents: the removal of the communities from the centers of command.

The Headquarters

I have identified eight locations that performed strategic military functions in the rebellion. Three of them were towns with a tributary tradition: Secce (sometimes written Seque or Sec-Sec), Aranhuay, and Huaillay, all three between 3,260 and 3,600 meters above sea level and thus in the suni ecological niche. The other five headquarters were haciendas or places without a tributary tradition: Uchuraccay and Cancaíllo, in the punas, Tucuvilca, in the suni, and Paraíso and Choimacota, in the montañas (see map 5). Let us first consider the towns.

Towns of Indians (and Spaniards): The Suni Villages

Secce stood out among all the others as a base of military operations. It figures most frequently as a "headquarters," followed by Aranhuay, which is referred to as a "command post,"[43] and, last, by Huaillay, the least important, as it appears only once as a "headquarters"[44] (see maps 5 and 6). One of the reasons for Secce's strategic military value was its location. The town lies on a very steep slope 3,262 meters above sea level. The roads from Secce to Huanta and the Mantaro valley can be seen in the distance, as can those which go in the direction of the punas.[45] Secce is a mere seventeen kilometers as the crow flies from the present community of Uchuraccay, at that time a hacienda and the most important headquarters. This distance is of course relative, for along this stretch the land abruptly rises nearly 1,000 meters. Proceeding along the edge

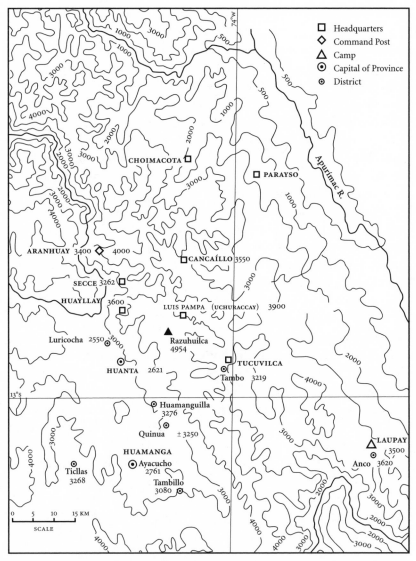

MAP 5. Ecology of the rebellion and main headquarters.

of the cordillera, a traveler who sets out from Secce on foot will walk for six hours before reaching Uchuraccay, which is itself on an incline above 4,000 meters (see maps 5 and 6). Secce was coveted by the forces of both sides for its strategic setting; shortly after the monarchists' defeat, the town was captured and converted into a headquarters for the republican army, which used the location to plan its incursions into Uchuraccay.

The tribute-paying population of Secce numbered only 20 individuals in 1801, and the same is true of Huaillay. Aranhuay, which, as noted, fulfilled the function of command post, was home to a larger tribute-paying population than those of the other two towns: 56 in 1801 and 42 in 1780. In all three cases tribute payers are defined as either *originarios* or *forasteros* "with lands."[46] The figures do not exhibit any exceptional features compared with those of the towns in the rest of the repartimiento. The towns with the smallest tributary populations had 4 to 5 tribute-paying indians, while the most populous were the capitals of doctrina, Tambo, Huanta, Guamanguilla, and Luricocha, whose tributary populations fluctuated between 153 and 350 individuals in 1801 (one must bear in mind that each tribute-paying person represented a family).[47]

Secce and Aranhuay would seem to differ little from the rest of the towns located above 3,000 meters. Nonetheless, they did possess features which rendered them distinct. In addition to their alcaldes de indios, these towns were governed by *alcaldes de españoles*, or "mayors of Spaniards."[48] Again, references to these mayors are elusive. Were they appointed by the montonero leaders in the course of the war? Or was there a dual system of authority before the rebellion? I believe both scenarios are possible. Dual, ethnically based authority systems were not uncommon in the Andes, particularly in larger towns. In the repartimiento of Huanta during the late colonial period, the larger towns, usually the capitals of doctrinas, had both alcaldes de indios *and* alcaldes de españoles.[49] The term *español*, however, as used in late colonial documentation, rarely denoted a peninsular Spaniard, as historian David Cahill reminds us, "but rather an American of Spanish ancestry" and could designate individuals ranging from "creole aristocrats" to "poor whites," including mestizos.[50] At any rate, and beyond physiognomy and ancestry, *español*, more broadly conceived, denoted cultural traits associated with Spaniards (Castilian language and European dress) rather than birthplace. The category of mestizo, in turn, although a legal one, was not a common form of self-identification, apparently because of its derogatory over-

On the road from Huanta to Secce. The houses have roofs made of *ichu*, a dry plant that grows abundantly in the punas. *Photograph by author, ca. 1994.*

tones, and it would not become widespread until the twentieth century. In practice, then, in Huanta as in most of Andean Peru, the language of ethnicity allowed little room for "middle ground" positions and tended to remain rather dichotomous, that is, based on the indian vs. Spanish opposition.[51] Spaniards from the Peninsula, on the other hand, were in turn called peninsular Spaniards (*españoles peninsulares*) or alluded to as being originally "from the kingdoms of Europe" or "from the kingdoms of Castilla," "Galicia," "Navarra," etc. This would change after Independence, when *español* began to acquire the national connotation it has now.

Españoles, then, in the more inclusive eighteenth-century and early nineteenth-century sense of the word, were part of the population of Secce and Aranhuay. Aranhuay was a gathering spot for the rebels. The priest Francisco Pacheco, in charge of the provision of arms, maintained one of his principal centers of operation in Aranhuay and would constantly write to Soregui and Huachaca from there; Huachaca also signed a dispatch from Aranhuay. In 1825, before the rebellion became more organized, the Spaniard Miguel Fariña and the Ayacuchan hacendado Marcelo Castro had led a peasant mobilization in Aranhuay that ended in the death of the town's governor. The political significance of the nonindian presence in Aranhuay was given even clearer expression in November 1827, when a handful of rebel caudillos there, several of them peninsular Spaniards, signed an oath of noncapitulation. The presence of an "alcalde de españoles" in the town is thus not surprising given the circumstances.

The information about an alcalde de españoles in Secce turns out to be still more revealing because it dates from 1831, that is, after the defeat of the rebellion. This means that if the appointment of alcaldes de españoles in Secce was initiated at the time of or prior to the rebellion, it was not a temporary measure. The presence of these mayors, nevertheless, did not nullify the position of mayor of indians. Two communities thus coexisted in the same town even after the rebellion.[52] We do not know what kind of relationship the two types of authorities established between themselves, but at the time of the uprising the supreme control of the town probably rested in the hands of the españoles. Soregui was in command in Secce—as he himself put it, "Only the band of armed men that I had in Seque gave orders"[53]—and the numerous communiqués signed by him at this headquarters suggest as much. The relative mildness of Secce's climate as compared with that of the punas, at nearly one thousand meters higher up, was perhaps one of the factors initially luring Europeans to the town, whose inhabitants today still refer disdainfully to the puna dwellers as chutos,[54] even though alcaldes de españoles have long since ceased to exist in the town. Puna, in turn, did not designate the neatly demarcated ecological niche it became in late twentieth-century geography textbooks; rather, it vaguely denoted "high lands," although these "heights" were always relative to who was speaking. Bureaucrats in Lima or Ayacucho city made no distinction between, say, Secce (or even lower towns) and Uchuraccay and referred to them generically as "puna," in accordance with the rather idiosyncratic sociogeographical scale still prevailing in Peru, whereby the higher up the town, the less its native inhabitants' social standing—and the more "indian."

In addition to the above, the presence of alcaldes de españoles in Secce and Aranhuay probably had to do with a series of orders issued by the Crown shortly before Independence in order to favor the colonization of the montañas of the vicinity (a royal warrant of 1816). In 1819, a group of Huanta vecinos (residents)—hacendados and military, Spaniards and Huantinos—had organized to secure the appointment of alcaldes de españoles in the montañas, where their haciendas were located (a task they accomplished after surmount-

The church of Secce. In the early nineteenth century Secce had both a mayor of indians and a mayor of Spaniards. *Photograph by author, ca. 1994.*

Huaillay, once a rebel headquarters. *Photograph by author, ca. 1997.*

ing several obstacles, to be analyzed in the following chapter). It is not known whether the españoles residing in Secce and Aranhuay made similar requests, but it is possible, and, if so, the presence of alcaldes de españoles in these towns would have preceded the rebellion and facilitated the formation of the alliances with the indigenous communities which materialized in the course of the uprising. We shall return to this question later. For now we must direct our attention to slightly higher elevations, to the punas, the location of the highest-ranking military command of the entire movement.

The Headquarters of Uchuraccay and the Elusiveness of Iquicha: The Punas

It was in the punas, at approximately 4,000 meters above sea level, that the rebels' most impregnable quarters were located. These included the headquarters of Cancaíllo, where Choque was in charge, and of Luis Pampa, or Uchuraccay, undeniably the most important of all command centers and under the command of Huachaca. Cancaíllo and Uchuraccay were haciendas. Unlike many other haciendas above 3,000 meters of altitude, they did not have tributary populations as of 1801.

The headquarters at Cancaíllo was simultaneously the hacienda of Choque and the center of military operations during the period of August 1826 to December 1827. The dispatches and communiqués signed by Choque during this period refer to military actions and the stockpiling of munitions. Cancaíllo is a place I have been unable to locate on the map, but I suspect it corresponds to the site currently referred to as Bramadero (map 5). From Cancaíllo Choque directed military operations in "seven towns" adjacent to Ccarhuahurán, just as Pascual Arancibia, "the second general" and owner of the hacienda Huayanay, controlled another "seven towns" adjacent to Luricocha.[55] In addition to Cancaíllo there was the hacienda Tucuvilca, near Tambo (3,291 meters or 10,797 feet in altitude, corresponding to the suni ecological niche). Although I have found no proof that the rebels produced documents in Tucuvilca, evidence that it served as another rebel headquarters is mounting. Tucuvilca was the hacienda-residence of the Ruiz family, and here the rebels planned their attacks on Tambo.[56] The steep slopes surrounding Tambo have, as does Secce, a most impressive view of the distant hills and valleys as well as of the cordilleras bordering the selva. It is no wonder the rebel caudillos chose this spot as a center of military operations (see illustrations on page 46 and map 5).

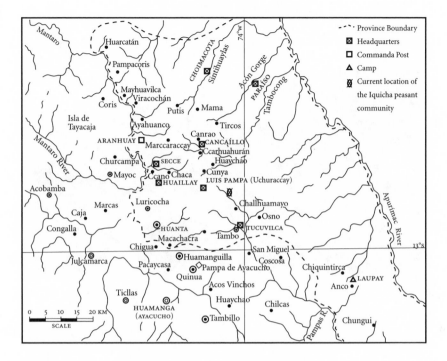

MAP 6. Rebel towns and headquarters.

Foremost was the headquarters of Luis Pampa, in the gorge of Uchuraccay, a place Commander Gabriel Quintanilla ironically, but not completely without reason, named "the palace of Huachaca." Located in the heart of the Huanta punas and partially hidden from sight by cavelike rocks which offer protection from the icy winds that scourge these altitudes, the barracks of Luis Pampa lacked the luxuries and comforts of a palace; yet it was, like a palace, a seat of power. Until the site was captured by troops of Commander Quintanilla's forces in March 1828, all of the operations of the monarchist war were centralized in Luis Pampa: it was to this location that prisoners were brought; it was here that justice was administered; and most of the military orders and communiqués issued by Huachaca came from here. Like Cancaíllo, Uchuraccay was a hacienda that has left no traces on either the tributary rolls or the most detailed maps of the period. That is, Uchuraccay, like Cancaíllo, did not record any individuals paying indian tribute between the end of the eighteenth and the beginning of the nineteenth century, and no other evidence brings to

Abandoned house at a location near Uchuraccay which villagers told the author was Luis Pampa. Notice the ichu growing wild. *Photograph by author, ca 1998.*

light the existence of a communal organization inside the boundaries of that hacienda. A document dating to 1805 refers to Uchuraccay as an hato, that is to say, as noted earlier, a hacienda dedicated to cattle raising. That year the Uchuraccay hato was sold by Antonio López to Captain Gabriel Ascarza for 3,734 pesos, and the purchase included "350 head of cattle, 1,383 Castilian cattle, 47 mares and horses and all of its lands, houses, and wages."[57] These were not inconsiderable quantities for the punas, where lands are generally ill-suited for agriculture, and the most prized commodity is precisely cattle. At the time of the rebellion, Ascarza apparently still owned Uchuraccay. His *mayordomo* (administrator), one Pedro Cárdenas, participated in the monarchist raids, leading one of the mobs to Tambo along with Benito Ruiz; he died in the final assault on Uchuraccay in March 1828.[58]

Although not incorporating existing tributary populations, the Uchuraccay hacienda was surrounded by them. Adjacent to Uchuraccay were the communities of Ninaquiro and Challhuamayo, home to the peasants who were to face off with Commander Quintanilla in his final assault on the Palace of Huachaca.[59] More important, Uchuraccay included a small area whose name, hitherto unknown beyond the local confines—or perhaps even nonexistent at the time—would soon acquire a mythical aura: Iquicha. Herein lies the importance of Uchuraccay, in addition to its strategic military role. The hacienda, as we shall see later, contained not only whatever "Iquicha" was at the time, but the legend it would become.

It is, indeed, paradoxical, that this place, which was to lend its name to the rebellion and the rebels, goes practically unmentioned in the hundreds of documents produced by the insurgents during the course of the war. I have been able to find only one reference to the "Headquarters at Iquicha."[60] Later documentation made clear that the name was just another designation for the Luis Pampa headquarters at Uchuraccay. Indeed, while references to the Iquichanos are omnipresent in government documents and rather scant in those of the rebels themselves, reference to Iquicha as a town or community is nonexistent in both. In fact, it is only toward the second half of the nineteenth century that the name Iquicha begins to appear on maps and in geographical dictionaries.[61]

Unlike the communities adjacent to Uchuraccay (Chalhuamayo, Ccano, and Ninaquiro), Iquicha was not registered on the tributary rolls between 1780 and 1801; it appears neither on the maps prepared by the Franciscans who traveled through these regions at the end of the eighteenth century nor on the exhaustive map produced by Intendant Demetrio O'Higgins on the basis of his visits to the Intendancy of Huamanga between 1802 and 1804. O'Higgins's is the most complete nineteenth-century map of Huamanga available. Neither is there mention of Iquicha in any of the descriptions accompanying these maps.[62] One notices a similar absence in testimonies emerging from the Independence struggles that make reference to the region. In the period before and after the battle of Ayacucho (December 9, 1824), when patriot officers reported harrying of republican troops by peasants from the Huanta punas, they referred not to Iquichanos, but to the "indians of Huanta." The same thing occurred in 1814 and 1815, when the people of the region mobilized to contain rebel troops that were nearing Huamanga from Cuzco.[63] In short, it would seem that until 1825 no one had heard of either Iquicha or Iquichanos.[64]

It was only with the start of the rebellion in 1825 and as a result of the dissemination of the first monarchist proclamations written principally by Spanish *capitulados* that the inhabitants of the communities situated in the highlands of Huanta began to be called Iquichanos. As noted in chapter 4, one of these proclamations, intended to be disseminated in Huancavelica, bore the signature, "The Yquichano Lover of the King." Brought to trial, a former officer of the Royal Army, the Spaniard Francisco Garay, confessed, as we recall, that he had written this piece and various others, although he claimed not to be their author.[65]

Why the name Iquichano, heretofore insignificant and elusive, suddenly became important remains unclear. Until new evidence contradicts my findings (or, rather, what I have not found), I propose the following explanation. Why select the appellative Iquichanos, rather than Ccarhuahuranenses, Ucchuraccayinos, or Ninaquirenses? Perhaps because, while Ccarhuahurán, Uchuraccay, and Ninaquiro were existing entities, whether villages or haciendas, Iquicha was not; and precisely because it was not, it lent itself to being created with an identity all its own. The ambiguity of the term *Iquichano*, its possible multivalence, is too deliberate to be merely coincidental. Iquichanos were the inhabitants of no town until 1825, yet the mass of peasants who embraced the restorationist cause came to be known as Iquichanos thereafter. The proof is to be found, as I have said, in the fact that "the indians of the Huanta punas" came to be called Iquichanos only at the outbreak of the rebellion. Ironically, the monarchist Spaniards were the ones who contributed, through their pamphlets and proclamations signed by "anonymous" Iquichanos, to the construction of an image of "resistance" and rebellion among the Huanta peasantry, that was to have a lasting impact on the region. Huanta peasants' fame as a fearsome people became established as early as 1828. Visiting Ayacucho that year, the German traveler Heinrich Witt wrote about "the mountains that inspired fear, those of Iquicha."[66]

Understandably, the villagers refused to identify themselves as Iquichanos. This was evidently a new and, after all, improper designation for people who had always felt more of an identification with Ccarhuahurán, Ninaquiro, Ayahuanco, Secce, Tircos, or whatever their town of origin. And since the name Iquichano began to be associated with the quality of being a rebel or "traitor to the Patria" or even a "barbarian," it is obvious why peasants would refuse to be identified as such. All the same, this situation was to be reversed years later with the establishment of a new relation between Huanta peasants and the republican state. That, however, is the subject of another chapter. Let us again take up the description of the headquarters, moving from the punas to the lower-elevation montañas, the last refuge of the fugitive rebels and site of two other headquarters.

Choimacota and Paraíso: The Coca Montañas

The rim of the forest, or montaña, entails a change not only in altitude, flora, and climate, which become increasingly lower, greener, and warmer, but also in the type of production and settlement patterns. Unlike the quechuas, sunis, and punas, where most of the communities were concentrated, this ecological niche was home to individual property owners who were mainly coca growers. It was also the area where the headquarters of Parayso and Choimacota were established.

Depending on their size and on the interests their owners wished to defend, coca plantations were alternately called haciendas, *cocalitos* ("little coca plantations") or *plantaditos* ("small planted plots"). In the official records, however, *hacienda* was the term most widely used, regardless of property size or value. Between 1802 and 1804, 233 requests were made for land grants in the montañas of Choimacota, Acón, and Buena, as part of the process of *composición de tierras* (land settlements) mandated by the Crown—through these composiciones, landowners were required to certify official ownership of the lands they cultivated by buying their respective titles from the Crown. Owners were mostly residents of the town of Huanta and to a lesser extent of Luricocha. Among the landowners were officers and *cívicos* (civilian corps) from the royal militia, some priests, and three "tribute-paying indians from the town of Huanta." The haciendas varied markedly in size and value. The most costly was appraised at 20,000 pesos, "for being a very luxuriant hacienda"; its owner, Ignacio Ballejo, was a captain of Huanta. The most modest property belonged to Leonardo Loaiza, a tax-paying indian from the town of Huanta, whose "cocalito" in Acón was appraised at only 10 pesos. Gaspar Huaycaña (or Vicaña), another "tribute-paying indian of the town of Huanta from the ayllu Cocha," had "a plot of woodland" appraised at 100 pesos, and Mariano Llimpe, likewise "a tribute-paying indian" from Huanta, owned a "cocalito" in the Acón gorge that was appraised at 1,000 pesos.[67]

The documents originating from the Huanta rebels at Choimacota headquarters date from May 1827, but the area remained under their control until at least February 1828.[68] Whether the Choimacota headquarters fell within the domain of any one hacienda is unclear since the documents refer simply to the "Choimacota gorge," but this may not matter. Many landowners refused to regularize the ownership of their lands in accordance with the arrangements drawn up for this purpose, so the boundaries between haciendas were often ambiguous or a matter of dispute. Moreover, a fair number of landowners spent considerable time away from their haciendas, probably owing to the diversification of their activities.[69] This factor most likely facilitated rebel control of the area, and it is not improbable that the location in which they established the Choimacota headquarters was a semiabandoned spot or one of ill-defined or disputed ownership.

Unlike the headquarters located at the higher elevations, which fulfilled above all military and "governmental" functions, Choimacota and Parayso carried out economic functions, centralizing the collection of the most valuable tithe in the repartimiento of Huanta: coca. The entire crop was produced in the montañas. In February 1828 the tithe collector of Choimacota was Juan Barragán,[70] while Manuel Leandro had exercised the same function a few years earlier in Parayso. Regarding the latter headquarters, more information is available.

Parayso was a coca-growing hacienda that had been bought from the Crown in 1802 and that at the onset of the rebellion was the subject of litigation between its owner and a leaseholder. The owner had filed suit against the leaseholder, a muleteer named Manuel Leandro (who identified himself before the tribunals as an "indian"), accusing him of failure to pay the debts contracted in the lease. For his part, Leandro claimed to have been swindled by the owner with regard to the value and yield of the coca plantation. Humiliated by a public flogging and subsequent incarceration, Leandro appealed to the intendant of Huamanga, charging the owner of the coca plantation with fraud. But the sluggishness and inefficiency of the "justice of the Patria" discouraged him. Freed from jail but with a verdict recorded against him, Leandro ended up appealing to Huachaca, the caudillo who by that time was a major presence in the region and whom Leandro knew through the muleteering trade. Huachaca seized the plantation and converted it into a headquarters. He legitimized Leandro's status as its leaseholder and, perhaps in an attempt to compensate him for past humiliations, appointed him "governor and subdelegate" of the Acón gorge, a post that Leandro occupied for six months. Meanwhile, the plantation owner abandoned the litigation he had brought against Leandro and retired to Ayacucho.[71]

The history of Parayso, which I shall examine in more detail in the following chapter, is the best documented of all the headquarters' histories considered thus far. Accordingly, it most clearly expresses a process which the histories of

Uchuraccay, Choimacota, and Cancaíllo allow us merely to guess at: the montonero chiefs of the Iquichanos, their lieutenants and secretaries, were taking the place of the hacendados, if they did not already occupy it.

We may now summarize some of the ideas presented thus far. The repartimiento of Huanta contained the largest number of communities in Huanta province, that is, ayllus or villages organized into ayllus and settlements classified as pueblos. The presence of a community peasantry is reflected in the monarchist rebellion, especially in the composition of the army. Even so, their direct representatives, the indigenous mayors, did not occupy the highest ranks; these were occupied by muleteers, merchants, hacendados, and noncommunity peasants. Likewise, only three of the eight headquarters were villages with a tributary tradition, and of these three, two had mayors of Spaniards, or more properly speaking, "alcades de españoles"—españoles in this context meaning not so much European-born individuals as "nonindians"—in addition to their mayors of indians. Finally, the rebels' ultimate seat of power was a hacienda without a community-tributary tradition: Uchuraccay. The communities, then, participated in the rebellion but were excluded from the highest leadership; they dominated the geography but did not control the war.

Recognition of these facts does not, however, amount to asserting that the rebellion was led by individuals who lacked ties with the communities. As I demonstrate in what follows, with the exception of the recently arrived Spanish capitulados, the "Iquichano" montonero leaders were not outsiders but part of the peasant community world. The peasants of the communities were linked to muleteers, hacendados, and merchants through trading and muleteering networks, the proximity of their lands, and the control that the latter could exert over their resources and labor, all relationships involving mutual, yet asymmetric, dependencies. The villages of Huanta were places where it was not just possible but seemingly common for people to own private property; inhabitants lived in permanent, if uneasy, interaction with residents of the larger (and lower-elevation) towns as well as with the landowners in the coca-growing montañas, where many of the highland villagers worked as farmhands. Chief among the large towns was the villa of Huanta, where the main authorities of the province and the wealthiest vecinos resided.

Villagers, Muleteers, and Hacendados: A World of Networks

In the present section I should like to discuss briefly some features of, first, the ownership of land and other agricultural resources in the world of Huanta's community peasants; and, second, of the communities' insertion into the regional circuits of muleteering and commerce. The first features serve to illustrate the less corporate side of the communities; the second shed light on the more dynamic side of their relation with other social sectors in the region. Both features point toward (little-known) instances in which the community manifests itself through its individuals and becomes diffused into a wider universe. Despite its fragmentary character, the evidence forcefully conveys an image of the communities as "open worlds," rather than the socially and ethnically self-contained entities still pictured by much of the historiography of the period.[72] And this openness, while explaining the communities' links with the broader local and regional society, also helps one discern the possible roots of their fragility and subordination.

Property, Spaces, and Resources

I have noted earlier that some communities were contained within the territory of the haciendas, whereas others were not. But in fact, the problem of property, landholding, and settlement patterns in Huanta is considerably more complex. Chacabamba, a location near Tambo that contributed significant contingents of montoneros to the uprising, is an exemplary case.

At the beginning of the nineteenth century Chacabamba was classified as an estancia with a tributary population. Years later the site would be referred to as a hacienda, while still containing a community organization.[73] Still, within the boundaries of the Chacabamba hacienda and among the lands occupied by the community there existed the "hacienda" of Esteban Meneses, an *arriero* (muleteer), coca merchant, and owner of coca-producing lands in the montaña of Tamboconga. Because of the strategic placement of his landholdings and his position as a muleteer, coupled with his status as a bilingual and literate individual in a mostly Quechua-speaking, and nonliterate, world, Meneses exercised an important brokering role in the rebellion.[74] Several witnesses describe him as close to Huachaca, imparting his orders and "dining at his table." Meneses was later prosecuted for being Huachaca's secretary. He denied the charges but admitted having written to Huachaca "obliged by the indians . . . on whose lands his estate stands."[75] Meneses explained as well that the reason people associated him with Huachaca and claimed he was his secretary was a long-standing friendship Huachaca had with his father, himself an arriero for whom Huachaca had worked as an assistant arriero. Thus, admitted Meneses, Huachaca was fond of him "and constantly called on him and even forced him to eat with him, and for that reason people said that he was his secretary." Meneses insisted that his intention was not to join the revolutionaries. But if that was so, the tribunal asked, why did he not surrender in exchange for a pardon when he had the chance to do so? He explained that "he had interests [that is, businesses] in the punas."[76]

The case of Esteban Meneses stands out because of his familiarity with Huachaca. Yet Meneses was not the only one to possess (or cultivate) a piece of property within community lands. The presence of individuals who formed haciendas within or among territories originally belonging to the ayllus can be traced from very early on during the colonial period.[77] Although the first hacendados in Huanta were (predictably) Spanish *encomenderos* and their descendants, in time and notably since the second half of the seventeenth century, native ruling elites, the kurakas, would also start turning ayllu lands into private holdings, either because they sold—or retained for themselves—communal lands in order to meet the debts they frequently contracted as collateral for the indian tribute of the communities they ruled over, or simply as a means of capitalization, replicating the economic patterns established by the colonizers.[78] Whatever the case, patterns of private property ownership were firmly entrenched in Huanta's rural economy by the early nineteenth century. Yet, despite having lost significant amounts of land to haciendas, indian tribute payers "with lands" still constituted more than 50 percent of the indian tributary population in the repartimiento of Huanta as of 1801—53.2 percent, to be precise. Twenty years earlier, the percentages were 60.6 percent landed and 39.4 percent landless indian tribute payers.[79] The number of tribute payers without land thus tended to increase toward the end of the eighteenth century.

The growth of private landholdings in Huanta is likely to have accelerated over the course of the second decade of the nineteenth century, driven by incentives for the colonization of Huanta's coca-growing region granted by royal warrant in 1816. The warrant lured newcomers to the area by exempting prospective landowners from a series of fiscal obligations for a period of ten years; it also extended special terms to them for the acquisition of plots in the montañas.[80] Although the measure affected only Huanta's coca-growing region and not its highlands, villagers established in the latter area were likely to have been affected by the royal warrant of 1816 in various ways. First, their lands were a crucial point of entry into the montañas, so contact and coexistence with the newcomers was inevitable. Second, if high-altitude communities held lands in the montañas that were not properly secured by legal titles, they ran the risk of losing them to the colonizers.[81] Third, and no less important, ayllu members and other inhabitants of the high-altitude villages could themselves become private landowners in the montañas, especially since one of the clauses in the royal provision gave special prerogatives regarding the distribution and colonization of montaña lands "first to the indian."[82] One such case of a high-altitude villager with private ownership in the montaña was that of Ildefonsa Belarde, from Marccaraccay.

By 1801, Marccaraccay was a town with two ayllus and a population of 58 landed tribute payers who appear to have been free of the control of any hacienda. And as was the case with Chacabamba, the villagers of Marccaraccay were active participants in the rebellion. With the upheaval already under way, Ildefonsa Belarde, a resident of the town and "legitimate wife of the Grenadier lieutenant in His Majesty's provincial urban militias of Huanta," requested Huachaca's intercession in order to recover a "cocalito" in the montañas that she claimed to have inherited.[83] Belarde's case, like that of Meneses, stands out because of the contacts she made with the Uchuraccay caudillo. Nevertheless, she was not the only resident of a tributary town to possess private lands in the montañas. At least three tribute-paying indians from the town of Huanta—Leonardo Loaiza, Mariano Llimpe, and Gaspar Vicaña, the latter a member of the ayllu Cocha—had sought legalization of their titles to coca lands as part of the above-mentioned 233 land requests submitted for the montañas of Huanta between 1802 and 1804.[84] Three out of 233 constitute, to be sure, an extremely small percentage (and undoubtedly one finds in the record many more references to indians as farmhands than as private owners in the montañas); nonetheless, it is significant that it was both possible and legal to be simultaneously a tributary indian, a member of an ayllu, and an owner of private lands beyond the confines of one's community.

Land was not the only good that Huanta villagers could own on an individual basis. There was also livestock, a no less vital resource. Ysidora Urbano, together with the Mayor Fernando Curiñaupa and Elifonso Chagua, "indians from the town of Ayguanco [Ayahuanco]," accused the hacendado José Antonio de la Barreda of stealing their livestock.[85] Shortly before, Urbano had lodged a similar complaint against Barreda in the name of her relatives, residents of the locality of Chupas, in the doctrina of Ccarhuahurán.[86] In the first instance (that of Ayahuanco), according to the plaintiffs, the stolen livestock amounted to 300 head belonging to Mayor Curiñaupa and Elifonso Chagua; in the second case (Chupas), the livestock numbered "42 head between cows and bulls, thirteen beasts between horses, capons, and mares."[87] Ayahuanco and Ccarhuahurán, of which Chupas was an anexo, were tributary towns organized around ayllus; they were among the most densely settled in the repartimiento of Huanta and were not part of a hacienda.[88] As in prior cases, both towns supplied montoneros for the restorationist war.

The first intriguing aspect of Ysidora Urbano's legal claims pertains not so much to her alleged dual residency, as to the fact that she was defending private interests in both villages. In Ayahuanco the livestock was, as she stated, "the property of the mayor and the second petitioner," while in Chupas it belonged to her relatives.[89] The second and most important aspect is the amount of livestock claimed. In Chupas 55 farm animals belonged to just three villagers, while in Ayahuanco 300 head of cattle belonged to two individuals alone, one of them the community mayor. These are unusually large herds by present-day standards; a community peasant is considered well off if he or she manages to own eight head of cattle.[90] But even in the early nineteenth century the two herds must have been deemed quite large. Some 350 head of cattle were, without question, a herd worthy of a hacienda.

Ysidora Urbano's claims are, therefore, just another example of the private accumulation of resources within the ayllu. Individual villagers who succeeded in accumulating resources, particularly cattle, commonly fell prey to rustlers (*abigeos*), as was the case with Urbano. The man whom she accused of rustling her cattle was none other than José Antonio de la Barreda, a hacendado with lands in the montañas of Huanta and an active supporter of Huachaca until he passed over to the government side to fight against the rebels. Barreda was, indeed, a ruthless and well-known rustler whose lands in the montañas he "had always maintained at the expense of poor wretches [indians]," according to Urbano's denunciation. Many others confirmed her claim:[91] "Barreda . . . from time immemorial . . . has behaved in an oppressive way toward the poor inhabitants of the montaña, availing himself of a thousand wicked pretexts in order not to pay them for their work."[92] But other villagers defended Barreda or remained silent in order to avoid compromising their own positions as beneficiaries of his raids. In fact, Barreda had stolen livestock from "wealthy" peasants in Ayahuanco and Chupas and had sold it to needier peasants in Secce and Marccaraccay, undoubtedly at prices well below market value or else in exchange for loyalty, as recorded in the confession of one Melchor Gente. The indigenous *regidor* (alderman) of Marccaraccay was another client of Barreda's, willing even to come to his defense by affirming "that he had no knowledge of any harm done by [Barreda] despite being a vara official."[93]

The case of Barreda is a telling example of the way in which relationships among individuals of different villages could be mediated by nonvillagers who used their social and economic position to form alliances with villagers from a given town (including its own communal authorities) to the detriment of those from other towns. Barreda, in a word, was no stranger to the world of peasant communities, but rather part of a larger network of power, labor, and economic relationships in which peasants, willingly or not, operated. If to some he was a thief, to others he was a patron or protector. In essence, he was an agent of the forced transfer of resources from some community peasants to others. In this regard, Huanta seems to fit a pattern scholars have detected in rural areas where state presence is weak and where cattle rustling is not an occupation of outcast persons but a systemic form of channeling economic surplus, of establishing clientele networks, of legitimizing local power and even local office.[94] Barreda himself, despite having been a "colonel" in the rebel army and operating as a rustler, evaded trial and conviction. He went on to serve with the "peace-keeping" troops of one Commander Sarrio, attached to the headquarters of Secce and holding the post of governor and civilian military commander. In reprisal for his treason, Huachaca ordered Barreda's haciendas to be burned to the ground.[95]

Barreda's might be an extreme case but certainly not an isolated one. In less violent ways, other montonero leaders carried out similar functions: they were intermediaries in the transfer of resources between peasants of various communities. Indeed, increasingly more than hacendados, the Huanta rebellion's most prominent leaders were merchants and muleteers. Eventually, some of them, including Huachaca himself, would be accused of cattle rustling (*abigeato*).[96] The nature of the relationships between montonero leaders and peasants does not appear in the record as neatly as one would desire. Still, evidence suggests that the realm of circulation, distribution, and allocation of resources was more important than the realm of production per se.

"Indian muleteer" reads the caption of this nineteenth-century lithograph reproduced from Manuel Atanasio Fuentes, *Lima. Esquisses Historiques, Statistiques, Administratives, Commerciales et Morales* (Paris: Librairie de firmín Didot, frerés, fils & cie., 1866), 78.

If one point stands out clearly, it is that, economically and politically, the most dynamic sector of the province—that which assumed the leadership of the monarchist rebellion—was based not in the community or the hacienda alone, but in trade, muleteering, and other forms of resource allocation and redistribution of surpluses.

Trade and Muleteering

Although the haciendas indeed predominated as spaces of military and political power during the rebellion, the hacendados apparently were not that strong as a politically empowered class. This does not mean that land did not confer wealth and power. The wealthiest of the Europeans to participate in the uprising was in all likelihood the hacendado Juan Cantón, who owned four haciendas of coca in the montaña of Acón and a house in Huanta and who was married to Gertrudis Lazón, a member of a renowned family of Huanta hacendados. His haciendas Santa Gertrudis and Culluchaca, in particular, provided food, arms, and men for the rebel army and shelter and interpreters for the fugitive rebel leaders on their way to the selvas of the Apurímac. But before being a hacendado, Cantón had been a merchant and worked as an administrator in Huamanga's and Huanta's customs houses. Part of his capital thus derived from his commercial activities and his participation in the management of the region's commercial surpluses—at that time public officials had no fixed salary but earned a percentage of the revenues they collected. Cantón had arrived in Huamanga around 1812. His commercial links here were not just with local people but also with merchants from Cádiz who at the time traded frequently in Huamanga and Lima.[97] In 1814, he was working as *vista* (inspector) of the Aduana Nacional de Huamanga and then moved to Huanta where, from roughly 1819 to 1822, he was the "lieutenant administrator" (*teniente administrador*) of the town's customs house. The Basque Navarran Nicolás Soregui, the other European to play a major role in the rebellion, had been an even more renowned merchant than Cantón, having engaged in prosperous trading in Lima. Unlike Cantón, however, Soregui owned no haciendas and had arrived in Huamanga relatively recently, in 1822; penniless, he was attempting to start a new life after losing his fortune to a number of debtors in La Paz, Lima, Chincha, Cuzco, and Huancavelica and even to the defeated Spanish army, in which he was an officer until 1823.[98]

Though lacking Cantón's unusually good fortune, other figures in the rebellion's leadership had something in common with him: diversification of activities, generally in the direction of trade. We have already noted how Esteban Meneses, erstwhile secretary of Huachaca, was both muleteer and hacendado. Similarly, Leandro was a muleteer and coca merchant who served as governor and subdelegate of Acón and who was likewise acquainted with Huachaca through muleteering, although, unlike Meneses, he was landless. Another example is the Ruiz family, whose sons Benito and José collaborated with the rebellion, the former leading montoneras in Tambo with the rank of colonel, the latter involved in minor logistical tasks.[99] The Ruizes were owners of the Tucuvilca hacienda, where they raised livestock and where Huachaca and other caudillos planned their attacks on Tambo; they also possessed a coca plantation in the Sintiguailas montañas[100] and "openly traded with" rebel caudillos.[101] It would not have been unusual for their transactions to have involved community peasants of the Chacabamba hacienda, their neighbors, whose mobilization and then demobilization they influenced.[102] The Ruizes' familiarity with the peasants of Chacabamba was admitted by the peasants themselves, who were interrogated as witnesses at the trial of José and Benito. Martín Qquente, for example, declared that he "knew Benito and José Ruiz on account of the small distance between Tucubilca, the Ruizes' residence, and Chacabamba, the residence of the deponent."[103] The same assertion about the Ruiz family seems plausible in connection with Huachaca's "second general," Arancibia. In addition to his hacienda Huayanay, he owned lands in the montañas. The types of transactions that Arancibia engaged in with peasants from the communities are not clear. However, it is certain that his dealings with the towns' mayors were quite informal and based upon the business he established with them. As the indian mayors of the towns of Ayahuanco and Marccaraccay themselves declared, Arancibia was in the habit of summoning them, when he visited their towns, "for his private business in the montaña."[104]

Although far less abundant than one would like, evidence on the supreme commander, Antonio Abad Huachaca, is adequate. His exact birthplace is not mentioned, but he was no doubt of humble Huantino origin.[105] Huachaca initiated himself into *arriería* (muleteering) from below, as an assistant of a certain muleteer Meneses, whose son, Esteban, was also an *arriero*. As mentioned above, Esteban would eventually serve Huachaca as a secretary in the course of the uprising. Muleteer and trader in livestock, potatoes, vegetables, cigarettes, and liquor, Huachaca carried out his activities within a network that extended from the most remote towns and hamlets of the punas all the way to the montañas, on the one hand, and to the cities of Huanta and Ayacucho, on the other. He was a well-known figure, by hearsay if not by sight, among the inhabitants of the various towns of Huanta and the residents of Huamanga. Accompanied by his pack of nine mules, Huachaca would arrive in town, distribute his freight, and trade in livestock, assisted by his muleteer partners, like Leandro and Meneses, or his closest collaborators, Andrés Hacha and Antonio Huamán. Huachaca's clients were people from a wide social spectrum. Among those in the montaña who purchased oxen from Huachaca through Hacha and Huamán were Huachaca's "brother-in-law" Anotlín Cárdenas, a twenty-eight-year-old illiterate *labrador* (landless farmer) and ex-soldier in the Spanish army; Narciso Choque, possibly a relative of the caudillo Tadeo Choque; and the highly educated priest Manuel Navarro.[106] In contrast to Leandro and Meneses, Hacha and Huamán, whom various witnesses referred to as "indians," never appeared before a tribunal. Beyond the fear of possible reprisals (though this is sheer speculation), the reason they eluded capture may lie, as in Huachaca's case, in the strength of the ties they had established with the peasant populations with whom they had dealings. Conceivably Huachaca's influence over them was based on these same ties, that is, on the villagers' need, among others, for provisions, and not solely on his military power. Huachaca's influence was also felt at the level of everyday life in the villages, in the form of certain ethical and juridical criteria as well as cultural practices, as we shall see later.[107]

The routes traveled by Huachaca and his partners were not exactly new and were far from exclusive. These corridors had a long history and were shared by many other peasants. Whether traveling southward in the direction of the towns of Huanta, Tambo, and Ayacucho or toward the coca-producing montañas in the north and east where many worked as temporary day-laborers, peasants rested or slept in neighboring towns and lodging houses, met with other peasants, muleteers, and merchants, and talked with messengers who were going from one location to another bearing news of occurrences they had either seen or knew about through hearsay.[108]

The interaction between settlers of the Huanta highlands and inhabitants of the montañas and selvas of Marañón and Apurímac, although seemingly more sporadic, can be traced to the pre-Columbian era and continued on into the colonial period, when the coca haciendas were established.[109] The other circuit, connecting Huanta's high-altitude communities with the cities of Huanta and Ayacucho, had an old colonial tradition as well. Toward the middle of the eighteenth century, peasants from the outskirts of Huamanga were virtually the only suppliers of foodstuffs for its inhabitants.[110] These circuits, while no doubt disturbed by the wars of Independence, continued to be active in the midst of the upheaval provoked by the restorationist war, at least as far as the suppliers of Huanta were concerned. In 1826, local authorities reported, "Guachaca has trade with Ayacucho, sends cargo potatoes, and does not miss liquor, cigarettes, and other [sic] vegetables."[111] The circuits persisted, as the traveler Clements Markham reported several years after the monarchist rebellion: "The Iquichanos now come into Huanta to buy cotton and sell their wool and vegetables. I saw several of them in the plaza."[112]

By the beginning of the nineteenth century the great caravans of merchants

Muleteers with the Peruvian flag. Watercolor by Léonce Angrand. Reproduced with permission from Léonce Angrand, *Imagen del Perú en el siglo XIX,* edited by Carlos Milla Batres (Lima: Milla Batres, 1972).

and muleteers that journeyed from Lima to Potosí toward the thriving mines of the southern Andes and vice-versa were no longer to be seen in Huanta. The mule and trade circuit of Huanta and Huamanga had diminished with the decline of the Potosí mines; it was now a more regional circuit, more restricted to the central sierra and the Ica coast.[113] Yet this development, far from far reducing the local arrieros' power, may well have augmented it by eliminating competition along the larger routes. In other words, an arriero like Huachaca, formerly a middling figure, would have become quite formidable, a master and overseer of contacts and routes and, as a result, socially more influential.

We may now recapitulate some of the ideas that can be drawn from the preceding analysis. Despite having provided the bulk of the montoneros for the monarchist uprising, and despite being present in the repartimiento of Huanta in greater numbers than in the other three repartimientos of Huanta province, the peasant communities do not appear to have been on very solid ground in institutional and economic terms. Something similar could be said for the hacienda. While militarily and logistically central to the uprising, and the predominant form of land possession in the ceja de selva, the hacienda did not, in itself, confer upon hacendados complete control over labor and economic networks.

In Huanta's high-altitude villages, community structures coexisted alongside the private accumulation of resources; communities themselves were located in the midst of private landholdings or haciendas and, in some cases, formed a part of them; they were in proximity to the coca-growing montañas and constituted an indispensable bridge to them. All of these factors lay the groundwork for the contacts and coexistence between community peasants and the muleteers, and hacendados, including even cattle rustlers, persons who, although they did not belong to the communities, formed a part of the villagers' network of labor, economic, and social relations.

The production of coca, the most important agricultural resource of the region, was not controlled directly by highland communities but by private owners of coca plantations in the montañas, while its marketing was the responsibility of muleteers, independent of racial or ethnic makeup.[114] Although the better-off community peasants and villagers could also own private coca lands in the montañas, most did not; their participation in the coca circuits was for the most part subordinate, either as temporary day-laborers in the coca haciendas or as buyers and consumers of coca leaves. This subordination was in turn reflected in the military hierarchies of the rebellion. And though indigenous mayors were the foremost representatives of the communities, they themselves did not occupy the highest military ranks in the rebel organization. In effect, the community peasants' only real advantage may have been achieved in the geostrategic sphere, since their villages were situated along the vital route that led to the coca-growing montañas. This location conferred upon them an indisputable central role in times of war and militarization and also gave them space to maneuver in their everyday relationships with montaña hacendados, government authorities, and muleteers.[115]

The inhabitants of Huanta's punas, quechuas, and sunis commonly have been referred to as "Iquichanos" and perceived as an "ancient" "ethnic group," endowed with a strong sense of "tribal, ethnic, identity" and having "lived aloof and forgotten since pre-Hispanic times."[116] The evidence at hand does not support this characterization. "Iquichano" is a rather recent denomination, created in the course of the monarchist uprising to designate the Huanta highland communities involved (or presumed to have been involved) in the rebellion as well as their military commanders, regardless of whether they belonged to a community. But even if one takes the label "Iquichanos" to designate the ayllus of the Huanta highlands (as villagers of the area have sometimes done), it would be a misconception to attach to them an "autonomous," "ethnic," or "tribal" identity. The ayllus of Huanta were hardly self-contained entities that related one to another without intermediation. Rather, relationships between ayllus and villages were constantly mediated by muleteers who supplied them with provisions, by hacendados who superimposed themselves upon (and sometimes, evidently, within) their lands; and even by hacendados-turned-cattle-rustlers, who raided "wealthy" villagers in order to sell below market value their plunder to poorer villagers in other towns.

The relationships established among all these characters could be best defined in terms of asymmetrical interdependencies. That is, even the most wealthy hacendado from the montaña needed to be on good terms both with highland villagers and muleteers; with the former because they provided a pool of seasonal labor for their coca haciendas; with the latter because they controlled the routes and means through which the coca crop from the haciendas was transported and marketed. Such control could also be wielded by highland villagers, given the strategic location of their communities and their mastery over a generally harsh terrain.

In addition to the economic and labor relations, there was an important level of cultural mediation involved in these relationships. Muleteers like Esteban Meneses, who owned lands in the puna, or Manuel Leandro, who leased a plot to cultivate coca in the montaña, were usually bilingual and sometimes literate. Both monolingual Spanish-speaking hacendados in the montañas and monolingual Quechua-speaking peasants from the ayllus had to rely on these muleteers, not to mention those who may have descended as far as the selva, where additional linguistic skills would have been required.

In sum, geographic and ecological factors, demographic distributions, and patterns of landownership and settlement created the ideal terrain for strengthening the "middling" sectors: those muleteer-merchants and small or middle-size landowners who would become the most important montonero leaders and who appear to be the ones wielding local power at the time of the monarchist rebellion and for years thereafter.

6

Government in Uchuraccay

It is usually said that "in Peru no one knows how to obey"; but we think it fairer to say that "in Peru no one knows how to command." For this reason, all the evils of Peru have come from the top down, not from the bottom up.—Francisco Laso, "Croquis sobre el carácter peruano." 1860

One of the most distinctive features of the Huanta rebellion was the heterogeneity of its protagonists: former soldiers and officers in the Royal Army, Spanish and mestizo merchant-hacendados, local muleteers, peasants from communities and haciendas, deserters from the republican army, and priests. An alliance that brought together such disparate groups could hardly be free of conflict. Class, cultural, national, and regional differences were sometimes cast in racial or "ethnic" terms. It was not unusual for the Spaniards and the local *españoles* to fancy themselves as antagonists of those whom they considered indian. Ethnic slurs against Europeans were rare, but Quechua-speaking caudillos found other ways to convey class (and possibly) "ethnic" tensions. Huachaca, for example, showed little reluctance in openly expressing his hostility toward the hacendados, even though some of them had joined the rebellion.[1] Likewise, some Spaniards were visibly ill at ease with obeying the supreme Uchuraccay caudillo but did not hesitate to place themselves at the service of the French-Basque Nicolás Soregui.[2] At his trial, the cleric Francisco Pacheco of Cuzco attributed the Spaniard Juan Fernández's unfavorable statements about him to the fact that "as he is a Spaniard and mine enemy he has no doubt declared as he did and it is not true."[3]

Beyond the understandable suspicions between individuals of such diverse social and cultural environments, tensions were also felt among leaders of similar social and cultural backgrounds. Shortly before the invasion of Huanta, Huachaca was allegedly "relieved of his command" for not having heeded reports announcing that "the Royal Army was near" and having opposed invasion; as a result, Tadeo Choque came to assume the post of "General in Chief," which until then had been held by Huachaca.[4] This was but one of the ways in which a long-lasting rivalry between the two caudillos was manifest. A dispatch signed by Choque and his secretary in Cancaíllo says more about these tensions: "The seven towns are under our authority, Huachaca no longer interferes in this division[;] besides he has 8 towns of his under an official note."[5] Not long afterward, we read: "Guachaca wants to remove don Tadeo Choque from his jurisdiction and take away his position."[6]

The rivalries exhibited among the movement's highest leadership were mirrored at the middle levels of command. Mayor Feliciano Guillén, for instance, refused to obey orders from Choque and Arancibia that were relayed by the Spaniard Juan Cantón, to the effect that the people be summoned and a proclamation read. Guillén argued that he was authorized to obey only Huachaca's orders.[7]

Added to this discord among the leaders were disagreements that arose between them and the peasants, whose compliance was never total. One witness reported that "the indians" refused to obey Soregui's orders to attack Huanta,[8] while Huachaca announced reprisals against four towns "because the four towns in the indictment have been shown to be against the Royal Monarch and his Generals."[9] On a later occasion, when rebel troops were fleeing toward the punas of Huanta after the thwarted attack on Ayacucho, "Huachaca ordered his followers to set fire to the area [Huanta], but fortunately this time no one obeyed the order."[10] Comparable incidents of "insubordination" happened at an individual level, as when a villager refused to continue serving as messenger for a priest and a Spaniard during one of the rebellion's most crucial moments.[11]

Despite these frictions, the alliance that made the rebellion possible remained operative because its members undoubtedly had common interests, the most visible being the appropriation of agricultural surpluses, mainly coca, which in that region were synonymous with tithes. Furthermore, arms, munitions, and supplies were paid for with the coca tithes, as were the salaries and rations of the *montoneros*. In short, coca tithes financed the entire rebellion.

The appropriation of the tithes did not, however, take the form of sheer looting. Neither was the expropriated coca merely war booty. Its collection required an infrastructure, a calendar, authorities who administered its payment, and tithe collectors who forwarded the stipulated quantities to the chapter board (*mesa capitular*), just as was done at the legal level. Finally, the appropriated tithes had to be redistributed: the appropriation, in other words, required an organization. In fact, what the sources reveal with disconcerting clarity is not only that this organization existed, but that its objectives and powers far surpassed the collection of tithes. It involved a political infrastructure of remarkable scope, a regional government of sorts run by its own laws and ruled by its own authorities. Antonio Huachaca stood as its commander-in-chief, and its principal headquarters were located at Luis Pampa, in the punas of Uchuraccay. Besides tithe collection (and at times that of "sales taxes") the functions of this government (or "my government," as Huachaca called it) included the administration of justice, the mobilization of manpower, the repair of bridges and roads, and the regulation of "public order." They included, in addition, military tasks, chiefly recruitment for the restorationist army.

As it exercised control over a broad stretch of territory, the rebel organization carried out the functions ordinarily filled by a state. Moreover, the carrying out of these very functions enabled the rebels not only to establish their power in the region, but above all to maintain it. This chapter describes and analyzes this political organization, which I shall be referring to as the "Government in Uchuraccay," since its principal headquarters was located in this area. An analysis of the Government in Uchuraccay will uncover the deeper motivations behind the monarchist rebellion, beyond the juncture that explains the outbreak: the political, economic, and social reasons that made it possible to prolong and maintain it; its social bases; the legitimacy of its leaders; and the reasons it was silently supported by a majority of Huantinos.

The chapter is divided into two parts. The first provides an account of the infrastructure by which the Government in Uchuraccay operated, focusing specifically on the system of tithe expropriation. The second part covers the whole spectrum of other functions assumed by the Uchuraccay government, in particular the administration of justice. In addressing the courts of Uchuraccay, we shall consider which cases were pursued, that is, which litigants had recourse to them and why. With regard to the judges and the rest of the "bureaucracy," the analysis offers a possible explanation of the basis for their legitimacy and power, concluding with a political analysis of the meaning and hierarchies of this peculiar government. As a whole, the chapter aims to explore not only the social basis of the government in Uchuraccay, but its social and political significance within the context of the nascent Republic.

The Revolution of the Tithes

[This branch] is for the aid of my worthy troops of the King [,]
may God save him.—Huachaca

Those who invented the idea of the oath [not to surrender] were the
generals and those who had interests in the tithes.
—Deposition of Juan Fernández

The tithe was the 10 percent tax on agricultural production to which rural landowners were subject. Established during the colonial era, the tithe, like the indigenous tribute and other colonial taxes, remained in force throughout the first decades of the Republic. Despite the tithe being an ecclesiastical tax, the state involved itself in its administration and retained a percentage of what was collected. State intervention increased over the course of the republican period—the prefect in each department acted as president of the Board of Tithes, in the same capacity that the intendant had functioned in the colonial era.[12] And the state retained a greater percentage of the tithe for itself: 11 percent at the end of the colonial era as opposed to 22 percent in the first decades of the Republic.[13]

The office of tithe collector was far from being a bureaucratic post in the modern sense. Like many other functionaries toward the end of the colonial period and the beginning of the Republic, the tithe collector received no salary. His earnings derived from his ability to retain a percentage of the tax that was taken in. The right to collect the tithe from each *partido* (a territorial unit during the colonial era, equivalent to a province during the Republic) was auctioned off at a chapter board, the top bidder earning the position of tithe collector. The tithe collectors, in other words, were bankers of sorts, lending the state the sum of tithes whose collection (in kind) would then accrue to them. Their importance, therefore, went beyond the strictly fiscal realm. On the one hand, tithe collectors furnished public administrators with a currency that was as scarce as it was precious, while on the other they constituted a critical link in rural economies.

The Uchuraccay rebels reproduced this system at a regional level, arrogating to themselves state powers and retaining possession of the income that was theoretically owed the state and the Church. Imitating the official system, the position of tithe collector was likewise auctioned off at a chapter board,[14] with the individual who won the bidding and became the tithe collector advancing part or all of the stipulated amount, in pesos, to the rebel generals; he would then collect the tithe in agricultural products, chiefly coca. Although the tithe auctions in the rebel camp were formal public events, often the sums would be agreed upon in advance and the bidders preselected; the office of tithe collector was not assigned to any ethnic, social, or racial category, but it did require a rudimentary knowledge of writing and arithmetic. Aside from the *indígena* Manuel Leandro, appointed by Huachaca governor and mayor of Acón, several other individuals, both Spaniards and locals, held the post of tithe collector. They included Juan Barragán, José Pérez del Valle, Ignacio Girón, Juan Heredia, Melchor Porras, Pedro Porras, Rafael Aristizábal, José Quintanilla, Antonio Bellido, and Rafael de Castro.

The rebels' appropriation of tithes was notable for its level of organization, considering the context of war in which it was carried out. In theory, at least, even the generals themselves and other authorities of the Government at Uchuraccay were forced to pay it. A list of 169 hacendados in Leandro's possession included the names of secretaries, hacendados, and other collaborators in the rebellion on whom the tithe was levied.[15] The sanctions against those who refused to pay it consisted of the seizure of haciendas and belongings.[16]

Yet over and above the severity of the sanctions and arbitrary acts sometimes committed as part of its collection, the tithe system imposed by the insurgents was apparently complied with without any major misgivings. The passivity, or perhaps silent obsequiousness, of the hacendados, who were the ones most affected by the tithe, appears less surprising in light of the fact that the tithe system the rebels instituted offered advantages to hacendados and peasants alike. Whereas under colonial legislation still operative during the Republic the tithe was assessed on the gross sum of a hacienda's earnings, the rebels' tithe was levied on the net total of a hacienda's earnings after the costs of wages paid to the farmhands were deducted. That is to say, if the hacienda yielded one hundred *arrobas* of coca (approximately twenty-five pounds) and the hacendado spent twenty arrobas in paying his laborers, the rebels assessed a tithe on eighty arrobas, not one hundred. Faced with two equally coercive tax systems and possible extortion, the hacendados opted for the least harmful one, which was imposed by the rebels in 1826.

In the end, the rebellion's system of tithe collection benefited the hacendados, for when calm was restored to the punas they refused to return to the official system of tithes and insisted on paying them in accordance with the practice established by the rebels. Hence the denunciation, in the latter half of 1828, by José Ramírez, the *mayordomo* of the tithe collector for the Acón gorge to the effect that "the hacendados refuse to pay me the total for the tithes[,] preferring to deduct for themselves the whole amount of the wages that are incurred in every *mita* [pay period]. From what I have found out *this was not the custom*[,] but rather to pay on the total of the hacienda and all that comes out of it and that this vicious practice only began with Guachaca."[17]

These same changes were noted with alarm by Prefect Domingo Tristán: "For Guachaca has caused many disturbances in the coca haciendas," he wrote in an official letter to the minister of government on February 16, 1828. Characteristically, the prefect found in these disturbances one of his primary reasons for keeping the recently pacified zone under military surveillance.[18] The success of the revolution of the tithes can be measured by the endurance of its effects. As late as 1844, nearly twenty years after the start of the monarchist war, hacendados continued to uphold the system of tithes established by the Government of Uchuraccay, in the face of which official tithe collectors and the state remained impotent.[19]

Besides proving less burdensome to the hacendados, this "vicious practice" instituted by Huachaca favored the coca workers because it ensured they would receive their wages on time, which were generally paid in coca under the name of *avíos*. The hacendados were often reluctant to pay the wage to their workers, but only those who could prove that they had paid them (by showing their respective receipts) had the right to deduct the expenditures from the total on which they were to pay the tithe. Significantly, when the system was newly implemented, Huachaca himself supervised its operation. So reported Manuel Leandro, the rebel tithe collector for Acón: "Guachaca would give little scraps of paper to the indians, so that they would take the coca, the deponent collected them and gave a ticket to the hacendados."[20] This brief but immensely suggestive quotation suggests that instead of getting paid by the hacendados, the workers simply took their wages in kind, with the authorization and protection of their caudillo Huachaca. The rebels thereby put an end to, or at least curbed, arbitrary acts by those hacendados who would leave their laborers without pay.[21]

Considering that laborers who worked on coca haciendas were mostly temporary workers from high-altitude communities and settlements dispersed throughout the montañas and selvas around the Marañón and Apurímac rivers,[22] it is understandable that the revolt, and its most charismatic caudillo, would attain such popularity over this vast—economically, ecologically, and culturally heterogeneous—area. Yet it was perhaps the very breadth of its social base that fueled situations that proved somewhat unmanageable for the leadership of the movement. Indeed, the appropriation of tithes did not always follow the established channels mandated by the rebel organization. The peasants, feeling secure under the benefits they enjoyed from the system, seemingly carried out their own coca requisitioning beyond the control of the rebellion's generals. For example, the Spaniard José Murrieta, a merchant and owner of coca haciendas in Choimacota, declared that "whatever coca he sent off [with his muleteers] was taken away from him by the indians, and they even threatened to seize his hacienda."[23] The rebellion, in other words, in all likelihood led to direct seizure of produce by the peasants.

In the midst of this conflict, the state, in concert with the Church, appeared not as an established institutional power, but rather as just one more party contending for the highly contested surplus.[24] Its means of exerting administrative pressure were not particularly efficient, and its capacity for collecting tithes depended entirely upon the official collectors, whose authority was constantly being challenged by those who served the rebels, even after the final battle of the monarchist rebellion had been waged. As a distraught Rafael Quisoruco, who was collecting the tithe in the same area Leandro had covered only a short time before, declared, "They [the tithe collectors appointed by Huachaca] give their little bits of paper to each day-laborer[,] two or three arrobas that do not include the tithe."[25]

A profound irony underlies the state's role in the conflict. If Independence brought a change to the region that truly revolutionized "the established order" of colonial society, the change occurred in spite of, not because of, those who fought so hard for the cause of Independence. It was in fact the monarchist peasants who, in their response to the Patria, completely revolutionized the fiscal system, "altering the established custom from time immemorial."[26] Ironically, this was the very custom that a state professing to break with "a past of servitude" (*pasado de esclavitud*, an expression of the time) was most determined to perpetuate. In contrast to the *ayllus* of northern Potosí, in today's Bolivia, which demanded that the republican state continue the colonial "tributary pact" (considering it a guarantee of their rights over communal lands),[27] Huanta's peasants, though seemingly staunch defenders of the colonial order, in practice defied some of the legal foundations upon which this order was founded. Furthermore, to the revolution of the tithes one must add their resistance to the payment of tribute.

The royalism of Huachaca and his followers in Huanta, then, turns out to be more than a blind defense of the colonial order—their rejection of the republican order ought not be attributed to peasants' "inability" to perceive their "own interests."[28] Their monarchism can hardly be defined as opposition to a liberal project. Moreover, the founders of the Republic that Simón Bolívar abandoned in frustration confronted more than just the contradictory task of administering a newly liberated country without repudiating the colonial mechanisms that had enslaved it. They also had to combat, over a period of three years, a monarchist alliance nourished by what appeared to be highly competitive market-oriented agricultural sectors of the sierra. Once again, the available evidence calls into question received myths. If Ayacucho is to be considered part of Peru's southern Andes, then the image of the Andean south as economically and ideologically "backward and feudal"—its subservient indians and autarkic economies typically counterpoised to a central sierra of dynamic peasant communities successfully incorporated into the market[29]— must, in light of the new evidence now at our disposal, be called into question.

Beyond the Tithes: The Dispute over Parayso

The appropriation of tithes was the most unambiguous social enterprise promoted by the rebels, but it was by no means the only one. Basing their efforts on this appropriation, the monarchist rebels established a political organization of remarkable scope. Huachaca's government exercised a range of functions, the most important being the administration of justice. Trials in Uchuraccay involved muleteers, peasants, small landowners, and even priests. Problems ranged from disputes over the ownership of coca lands to complaints about the moral authority of a priest, the behavior of certain women, petty theft, and other minor offenses. The authority through whom the leader of this government legitimated his exercise of power was the king. Some of the requests brought before this royal tribunal as well as other internal documents produced by it bore the preamble, "By the authority of the reign of don Fernando VII for the years 1827 and 1828."[30]

The powers of the Uchuraccay government went so far as to include authority over the mobilization of manpower for "the repair of roads and bridges" and the regulation of "law and order," establishing standards of conduct for individuals under their jurisdiction. In other words, besides administering jus-tice, collecting taxes, and organizing the restorationist armies, the Uchuraccay government arrogated to itself powers that corresponded to a municipality or prefecture—it was no coincidence that the designations "Headquarters of Luis Pampa" and "Prefecture of Luis Pampa" were used interchangeably in rebel documents. Take, for example, the eloquent document appointing Leandro governor and subdelegate of Acón:

> Prefecture of Luis Pampa, 26 March, 1827.
>
> José Antonio Abad Guachaca, Brigadier and General in Chief of the Royal Armies of the Reserve Division Defenders of the faith[.] It being advisable to appoint a Governor and Subdelegate in the Acón gorge, the previous one finding himself disabled by the illness that God had given him and since the necessary qualities are present in Manuel Leandro I choose and appoint his person, for his good conduct and honorable comportment[,] *to rule and govern all individuals of this gorge, Spaniards as well as natives [naturales]* obeying all of his commands[,] as he shall order the maintenance of roads, bridges, and other works in favor of the human species that passes through this gorge; he shall watch over those publicly living in illicit union and as many other evil occupations [*mal entretenidos*], punishing them severely in accordance with the laws that allow arbitrary penalties[.] On my order and command all those individuals shall consider him and have him as such, [the] Subdelegate[,] and if anyone should not obey him in his orders they shall be punished, and fined, fifty pesos for the aid, of these my worthy troops and so that they do not plead ignorance this shall be published as a decree[.] I place my signature hereon in this Headquarters at Luis Pampa 17 April, 1827. Huachaca. I the second Gen-eral Pascual Arancibia. For lack of notary Rafael de Castro. Witness Bernar-dino Galindo.[31]

Yet this document is more than an example; it displays a particular richness that transcends the text. In fact, it is one of the most contextualizable (so to speak) of all the surviving decrees, proclamations, orders, appointments, and sentences the Uchuraccay government has left us. Leandro was especially close to Huachaca. When he was captured, the authorities seized, in addition to the above document recording his appointment, various others equally valuable and compromising. Following is an examination of the circumstances prior to Leandro's appointment and of the documents seized from him.

Besides addressing the operational logic of the government in Uchuraccay, this analysis will bring into relief the bureaucratic, judicial, economic, and, in short, human problems that led the inhabitants of Huanta to turn to its courts.

Leandro was a forty-year-old married *arriero* and coca merchant from Huanta. Like other landless muleteers, he leased a *cocalito* (small coca plantation) in the *ceja de selva* to supplement his income. The coca plantation, located in the montaña of Acón, was called Parayso, and it was owned by José Tholedo, also a resident of Huanta. Shortly after beginning work on the leased lands, Leandro discovered he had been swindled. Tholedo had assured him that the coca plantation yielded two hundred *arrobas* of coca, but the truth, Leandro convincingly argued, was that it produced no more than sixty. The plantation, Leandro insisted, had been turned over to him in poor condition, so he had to invest money in cleanup and other fitting-out costs, which led him to withhold payment on the lease. Tholedo then brought charges against him, evidently under instigation of a third individual, the hacendado José Ruiz, with whom Tholedo had an outstanding debt of some one thousand pesos. Ruiz's intention was evidently to appropriate the coca plantation that Tholedo had leased to Leandro on account of the debt, taking advantage of the fact that the arriero had invested his own funds in fitting out the lands. "The self-seeking Don José Ruis," wrote Leandro, "without considering the excessive work that I had contracted managed to interrupt my work. . . . not happy enough with the cruel suffering to which he had persuaded me . . . he had the audacity to raise his violent hands and snatch [the plantation] from me by force." All the same, it was not Ruiz but Leandro who ended up in jail, where he remained for two months. While in jail, he wrote a letter to the intendant, asking to be set free and expressing his desire to reach "a reasonable agreement with said Tholedo," who "ha[d] left for Ayacucho, abandoning the lawsuit." The intendant's reply advised him to begin proceedings to obtain freedom on bail, but Leandro was too demoralized to undertake any action: "My heart never permitted me to draw up any papers."[32] It was then, and not before "experiencing as improper harassment . . . as has been endured from the justice of the Patria" (including a public flogging), that Leandro turned to Huachaca, with whom he had ties based on personal friendship and *arriería*.

The rebellion had begun while all of this litigation was taking place, and Huachaca's intervention could be decisive. In a document in his own handwriting, under the preamble "Valid for the reign of Fernando VII for the years 1827 and 1828," Leandro petitioned the caudillo for justice:

> I beg of your invulnerable justification that you be of help and order that the above mentioned Ruyis [sic] pay me the last bit that I had spent in that cleaning of the hacienda mentioned or of [i.e., if] not[,] that I be allowed to enter the hacienda, with whose produce I shall fulfill the amount that this Tholedo owes to this Ruis, whose fulfillment even though I have not [sic] it must be by means of your uprightness[.] [As] for greater payment I of course concede an obligation for its fulfillment.[33]

Huachaca responded with a vigorous defense of Leandro: "Headquarters at Luis Pampa, 3 [sic], 1827. Let this appeal be delivered to Señor Subdelegate José del Balle: without any excuse or argument you shall administer justice without omission or hesitation, principally [by] seizing the hacienda; do as requested. If you have any obstacles make this known to the mayor don Ysidro Castillo. Huachaca [signature and mark] Pedro José Cza de Ezcurra, acting CL. GL. E. M. GL."[34]

One month after ordering the seizure of the Parayso coca plantation, Huachaca appointed Leandro governor and subdelegate of the "district" of Acón, by means of the document transcribed above.

The outcome of the case could not have proven more favorable to Leandro, who not only succeeded in recovering the leased coca plantation, but also became a political authority under the government of Uchuraccay. Furthermore, soon afterward he also became beneficiary, along with Rafael Castro, of the tithe corresponding to the gorge of El Rosario for two *mitas*, auctioned off in the amount of four hundred pesos in August 1827. That is to say, in addition to being governor and subdelegate, Leandro had now become a tithe collector.

Yet the case was also beneficial for Huachaca, who not only won an unconditional follower, but added new territory to his domains. Indeed, Parayso, the coca plantation under litigation, would from then on become a new rebel headquarters in the ceja de selva (see maps, chapter 5).

At least three important ideas can be drawn from the case of Parayso. First, compared to rebel justice, the justice of the Patria, which made the plaintiff suffer and required burdensome proceedings, Huachaca's justice proved to be more accessible and more expeditious. The court of Uchuraccay settled cases involving everyday conflicts among the area's inhabitants. It would seem to have been, in short, more within popular reach than the courts of the Patria.

Second, the "power vacuum" or recomposition of local elites is highlighted. In the midst of litigation, Parayso's owner left for Ayacucho, "abandoning the lawsuit." His desertion facilitated Leandro's case before both courts, that of Huachaca and that of the Patria, as well as the execution of Huachaca's final sentence, that is, the seizure of the coca plantation. The third figure in the case, José Ruiz, who had instigated Tholedo to sue Leandro and deprive him of his coca plantation, likewise left the area. The cause of the muleteers won out over that of the landowners. Huachaca's system of justice prevailed not only because it was more accessible than that of the Republic, but because there seemed not to have been groups powerful enough to contest its hegemony. When Huachaca issued a sentence, no one got in the way of its execution. The Uchuraccay rebels attained their supremacy with relative ease because they were able to fill a "power vacuum."

Third, the case shows the predominance of "indian" ways, or the dissolution of ethnicities. Leandro was regarded as an *indígena* by the institutions of the Republic, and he himself assumed this identity when he had to litigate in its courts; this makes his subsequent appointment as governor and subdelegate much more significant. Leandro was an indian, yet his office was not that of an "ethnic" authority. His duties as governor and subdelegate of Acón went beyond communities and ethnicities. Huachaca had decreed that it be so, upon giving Leandro power to "rule and govern *all the individuals of this gorge, Spaniards as well as natives.*"

Once again, as in the case of the revolution of the tithes, defense of the king did not necessarily imply acceptance of ethnic hierarchies inherent in colonialism, that is, a "republic of indians" subordinate to one of Spaniards. Rather, indian elements prevailed over all the rest. Moreover, although the caudillos of Uchuraccay never explicitly admitted as much, the hierarchical and bureaucratic structure of the rebel government did in fact contain elements of an ethnic vindication. But it was a vindication that, precisely because it remained unspoken, distanced itself from any discursive strategy (whether official or popular) endorsing the dualist conception of a separation of republics. Although the dualist conception that divided the society into a "republic of Indians" and a "republic of Spaniards"—each with its own distinctive laws— gave native Andeans the opportunity to reclaim their rights and defend themselves before the tribunals, it implicitly assumed they would accept the condition of being indian (that is, the "colonized"), which the Iquichano generals never claimed for either their movement or themselves. The critical importance of these three aspects warrants a more detailed look of each one.

Government in Uchuraccay

Before there was no one who could carry out my governance.
Now those who did not back the Sovereign King want to be granted a hearing.
—Antonio Huachaca, Headquarters at Luis Pampa, February, 1827

The cases I present below are based on documents confiscated from Leandro. They concern trials that arose before and during his tenure as subdelegate and governor of Acón, a post he held for some four to six months in 1827. Accusations and requests were addressed to him as well as to his predecessor in the position, the Spaniard José Pérez del Valle; to his successor, Manuel Ynga; and to Huachaca himself, who had the final word in all verdicts.

The terms I use to designate the various (juridical) echelons and offices of the Uchuraccay government will seem somewhat imprecise, for the documents themselves convey this imprecision. Leandro was appointed governor and subdelegate, and therefore I shall refer to "Leandro's government." Nevertheless, he was also referred to as "mayor." Along the same lines, Valle, whom Huachaca called "my subdelegate lieutenant colonel," signed his documents "Military Political Judge and Colonel of the Royal Army." Leandro's government, with headquarters in the gorge of Acón (which the rebels also called the "district of Acón"), was subordinated, of course, to Huachaca's government, whose center, the headquarters at Luis Pampa in Uchuraccay, was occasionally referred to as the "Prefecture of Luis Pampa." It is the entirety of these imprecisely delimited political entities, of which the governance of Acón was but one part, that I have been calling the "Government of Uchuraccay."

The terminological imprecision in the Uchuraccay government documents is not surprising when viewed in light of the bureaucratic terminology of the period. The transition from a colonial to a national regime and the political turbulence inherent in the first years of the Republic found expression in diverse forms, among them the increasing ambiguity of bureaucratic terminology. Colonial subdelegates gave way to republican subprefects, and intendants to prefects, albeit without the judicial powers of the former, which would be assumed by judges of the court of first instance.[35] However, in 1827 these changes were still far from being consolidated, and it was not unusual to find both parallel authorities and republican authorities designated by their old colonial names (a confusion that could only benefit the Uchuraccay rebels, who appointed their own authorities). Yet beyond the confusion, what strikes us as "ambiguity," as exemplified in the superimposition and interchangeability of offices and functions in one individual, in fact reflected an administrative system of limited division of labor and, hence, of high concentration of power. This state of affairs, which was valid in official legal proceedings of the Republic (and even more so during the colonial period), was reproduced almost to the letter in the bureaucratic proceedings of the Uchuraccay government.

In order to grasp the scope of the political and judicial powers of the rebel government, I have classified the court cases into three groups: (a) litigation over coca lands; (b) crimes concerning inheritance and sexual conduct; and (c) issues related to the allocation of labor.

Litigation over Coca Lands

Leandro's government decided cases originating in land disputes. Because his administration fell in montaña territory, most disputes concerned coca lands, and litigants were generally coca plot owners. Thus Leandro settles a dispute between Don Gregorio Sebrón and Don Bernardo Chilenos, who were fighting over a "montaña plot in which they have undertaken the cultivation of coca. . . . And as these wanted to take away between themselves [sic] said land[,] one wanted more than the other,"[36] Leandro determined the exact limits of each man's land. The verdict was signed by "el Sr. Gr. [Señor Gobernador] Dn. Manuel Leandro" as well as by two mayors and another authority.[37]

The second case concerning lands had been initiated before Leandro assumed the governance of Acón. Eustaquio Miranda, "a poor wretch, burdened with six male children," requested that Leandro annul the distrainer of his hacienda, which had been seized by the court of Uchuraccay. Miranda had the backing of Huachaca, but Leandro refused to act without a written order from his caudillo. Miranda then turned to Huachaca:

Eustaquio Miranda, at my lord's feet [Huachaca's] with the utmost devotion and due humility[,] I say that I went to the montaña of Acón to my hacienda named Yauchuanay with the permission and word given by my lord to have them turn my hacienda over to me[.] Señor Governor [Leandro] remonstrated [,] he tells to bring a firm order from my lord to release my hacienda and I here surrender myself to you and so hand it to me and therefore, Sire, at least for the male sons you have [,] do this act of charity for a poor wretch burdened with six male children [,] giving me a firm order for the Señor Governor so that he will cancel the seizure and release my hacienda to me[.] God will reward my lord.[38]

The Uchuraccay caudillo was clear and emphatic in his reply:

Prefecture of Luis Pampa 26 March 1827. The mayor of the Acón gorge with sufficient mandate [from] Don Manuel Leandro shall in all justice attend to the petitioner *guiding himself with the testament that he bears as proof which speaks in favor of its presenter Miranda*[,] and the hacienda shall be handed over so that he may work and if his counterpart should have any complaint he shall present it to my government so that both sides may be served with justice[.] I order and command thus . . . Huachaca [signature and mark].[39]

Huachaca's word was not questioned, but written proof of it was required, which arrived forthwith. Huachaca not only formalized his sentence on paper, but also substantiated it by referring to another written document, a testament. The case in question not only conveys the weight of the written document in the Uchuraccay courts: it confirms Huachaca's unquestioned leadership.

The third case involving lands featured a woman as its protagonist, Ildefonsa Belarde, "lawfully wedded wife of the Lieutenant of Grenadiers of the provincial urban Militias of Huanta for His Majesty." Belarde appealed to Huachaca with the formal salute, "*Señor Brigadier General*," to intercede on her behalf in connection with a coca plantation she claimed to have inherited. Her request arose as a result of the emergence of an adversary who sought to appropriate the plantation. Belarde claimed that the probative document for the donation had "suffered damage" in Marccaraccay, where "the opposing troops burned my house," but insisted that the original was in the archive "of the Town of Huanta." What she asked of Huachaca was to have the hacienda placed in escrow until she succeeded in proving her claim "with qualifying documents and justificatory testimonies from the gorge's residents themselves." Huachaca directed the case to Leandro, who in turn authorized Mayor Feliciano Guillén to set aside "all of the [owner's] possessions until both the plaintiff and the defendant clarify and present an account to this headquarters." The document, signed by Leandro, was dated in Parayso, May 13, 1827.[40]

A Sinful Priest, Guilty Women

In contrast to the cases presented thus far, which in contemporary terminology are civil suits, the following one might fall within the sphere of criminal cases, or perhaps minor offenses—those of the kind that would eventually fall under the jurisdiction of justices of the peace.

Isidro Castillo, *alcalde ordinario* of the Acón gorge, accused Lucas Retamoso, the priest of Choimacota, on a variety of charges, first of all, of having stolen a small bell and an altar cloth from his oratory and neglected the obligations of his ministry: "The priest collects two arrobas [of coca] of the first crop without administering the last rites in this gorge during the first year[;] in the present year [he has administered them] only on account of having been notified by several commissioners." Second, he reprimanded him for marrying couples without having confessed them and for not having "made the proclamations as is customary and ordered by the church for holidays." The third accusation was political: "This said priest," alleged Castillo, "before the King's commissioners and Señor General Huachaca arrived[,] was speaking out against the Generals[,] saying that they were just thieving *godo* [derogatory for Spanish] indians, and vile, and who were only fit to be burned and that all of them who died went to hell, because they were against the patria and did not deserve God's temple."[41] The fourth and final accusation referred to the priest's sexual conduct: "This priest lives maritally with a woman named Andrea so and so and they are in Choimacota setting an example for us even though in a note of his he treats us as immoral as if he were pure, he is purified [*sic*] with his lover since in [that is, by] her he has several sacrilegious children, these are the lessons that he gives us and the gospel that he explains to us so that we sinners follow in his tracks and go into the abysses of hell."[42]

The accusations were addressed to Señor Colonel José Pérez del Valle, who, upon receiving them, directed them to "Reverend Friar Juan Basques Chaplain of the Royal Army so that he may obtain summary information . . . in accordance with ecclesiastical laws[,] as it does not belong to my jurisdiction. . . ." Valle signed as "Military Political Judge and Colonel of the Royal

Army."[43] This transfer did not take place, and, a bit more than a month later, Huachaca decided that Valle ("my subdelegate lieutenant Colonel") should again take on the case or, in the latter's absence, "Don Manuel Leandro."[44] Valle retook the case. Oddly, the records contain no evidence that an investigation of the charges was ever carried out. However, there is a brief statement by the cleric Retamoso in which he defends himself against the charges: "I owe nothing to that swine of a plaintiff, I pay no attention to these useless affairs," the priest wrote arrogantly to Valle, making no effort to conceal his irritation. As for the objects he was accused of having stolen, he maintained that they had been donated to his church by the faithful and that "it is not right for anyone to have the things from my church." He did not address the other charges.[45]

If, as I believe, form reveals as much as (and sometimes even more than) content, this holds especially true for the form in these particular documents, in which the most minute detail can fill in an enormous gap of information. The tone of Retamoso's reply and the laconic character of his defense are as revealing as his arguments, if not more so. In effect, by belittling and even ignoring the charges brought against him, the priest was calling into question not only his accusers' credibility, but also the judges' authority. Retamoso did not address himself to Valle in the deferential manner of the other litigants in the Uchuraccay courts ("Señor Colonel"), but rather in the colloquial "don José del Valle" and "Dear Friend." The priest did not recognize the appointed authorities of the Uchuraccay government or show any interest in defending himself against the accusations of people he openly scorned.

Justice in Uchuraccay was less than expeditious on this occasion, and the plaintiff Castillo was forced to make a new appeal, this time to "Señor General" Huachaca himself. In the appeal Castillo repeated his accusations against the priest, but this time his charges implicated two women, allegedly the "instigators" of the priest's transgressions and theft. The first was one Andrea, the priest's "lover and cook," who had been mentioned collaterally in the first charges, and the other, Bárbara Torre. Castillo demanded once again the return of his goods and reiterated his concern regarding the priest's failure to administer the sacrament: "For two years none of us parishioners have been confessed." He also asked that Retamoso be tried "by means of your judges" and that "these seducers [the two women] likewise be punished as an example and lesson to others." Last, in a gesture of loyalty toward (or adulation of) Huachaca, Castillo reiterated his dismay at the disrespectful manner in which the priest had referred to the caudillo: "*Se ha rajado contra de Vs. indispensable-*

mente de que Vs. no es nada para el" (He has lashed out against you essentially because you are nothing to him).[46]

Unlike the trials dealing with the land disputes, in this particular case the Uchuraccay justices proceeded without a shred of evidence. Following up on Castillo's second letter, Huachaca immediately decreed, "The altar cloth, the bell, being his must be returned."[47] But he did not demand any punishment for the priest. At the same time, partially obliging the plaintiff, he ordered that the two women named as the priest's "seducers" be arrested and tried: "[They] shall consign the women Andrea, the cook, and Bárbara Torre to well-guarded custody at the disposal of this court[,] conveyance to which shall be carried out at the delinquents' expense."[48] The letter, dated at Luis Pampa on January, 8, 1827, was addressed to Colonel Valle and two other subdelegates and was corroborated by another letter dated February 22, written at the same location and likewise signed by Huachaca. In the latter document the caudillo was particularly harsh on one of the two women: "As for Bárbara Torre, this woman shall be sent in accordance with the previous order[,] well bound in her resistance. . . . When this preliminary hearing has been carried out it shall be attached to the communiqués of the transcript for the definitive ruling[,] the proceedings of which shall be executed with the abstention of both sides."[49]

Was the judgment ever carried out? Or were the women simply punished as Castillo had requested? The documents do not say, yet it is not difficult to imagine the outcome. The reference to the women, at first incidental to the charge, turned into an accusation, and the accusation into a guilty verdict. The order that they appear before the court ("at the delinquent's expense" and "well bound") resonates with the severity and intent to humiliate normally reserved for those accused of witchcraft and proven delinquents.[50] The women endured discriminatory treatment even from the plaintiff, who in his second petition asked for justice for the priest ("by means of your judges") while prescribing punishment for the women ("these seducers . . . [must] be punished as an example"). Ironically, whereas the accused would have had the right to defend himself, the alleged accomplices were presumed guilty. Significantly, the plaintiff was the alcalde ordinario of Acón, that is, a recognized authority, so it is equally significant that the court at Uchuraccay complied with his requests.

The case sheds light on still other aspects of rebel jurisprudence. First of all, the government of Uchuraccay passed judgment on a member of the Church. This is astonishing in an era in which priests could be tried only under their *fueros*, that is, by the Church's own code of laws. Huachaca was not unaware of the Church's authority. In fact, he seemed to have hoped that a religious from within his ranks would intervene in solving Retamoso's case; thus his orders: "They will make the inquiry with extreme care, and once done and over they will give me a report *so that in the same way I may give a report to the ecclesiastical chapter.*"[51] It is telling also that Valle, the first Uchuraccay judge to preside over the accusation against the priest, refrained from taking action, arguing that the case did not fall within his jurisdiction: "Let it be referred to Reverend Friar Juan Basques Chaplain of the Royal Army so that he may obtain summary information with extreme care in accordance with ecclesiastical laws[,] as it does not belong to my jurisdiction and on account of his powers *as the only clergyman* that there is in this gorge. Acon, and 23 January of 1827."[52] Despite the Uchuraccay judges' intention to refer Retamoso to a clergyman for trial, no such person seems to have appeared, so Huachaca ended up hearing the case himself. The suit demonstrates the institutional fragility of the Church in Huanta. Its high-ranking officials having been largely absent from the region, the Church did not come forward to protect its ministers. Second, the case proves yet again Huachaca's skill in arriving at Solomonic solutions to conflicts. Both sides could consider themselves satisfied. Mayor Castillo succeeded in recuperating the objects the cleric had stolen. The cleric returned the items but avoided punishment. Justice was done for the men. Huachaca did not need to make any male enemies, though in the process he most certainly made some female ones. Justice in Uchuraccay turned out to be, in the third place, effective for the men, though not so much for the women.

This was not the only case in which Huachaca's justice was merciless toward women. It would happen again in the course of the rebellion, when a woman accused of witchcraft was murdered by villagers from Mayhuavilca and other towns acting under the order of their alcaldes, who in turn claimed to be carrying out Huachaca's orders:

On more or less January 20, [Juan Heredia] was in the town of Mayhuavilca, and there one Herrero told him that the indians had an old woman bound up naked, and that they were tormenting and flogging her every day, and having seen her, he asked the mayors why they were doing that, and they answered that she was a witch who had left many bewitched and sick, and that they were going to kill her. He then said to them that they should do no such thing, and that they should send her to the priest Pacheco, to which they replied that he [Pacheco] had previously defended her, and it was necessary to teach a lesson with her, *and then the mayor of Huarcatán came and said that he was bringing Huachaca's order to shoot her, whereupon they executed her in the presence of the declarant and threw her cadaver in the river, the whole population taking an interest in this.*[53]

This quote constitutes one of the most direct testimonies of villagers, their mayors, and Huachaca acting in concert under the rubric of what appear to have been shared beliefs or cultural practices. If the mayors were, in fact, "obeying orders of Huachaca," one should also note that "the whole population [took] an interest in this." The testimony powerfully shows the extent of the caudillo's moral influence among the *comuneros*. If in the courts of Uchuraccay, litigants presented their pleas individually and always in written form, in this case a more informal type of justice seems to have been at work, one perhaps related to unwritten moral codes shared collectively by the communities and Huachaca. The testimony is, on the other hand, meaningful when contrasted with the previous case, in which Huachaca appears open to priestly advice and respectful of the investiture of a religious. Conversely, in this case neither Huachaca nor the villagers show any interest in heeding Father Francisco Pacheco's admonitions to spare the woman's life, who is eventually executed by villagers acting on orders of their caudillo Huachaca. The punas thus emerge from this testimony as the antithesis of the "safe haven" for witches that Irene Silverblatt has depicted for an earlier period.[54]

Not surprisingly, the women of Huanta, when not adopting a neutral or pacifist stance, were more inclined to side with the patriots. Doña Teresa Arbizu is a good example of someone who adopted a "neutral" attitude. The sister of the rebel leader Aguinaga and of Juan Barragán, a tithe collector for the rebels, Arbizu was on familiar terms with some important leaders of the monarchist rebellion; she was at the same time one of Pascual Arancibia's tenant farmers before the outbreak of the uprising. Her house in Huanta was used to hold prisoners when monarchist forces occupied the town in November 1827. Her treatment of the patriot prisoners was reportedly so cordial and friendly that it aroused suspicion among her relatives and royalist friends. At war's end, the Republic found no charge on which to convict her. Among many who testified in her favor was Don Francisco Torres, who said that "Teresa Arviso [*sic*], although she had an opinion favorable to the rebels, this individual behaved well toward [him] and other additional individuals, who were held prisoner in her house, by order of the caudillos on the night of the twelfth day of last November, with the greatest affection and attention favoring [us] in [our] nourishment and taking pains to get [us] released as in fact occurred by dint of her continuous determination."[55] Another woman who served as intermediary between the two sides was Magdalena Pons, owner of the Marcarí hacienda, who was commissioned by Prefect Tristán to take an offer of pardon to Soregui, a fugitive at the time.

There is even greater evidence for Huanta women explicitly serving the patriot cause during the monarchist war. In 1826, Huanta women "of the common people," or *la plebe*, rose in protest against the departure of the patriot sympathizer Mariano Maldonado from his position as intendant of Huamanga.[56] Likewise, during the rebellion, a woman described as being an "indian" provided Commander Quintanilla with valuable clues as to the whereabouts of Huachaca.[57] Regardless, patriot officers and civil authorities related how, in the midst of the Independence campaigns, "indian women" of Huanta offered them support, supplying them with resources and information. Brigadier and General Commander Antonio Gutiérrez de la Fuente wrote to Bolívar, "Because of several women from this town who have come to Huanta I know that the [royalist] enemies have continued their march toward Cuzco."[58] Fermín Lino Enriquez, governor of Palpa, wrote in turn to Gutiérrez de la Fuente, "The town of Huanta that revolted has suffered the punishment that corresponds to its crime; the indian women of these towns have been rewarded because they persistently strove to cooperate with the maneuvers of the Liberation Army."[59] Revealingly, and consistent with the testimonies quoted thus far, whereas the presence of women among the patriotic armies of Ayacucho was considerable, it was all but imperceptible among royalist forces and completely nonexistent in positions of power in the Uchuraccay government.[60]

Women were not, however, completely marginalized by the monarchists. We have seen how at least two women, Ildefonsa Belarde and Ysidora Urbano (see chapter 5 for the latter), were given a hearing in Huachaca's courts, with seemingly favorable outcomes. But no source attests to the presence of women in the leadership of the movement. Huachaca had a wife and children, yet references to his spouse are always tangential—the available documents do not disclose even her name. Such noninvolvement stands in stark contrast to the conspicuously prominent role that wives of prior Andean rebel caudillos exercised in the course of other uprisings, notably, the celebrated wife of José

Gabriel Condorcanqui (Túpac Amaru II), Micaela Bastidas, who played a paramount role in the logistics of the rebel army in Cuzco in 1780 and 1781.

It would be presumptuous, however, to infer that the Republic had suddenly committed itself to the vindication of women, or at least to their right to be judged by the same criteria as men—too little time had elapsed for such an evolution to have taken place. Nevertheless, patriot attitudes toward women deserve to be studied, especially in light of the contrasting treatment they received from the royalists during the wars of Independence and from the government of Uchuraccay during the Huanta uprising. It would perhaps be worthwhile to devote more attention to the role played by the *rabonas*, or women who accompanied soldiers during their movements and who took charge, to an extraordinary degree, of the armies' subsistence infrastructure.[61] Likewise, new data on the Huanta uprising would help us understand better (or qualify) the marginal role of women as it is depicted in the evidence so far.

Labor and Military Power

Other documents confiscated from Leandro disclose additional aspects of his powers and those of the Uchuraccay government in general. In this instance they do not concern trials, but orders received and executed by Leandro. Thanks to these documents we know that the subdelegate and governor of Acón interfered in the mobility of the population within his districts. Thus, for example, the subdelegate from Choimacota asked Leandro "to turn over to Colonel don José Antonio de la Barreda's mayordomo three laborers who have fled from his Carmelo hacienda," along with two women who escaped with them.[62] Acting as an officially established civil authority would, Leandro had to ensure "public order," taking charge of cases of escapees like the aforementioned as well as of the "maintenance of roads, bridges and [the] watch over those publicly living in illicit union," as stated in the appointment cited above. In addition, his powers extended, though to a limited extent, to the military sphere. Leandro carried out Huachaca's and Arancibia's orders concerning the logistics and recruitment of personnel for the restorationist war.[63]

In short, the powers of the Uchuraccay government covered everything from problems of landownership to ethical, sexual, religious, municipal, labor, and even military affairs. Of all these issues, however, only the last two had a direct bearing on political objectives: the mobilization of men for the restorationist army. The rest were everyday matters. The evidence, incomplete yet convincing, seems to indicate that people who turned to the courts at Uchuraccay did so above all in the hope of solving problems left unresolved by the inefficiency (or nonexistence) of the Republic's authorities and system of justice. There were no ideological questions at stake here. Not that the court at Uchuraccay was not concerned with sanctioning rebel detractors; we have seen how severe Huachaca's threats toward deserters of his movement were. But, as the documents confiscated from Leandro show, this was far from the Uchuraccay tribunal's unique or primary goal. People who turned to the courts at Uchuraccay did so out of need, not fear. It was precisely the goal of satisfying, if only in small measure, an ordinary demand for justice and government among one sector of the population that led the Uchuraccay rebels to exercise and especially legitimize their power, while at the same time enabling them to recruit some of their most loyal supporters.

Huachaca was undoubtedly conscious of the role his courts played. Thus he proudly declared, soon after having ordered the arrest of the women implicated in the accusation against the priest Retamoso (and aware perhaps of the growing popularity of his courts among the men), "Before there was no one who could carry out my governance, now those who did not back the Sovereign King want to be granted a hearing."[64] The evidence indeed lends a modicum of credibility to this claim, as we shall see.

Misgovernment and the "Power Vacuum," or the Recomposition of Local Elites

No one maintains respect for an individual[,] neither pays him what he owes him[,] nor fulfills the contracts he has with him[.] Everyone usurps an individual's rights and actions because they know that there is no judge who could do justice to those who have their rights so usurped. This is why they often pester Your Excellency's superior justification[,] presenting their needs and grievances to you; as a result of which the residents of this town would perhaps be considered litigious and disturbers of the peace.
—José Aguilar y Vílchez and other vecinos of Huanta, 1819

We lack justice and someone to rule over us.
—Gregorio Ydalgo, vecino and hacendado of the Viscatán gorge, 1819

To return for a moment to the story of the Parayso coca plantation, in the midst of the litigation he himself had initiated, José Tholedo, the owner of the plantation, abandoned the lawsuit. His accomplice, José Ruiz, did the same. The coca plantation was left in the hands of the Uchuraccay rebels, who seized it and established therein a new headquarters. Why did no one prevent Huachaca's ruling in this case? The explanation, I believe, goes beyond the usual premise of intimidation. For while the government of Uchuraccay relied, admittedly, on an army to guarantee observance of its laws, need alone compelled the inhabitants to call on its courts. The government of Uchuraccay responded to a demand that originated with them. Huachaca imposed his own brand of justice in a region that for decades had been clamoring for justice and government. His claim that "before there was no one who could carry out my governance" was triumphalist and rhetorical but could all the same be justified historically. The complaints and charges over lack of authority and justice in Huamanga in general and Huanta in particular in fact preceded the outbreak of the restorationist war. They came from various sectors and began in the last decades of the colonial era, so far as I have been able to track them. The most telling examples emerge from troops who participated in the Ayacucho campaign. The soldiers lamented the impossibility of coordinating their actions because of a dearth of town authorities in the region: "Here I find myself with absolutely no one to take command," José Caceda remarked to the intendant in Huangazca just a few weeks prior to the Battle of Ayacucho, "because there is neither a mayor, nor an alderman, since all have fled; the disobedience in these towns is great."[65] Identical complaints were expressed a week after the battle: "The scandalous lack of leaders, governors, and headmen in these towns is great," said the guerrilla commander of the province of Anco, Juan de Dios Castilla, writing to Marshall Antonio José de Sucre, "for, as Mr. Governor Provider of the Bishopric and the military chiefs who have passed through this province will inform Your Lordship[,] there is no one in command nor any one to help us, as a result of which its inhabitants still find themselves without any government at all."[66] A few weeks later, the intendant governor of the province of Castrovirreina informed the prefect of Huancavelica, "I had scarcely glanced at the capital of the province and found that the town was leaderless[,] with neither a priest nor a mayor."[67]

The fact that these testimonies were pronounced in the midst of a war and that their authors were mainly guerrilla commanders, military officers, and newly appointed civilian authorities who were generally strangers to the localities may explain the clarity with which they express the problem of lack of authority. Even so, similar opinions came to be expressed from other quarters and on other occasions. One such instance was the establishment of intendancies in 1782. This administrative change was felt throughout the viceroyalty and gave rise to an intense struggle between the civil and ecclesiastical powers. Yet in no region was the strife as fierce as in Huamanga. In 1785, Inspector (*Visitador*) Escobedo had noted that on account of the "cliques and dissensions among which Guamanga was divided . . . they were all reluctant to take charge of that city."[68] Or, as Fisher put it, "Huamanga in fact, was so notoriously difficult to govern, that, according to Escobedo it was the least desirable of the intendancies."[69] Two years later the bishop of Huamanga resigned, complaining bitterly about a diocese so "full of thorns and weeds."[70]

In the first years of the nineteenth century, Visitador Demetrio O'Higgins added his own brushstrokes to the picture of supposed "misgovernment" portrayed by his predecessors. O'Higgins blamed the authorities, and in particular the priests, for the neglect that characterized the province of Huanta.[71] He noted the lack of authorities such as the *Protector de Naturales* (protector of indians) and deplored the spirit of "vilification of authority" among the inhabitants.[72] O'Higgins's reports were not without personal interest (and his mission as a visitador was undoubtedly to denounce the "bad government"), but this fact by no means mars the truth they contained.

In a letter to the intendant in 1819, more than ten years after O'Higgins's last *visita* (inspection) of Huamanga, a group of eleven hacendados added their voices to the historical succession of complaints about misgovernment. Their allegations included a proposal for a resolution of their problems. The hacendados asked for the appointment of four *alcaldes de españoles* for the town of Huanta and the two montañas of Choimacota and Acón, where their coca haciendas were located. They were joined by Gregorio Hidalgo, who identified himself as *español*, in another petition, this one in the name of the residents and hacendados of the Viscatán gorge, also located in the montañas of Huanta. "For four years this gorge has been without anyone to govern it, such as a mayor, during which time there have been murders, robberies, and what is more the roads, and bridges [are] impassable," Hidalgo pointed out. His protest, along with that of the other hacendados, was summarized in one of Hidalgo's own phrases: "We lack justice and someone to rule over us."[73]

While the tone and content of the hacendados' charges in 1819 were similar to those of the denunciations considered thus far, their arguments are noteworthy as to the authors' identity: they were neither bureaucrats nor soldiers on military campaign, but residents (*vecinos*) of Huanta. Also noteworthy is the forwardness of their proposal: the appointment of alcaldes de españoles. Above all, however, the accusations stand out by virtue of the clarity with which they defined misgovernment. For these hacendados, the explanation for misgovernment was not so much the authorities' physical absence (as it might seem at first glance) as the private use of public positions and, above all, the concentration of power.

The hacendados of 1819 argued, first of all, that the subdelegate of Huanta could not keep up with the peoples' requests. Despite the size of the province, "which covers thirty leagues of latitude and another thirty or more of longitude," and the high number of españoles who resided in its gorges (fourteen thousand, according to them) "there is but one judge as an interim subdelegate [who] cannot keep up with the events requiring justice."[74] The subdelegate-judge in question was Pedro José Lazón, a Huanta hacendado who was accused of *paisanismo* (favoring his *paisanos*, or close acquaintances and people from his hometown): "As a son and native of this town he [Lazón] has abundant relations and acquaintances that prevent him from properly administering justice; on the other hand his business dealings and estates are so many other ties that cloud other party's reason."[75] Similar accusations fell on Melchor Porras, mayor of the Viscatán gorge and Lazón's protégé:

> The gorge is without anyone to govern it because even though we have Melchor Porras [who rules] with the name of Mayor, there is no doubt that he governed well during the first year[,] keeping a watchful eye on concubinages[,] readying roads and bridges, yet in the three following years he has been nothing but a thief who never administers justice to anyone, so that even if we kill each other, and rob from one another there is no one to pass judgment on the delinquent to decide his punishment.[76]

What the hacendado Hidalgo meant in saying that "the gorge is without anyone to govern it" was not, then, that Viscatán lacked a mayor, but that the mayor in office did not impart justice; this state of affairs was only exacerbated by the dubious legitimacy of his post: "He usurps jurisdiction without the appropriate title."[77] Likewise, the charge against the hacendado and subdelegate-judge Lazón was a protest against the monopolization of power which the hacendados signing the 1819 requests deemed to be at the root of arbitrary acts and injustices. Hence, the absence of government was not so much a lack of authorities as a lack of justice. The phrase "we lack justice and someone to rule over us" must be read, therefore, not as an accusation motivated by the physical absence of authorities, but by the absence of just authorities. The demand for government was, then, a demand for justice and consequently a demand for representation and a share of power. Yet it was not framed in the abstract: hacendado charges in 1819 were accompanied by petitions for the appointment of mayors, whom the petitioners themselves had elected through voting.[78]

After an initial unfavorable ruling and a full year of appeals, Huanta hacendados finally succeeded in getting their demands met. Their success set an important legal precedent in the balance of local power. However, their problems were far from over. Only a few years later, several of them became involved in conspiracies to obtain public office. For example, the Huantino Manuel Segundo Cabrera led a coup against the current intendant of Huamanga, Manuel Químper, taking over his position, only a few weeks after the Battle of Ayacucho. Cabrera's major collaborator in the plot was a twenty-year-old lieutenant, Juan Ramos, who eventually joined the monarchist rebellion.[79] The relation between the hacendado demands of 1819 and the motives of the monarchist rebels can be even more readily observed in light of the open, militant incorporation of another of the hacendados, the Spaniard and former officer of the Royal Army Miguel Fariña, into the restorationist ranks. Yet this relation became still more apparent when Huachaca himself, already involved in a leadership role in the first monarchist hostilities, pointed to Subdelegate Pedro José Lazón's and his family's monopolistic attitude as one of the reasons for his rebellion. Thus, everything indicates that Huachaca, along with an important sector of village peasants, small landowners, and muleteers whom he represented, was affected by the same problems afflicting the hacendados who requested the appointment of alcaldes de españoles in 1819. He expressed as much in a letter of March 1826, cosigned by his lieutenant, Pablo Guamán, and addressed to the prefect: "We are very disheartened because of Mr. Vilchez *and other lasones* [Lazones] who only dedicate themselves to humiliating us *without allowing us to conduct our business, the coca haciendas going to waste.*"[80]

Like the hacendado plaintiffs of 1819, Huachaca and Guamán directed their accusations at Subdelegate Lazón, his relatives, and protégées. However, in contrast to the hacendados, who claimed to be suffering from the consequences of that family's political empire, Huachaca and Guamán denounced the harmful effects of their economic monopoly ("without allowing us to conduct our business, the coca haciendas going to waste"). Both groups' complaints, at any rate, represented aspects of the same problem.

Pedro José Lazón did indeed belong to an extensive family of creole Huanta landowners. Alluded to as a patrician in the documents, he owned haciendas in Huanta, served as colonel in the Royal Army, and worked for a number of years as a subdelegate.[81] As the intendant's provincial representative, the subdelegate had great power, his jurisdiction covering everything from collection of tribute, to issues of justice and war, to control over the resources and political life of indian populations.[82] Just as much as his hated predecessor, the *corregidor*, a subdelegate enjoyed the possibility of amassing personal fortune from his office. It was, accordingly, no accident that Lazón aroused so much resentment among such a broad and disparate sector of Huanta's population. Even so, everything suggests that his power had ceased to be all-encompassing by the final years of colonial domination. First called into question by a faction of hacendados in 1819, Lazón saw his power further diminished by Huachaca's affront, the sectors whom he represented, and the rebel organization itself.

These awkward alliances arising, in this instance, from a need to unify in the face of a common enemy, invalidate any attempt to interpret the hacendados' requests for alcaldes de españoles as being ethnically oriented. Here my analysis differs from Mark Thurner's hypothesis vis-à-vis the province of Huaylas (Ancash) in the same period. Finding petitions in Huaylas that bear a striking resemblance to those I have located in Huanta in connection with the appointment of alcaldes de españoles," Thurner suggests that they originated as buffers against the power of the *alcaldes de indios*.[83] This Spanish and indian opposition is irrelevant in Huanta, where circumstances pitted a sector of the local people self-defined as españoles and recently arrived Spaniards, on the one hand, with the traditional, established creole elites, on the other. Indeed, several, if not most, of the hacendados requesting the alcaldes de españoles were Huantinos, probably mestizos; some were military men drawn to Huanta by laws promoting trade and the colonization of the area's montañas.[84] Their request arose not from any rivalry with indian mayors, with whom in fact they would end up forming alliances, but rather one with established, "aristocratic" creole hacendados represented by Lazón's clique.[85]

Why Lazón and his supporters succumbed to the new merchant-hacendado sectors and muleteers who ultimately coalesced in the monarchist rebellion and at courts in Uchuraccay is far from obvious. Why did these formerly powerful hacendados choose to withdraw, to the point of abandoning their haciendas in some instances, instead of assembling private armies to confront the "upstarts" who for some time had been challenging them? Were their properties depreciating? Was there already little left for them to defend? Was this a manifestation of an imminent economic decline? Informed replies to these questions would require a more detailed inquiry. What is certain is that the collapse of this group (temporarily, at least) was inevitable. Once the most powerful landowners of Huanta, they gave way to a faction of montoneros, including merchant-hacendados of more recent fortune and Quechua-speaking muleteers who signed edicts and administered justice in the name of the king.

This transition, the decline of the old landowner class and the conflictive rise to power of a culturally and ethnically heterogeneous sector, must also be taken into account, along with the other factors thus far mentioned, in understanding the background of "misgovernment." While the traditional class, whose power was increasingly called into question, did not collapse altogether, the new groups failed to establish themselves completely within the region's economic and political power structures. One must add to all of these factors the crisis brought on by the wars of Independence, in which Ayacucho was the final, decisive scene. In the midst of such chaos the need for some order inevitably arose. Increasingly, such order was emanating, with drastic and sometimes overwhelming force, from the headquarters at Luis Pampa in the punas of Uchuraccay.

The Predominance of Indian Elements, or the "Dissolution of Ethnicities"

Composed in Spanish and observing the protocol common to colonial bureaucratic records, the documents produced by the Uchuraccay government display a marked influence of Quechua syntax and phonology. Regrettably, such traits are impossible to convey in translation, but they testify to the indigenous, or at least mestizo, origin of those who created them, namely, authorities, secretaries, and litigants in the courts. The predominance of "indian" hues, however, went far beyond these papers.

The presence of Europeans in the highest administrative positions of the rebel government is hardly perceptible. Huachaca, by all accounts the highest

Uchuraccay magistrate, entrusted Leandro, another "indian" muleteer, with the authority to rule over "Spaniards and natives," in one of the rebellion's key zones, as noted. Manuel Meneses, a Huantino coca merchant, was secretary and right hand of the indigenous caudillo. The priests, who were among Huachaca's more reliable advisors, were also natives of the Ayacuchano backwaters, or at least Peruvian. No Spaniard came to hold the status of general, the rank attained by Huachaca, Choque, Huamán, and Arancibia, all of whom, except for Arancibia, were referred to as *indígenas* by republican authorities. It is true that the Europeans played an important role in the organization and inception of the movement, above all in the production and dissemination of proclamations and manifestos, as noted in chapter 5. They also participated in the rebel government, as was the case of Pérez del Valle, tithe collector for the rebels, whom Huachaca called "my subdelegate lieutenant Colonel"; and complemented the logistical position of the rebel army in crucial ways, as in the case of the hacendado Juan Cantón (see chapter 5). Still, even Soregui, the most prominent European leader, had to submit to the authority of General Huachaca, who promoted him with the rank of "Brigadier of the Royal Army" (see chapter 2).[86]

The subordinate position of the Spanish was not limited to the military realm. Some were in the service of caudillos whom republican authorities deemed indígenas, often working as secretaries. Such was the case of the *capitulado* Gregorio Guijas, secretary to Tadeo Choque.[87] Antonio García and Francisco Garay fulfilled similar functions. An analogous hierarchizing took place between "mestizos" and "indians," the former being relegated to a subordinate role. Thus, for example, Martín Ccente (or Qqente), "indígena" from the Chacabamba hacienda and commander of guerrillas in the rebellion, made use of the Ruiz hacendados from the neighboring Tucuvilca hacienda in replying to his correspondence, since he himself could not read or write.[88]

Here we see once again how the Huanta rebellion openly and forcefully defied criterias of ethnic hierarchization inherent in imperial rule: a republic of indians subordinated to one of Spaniards. The old order now found itself subverted by the rebellion, and therein likewise lay the rebellion's subversive potential vis-à-vis the Republic. To complete the paradox, in the Túpac Amaru rebellion the opposite phenomenon occurred. As Scarlett O'Phelan has correctly emphasized, the Túpac Amaru rebellion, which most scholars regard as anticolonial, to a large extent reproduced, ironically enough, the social hierarchy of colonial society. The organization of its armies attests to that fact:

noble indians and creoles occupied the highest command, *indios de común* (commoner indians) filled the rank and file, and blacks were assigned to perform menial labor.[89]

The Huanta rebellion's subversion of ethnic hierarchies was never explicitly acknowledged. The most conspicuous indigenous leaders of the monarchist rebellion, Huachaca and Choque, never defined themselves as indians. Their discourse, accordingly, differed as much from that of their peasant followers who assumed indian status so as to obtain the legal advantages inherent in it, as from that of *kurakas*, who in earlier times demanded rights as representatives of *kurakazgos*, the indian groups they ruled over and which also functioned as tributary units. Historians have at times referred to them as *etnías*, or "ethnic groups."[90]

Nevertheless, the fact that the discourse of the Iquichano generals was devoid of ethnic allusions does not detract from, but rather underscores, the "ethnic" vindication of their actions. As Foucault put it: "Silence itself—the things one declines to say . . . is . . . an element that functions alongside with things said."[91] In other words, what remained unsaid was realized; or, to put it in Foucauldian terms, it was "said in a different way."[92] This "different way" was the logic behind the hierarchies of the rebel government and army and the character and powers of their authorities—above all, in comparison with those then in existence, to which I now turn. Whereas Pedro José Lazón, a landowner from the white, creole elite, was a former colonel and subdelegate who appointed mayors, Huachaca, an illiterate Quechua-speaking mule driver from the punas, was a general who appointed subdelegates (in addition to governors and mayors). This was not, of course, the first time in the history of the viceroyalty and the nascent Republic that a Spaniard or creole had been subordinated to a person deemed indian. The phenomenon also occurred in the colonial era, but in rather isolated instances and in the context of economic relations.[93] The revolutionary dimension of the Huanta rebellion lay in the fact that the subversion of colonial ethnic hierarchies was profoundly political; it was part of a government strategy, though not articulated as such. Obvious in the appointments that we have analyzed thus far, this political subversion of ethnic hierarchies will be understood even better in light of the legal terms the Uchuraccay government used to categorize its authorities (subdelegates, governors, and mayors) and of the meaning that such categories acquired when assumed by these authorities.

The position of subdelegate had been created alongside the system of intendancies in 1782. Subdelegates replaced the old *corregidores* and *alcaldes mayores* and were in charge of governing separate *partidos*.[94] Besides overseeing the collection of indian tribute, subdelegates were responsible for the administration of justice.[95] For this reason they were also called judges.[96] Their third most important function involved supervision of the political life of indian communities: "The Yndian caste, which is the most plentiful one in the Partidos, most especially needs the dedication of the subdelegates, and besides that[,] which they must have in all respects so that they live honestly and without idleness, vices or miseries, *the subdelegate shall watch over the formation of their Republics, and their elections of mayors, and the officials that comprise them* [that is, their republics] . . . the subdelegate must see that this class of natives progresses."[97]

The determination to control the political life of the republic of indians, already quite explicit in the paragraph from the Directions for Subdelegates of 1784 cited above, is expressed even more unequivocally in the fourth clause of that document. The clause specifies that the subdelegate must not only personally supervise the election of indian authorities, but also preside over them. Furthermore,

> it is the subdelegates' duty[,] which as an express charge from his Majesty they must never neglect[,] *not to allow the Yndians to assemble on their own for the election* of[,] and to actually elect the officials of their republic, and when it is time for these assemblies on the days and in the towns that are accustomed to having them, concerning which there shall be no innovations, *my subdelegate shall always attend them, and preside over them*, and only because of a legitimate impediment may some other Spaniard be appointed commissioner for this purpose, without this condition, any elections that take place shall be null and void and I shall be informed thereof.[98]

Thus, the law granted subdelegates a not inconsiderable power over indian communities, whose margin of political autonomy remained legally curtailed, not coincidentally, starting with the backlash from the Túpac Amaru rebellion.[99] Governors, for their part, represented a much more complex category. In accordance with colonial legislation from the end of the eighteenth century, "governor" was but another name for the mayor of indians.[100] However, at the onset of the Republic, "governor" was the name given to the former subdelegate.[101] A similar complexity appears in connection with mayors or *alcaldes*. There was the "mayor of indians," established early in the colonial period as the maximum authority over indian communities or ayllus that had been grouped together in *reducciones*. But there was also the "mayor of Spaniards" (see chapter 5). To further complicate matters, the term *alcaldes mayores* (high indian magistrates) was sometimes employed as a synonym for *corregidor*;[102] and although the term *corregidor* may have fallen into disuse by the early nineteenth century, not unlikely it still had a certain resonance.

In conferring upon Leandro the title of subdelegate, Huachaca was delegating a position hitherto reserved for Spaniards under the colonial state to a man whom the Republic considered an indígena.[103] The language of the old bureaucratic hierarchies was being emulated, but the content was substantially different. It is no accident that the documents called the main headquarters the Prefecture of Luis Pampa and on a few occasions even the Royal Prefecture of Luis Pampa![104] The ambiguity, far from diminishing, reinforces the clarity of the intent. The subdelegate, who during the Republic would become the subprefect, was after all subordinate to the intendant, who during the Republic would become the prefect; and, by law subdelegates were appointed by intendants. This in fact is what Huachaca (who was a general, as prefects used to be) did with Leandro. If Huachaca's functions were similar to those of the (colonial) intendant and, therefore, of those of the republican prefect, it was only to be expected that his headquarters should be a prefecture; likewise, if his slogan was the defense of the king, "royal prefecture" was a fitting title.[105]

The nature of the powers with which Huachaca invested Leandro parallels the type of powers that the Directions of 1784 established for subdelegates: to look after "public cleanliness," to tend to the preservation of bridges and roads and "public order," to assure that "in the territories there are neither vagabonds nor idle folks, nor people with unwholesome diversions."[106] In designating him both governor and mayor, however, Huachaca endowed the position with an ambiguity that could only enhance the range of Leandro's powers.[107] For while the term *subdelegate* did not lend itself to any misunderstanding, *governor* and *mayor* did; they were multivalent terms: they could designate any one of a wide range of offices, including that of *alcaldes vara*, or indian mayors.

The theme is crucial: Leandro's appointment created a position that united the powers of the colonial subdelegate, the mayor of Spaniards, and those of the governor, or mayor of indians. The post had few, if any, precedents in colonial history. By means of his order that Leandro "rule and govern all individuals of this gorge, *Spaniards as well as natives*," Huachaca brought about the convergence, in a single individual, of functions that were hierarchically delimited in colonial law, not only administratively but also ethnically.[108] The subdelegate was a colonial functionary: his realm belonged within the republic of Spaniards, which included creoles and could include mestizos, yet he also had authority over the republic of indians.[109] The governor, or "indian mayor," on the other hand, was an ethnic authority: his powers were confined to the republic of indians and, more specifically, to an indian village, or the ayllu(s) within a village. This division did not exist in the bureaucracy of Uchuraccay. Leandro was not the alcalde de españoles the Huanta hacendados were requesting in 1819: he was a subdelegate with the powers of a mayor (with all the ambiguity that this implies).[110] A Quechua-speaking muleteer thus came to occupy, thanks to the heterodox practices condoned by the Uchuraccay bureaucracy, the same post that only eight years earlier had been held by the white patrician Lazón. What is more, Leandro was not the only one to hold this position.[111]

The magnitude of the upheaval that the Iquichano insurrection visited upon Huantan society should now be more visible, and so should the error of viewing the phenomenon as an effort to restore the legal fictions of the "old regime." For, in addition to nullifying the ethnic hierarchy inherent in the colonial order, the Uchuraccay government broke with a post–Tupac Amaru colonial legislation that insisted that indians be supervised by Spanish or creole officials, especially in regard to the subdelegate.[112] A subdelegate could now be an indian, a Leandro or an Ynga. In other words, the Uchuraccay government rendered obsolete the imperial legal fiction separating society into two republics (indians / Spaniards), each with its own laws and one subordinated to the other. If indian elements enjoyed a de facto predominance, they were not thought of as being separate. Indians, Spaniards, and mestizos were all part of the same political and legislative universe, perhaps because, after all, they also participated in the same economic circuits and lived in contact with one another.[113]

In short, what the rebels of Uchuraccay proposed through the eloquent coarseness of their lexicon, the meaning and logic of their appointments, and the force of their deeds was something conceivably much more subversive than the preeminence of "indian" elements: the dissolution of ethnicities. It proved to be subversive because any ordainment of the mere superiority of things indian would have meant nothing more than an inversion of existing hierarchies and legal structures. By contrast, the dissolution of ethnicities implied a new order, the laws for which did not yet exist or were still being formulated. Moreover, this new order was more in keeping with local, re-gional, and national everyday political practices than any legal fiction could have possibly been. Unmistakably, this adaptation and approximation of rebel practices and discourse to the political realities of Huanta contributed to the legitimacy of the rebellion's leaders and to their success in retaining power.

A monarchist rebellion with restorationist pretensions thus managed to undermine the bases of the colonial order in a way that the Republic itself had not. There was little defense of the "old regime" here; there was little of the "naive monarchism" and redemptory messianism (or some alleged "conserva-tive" and "retrograde" ideology) that many have associated with the monar-chist sympathies of the peasants and rural poor in other contexts.[114] Nor was there much of the "ethnic hatred" (indians against whites) that others have perceived behind the defense of the king in the great Andean rebellions of the eighteenth century.[115]

7

The Plebeian Republic

In 1838, on passing through that location [the Huanta punas], the Protector Grand Marshal General Santa Cruz presented a general's uniform to one indian Huachaca.—*El Debate*, November 6, 1896

The Huanta rebels' failed assault on Ayacucho in November 1827 marked the beginning of the end of the restorationist venture. Following this setback, the rebels retreated to the punas, where the most resolved among them would continue to do battle throughout the ensuing months. Others, however, began to turn themselves in, enticed by the pardons the government offered to those who surrendered. Some of the most outspoken rebel caudillos were in this group, including Pascual Arancibia, Tadeo Choque, Antonio de la Barreda, and Juan Ramos, all of whom, after being interrogated, were set free. By June 1828, after enduring seven months of raids and persecutions, fifty people were captured in the *ceja de selva* on the banks of the Apurímac, among them some of the foremost rebel leaders.

Most of the European chiefs, including Nicolás Soregui and Francisco Garay, were sentenced to exile; the cleric Francisco Pacheco was excommunicated; Huantan hacendados and muleteers like Esteban Meneses received prison sentences of various lengths. "Indians" taken prisoner were sentenced to military service, for, according to the paternalist mentality of the time, they were not deemed responsible for their actions. This "leniency" toward those regarded as indian was, however, deceiving, if the case of Manuel Leandro, who fell within this category, serves as an example. Leandro, the landless muleteer and coca grower who served in the government at Uchuraccay as a tithe collector, governor, and subdelegate, was publicly flogged upon being captured and then tried and sentenced to serve in the army's Division of the North.[1] Remarkably, however, most of the Peruvian-born high commanders, secretaries, and active supporters of the rebellion were ultimately pardoned, either by commutation of their death sentences or by reduction of their prison terms. Moreover, only a few years later some were actively engaged in the public life of Huanta, not a few of them occupying public office. This was not the fate of most Spaniards, even those who had played minor roles in the rebellion, for, according to the emerging anti-Spanish rhetoric of the newly founded Republic, Spaniards deserved no mercy. Yet some, undoubtedly the wealthiest and most established, escaped such retribution. Juan Cantón, for example, one of the most committed and by all appearances the wealthiest hacendado of the rebellion was ultimately pardoned.[2]

The most influential of the peasant leaders, General in Chief Antonio Abad Huachaca, neither surrendered nor was captured. Together with his fellow general Mariano Méndez, he was seen walking about the streets of Huanta early in 1830 with impunity and protected by guards. The department's prefect, Colonel Juan Antonio Gonzales, received reports that Huachaca and Méndez had set up permanent residence in Huanta and that "from there, escorted by six men, they go to Carhuaurán [sic] (and who knows where else in the Punas) to form clandestinely what they call their cabildos, or their infernal juntas, whose results are easy to foresee."[3] The prefect, perceiving some "haughtiness among the indigenous highlanders," attributed it to Huachaca's and Méndez's frequent visits to town.[4] That very same year he issued an edict offering two thousand pesos to anyone who captured the two caudillos alive — but to no avail. Three years later he was killed in a new insurrection.

Prefect Colonel Gonzales's uneasiness about Huachaca's and Méndez's presence in town was probably warranted. But he incorrectly targeted them as being the chief source of unrest because during those turbulent years of the Republic, plots and conspiracies were being cooked up more often than not within military circles. Those who killed Gonzales were not the *montonero* leaders he was so intent on capturing but more intimate enemies: a group of officers in the Ayacucho garrison. The prefect was in fact murdered during an anti-Gamarrista military mutiny of July 1833, which passed into history as "the revolution of the Callao Battalion."[5] Yet newer waves of unrest were to ravage Ayacucho, some of them involving the so-called Iquichanos. But the new unrest, which no longer bore restorationist aspirations, would not be alien to the ambitions of the national *caudillos* and the various political factions striving for state power. In this chapter I look at this new turmoil, in particular at the novel set of relations that the onetime royalist peasants of Huanta established with the *caudillista* state.

How did Huanta peasants and their montonero leaders manage not only to adapt and relate to, but also to coexist with a state they had once so blatantly rejected? What impact did the monarchist rebellion and subsequent confrontations between caudillos striving for state power have in the life and political consciousness of Ayacucho villagers? These are the guiding questions of this chapter. My answers will take two directions: first, the military pacts established between national caudillos and former royalist montoneros; second, the peaceful and legal means by which community peasants presented their claims to the state. Military and peaceful approaches did not, however, necessarily exclude one another. The peasants who sought legal and peaceful solutions in many cases turned out to be the same ones who had been involved in armed conflicts. Their legal claims are revealing precisely because they disclose their perception of the role they had performed in those conflicts.

At the center of this analysis are the peasants and montoneros of Huanta who took part in the monarchist uprising and who subsequently engaged in a series of politico-military alliances with the national state. However, peasants who fought against them are no lesser protagonists. The La Mar government's defeat of the 1826–28 uprising was mainly owing to the support of the inhabitants of the provinces of Huamanga and Cangallo, to the south of Huanta, as well as of towns in Huanta province itself, in the southeastern district of San Miguel (an area which today lies in the province of La Mar). Understanding their voices is essential to grasping both the meaning and consequences of the monarchist rebellion and subsequent caudillo confrontations in the region and, more broadly, the role played by rural populations in the making of the early republican state.

Military Ways: The President and the Montoneros

In those days, it was impossible for the Peruvian military to be subdued.
—Heinrich Witt, *Diario*

Two critical moments marked the 1830s in Peru. The first was the civil war of 1834, which pitted the armies of the recently elected provisional president, General Luis José Orbegoso, against those of Marshal Agustín Gamarra, the outgoing president. Gamarra launched a full-scale war against Orbegoso after failing to wrest command from him in an aborted and highly unpopular coup.

We shall call this moment "the guerrillas of 1834." The second moment took place a few years later, in the context of the Peruvian-Bolivian Confederation (1836–39).

In the early days of the Republic, guerrillas were irregular armies made up of armed civilians who usually fought alongside the regular army. This form of combat originated with the Independence wars. Although the terms *montonera* and *guerrilla* were used somewhat interchangeably during the Independence wars, in the 1830s they started to acquire different meanings. During that decade, montoneras (bands of armed men) and montoneros (the men who belonged to them) were most commonly associated with banditry, revolution, and rebelliousness, and sometimes they were even linked to liberals by conservative politicians. To put it differently, the term *montonera* usually stood for bands of armed men acting either on their own or alongside local powers, whereas the term *guerrilla* was most commonly reserved for irregular armies acting as auxiliary forces of the regular army, that is, as allies of the state—a far cry from the present-day concept of guerrilla. Although the armed groups that fought in Huanta during the civil war functioned as a guerrilla force insofar as they supported the elected president, Orbegoso, they also exhibited some of the features of montoneras. Hence, whenever appropriate, I shall also refer to them as montoneros.

The Guerrillas of 1834

For the first time, in a street fight, the people had defeated the army.
—Jorge Basadre, *Historia de La República*, 1983

In December 1833 the presidency of Agustín Gamarra was coming to an end. Beleaguered during his term in office by seventeen conspiracies and uprisings, eight of them in 1833 alone, including one in Ayacucho,[6] Gamarra was stepping down. The fact that his four-year term (1829–33) had expired as scheduled can be considered a political success, given how unusual it then was for presidents to complete their terms of office. Yet the number of upheavals he faced suggests at the same time that the stability achieved during his tenure came not without political cost. Shortly after being elected provisional president by the National Convention on December 20, 1833, General Luis José Orbegoso took office.[7] Politically, Orbegoso was backed by Peru's first generation of doctrinaire liberals (Francisco Javier de Luna Pizarro, Francisco de Paula Gonzales

General Agustín Gamarra, by an unknown artist. Reproduced with permission from the Museo Nacional de Arqueología, Antropología e Historia del Perú, Lima. *Photograph by Daniel Giannoni.*

Vigil, and Francisco Javier Mariátegui), who stressed the primacy of law over the will of the executive and the importance of keeping a balance between the state powers. Gamarra, by contrast, the epitome of military authoritarianism, was supported by conservatives, who endorsed thoroughly authoritarian principles and stressed the need for "order" and a strong executive (José María Pando, Bartolomé Herrera, Felipe Pardo y Aliaga).[8]

During his presidency, Gamarra had established a policy of prebends among the military, which, coupled with his notorious disregard for the Congress and the constitution, had allowed him to retain power notwithstanding escalating opposition. Gamarra rewarded loyalty with promotions and high salaries, allowing provincial chiefs relative freedom as long as they remained submissive to his government. His methods led to the formation of what historian

Jorge Basadre has called a "military aristocracy"; during his administration the military attained unprecedented status in public life.[9] Although by the end of his term it was evident that Gamarra had made many enemies, the military oligarchy that he had created was prepared to back any attempts to perpetuate his presidential power. On January 3, 1834, less than two weeks after Orbegoso had taken office, Gamarra orchestrated a coup that ousted him and installed General Pedro Bermúdez as provisional head of the Peruvian state. But the coup proved highly unpopular, occasioning popular protests in Lima in which multitudes confronted the military in the streets. So strong was the popular mobilization that it forced the putschist military out of Lima. "For the first time, in a street fight, the people had defeated the army,"[10] wrote Basadre, who saw this as the first popular mobilization against militarism in the history of Peru.[11] On January 29, 1834, Orbegoso, who had taken refuge in Callao, returned triumphantly to the capital preceded by a group of montoneros and swept along by the din of its inhabitants.[12]

But Gamarra did not concede defeat. Acknowledging his failure in Lima, he launched a war against Orbegoso in the countryside. Orbegoso organized his forces. In command of his armies were some of the most prestigious veterans of the Independence wars, including generals Guillermo Miller and Mariano Necochea as well as the ex-prefect of Ayacucho Domingo Tristán, also a veteran. In addition to their experience in commanding guerrillas, these officers were aided by the popular support shown their cause among the civilian populations, whereas Gamarra had force on his side. Prefects loyal to him included those from Puno, Cuzco, Ayacucho, and some from the north, all of them military officers.[13] By mid-March of 1834, Miller's guerrillas had dealt Gamarra's forces an important defeat at Huaylacucho (in the present-day department of Huancavelica), forcing them to retreat toward Ayacucho city. Tristán, writing later from Lunahuaná, in the sierra of Lima, also reported on the positive response he received in the towns of Viñac, Chupamarca, and Turpo, situated in the highlands of Lima and in the current department of Huancavelica.[14] Keenly aware of the tenacity and military prowess of Huanta peasants, the Orbegosista generals were no less mindful of the advantages that could be accrued from winning them over to their camp, now that the Gamarrista forces were nearing Ayacucho. Forgetting, whether genuinely or not, whatever contempt they may have felt for the Huanta peasants in the past, Orbegoso and his generals requested their support in the most deferential terms, as a series of letters they addressed to the chiefs of the formerly monarchist montoneros demonstrate. In addition to praising their bravery, the generals insisted on the legitimacy of the Orbegosista struggle and the urgency of its mission for "saving the nation" from falling into the tyrant Gamarra's hands. The state, which by way of its highest representatives had until very recently mocked the military ranks that the Huanta montoneros claimed to have received from the king, now granted them humble recognition. Given their eloquence and uniqueness as historical documents, these letters deserve extensive citation. Take, for instance, President Orbegoso's appeal to Tadeo Choque:

Sr Dn. Tadeo Choque:
Dear Sir, although you have been living in retirement, word has reached you of the criminal conduct of Gamarra and Bermudes, who, by *attacking the law*, have incited a revolution which has done immense harm to the Patria. Having been named President of the Republic, I have not ceased to do everything in my power to reestablish order and punish the seditionists. I have relied on the opinion of the people, whose good sense has led them to side with justice, and I am certain that the result cannot but be favorable. It is essential, then, that you take advantage of this opportunity, as you have done to win the gratitude of your fellow countrymen, and *make yourself worthy of the rewards which the Patria grants to those who render it distinguished service*. You must use the influence which you have among your compatriots to make them participate actively against the subversives, blocking their communications, depriving them of resources, and surprising and attacking them, so that they find no repose, while I advance with the Army, which you will soon see. I hope that you, who have already on other occasions displayed your bravery, will employ it now that you have the opportunity to fight on behalf of *so just a cause* . . . SS. L. J. Orbegoso.[15]

In a previous letter dated March 14, General Blas Cerdeña likewise implored the unyielding Antonio Huachaca to lend his support to Obregoso. Huachaca had become a highly esteemed leader among the Huantinos because, unlike Choque, he never allowed himself to be seduced by the pardons offered at the time of the monarchist rebellion. Cerdeña addressed Huachaca as *"don"* and "Sir Major Colonel" (*Señor Mayor Coronel don*); he urged him to join the fight to defeat the "tyrant" Gamarra and concluded by announcing that "[he] who holds the greatest esteem for you, would have the satisfaction of greeting and meeting you. Your humble servant, Q.B.S.M. B. Cerdeña."[16] The acronym Q.B.S.M. (*que besa su mano*, that is, "he who kisses your hand") was a gracious formalism of the period, but a mere six years earlier it would have been unthinkable for a government authority to have used it to address Huachaca. General Miller, the Independence hero who, unlike Cerdeña, was personally acquainted with the Iquicha montoneros, having met them on the battlefield, implored them in similar terms:

> Brave Iquichanos:
> The enemies of the Nation, the subversives Bermudes and Gamarra, are fleeing in terror to your lands, having been taught a harsh lesson at the Huipacha bridge on the 24 and 25 [of March]. The victorious troops under my command are pursuing them, and I, who know you and remember your bravery, do not doubt that you will spare no pains to hinder their shameful flight. So cooperate in their extermination and the fruit of your labor will be the restoration of the peace and tranquility they have stolen, sparing yourselves the evils of war in which they wish to involve you. You *shall make yourselves worthy of the Nation's gratitude* as well as the admiration with which your old friend Guillermo Miller looks upon you. Lloyla Pampa [Lloclla Pampa], March 29, 1834.[17]

Even more astounding is the letter addressed by the ex-prefect Domingo Tristán to Huachaca (now signing his name as Antonio Navala Huachaca), for whom he had hitherto expressed only the greatest contempt. A now ingratiating Tristán wrote,

> Sr. Dn. José Antonio Naval [*sic*] Huachaca. My dear friend: Having been named Prefect of Ayacucho by His Excellency the President, I feel a boundless satisfaction on going to meet with *citizens so fond of their Patria's happiness*, this is the most brilliant epoch presented to us for our exertions, as we arm ourselves to destroy those villains Gamarra and Bermudes and their vile henchmen, very soon they will reach those surroundings with five or six thousand men, and all the traitors will disappear from among us. He who places this in your hands shall instruct you in all the particulars of what I have said to you. Regards to all our dear friends, tell them that all are in my heart and I long only to embrace them in my arms, your true friend, D. Tristán.[18]

Tristán's letter, dated in Lunahuaná on March 4, 1834, is the earliest of the series quoted above. Whether Huachaca answered it is hard to tell. But only two days later, possibly before he had seen it (and surely before the other letters were written), Huachaca and other montonero chiefs from the punas, in tandem with the authorities and *vecinos* of Huanta, had already cast their lots with Orbegoso and were rallying their forces to defend Ayacucho from the impending invasion by Gamarra's troops. By means of two separate but evidently well-coordinated documents, referred to by their authors as "acts," the montoneros of Uchuraccay, on the one hand, and the civilian authorities and *vecinos notables* (notable residents) of the *villa* of Huanta, on the other, appointed the Huanta hacendado José Urbina as their supreme commander. Urbina was appointed first by the montoneros, "General Don José Antonio Naval [sic] Huachaca, Colonel Don Tadeo Choque, and Lieutenant Colonel Don Mariano Mendes" through an act signed at the "Headquarters at Uchuraccay" on March 6, 1834. Citing "citizen Urbina's publicly known services in defense of the Avenging Law," Huachaca and his associates proclaimed him "Commander General of Army [sic]."[19] Two days later, on March 8, the governor, a group of municipal authorities, and other vecinos notables of the villa of Huanta met in the town of Luricocha, in the vicinity of Huanta, to endorse the appointment of Urbina as chief commander made by the "señores Generals, commanders and other individuals of the punas of Yquicha." In addition to recognizing Urbina's military authority, Huantan authorities and vecinos named him "Commander in Chief of the Province." Proclaiming their "blind faith" in Urbina, they likewise authorized him to "make the invasions he may find convenient, timely and necessary . . . in order to destroy and harass the enemies [the armies of Gamarra, which were already occupying Huanta and Ayacucho]."[20] They also pledged their "voluntary support to the competent authority elected by the National Convention [Orbegoso]" and their commitment to "defend the laws at whatever cost." Finally, they committed themselves "to sacrific[e] their lives and interests, if need be, so as to save the nation from the peril that endangers it."[21] The document was signed by twelve individuals, including the secretary, Rafael de Castro.

Unlike the men who signed the act of Uchuraccay, most of those who endorsed the pronouncement of Luricocha had not been involved (at least, not openly) in the monarchist rebellion.[22] Don José Urbina was a twenty-eight-year-old hacendado and captain in the Civic Militias of Huanta. At the time of

Abandoned house in Luricocha, decorated with early nineteenth-century paintings. It probably belonged to one of the hacendados or "notables" of the town. *Photograph by author, ca. 1994.*

the monarchist rebellion he had been a member of Huanta's city council (a *regidor,* or alderman) remaining loyal to the government.[23] Nevertheless, he was evidently held in high esteem by both the montoneros and the notables of Huanta. Although Huantinos had appointed him as a military and political authority, Urbina's main functions were apparently financial. In fact, he became the main provisioner and coordinator of supplies for the guerrillas. He committed his own resources, which he would later reclaim from the state, to the acquisition of arms, munitions, food, and sometimes clothes for the guerrillas. Additionally, he handed out stipends for soldiers, officers, messengers, and even spies. Urbina also siphoned off resources from other providers and hacendados for the war effort, including livestock, horses, coca leaves, food, and money, with the understanding that should their cause result in victory they would be reimbursed by the state; only those indebted to the state were ineligible for repayment. The army raised by the Huantinos on this occasion numbered over four thousand individuals at a cost of 3,262 pesos, 519 of which were provided in currency by Urbina, the rest coming from in-kind and monetary payments by other suppliers.[24] This army was larger than the one that rallied around the monarchist cause and operated beyond the boundaries of Huanta province, venturing into Huamanga and several towns in the neighboring department of Huancavelica.

And it proved successful. By mid-March, taking advantage of the absence of General José María Frías, the Gamarrista prefect of Ayacucho, the Iquichanos, as the army of montoneros was constantly referred to, seized the capital city and embarked on a string of military victories that would result in the final defeat of Gamarra's forces in Huanta and Ayacucho.[25] These successes ultimately strengthened Orbegoso's position nationwide, ending the civil war, albeit temporarily, early in May. Once again, Orbegoso returned to the presidential palace in Lima amidst enthusiastic expressions of support.

The Uchuraccay montoneros and the Huanta people in general had played a central role in restoring Orbegoso to power following Gamarra's coup, and that naturally earned them the government's gratitude. The first words of praise on record came from an unlikely source. On May 30, 1834, Domingo Tristán, back in charge of the prefecture of Ayacucho, wrote an official letter to the minister of war "applauding the laudable conduct and services that *citizens* Huachaca, Mendez, and Choque have lent to the *just cause*" and expressing his willingness to "lend whatever assistance necessary to these individuals so that they may proceed to the capital to introduce themselves to His Excellency the Council of Government."[26] The montonero chiefs, now (tellingly) treated as citizens, may in fact have reported to the Council of Government in Lima, as Tristán suggested, although I have no proof of this not unlikely encounter. But one thing known for sure is that the government staged at least one ritual act of recognition for the montoneros, the initiative coming from the president himself. As part of a trip he took to southern Peru toward the end of 1834, Orbegoso paid a visit to Huanta, where he was received with lavish celebrations. At a banquet offered in his honor, the president met with the authorities and other notables from the area as well as with "the Iquichano chiefs whom he feted, and he also promised to take charge of the education of Huachaca's son."[27] Early the next day, as he was preparing to set off for Ayacucho city, the president, in the words of the chaplain accompanying him, "missed the Iquichano indian Huachaca, who disappeared, believing no doubt that he [Huachaca] might be done a disservice in Ayacucho."[28]

Beyond its purely anecdotal interest, the encounter between the montonero chief and the president of the Republic is significant. The president wished to reward the montonero and then "missed him." But the montonero had "disappeared." Huachaca apparently did not wish to engage in a "classic" cliental relationship with Orbegoso. Orbegoso likely offered to take charge of Huachaca's son's education because he would not have dared offer him, an illiterate Quechua-speaking *arriero* from the punas, a high post in the public administration or the army (not uncommon political prebends in those days). Huachaca undoubtedly knew how to profit from gestures of appreciation conferred upon him by high authorities; a case in point is his consistent use of the title general, allegedly given to him by a viceroy, and to this we shall return. But being subservient was not part of his character, and even if he were fond of the president, experience had taught him to be wary of easy praise. Perhaps most importantly, the president's "reward" may not have seemed particularly flattering to Huachaca. On the contrary, Orbegoso's offer to educate his son implied that Huachaca's son was deficiently educated or that Huachaca was not "fit" to undertake the task himself. Orbegoso's chaplain, José María Blanco, referred to Huachaca quite derogatorily as a "drunkard" and to the Iquichano chiefs in general as "vicious and degraded indians," "murderers," and "professional thieves."[29] The president's "recompense," in other words, implicitly conveyed a sense of cultural and even moral hierarchy that Huachaca may well not have been willing to accept. Although there is obviously no way to know how Huachaca actually felt about Orbegoso, one may picture the following scenario in reinforcement of this interpretation. Would the president have made Urbina the same offer he made Huachaca? Most likely not, because the president's expectation in the case of Urbina, a hacendado, a wealthy person, and a "vecino notable" from Huanta, would have been that his sons' education was guaranteed by Urbina's economic, cultural, intellectual, and social standing. Indeed, though Urbina was not, to my knowledge, symbolically rewarded for having played such a prominent role in the organization and funding of the army that backed Orbegoso in Ayacucho, he did eventually take a post in the provincial bureaucracy as the *apoderado fiscal* of Huanta (that is, the officer in charge of assessing the taxes) by express recommendation of General Tristán.[30]

Yet regardless of how much Huachaca, his peers, and followers may have appreciated Orbegoso, their support for him was rooted in causes that transcended their expectation of paternalistic recompense. In fact, their support stemmed from deeper political experiences and understandings. Huantans were well aware that Orbegoso, his upper-class creole social origins notwithstanding, was aligned with the liberals, and liberals were known (and even

jeered at by conservatives) for their willingness and ability to establish effective political alliances with marginal sectors of society, including bandits and
montoneros.[31] Secondly, and related to this, Orbegoso's newly inaugurated
government represented for Huantinos a hopeful alternative to the "feudal
despotism" that Gamarra had instituted (or condoned) in Ayacucho.[32] Indeed,
for most of Gamarra's term, the civilian authorities of Huanta, including
governors and municipal officials, were constantly harassed, bypassed, or ignored by the political authorities appointed by Gamarra, invariably military
officers; these included the prefect (the highest political authority of a department and usually a colonel or general) and the subprefect (the prefect's provincial representative, also a military officer). Even before the guerrillas of 1834,
Huanta's town council was expressing its repudiation of Gamarra's government through acts of what for lack of a better term we shall call "civil disobedience." In 1831, when Gamarra visited the town, municipal authorities refused to welcome him. As a result, they were imprisoned by the department
prefect and the province subprefect for the "disrespect with which they treated
the First Chief of the Republic, without even coming to receive him when he
entered town, refraining themselves from paying their respects to the president, not even showing up at the door of the president's lodging."[33] By the end
of Gamarra's term in office, it was becoming evident that the military too felt
alienated, and not only in Huanta. In July 1833, as mentioned, a group of
soldiers and officers from the Callao Batallion who were stationed at the
Ayacucho city barracks mutinied and killed the department prefect. They
alleged he was trying to fix the upcoming popular presidential election for
Gamarra.[34]

Orbegoso's administration did not last long enough to allow one to determine whether his honeymoon with the Iquichano chiefs would have endured.
He transferred his "presidential powers" to Marshal Andrés de Santa Cruz in
the midst of a new political crisis in June 1835. Yet in the "real" world of politics
(that is, beyond political ritual), things looked less promising for Huantinos
and particularly for tribute-paying indians. In the highest echelons of Orbegoso's administration, a political double standard was the order of the day.
Two and a half months after Tristán delivered his letter of March 4 to Huachaca, the one in which he called him a "friend" and his followers "citizens so
fond of their Patria's happiness," and not long after "applauding the laudable
conduct and services that citizens Huachaca, Mendez, and Choque have lent
the just cause," the very same Tristán was frustrated at being unable to deal

with the department's "deplorable situation," a state of affairs he attributed to the "Iquichanos' demoralization and my inability, for lack of armed forces, to suppress the excesses which those barbarians are committing daily, and nip in the bud the corrupting seed of scandals which could later produce baneful results for the patria."[35] Then the subprefect of Huanta, Manuel Segundo Cabrera, presented a report to the government suggesting measures "to instill order in the towns of Iquicha."[36] He regretted that, "made arrogant by the services they just rendered to the nation," they "had become too uppity [*absolutos*] and among other favors they demand to be freed from tribute for five or six years."[37] Soon thereafter, Tristán reported once again on the "ruins to which the province of Huanta ha[d] been reduced because of the Iquichanos' obstinate refusal to pay their taxes and the bad example which has spread among the neighboring towns."[38]

Exemption from the indian tax, or *contribución personal de indígenas* (sometimes still called *tributo*), was commonly offered during the Independence wars by military chiefs in the field as a means of enticing rural populations to join the fight, and it continued to be used by various caudillos during the ensuing civil wars. Tax relief was granted on the grounds that military action was an alternative form of rendering services to the nation, that is, of complying with a citizen's duty—or so the military commanders strived to convince the peasants. Not uncommonly, tax relief offers were verbal, which hampered peasants' attempts to ensure they were met. The Orbegosista generals in all likelihood made such verbal offers to Huanta peasants during the civil war of 1834. At any rate, the policy of tax exemptions continued under Santa Cruz— an Orbegoso ally—during the wars leading to the Peruvian-Bolivian Confederation. A decree from the highest level of government (*decreto supremo*) of November 1835, at which time Santa Cruz controlled part of Peru, exempted the communities of Huanta from payment of their contribuciones. The new prefect of Ayacucho, the Santacrucista Francisco Méndez, instructed the subprefect of Huanta to "inform these brave men that they remain exempt from the personal tax so long as they adhere to the same conduct as that which they have just displayed in teaching a bitter lesson to those rebels [apparently, Gamarristas] who sought to overrun them."[39]

From this perspective, Huanta peasant requests to be exempted from contribuciones and their refusal to pay them were not unilateral acts of "stubbornness" or "uppityness," as the official sources described them. Peasants had not invented the policy of tax exemptions; they were simply demanding that the state live up to its promises. Put another way, they had assimilated what had become a de facto state policy toward the rural masses in the founding years of the Republic and were demanding political consistency from the state.

In brief, Orbegoso's short-lived provisional government was aware of the need to reward Huanta's montonero chiefs for the services they rendered to the state. But as to the tribute-paying peasants who formed the bulk of their armies, there seems to have been an assumption that they were merely performing their duty and thus did not need to be recompensed. Hence, while the government was calling on peasants to brandish their weapons against "the nation's enemies," on the one hand, it was demanding that they be compliant, on the other. In reality, the two appeals were mutually incompatible.

The excesses that Tristán attributed to the peasants in the letter quoted above consisted not only of their refusal to pay the contribución, but of the appropriation of the product of the tithes which, according to the tithe collector, peasants had seized for themselves. These disturbances occurred between March and May of 1834, that is, at the same time that the government was sponsoring guerrilla movements against Gamarra and Bermúdez. Manuel Santa Cruz de la Vega, the tithe collector involved, denounced the peasants in the following terms: "The Yquicha indígenas, authorized by their spokesmen Huachaca, Mendes, Choque, and Huaman, took all of the *arrobas* of coca through a public plunder, on alarm over the generals Bermúdez and Frias [the prefect of Ayacucho] last March."[40] Furthermore, he declared, "The Iquicha punas produce nothing but potatoes and sheep and cattle, the tithe of which was mostly collected by the self-styled generals Huachaca, Mendes, Choque, and Huamán, by claiming that since the tithes belonged to the state, and since they defended the nation, they had the right to take hold of all its resources *to uphold and defend the laws.*"[41]

Santa Cruz de la Vega was describing a familiar scenario: peasants were appropriating tithes again in March, just as they had during the monarchist rebellion. But this time the political circumstances and justification were different. Huanta villagers had taken up arms not to fight but to defend the state—a state that calling them citizens had summoned them to take up arms to defend the "Patria," the "nation," and "its laws." Thus, the peasants' response to Santa Cruz de la Vega was a well-reasoned one. Keenly aware that "the tithes belonged to the state," they felt entitled to them nevertheless, for, as they put it, "they defended the nation [and] they had the right to take hold of all its resources to uphold and defend the laws." Bearing in mind that, since the founding of the Republic, peasants had rendered the state much more than they had received in return—in the form of contribución de indígenas, tribute, military service, and even unpaid labor—it was only to be expected that in the midst of the turmoil of war, a war in which their lives and resources were compromised on the state's behalf, some appropriation of the tithe produce occur. And yet, what lent their actions even greater legitimacy—and cautions one not to think of the peasants as undertaking a "public plunder," as the official tax collector put it—is the fact the state itself had authorized José Urbina, the commander in chief of the pro-Orbegosista guerrillas, to help himself to the produce of the tithes, if need be, in order to supply his troops. This, at any rate, is what Urbina said to reassure Huachaca after a hacendado had complained that one of the commanders in Huachaca's montonera had taken several head of cattle from his hacienda. Urbina cautioned Huachaca: "He [Huachaca] and his troops should march without harming the hacendados . . . for *there are special provisions that [the guerrillas] make use of the produce from the tithes or from some state creditors for this effect.*"[42]

"Defense of the law," the other argument employed by the guerrillas to justify their seizure of tithes, had been widely invoked by the Orbegoso generals in their proselytizing campaign against Gamarra; it was probably the most easily graspable of the slogans they used to rally support. Unlike the notions of "state," "nation," and "Patria," which lent themselves to more abstract interpretations, "defense of the law" pointed to more concrete circumstances in the context of the Orbegoso-Gamarra civil war. It did not take a well-educated person to identify Gamarra as the lawbreaker and Orbegoso as the keeper of the law: attention to national events and minimal exposure to military arbitrariness at the local level would have sufficed. "Defense of the law" had also served as a familiar slogan for the montoneros of Huanta at the time of the monarchist rebellion. One of Huachaca's signatures at that time read, "Brigadier and General in Chief of the Royal Army of Volunteer Upholders of the Law of the field of Yquicha."[43] By 1834 the signature had evolved to reflect new political circumstances and causes that were defended by the montoneros. In addition to dropping of the reference to "Royal Army," the most significant innovation in Huachaca's titles was the addition of the word *citizen*, a neologism concomitant with the birth of the Republic, and one used repeatedly by the Orbegosista generals to address the montoneros. By 1834, one of Huachaca's signatures read as follows: "The citizen J. Antonio Nav. Huachaca, General in Chief of the Restorers of the Law Division of the

Valiant and Brave Equichano Defenders of the Just Cause."[44] Huachaca's titles overlapped, as well, with that of the officers who, calling themselves "The Avengers of the Law Division," mutinied in July 1833 against Gamarra in Ayacucho. Again, it is important to note that the signature employed the very same terms with which the Orbegosista generals Tristán and Miller had summoned the montoneros, as the letters quoted above show: "valiant," "brave," and "just cause."

To summarize, the facts of the civil war of 1834 reveal the Huanta montonero leaders' acute awareness of the national political process, their creative understanding and appropriation of linguistic resources ushered in by the state's incipient nationalist rhetoric, their capacity to make effective alliances with the state in concert with the urban sectors of their society (the notables and municipal authorities of Huanta), and, finally, their ability to mobilize the peasants and act in unison with them and the notables to the point of becoming a regional force with a national voice. The facts of the conflict illustrate as well the speed with which the political language generated from within the highest echelons of the state administration was effectively appropriated by the rural peoples of Huanta. Though generally illiterate and no masters of the language of power, Spanish, they were nonetheless fully able to reclaim, to the extent of seizing with their own hands, the payment that they felt entitled to in recompense for the services they had rendered to the state at a most critical moment in Peru's early state-making process.

The Peruvian-Bolivian Confederation (1836–39)

Although . . . the indian or highlander abhors serving in the militia, General Santa Cruz has managed to make them soldiers that I doubt would find match in the world with regards to sobriety, indefatigability in the marches, and resistance to all outdoors adversities. These men, certainly admired in this, make journeys of 25 to 30 leagues on the most difficult roads as are those of the sierra and on the sands of the coast; but this is not a matter of one day, they march 15, 20, and more days continuously, and after a march of 1,300 leagues . . . we have seen them as fresh and agile as though they had walked not at all. Peruvian leagues are 10 to 15,000 *varas*, and one needs to walk from sunrise to sunset to make a 14- to 18-league journey—so bad is the terrain. With regard to frugality, it should suffice to say that with a bit of toasted maize and another bit of coca, they have enough for a day, so they can carry their food for fifteen days with no difficulty. Neither rain nor cold nor heat stops them in their marches. Now, with an army that walks more than 100 leagues in four days and arrives fresh and ready to give battle, an army of whose maintenance you need not worry as long as you give a soldier 2 *reales* a day as all salary and food, and an army that will not be stopped by any obstacle, what cannot be done in any part of the world?

—Juan Espinosa to Juan Mauricio Rugendas, Arequipa, July 1, 1838

A situation similar to that of 1834 arose during the closing stages of the Peruvian-Bolivian Confederation. The Confederation was a short-lived and conflict-ridden, albeit meaningful, political experiment whereby the republics of Peru and Bolivia were merged into a single polity comprising three "confederate states": North Peru, South Peru, and Bolivia. It lasted barely three years (from February 1836 to January 1839), and its supreme chief, ideologue, and founder was the La Paz–born Marshal Andrés de Santa Cruz. Like most Peruvian military caudillos of the time, Santa Cruz had risen to prominence fighting for Spain during the wars of Independence; in 1820, he switched sides in order to join the armies of San Martín, as did many of his peers. Before Bolivia was constituted as an independent republic in 1825 and before Santa Cruz became one of its first presidents, he had been actively involved in the highest political circles in Peru and even held high office. Santa Cruz, the offspring of an Aymara *cacica* and a creole father born in Huamanga, became the head of Bolívar's Government Council in 1826 and later on ran unsuccessfully for the presidency of Peru. He then returned to his native Bolivia, where he became president. From there, he kept abreast of political events in Peru, spying where possible, lobbying when necessary, in order to make his confederation plan viable.

The idea of a confederate state unifying Peru and Bolivia was not exclusively his. Gamarra's own political career was marked by an open desire to annex Bolivia, a country he invaded on several occasions and in which he was to die in battle. But beyond the caudillos' personal ambitions, the idea of a joint state for Peru and Bolivia had been discussed in the Peruvian Congress since the late 1820s and was favored by some of the most prominent liberal congresspersons, including Luna Pizarro. Yet Santa Cruz was by far the most determined politician to push for it. The climate seemed propitious in 1835, as Peru was again being torn by civil war and found itself engulfed in one of the worst waves of anarchy in its republican history. President Orbegoso was left virtually without power after a young caudillo, Lima-born Felipe Santiago Salaverry, took over the Real Felipe fortress in a new coup in February 1835, proclaiming himself Supreme Chief of the Republic. By March of that year, parts of the country had pronounced themselves for Salaverry, while lawlessness wracked the capital city, as the self-appointed president left Lima in order to contain a wave of mutinies in the provinces. In the meantime, Gamarra continued his relentless struggle to reclaim the presidency, courting Salaverry and Santa Cruz simultaneously but ultimately turning against the latter. By February 1835, Peru had two presidents and one ex-president who was aggressively fighting his way back into power. So extreme was the anarchy that it is said that one day the famed mulatto bandit León Escobar entered the capital along with his montoneros, ousted municipal officials from their positions, and installed themselves in their place.[45]

Under these circumstances, Orbegoso, supported by a mostly liberal National Convention, extended an official invitation to Santa Cruz to enter Peru with his army in order to assist what remained of the legal Peruvian state in dealing with the internal crisis. The day Santa Cruz had been preparing for all his life had finally arrived. In July 1835, Orbegoso, "like a deposed king, passed on to Santa Cruz the insignias of his chimerical power, by transferring to him in a letter the extraordinary faculties with which he was invested."[46] Following seven months of warfare, Gamarra was defeated, Salaverry was executed, and the Peruvian-Bolivian Confederation came into being.

Despite its historic and symbolic importance, the Confederation remains a poorly known and even less understood episode in the history of Peru. The dominant interpretations in Peruvian historiography have portrayed Santa Cruz as an invader and Salaverry as a nationalist martyr, while praising Gamarra's leading role in defeating the Confederation. This interpretation was largely inspired by Santa Cruz's contemporary detractors, notably the celebrated Lima poet and writer Felipe Pardo y Aliaga, by far the most articulate and gifted of Santa Cruz's political adversaries in Peru. Like many other Lima aristocrats of his time, Pardo saw in Santa Cruz the specter of a "conquering indian," that is, one who had failed to remain in his "proper station." He spared no racist slur in casting him as a degraded and "stolid" Bolivian, guilty of being both a "foreigner" *and* an "Indian" with no right over Peruvian soil, which he and other self-proclaimed nationalists ironically referred to as "the land of the Incas." This interpretation of the Confederation as an "invasion," whose racist underpinnings I have discussed elsewhere,[47] demands qualification. There is no question that Santa Cruz had great political ambitions and never shied away from implementing draconian measures in order to meet his goals, as the events leading up to the establishment of the Confederation attest. As Basadre put it, "Those colonels, those generals felt . . . the totemic influence of Napoleon."[48] Yet the validity of labeling his armies' incursion into Peruvian soil an invasion is, at the very least, debatable, for, as mentioned above, Santa Cruz had been called in to Peru by the country's sole legally established powers. Moreover, the accusation of "foreigner" lacked substance in a time of still blurry national boundaries: several Independence heroes in Peru as well as one Peruvian president before Santa Cruz (José de la Mar) had been "foreigners" themselves.[49] Most importantly, this interpretation fails to address adequately the fact that "nationalist" resistance to the Confederation in Peru was not all that national. Just as Orbegoso had called in the Bolivian army to rescue the country from anarchy, so Santa Cruz's opponents, including both Salaverry and Gamarra, consistently relied on the Chilean army, which was to play a central part in the Confederation's ultimate defeat.[50]

The Peruvian-Bolivian Confederation project aimed at integrating the historically united territories of Peru and Bolivia through an internal market and the opening of free ports to the Pacific. It sought to restructure the old trading circuits that had joined these countries during the colonial period, while promoting free trade with the North Atlantic and the United States. In the Santa Cruz plan, "free trade" and the internal market would work in tandem to invigorate a region that for three centuries had been the economic backbone of the Spanish Empire in South America and, before the European invasion, the cradle of America's greatest civilizations. This plan was fairly well received in the southern departments of Peru, but met with resistance from the mercantile elites in Lima and along the northern coast, whose economic interests were secured by Pacific trade agreements with Chile that excluded Bolivia. The commercial arrangements that Santa Cruz's confederation threatened to dismantle were, in other words, the very same ones that Gamarra had so vigorously defended through xenophobic protectionist policies that seemed to have ultimately favored Lima and the northern coast more than his native Cuzco. And it was this "triple alliance"—of Lima and northern merchants joined by conservative politicians, Gamarra's Cuzco-centric and xenophobic aspiration to dominate the Altiplano, and Chile's economic and geostrategic interests—that would end up thwarting all of Santa Cruz's

General Andrés de Santa Cruz, by Francis Martin Drexel, ca. 1827. Reproduced with permission from the Museo Nacional de Arqueología, Antropología e Historia del Perú, Lima. *Photograph by Daniel Giannoni.*

economic and political measures. The alliance finally succeeded in defeating the Confederation on the fields of Yungay, department of Ancash, in northern Peru, in January 1839, after which Gamarra was again installed as Peru's president—though not for long. He was eventually killed in battle when he invaded Bolivia one last time in 1841.

Despite the Confederation's short-lived and conflict-ridden existence, the fact that Santa Cruz made it to power as he had envisioned and stood as supreme ruler of the Confederation for three years may well be considered a significant political achievement. To be sure, Peru's endemic factionalism assisted his success, but his strongest political asset was probably his army. Santa Cruz was ever mindful of the importance of a well-organized army in his plan for uniting Peru and Bolivia, for in the geostrategic order of things the confederation was Chile's worst fear and a source of concern for Argentina. And he had all the confidence that Bolívar notoriously lacked in native Andeans' intellectual abilities and especially in their potential as soldiers in a first-rate army.[51] When Santa Cruz followed Orbegoso's call and crossed the Peruvian border with his army of five thousand men, "he had been preparing them for years," writes Basadre.[52] Contemporaries described his armies as disciplined, indefatigable, and well equipped, while portraying Santa Cruz himself as a charismatic leader acutely concerned with the self-esteem of the rank and file, to the extent of contributing his own resources to supply uniforms for his troops. Santa Cruz also encouraged the presence of women in the army known as *rabonas* as both marital partners and cooks for the soldiers. It was said even that he would sit with the soldiers and eat the food prepared by the women. An Uruguayan officer living in Arequipa at the time of the Confederation described Santa Cruz's army as follows:

General Santa Cruz, who knows [indians] well, gives them one *peseta* (2 r.) every day, he dresses them at his own expense with a very strong, white and gray, close-woven woolen cloth, and he need not think whether the soldier eats or not, but just marches with him wherever and at whatever time. The soldier with the *peseta* he receives has enough to maintain himself and a woman of his caste. So there is no soldier who does not have one, for he who does not have one will get in trouble. These admirable women accompany the soldier in all of the troubles and hardships of a campaign. They are the army's vanguard. They are shown the location where the army is to stop at the end of the day, and they march ahead. When the soldier arrives at the encampment, after a 20-league march, he finds the food ready, eats, sleeps and before being called to continue on his route, the female companion who provided him with shelter during the night has already departed to again prepare his food for him 20 or 30 leagues farther on down. . . . The convenience that these women represent for the soldier makes them to be regarded as very useful. How many times the general in chief himself has eaten from what one of these women had cooked for her husband![53]

With all the above in mind, let us now take a look at Santa Cruz's relation to the peasants of Ayacucho and Huanta, in particular. As a veteran of Independence and a former royalist soldier himself, he was familiar with the so-called Iquichanos. As head of Bolívar's Government Council in Peru, he had personally directed the July 1826 peace negotiations with the Huanta monarchist rebels, having met with the hacendado Pascual Arancibia, a rebel caudillo with great influence among the villagers.[54] This experience, coupled with his political astuteness, made him conscious of the advantages of a possible alliance with the Huanta peasantry for his confederation project. Ayacucho constituted a strategic region in his plans, since the Pampas River basin served as a possible frontier between the hypothetical states of Northern and Southern Peru. Consequently, Santa Cruz did not lose track of Arancibia, who evidently became an agent of his in Huanta during the early 1830s.[55]

Later on, in September 1835, while serving as president of Bolivia, Santa Cruz instructed his spies regarding their role in Ayacucho: "The group which Gamarra has begun to gather there must be thrown into confusion," wrote Santa Cruz, adding that his agents must also "work to win over the party of Morochucos and Yquichanos who were always opposed to Gamarra."[56] In a subsequent letter, the Bolivian caudillo was even more emphatic: "I forbid you to proceed one step beyond the city of Ayacucho, or to use your arms against the Yquichanos, whom it is necessary to incite against Gamarra and Salaverry and to attract to our side by whatever means imaginable."[57]

Santa Cruz's plans could not have been better conceived and ended up producing their desired effect. The marshall from La Paz was able to count on Huanta peasants in the Confederation's decisive battles, retaining their loyalty even after the fall of the Confederation. But with Gamarra back in the presidency, revenge was not long in coming. Huanta villagers were persecuted; their towns were plundered and burned. It took nearly a year and much bloodshed to subdue them.

"Rabonas doing the laundry." Reproduced from
Manuel Atanasio Fuentes, *Lima. Esquisses Histo-*
riques, Statistiques, Administratives, Commerciales
et Morales (Paris: Librairie de firmín Didot,
frerés, fils & cie., 1866), 183.

Throughout the long months of resistance to Gamarra's troops and his Chilean
allies, Huanta peasants committed the same acts of defiance they had on previous
occasions: they refused to pay tribute and appropriated the produce of the tithes.
And once again, the official tithe collectors were the first ones to denounce them:

> Unfortunately it happens that the Iquichano *indíjenas* revolt, they take all
> the produce from these districts and attack the neighboring towns who are
> not in agreement with their subversive designs of denying the government's
> legitimacy and the republic's laws' authority, and they do not allow us to
> make our collection, let alone show ourselves in these places which they had
> sacked as much as they could and their eyes could see, after killing the most
> innocent there.[58]

Soldier and rabona. *Watercolor by Pancho Fierro. Reproduced with permission from the Banco Central de Reserva, Lima. Photograph by Daniel Giannoni.*

Cesilio Escobar and Domingo Cáseres, the authors of this letter to the Juez de Primera Instancia (judge of first instance), were subleasers of the tithe from Paccoracay and Rayán, in the jurisdiction of Tambo in the province of Huanta. They were not the only ones to voice such complaints in 1839. The hacendado Juan del Pozo, for example, tithe collector for the district of Aco, and several of his tithe subleasers, among them Hilario Cárdenas and Estevan Casas, "tribute-paying indígenas from the district of Tambo," also made themselves heard:

During the past two-year period of eighteen-hundred thirty-nine I, Hilario, took in sublease the tithe district named Cchachobamba, from don Juan Poso, in the amount of one-hundred forty pesos; and I, Estevan, the other district named Carhuac in thirty, both of us paying religiously during the first year of thirty-eight . . ., because we collected the grain and not the least surprise occurred in the collection of the tithe; yet in the following thirty-nine neither a single grain nor the least payment could be collected because the Iquicha dissidents established their encampments throughout the district of Aco, and in the six months that they posted themselves . . . in the district they consumed all of the grain and livestock, inundating even the town of Tambo, where they set the houses on fire and caused the havoc which to this day exists for the memory of the perversity of those defectors.[59]

It is quite likely, as these testimonies in some sense suggest, that peasant actions in 1839 exceeded the expectations of the high officers who had encouraged their mobilization, just as they had in the case of the guerrillas of 1834. The difference, however, is that in this instance the leader they supported had already been defeated, and the peasants were literally waging a war of resistance. They were not alone. They had pledged allegiance to one General Otero, a Santa Cruz loyalist who, refusing to recognize Gamarra's authority, had occupied Ayacucho city with his division.[60] In this context, the arguments given by the tithe collectors in singling out the peasants as the sole source of unrest require, once again, qualification. The peasants were not subdued until December 1839, after enduring intense persecution and engaging in violent clashes with a combined army of Chilean soldiers and Peruvian military officers loyal to Gamarra.[61]

Contributing to the villagers' capitulation was one of their own leaders: Tadeo Choque, the man who had served as general alongside Huachaca during the monarchist rebellion and as colonel during the guerrillas of 1834. At the time of the monarchist upheaval, Choque had given in to the government pardons, ultimately renouncing the enterprise (see chapter 2). On this occasion he was to switch sides again, evidently enticed by a Gamarrista chief who offered to make him "principal governor of all the punas" and seemingly a "captain" as well.[62] Thus, following his negotiations with the Gamarrista military chiefs, Choque led three hundred Huanta community peasants to the location of Yanallay, where on November 15, 1839, they swore allegiance to Gamarra's government. The event passed into history as the "Pact of Yanallay." Not long afterward, Choque assumed the duty of "picking up the arms and persecuting the caudillo Huachaca and other subalterns, who had taken refuge in the impassable *montes* [montañas] of Chunchaybamba."[63] But to no avail. Huachaca escaped once more, never to be found and never to surrender. One officer wrote, "We know for sure from reports by Choque's people that the *cabecilla* [leader] Huachaca with his sons and some fugitive Bolivians who were with him have vanished and that the Iquichano territory finds itself calm."[64]

The evidence of the inner workings of Santa Cruz's alliance with the Huanta peasants and the latter's motivations to serve in his ranks—aside from getting back at Gamarra—is not of the same caliber as that for the Huantino pact with Orbegoso. Yet there is no question that such an alliance existed. A series of violent, symbolically charged events that took place in Huanta following Santa Cruz's defeat at the battle of Yungay offer additional elements that may help us understand the extent of Huantinos' and, particularly, Huachaca's allegiance with the Confederation. Local accounts have it that Huachaca captured and killed his longtime persecutor, the subprefect of Huanta José Gabriel Quintanilla, who had joined Gamarra's side in the Confederation wars. After decapitating him, Huachaca reportedly "gave his head to the lancers of his troops. The indians then took the wretched man's body and cast it into the river. Following this, they captured the victim's wife . . . and marched on to Huanta."[65] The story continued in this vein:

> The dreadful procession paraded through the city's streets before the people's fear and consternation [and] amidst the acclamations to the supreme caudillo of the Iquichanos. . . . They marched in columns of four to the tunes of fifes and drums, in this order: First, the Flag of the Peruvian-Bolivian Confederation, then Quintanilla's head, affixed to the point of a spear, then the wife [of Quintanilla] Sra. Francisca Valdivia—one of the most beautiful women of the Ayacuchan aristocracy—mounting bareback a beast of burden and, at her side, General Antonio Navala Huachaca riding his famous battle horse "Rifle," then came the principal guerrilla chiefs riding the best *aguilillos* [horses], following them the infantry of the lancers and closing the parade the chivalry. They made a complete turn around the main square, firing their rifles at every corner and then fixed the head of the wretched Quintanilla at the main Church's atrium under the surveillance of guards armed with lances.[66]

There was, no doubt, an element of personal revenge in the theatrical deployment of violence that Huantan historian Luis E. Cavero describes with-

out disclosing his source. Huachaca's beheading of Quintanilla and his symbolic possession and subduing of the dead man's wife, are best understood in
light of an ongoing relationship between the two men. As the reader may
recall, Quintanilla had been a leading figure in the raids against the peasants of
Huanta when they first rebelled in the name of the king, during which he had
taken Huachaca's wife prisoner (see chapter 2). Huachaca may have sought a
political opportunity to avenge this personal offense. But the story was surely
not that simple, since the two men were bonded by more than just hatred.
They were *compadres* ("coparents"), meaning that at least one of them was
godfather of the other's child(ren), presumably Quintanilla of Huachaca's.
When one recalls that José Gabriel Túpac Amaru was also a compadre of the
very *corregidor* he was to send to the gallows not long after having dined with
him, in an act that sparked the Great Rebellion, the killing of Quintanilla does
not seem all that surprising. *Compadrazgo*, the most widespread form of ritual
kinship in the Andes, works as a "social leveler" of sorts; it entails a set of social
obligations between people of usually uneven social status and power. Quintanilla's death at the hands of Huachaca shows, no doubt, the limitations of
compadrazgo in achieving a much sought-after equilibrium between unequal
parties. Yet the very fact that the two men were linked by this relationship
challenges widespread assumptions that creole state representatives and Andean peasants belonged to two utterly unrelated and irreconcilable worlds.
Obvious as it may sound (and the relationship between Huachaca and Quintanilla is a case in point), violence ought to be considered a component of a
relationship, rather than an extraneous element that antagonizes it.[67]

In yet another way the deadly spectacle described by the anonymous witness finds analogies elsewhere. At that time, the public display of severed
heads was a widespread practice used as much for heralding victory as for
intimidating the enemy. By no means the exclusive purview of rebels in arms
or montoneros, the practice was carried out by both sides during the wars of
Independence and later on by republican authorities in their campaign against
the monarchist rebels of Huanta.[68] Finally, Huachaca's symbolic possession
and subduing of Quintanilla's wife also finds parallels in other caudillo wars in
South America.[69] By forcing the humiliated widow to ride by his side, Huachaca was asserting his manly power, thus probably eliciting the mixture of
revulsion and attraction that unrestrained uses of force not rarely provoke.
Politically, Huachaca was proclaiming with this gesture that he had, literally,
taken the place of the man who had been not only the highest politico-military

authority in Huanta province but who, moreover, embodied the party that had just claimed national victory: Gamarrismo. Thus, Huachaca's public insult reverberated beyond personal and local spheres alike.

The episode raises an important question: why did this celebration of death and victory take place under the flag of the Peruvian-Bolivian Confederation? In other words, what did the Confederation represent to the Huantinos, and why did Huachaca and his followers so staunchly support Santa Cruz?

One way to answer this question is by speculating on the material benefits that would have accrued to Ayacuchans from the Confederation. The Confederation was designed to bring new economic prosperity to the south of Peru, and in theory it was supposed to benefit Ayacucho. This was, at any rate, how it was advertised at the time.[70] In addition to lowering customs tariffs in order to expedite commerce with Bolivia, Santa Cruz foresaw the reactivation of mining in Ayacucho, virtually abandoned since the end of the colonial period. Huanta montoneros presumably were exposed to this discourse, and Santa Cruz could have resorted to it to win over their support.

Without writing off this hypothesis, one can establish with a lot more certainty the extramaterial factors that may have drawn Huantan villagers to the Bolivian caudillo. Santa Cruz, as we saw above, was keenly aware of the rank and file's needs: from food and uniforms to the company of women. Particularly evident was the personal care he took with the uniforms of the soldiers. "He dresses them at his own expense with a very strong, white and gray, close-woven cloth," wrote a witness, adding that he "has managed to make them [indians] soldiers that I doubt would find match in the world."[71] Although there is a lack of direct testimony regarding Santa Cruz's interaction with Huanta villagers, what is known about his concern for soldiers' self-esteem in general gives an idea of how such an interaction would have gone. Luckily, one eloquent anecdote bears directly on the history of Huanta and Huachaca. It is said that "in 1838 Santa Cruz, on passing through that location [the punas of Huanta], . . . presented a general's uniform to an indian Huachaca."[72] The anecdote is consistent with another testimonial, which likewise dates from the days of the Confederation: in 1836 Antonio Navala Huachaca was reportedly appointed "justice of the peace for the district of Ccarhuahurán or the area known as Iquicha."[73]

Although the report about the general's uniform hardly allows for confirmation, it is all the same quite credible. Such magnanimous gestures on the part of presidents were far from infrequent in that era, when presidents themselves conducted and supervised battles. Orbegoso, as we have seen, had sought to gratify publicly the Huanta montoneros, though his efforts proved less than successful. Politics, after all, is also—and sometimes even mainly—a matter of gestures. Bearing in mind that Huachaca held claim to the rank of General of the King's Armies since the first rebellion he had led, by giving him the uniform of a general Santa Cruz was not presenting him with anything new; rather, he was recognizing and legitimating a status and distinction Huachaca regarded himself as already possessing. Huachaca's appointment as justice of the peace held similar significance, given that he had been, as we have seen, the supreme magistrate of the courts of Uchuraccay. An appointment or a symbolic decoration did not necessarily increase the power of a montonero in his region, but it did heighten his prestige; it did not necessarily accord him additional power as much as it legitimized that which he already exerted.

Integrating the anecdote of Huachaca's uniform with the evidence attesting to Huantan villagers' support of Santa Cruz and their resistance to Gamarra's rule, one may draw the following conclusions. First, the villagers' refusal to pay their contribuciones and their appropriation of the tithes following the Confederation's defeat were, no doubt, acts of resistance. But this was not a resistance to "the state" in the abstract as much as to one of the various forms the state could take. Second, the peasants were not alone in their resistance; at least one high military officer in Ayacucho, General Otero, resisted Gamarra's victory over Santa Cruz in 1839 in equal measure. In this sense, Huantans' opposition to Gamarra in 1839 seems to have had a component similar to one that characterized their opposition to the same caudillo during the guerrillas of 1834, that is, a cross-class component. The nature of the Huanta peasants' relation with General Otero and the level of coordination they may (or may not?) have established with him remain blurry to us, but the possibility that peasants and military acted in concert against Gamarra in 1839 or, at the very least, that the peasants felt emboldened by the military's resistance cannot be discarded.

The inner workings of the Huantan–Santa Cruz alliance remain to be clarified. But one thing is certain: peasants took sides. And they did so because their experience of the state under Gamarra differed from that under Orbegoso and Santa Cruz. With the latter two, local authorities, peasants, and montoneros seem to have enjoyed a greater degree of political autonomy and legitimacy than when under the grip of Gamarra, in whose hands the state

General Andrés de Santa Cruz in old age, by an unknown artist. Reproduced with permission from the Museo Nacional de Arqueología, Antropología e Historia del Perú, Lima. *Photograph by Daniel Giannoni.*

took on a more centralized, authoritarian cast. The evident "calm" (as one testimony had it) in the Huanta punas during the Confederation years was the result of significant historical moments, such as Huachaca's acceptance of a general's uniform from the hands of Santa Cruz and his appointment as justice of the peace—that is, the moments when the supreme caudillo of Uchuraccay achieved symbolic recognition of his status, power, and military skills, as well as a concrete position in the local state administration.[74] All this reveals as much about Santa Cruz's political skills as it does about the Huanta peasant leader's aspirations. It is also significant that the most charismatic and unyielding of the Huantan montoneros, General in Chief Antonio Navala Huachaca, was not repulsed by the idea of being part of the state, just as his followers did not reject the state simply for being the state. But they were highly sensitive to the way in which the state and its caudillos responded to their needs, demands, and expectations.

Peaceful Means:
The *Caudillista* Wars in Peasant Consciousness

We, who did more than we had to (it must be said).
—The people of San Miguel and Chilcas, 1831

Thus far we have mainly referred to the leaders of the montoneras and the national caudillos. Behind them were the common villagers, a people not always eager to fight but quite aware that when they did fight they were entitled to some compensation for it. A whole series of petitions addressed by various villages to the state attest to this awareness. Although their claims were diverse, they mostly called for the fulfillment of the military commanders' promises, which usually consisted of exemptions from tribute. Yet villagers' experiences with warfare and their uses of the law were much more complex than this. The villagers' awareness of and peaceful response to the various politico-military confrontations that ensued in their region after the proclamation of Independence, including the monarchist rebellion, are illustrated in three cases that express varying degrees of peasant assimilation of political conflicts as well as the different options presented by the conflicts.

Addressed initially to prefects and intendants, that is, departmental authorities, claims initiated by the villagers not infrequently reached the highest judicial authorities in Lima, who rendered the final decision. Community petitions were drawn up chiefly by (or at least in the name of) their mayors, who represented the community or village as a whole. The petitions were presented by a single village in reference to one particular claim, but occasionally petitions emanating from various villages look very similar and can be found together in a single dossier. This phenomenon suggests that groups of communities acted in concert.

It is important to note that these claims were not necessarily presented in lieu of military action but sometimes paralleled it. For, in many instances, villagers engaging in battle were the same ones who insisted on certain rights which they claimed to deserve—either as fighters for the "nation" and the Patria or as "victims" of the rebels, as the case may be. Let us examine the three cases in greater detail.

Case One: Patriotic Peasants

The communities of peasants self-identified as patriots were located to the east and southeast of Huanta, in the districts of San Miguel, Chilcas, and Tambo, an area corresponding to the present-day provinces of Huamanga and La Mar (see maps 3 and 6). These villages sided with the patriots during the Independence struggles and also helped put down the monarchist uprising.

In 1827, the indigenous mayors and aldermen of the community of San Juan Bautista de Tambo presented a letter to the intendant requesting reduction of their debt for contribuciones corresponding to the Christmas semestral payment of 1826 and to midsummer (St. John's) of 1827. The mayors substantiated their request by appealing to damages they had suffered during the "pacification campaigns":

> The district finds itself exceedingly poor in resources, and still more backward because of the calamities that the *Yndigenas* from Yquicha and Caruhuran [*sic*] have perpetrated in the past year in the sowing and among the livestock; they have looted and burned almost all the district; most of their children have been killed and leaving blood-stained for the sake of the just cause of Independence the fields of [A]co and Carpampa, which have also distinguished themselves from the rest of the towns of the province by serving as Guerrillas in the pacification division under the command of Colonel Benavídez.[75]

The government acceded to their request. The same year the people of the district of San Miguel, adjacent to the area loosely referred to as Iquicha, presented a similar request for an exemption from a payment in arrears corresponding to their contribuciones of Christmas semester, "since the towns of Huanta and Luricocha have been exempted." On this occasion the request was also granted, on the grounds that, as the prefect put it, "their services and support [for the Patria] since the year 1814 are well known."[76] Four years later, in 1831, the people of San Miguel and the vice-parish of Chilcas again addressed the prefect, this time with a major request: an exemption from payment of contribuciones for four years. The Sanmiguelinos based their demand on promises made to them by General Tristán during the campaign against the Iquichanos. The petition read in part as follows:

> Attentive to the summons made to us in the past year of 1827, calling on us to take up arms against the rebels of Yquicha, we generally lent ourselves to this important service. . . . The enthusiasm, bravery and daring with which we, bearing all sorts of dangers, waged war on the Yquichanos, who were proud of the repeated victories which they had attained over the veteran troops, are only too well known. . . . In spite of this we were continually suspected of joining with the Yquicha dissidents solely because of our proximity to them; but also because of the seductive promises, with which they wanted to attract towns to their band of not having to pay either contribuciones or duties or the slightest tax. *Hence General Domingo Tristán, then Prefect of the Department, repeatedly promised us through the military commander of Tambo, don José de Quintanilla, that we would be exempted from the tax in reward for our sacrifices.*[77]

The settlers of San Miguel and Chilcas suspected that they, who had spared no sacrifice in aiding the government in its struggle against the rebels of Huanta, would have to continue paying their contribuciones, whereas the insurgents had been forgiven theirs:

> The rebels of Yquicha who stirred up the towns, upset order, broke the dikes of obedience, and caused immense damage to the nation, were excused from paying the contribución because of an excess of compassion from the government, and they have enjoyed this grace in full; and although their crimes were the cause of the harm which they have suffered, the *Madre patria*, though ruined by these perverse sons, has shown them consideration, extending its tender and beneficent hand to them to wipe away their tears. And we who with robust arm and dauntless heart stood up to the revolution, and broke the hard neck of this hydra, *we who did more than we had to (it must be said), serving at our own expense*, and having rid the nation of this source of scandal, have brought the rebels under control and back to their duties, shall we remain in a worse condition so that the favor which was promised us remain void and without effect?[78]

Before ending their letter, the petitioners emphasized, and not without reason, that if the government had been able to overcome the Iquichano insurrection it was not on account of its own merits, but rather thanks to those who, like themselves, had committed their resources: "We expect that . . . the supreme government . . . [,] calculating the savings of hundreds of thousands that would have been spent had the war of Yquicha been prosecuted and finished by the veteran Battalions, will find no objections to make to our request."[79]

This time the government's response showed greater deliberation. The lower instances rejected the request, adducing insufficient grounds "and because the critical circumstances of the national finances do not permit it." This, despite the fact that Commander Quintanilla himself, who had led the campaign, sent an official letter endorsing the petitioners' account. In order to reconsider the request, the Office of the Treasurer asked the petitioners for written proof of both the tax exemption offers to which they alluded and the damages they claimed to have suffered in the campaigns against the Iquichanos. Tristán's offers, however, had evidently been verbal only. The request was finally denied, and the patriotic San Miguelinos most likely felt deeply let down by a government for which they had done "more than they had to." Nonetheless, in the eyes of the fiscal authority handling their case, they had done no more than their duty.[80]

Case Two: Nine Towns Petition the Government: Seduced by the "Iquichanos"?

In 1831, the authorities from nine Huanta villages—Ccarhuahurán, Secce, Aranhuay, Ayahuanco, Mayhuavilca, Chaca, Huarcatán, Pampacoris, and Marcaraccay—addressed nine pleas to the prefect. Unlike the petitioners from San Miguel, these communities were located at the very core of the convulsed area during the monarchist uprising. The area was referred to by government officials and other contemporaries as the "Ccarhuahurán punas" or "punas of Iquicha." These communities certainly did not claim to be patriotic but presented themselves instead as victims of the war promoted by the "leaders of the Iquichano party," by whom they claimed to have been seduced. As a result, they asked to be exempted from their contribuciones for 1830 and 1831, arguing that they had suffered losses during that war. The mayor of Ccarhuahurán explained:

Being victims of seduction by the leaders [*corifeos*] of the Yquichano party which had expanded in those places, we have suffered the damages resulting from a destructive war. The pastures of those barren lands are not insulted [*sic*] by any domestic livestock, since the soldiers, be they friends or enemies, did away with all of it. The *chacras* [farmed lands] have become forests, for we have only recently taken up agriculture. On the other hand, we had no other choice for our subsistence than to raise some livestock or other, and to cultivate the lands of said town, which, as they are situated in the Punas, yield no more than barley, potatoes, broad beans, and quinoa, provisions which are not at all desirable.[81]

The dossier does not state whether the petitioners succeeded in their request, but this may matter less than the rationale supporting their arguments. The villagers truthfully stated that they had "suffered damages resulting from a destructive war," including the loss of their livestock to soldiers, "be they friends or enemies." Yet this phrase, meant to deflect blame from themselves, suggests that the petitioners had, in fact, taken sides. For, it was precisely for having supported the monarchist insurrection (their "friends") that the towns had taken the brunt of the beating during the government's (their "enemies' ") campaigns of repression.

But if these communities had been implicated in the monarchist insurrection to so great an extent, to the point that the authorities were already referring to them as "Iquichanos," what logic lay behind their expiatory claims? Who were those "leaders of the Iquichano party" of whom they declared themselves the victims? They were surely the principal caudillos of the monarchist uprising, including those Spanish officers who, as we saw in chapter 4, had first adopted the appellation "Iquichanos" in signing their anonymous proclamations inciting rebellion. Whether or not they were indeed "seduced," the peasants probably employed this argument in full awareness that it was consistent with the view held by the state. Inheritor of the paternalist colonial mentality, the republican government considered peasants—then designated indians or indígenas—to be naive creatures, easily susceptible to manipulation and deceit. When the peasants had to be judged for their participation in the monarchist rebellion, the political authorities advised the judges to avoid "possible misfortunes for the indígenas taken prisoner," recommending penalties like that of mandatory enlistment in the army, which were meant to instruct rather than punish. But no leniency was to be shown "those who ganged up, nor for the other caudillos, all of whom must be judged and sentenced in accordance with the law as an example to all who seek to emulate them."[82] Using the same logic, Prefect Tristán had appealed to the priest Manuel Navarro "to use shrewdness to rid the headmen of these errant indígenas of the delusion from which they suffer and so that they see the cautious way of thinking and turn over the foreign caudillos who seduced them in the devil's stead."[83]

The claim of the mayor of Ccarhuahurán that the peasants had been "victims of seduction" thus proved compatible with the logic and rhetoric of the government itself. Without making too great a leap in time or interpretation, I believe that this was the same attitude the peasants of Uchuraccay adopted when summoned by Vargas Llosa to reveal the details regarding the journalists' murder in 1983: they stressed repeatedly their inability to understand and consistently claimed, "We do not know any more," "We are ignorant."[84]

In the course of the 1830s, however, the very same petitioners who in 1831 so forcefully denied being associated with the Iquichanos would soon shift their strategy. The change came about as a result of the successful military support they offered first to President Orbegoso, in 1834, and then to Marshal Santa Cruz from 1836 to 1839. These generals, as we have seen, had actively campaigned in Ayacucho to persuade the once scorned Huanta peasants to join their side; having succeeded, the presidents publicly decorated the peasants, referring to them as "brave Iquichanos" and granting them fiscal exemptions. Henceforth, and borrowing the very language that the governments of Orbegoso and Santa Cruz had used to address them, the peasants from the nine villages of our story would claim they had "served the Patria" and "defended the nation," just as the patriotic San Miguelinos had. As a result of this new situation, they would not only come to identify themselves as Iquichanos, but even gain a certain pride in the name they had once utterly rejected.

In sum, if at first the inhabitants of the nine villages attempted to portray themselves as "poor deceived indígenas" in the hope of avoiding possible penal sanctions and, especially, payment of tribute, in time they would learn to profit from the fear which the population felt toward them as a result of the 1826–28 rebellion as well as from their newfound fame as courageous fighters, so as to serve similar ends. Yet the villagers would also exploit this fear to protect themselves from the misfortunes unleashed by the caudillista wars, which intensified in the region after the defeat of the Peruvian-Bolivian Confederation. These considerations inform my analysis of the evolution that Secce, one of the nine villages of our story, underwent during the years following the demise of the Confederation.

Case Three: The Resistance of Secce and the Birth of Iquicha

The village of Secce, officially belonging to the district of Tambo, had played a strategic role during the monarchist rebellion, first as a rebel headquarters, then as government military base. Its inhabitants had been paying the tribute, albeit irregularly, up until 1839—the same year in which the Confederation was defeated—at which time they stopped doing so. "There are [in Secce] very few people because they almost finished with it in the revolution [the Confederation wars] and there are no more than four or five people, and more than fifteen men are dead, and moreover the wretched people [*gentalla*] of this place are entirely ruined and some are about to leave for other lands because they are very poor."[85] With these words the indigenous mayor of Secce, Francisco Quispe, replied to the subprefect of Huanta in September 1841, upon being summoned to explain why the villagers of his town refused to pay tribute. The following year, commissioned by the subprefect, Anselmo Cordero and Juan Maldonado Alvarado, the governor and priest of Tambo, respectively, would corroborate the facts described by Quispe. Upon their arrival in Secce, they found only the new mayor, Bernardo Lapa,

> who apprised of the interrogation to which he was being subjected, replied that the rest of the indians were not in this hamlet [*estancia*] but in Pante, Marayniyocc and other places, and that even now they are gathering at the mayor's urging, and making their homes, that they are not paying their tributes because they are still recovering from their past losses, that they previously belonged to this district [Tambo], and that due to the recent revolutions, the *headmen [mandones] of that time had added them to Yquicha . . . and that so long as those of Yquicha begin to pay, so will they.*[86]

What these eloquent testimonies seem to be revealing is nothing less than the emergence of the district (and, possibly, the town) of Iquicha. Those who fled Secce (and eventually other towns) went on to colonize what had until then been a most inconspicuous area and, sheltered by a new denomination— "Iquichanos"—sought to protect themselves from the demands imposed by the caudillo wars, the local priests, and the burdens of the tribute. They refused to comply with both religious and civilian authorities in Tambo, and as a helpless governor of Tambo denounced: *"The dwellers of that hamlet [Secce] called themselves Yquichanos, and with this excuse they refrained from paying this district [Tambo], and even ceased to come to mass as indeed they have done. . . . For I say those of Secca [sic] never come to hear mass, nor do they pay the obligations which they owe for their unctions, marriages and funerals, and I do not know where they take them to but I assume that it is to Yquicha."*[87]

The authorities were aware of the repercussions that could result from the movements undertaken by the villagers of Secce as well as of the refusal of this and other villages to register in their original districts. In April 1842, the subprefect of Huanta claimed that in order to get them to pay the tribute, "it was first necessary to reconquer, by reason or force, the *estancia* of Secce, as those of Yquicha have extended their conquest that far."[88] The reality, however, was probably the reverse. I suspect that it was the inhabitants of the various villages and hamlets of the Huanta highlands who, through progressive displacements undertaken during the upheavals of the caudillo wars, began to conquer a spot hitherto omitted from the maps, until they transformed it into the village and, eventually, the district of Iquicha.

Whatever the name *Iquicha* stood for before those events (and, generally, prior to the republican era) or whether it even existed, we can only speculate: was it an *ayllu* of peasants and herders who managed to escape written records? the name of a hillside? a pasture area? a rivulet? Did it stem from the Aymara word *iki*, as some suggest? All this is likely, especially since before the Spanish invasion Aymara was spoken prior to Quechua, and alongside it, in many areas of the southern Andes, particularly, in the highest elevations.[89] The fact is that after two decades of eventful republican rule, this name had come to signify something greater and more visible than anything it could have thus far been: a core settlement around which groups of peoples, hitherto unrelated to this name or place, would establish and seek to identify themselves.

The identity of Iquicha (and of the Iquichanos) was to remain variable, however. As various other witnesses would continue to attest, with great eloquence, of the villagers of Secce: "sometimes . . . they call themselves Yquichanos, and . . . other times they [say] that they belong to the town of Huamanguilla, where they go to name their authorities, and present their offerings, for they say that they eat in the lands of Huamanguilla."[90] But this variability—and herein lies the richness of this testimony—seems to have been more than just a manipulative strategy to rid themselves of fiscal burdens; it seems as well to have been an expression of actual, very mobile, patterns of settlement, access to resources, and forms of local government among the various communities in Huanta. For, as our witness states, those of Secce may indeed have "eaten" (that is, farmed or owned lands), and performed ritual activity in Huamanguilla, which is situated in the northernmost corner of the province of Huamanga, some twenty-eight straight-line kilometers (seventeen miles) from Secce (see map 5).⁹¹ But this did not prevent them from establishing other, more or less permanent settlements on the less accessible northeastern slopes of Huanta's ceja de selva, an area which they would (sometimes) claim formed part of "Iquicha," and where, by the early 1840s, they would start building a chapel: "Those of Secc-secc [sic]," claimed the farmer (labrador) José Manuel Cárdenas, "are building themselves a chapel in Pantecc [located in the ceja de selva] so that the priest of Yquicha can go in due time for their festivities, and for this reason they no longer come to this town [Tambo]."⁹²

Hence, alongside the "itinerancy" that characterized Secce villagers' modus vivendi—and which so exasperated government officials trying to confine them to a single place—lay "sedentary aspects," so to speak. In the places where they moved to, the villagers built chapels, and chapels are by far the most enduring architectonic structures of Andean villages, around which an important part of community life took place. Moreover, chapels and churches were precisely what differentiated a village from other lesser types of settlements, according to the nineteenth-century geographer Mariano Felipe Paz Soldán. They were the most distinctive feature of a pueblo: "In Peru one calls pueblo any union of houses, as long as they are close to a chapel or church, however miserable it be, and where [people] gather on Sundays for religious festivities."⁹³ A church, that is, could make a "pueblo" out of the most inconspicuous settlement. And it is precisely in this sense that Secce villagers' migration to the rim of the forest in order to comply with the Catholic liturgy and build a chapel, while simultaneously claiming to belong to "Iquicha," is significant. It means that their refusal to comply with the state's dictates at the fiscal level cannot be interpreted as an attitude of blunt confrontation with either the state or the Church.⁹⁴ It may, moreover, mean that when they claimed to belong to "Iquicha," the Secce villagers were not necessarily deceiving government officials as much as expressing how forceful and effective a name could be in reshaping the ties they had established with other communities at the level of everyday practice. By claiming "Iquicha," that is, the peasants were redefining patterns of periodic migration and remolding the political and administrative landscape in the highlands of Huanta. Thus, a name which rose to prominence as a result of these communities' play of confrontation and alliance with the state ended up creating a place whose boundaries were to be continually recreated. Furthermore, given that in the Andes the concept of community has not necessarily been tied to the idea of a contiguous territory, but rather has coexisted with notions of noncontiguous territoriality and ever-flexible boundaries, the history of Iquicha may well be but one among many untold histories of Andean villages or districts which came into existence as a result of similar processes throughout the nineteenth century and perhaps even later.[95]

In response to this situation, the government took pains to "reconquer" these territories. First, because Secce—with its villagers constantly moving into other areas and especially into that which came to be known as "Iquicha"—refused to pay tribute for many more years, setting a precedent for other towns to follow, as Prefect Francisco del Barco reported in 1848; he claimed that the villagers of Palomayoc refused to pay tribute "on the pretext of it [Palomayoc] being in the district of Yquicha."[96] But secondly, and most importantly, because it was the government itself that acknowledged the villagers' "conquests." This time, however, it was not by means of symbols, ritual decorations, or promises of tributary exemptions, but rather through more worldly and permanent measures: the delimitation of new political boundaries. In the 1830s the authorities referred to the "district of Iquicha" even though it did not exist officially. As already mentioned, Iquicha was then just another name for "the punas of Ccarhuahurán" or "the district of Ccarhuahurán." In 1849, a guidebook lists the towns of Ccarhuauarán and Ayahuanco as "capitals of the famous district of Iquicha," showing the preponderance that the name had acquired by then as a regional denomination.[97] Sounder evidence of the existence of both a village and a district called Iquicha is, however, found only for the second half of the nineteenth century, coinciding, significantly, with a period of consolidation of state institutions in Peru. In 1853 a parish census for Ayacucho lists Iquicha as one of the six *doctrinas* making up Huanta province.[98] By the mid-1850s a court of the peace was firmly established in the "district of Iquicha," and in 1877, the historian and geographer Mariano Felipe Paz Soldán would estimate a population of 3,112 inhabitants for the same district, 308 of them corresponding to the pueblo of Iquicha, capital of the district.[99] A number of "verbal hearings" (*juicios verbales*) decided in the "court of the

Iquicha as seen on the road from Uchuraccay. Notice the change in flora. The increasing vegetation reveals an ecological niche which is distinct from the punas of Uchuraccay and suggests the proximity of the ceja de selva, or rim of the forest.

Iquicha, with the remains of its church, which was burned during the Shining Path war. *Both photographs by the author, 1999.*

peace of Iquicha" from 1855 to 1915, records for which are still kept in Huanta, attest to the fact that these administrative units were in operation.[100] According to local histories, the legendary muleteer and *montonero* General in Chief of the Royal Armies of Perú Antonio Navala Huachaca ended his days occupying the office of justice of the peace in Iquicha, one of the most coveted positions in local politics in any region.

By the second decade of the twentieth century one loses track of the district of Iquicha, as the whole area had fallen under a different jurisdiction by 1915.[101] It seems that the only Iquichano entity that survived the subsequent political demarcations was village-based, though to prove this assertion would take specific research of "Iquicha" into the twentieth century. Whatever the case, the name *Iquichano* had acquired such powerful resonance among local writers, travelers, and authorities since the end of the monarchist uprising, that the reach of the Iquichano identity and the boundaries of "Iquichano territory" would not cease to be expanded upon in written accounts. In 1838, an attorney in Ayacucho referred to the territory controlled by Justice of the Peace Huachaca as the "*republiqueta* [derogatorily diminutive for "republic"] of Iquicha."[102] In the early 1850s, upon his arrival in Ayacucho, the English traveler Clements R. Markham expressed great curiosity "to see the Iquichano Indians." His description of the area "to the eastward [of the town of Huanta]" as "the wild country of the Iquichanos" is highly telling of the reputation that the area and its people had by then attained.[103] A few decades later, in 1888, the Italian geographer Antonio Raimondi laid out a map of Peru in which he labeled the area corresponding to the provinces of Huanta and La Mar "*indios iquichanos*," doing likewise with the region comprising the province of Cangallo (also in the department of Ayacucho), which he termed "*indios morochucos*."[104] In doing so, Raimondi was projecting a relatively recent political history rather than the "ethnography" he purported—"Morochucos," as the reader may recall, was another name for the inhabitants of the province of Pampa Cangallo, who stood out for their patriotic militancy during the Independence wars and who were subsequently mobilized by the government to suppress the monarchist rebellion of Huanta.

Hence, what in actuality were rather fluid political identities forged in the heat of the Independence wars, the monarchist rebellion, and subsequent caudillo struggles, were converted into self-contained "indian groups," circumscribed within territories delimited by fixed boundaries.[105] By the same period, the idea of the Iquichanos as a special "indian group" originating in the pre-Hispanic Chanka Confederation began taking root among urban intellectuals.[106] The Iquichanos thus emerged in the imagination of the late nineteenth-century urban elites as an "indian group" existing outside the modern nation—brave yet backward, and invariably attached to "their" pre-Hispanic past.

Ironically, these identifications occurred at the very moment Huanta peasants were most unambiguously adopting a nationalist stance. Indeed, during the 1880s, the villagers of Huanta once again drew national attention, this time for their participation in the War of the Pacific (1879–84), when they rallied around would-be president Andrés Avelino Cáceres, leader of the resistance campaign against the invading Chilean army in the central sierra. And yet, the idea of the Iquichanos as having no past other than a remote one, no militaristic skills other than those inherited from their alleged "Chanka" past, and virtually no culture other than the "vestiges" of that past, not only persisted but acquired even more elaborate form during the twentieth century.[107]

The murder of eight journalists in Uchuraccay in January 1983 reinforced these constructs, which were embraced by both liberal and conservative commentators, Marxists and non-Marxists alike.[108] In summary, the myth of the backward peasant—brute or victim—I shall argue, was the most effective discursive strategy deployed by urban-based writers, journalists, and academicians to deny not only Huanta peasants' mental capacities and active engagement with the present, but their historicity as well and, in this sense, their contribution to the making of Peru's early republican state.[109] All the allusions made by travelers, authorities, and intellectuals would, in turn, inevitably affect the peasants' self-perception.

Today there is no district of Iquicha in the province of Huanta. And the district of (San José de) Secce, located within the area that the authorities of the nineteenth century referred to as "Iquicha," is now called (San José de) Santillana: a Quechua name having been (significantly) replaced by a Spanish one. Ccarhuahurán and Iquicha are, in turn, two clearly differentiated villages and share no apparent boundaries. While the administrative units of Huanta remain in constant flux and the presence of the government is more visible than ever following the defeat of the Shining Path in 1992, the most recent political demarcations have clearly tended toward fragmentation and even overlapping of local authority. As of today, however, a self-acknowledged Iquichano identity remains elusive (if existent at all) anywhere beyond the level of the village of Iquicha. The inhabitants of this hamlet achieved official recognition as a "peasant community" (*comunidad campesina*) as late as 1991, in the midst, and apropos, of the civil war that was then devastating Peru.[110] At that point, Uchuraccay was still struggling to achieve such recognition.

Epilogue

This book has followed the trajectory of the local leaders and participants in the Huanta rebellion more closely than that of the Spanish ones because, although the latter played a significant role in the conception and organization of the movement, the rebellion's supreme command remained in the hands of the local people. More importantly, the local leaders proved more resilient than their Spanish counterparts following the defeat of the uprising. It thus seems pertinent to begin these concluding pages by reflecting on the meaning of this resilience.

Unlike the Spanish leaders, most of whom received sentences of exile or imprisonment and eventually vanished from the local political scene, the highest Huantan commanders were either spared prison or had their sentences commuted and were ultimately released. Moreover, the rebellion's main indigenous leader, Antonio Huachaca, never surrendered and successfully eluded capture. Even more, far from becoming political outcasts, these ex-royalist *montoneros* eventually attained a new legitimacy by engaging in a series of military alliances with national caudillos and incorporating themselves into the lower echelons of the state administration. Tadeo Choque became governor of the district of Luricocha and then of Ccarhuahurán,[1] Huachaca was appointed justice of the peace in Iquicha. By assuming these positions, they did not, however, give up altogether their identity as montoneros. These men, both of whom were labeled *indígenas* by republican authorities, diverged greatly in their degree of political consistency, Huachaca proving invariably more loyal than Choque in his political alliances. Yet, by incorporating themselves into the local echelons of power within the early *caudillista* state, both constituted themselves in the local basis of support for Peru's earliest nation builders.[2] At the military level, their role as montoneros and guerrilla commanders accomplished a similar effect.

Given this outcome, I think it fair to say that although the Huanta rebellion was defeated militarily, dismantled as a monarchist alliance, and truncated as a restorationist project, the Huanta rebels themselves were not. Politically, they were successful. And their success acquires special significance in light of

Peruvian historiography's traditional portrayal of Peru in defeatist terms; that is, as a series of crushed rebellions, lost opportunities, and aborted political projects.[3]

The aftermath of the Huanta monarchist rebellion, in this sense, runs counter to the aftermaths of the better-known "anticolonial" rebellions of the late eighteenth century, which were brutally suppressed and whose leaders almost invariably met severe punishment, including death. The most emblematic of these reprisals was of course that inflicted upon Túpac Amaru, which has left a trail in Peru's historical memory that in many ways still affects the present. More than these late eighteenth-century Andean rebels, however, the Huanta rebels' trajectory mirrors that of early nineteenth-century creole and mestizo national caudillos. Like the petty caudillos of Huanta, most of Peru's national caudillos of the early republican period had militant (and military) royalist pasts, which they eventually relinquished altogether in order to participate in the creation of the republican state. In so doing, they became Peru's first nation builders.

On the other hand, the contrast between the outcome of the Huanta monarchist rebellion and the outcomes of late eighteenth-century anticolonial uprisings illustrates the extent to which the early national state differed from its late-colonial predecessor, while at the same time exemplifying some of the continuities. Both aspects are highly intermingled, though most striking are the differences. Indeed, what allowed the most important Huantan rebel leaders to be so graciously pardoned, as well as what allowed "indian" villagers to be conscribed to the army rather than sent to prison, was a blend of colonial legacies and new republican elements. Significantly, more rigorous punishments (rhetorically, at least) were being meted out to the "foreign caudillos" involved. The idea that indians were minors of sorts and therefore not totally accountable for their actions was a centerpiece of Spanish imperial ideology since the sixteenth century. Yet the concomitant harsher treatment of "foreign caudillos" who were held responsible for "seducing the indians" was an expression of an incipient anti-Spanish nationalism. As one historian put it, "Peru of the Independence struggles was hardly nationalistic, but postindependent Peru was increasingly so."[4] Granted, the anti-Spanish rhetoric that permeated virtually all political manifestos of the early republican decades hardly ever translated into a renunciation of the Spanish ethos, as Basadre rightly reminded us. Nevertheless, rhetorical anti-Spanish nationalism, when coupled

with condescending paternalism toward indians, could lead to concrete action, as the relative leniency toward the indigenous participants in the monarchist uprising attests. It is precisely at this politico-juridical level that the divide
between the Bourbon imperial state project and the early republican state
policies seems most readily apparent.

The Bourbon state punished Túpac Amaru's affront with an exuberant
display of cruelty: it tortured and then executed the rebel leader, his wife and
children; it forbade native Andeans to enact the memory of the Incas, play Inca
music, display noble Inca portraits, insignias, and dresses; it prohibited them
from signing their names as Incas and banned the hereditary title of cacique to
caciques who allegedly supported the rebellion, all of which led to the even-
tual dismantling of the native nobility. In all of these endeavors, the Bourbon
state succeeded. And although Inca-inspired symbols, history, and artistic representations did not vanish, they would be appropriated by the creoles, and
integrated into the official rhetoric as a means of neutralizing "the political
content of the cultural elements of indian origin,"[5] that is, their subversive
potential. In the aftermath of Independence, with the native leadership long
departed, Inca-inspired symbols and artistic representations were to become
the fashions and archaeological objects of the elite. Inca deeds and names
would provide the rhetorical tools and themes for patriotic poets and nationalist caudillos. In the official rhetoric, the Incas became the "founders of Peru,"
and Peru was referred to as "the land of the Incas," a "sacred land," as nationalist caudillos boasted time and again to contest their alleged antinationalist
rivals. The Incas did become all this. And the more they did so, the less they
had to do with living indians.[6]

Conversely, the early republican state, faced with its first and only peasant
rebellion in forty years of republican rule—the Huanta rebellion—condoned,
forgave, and granted pardons. Later on, it rallied around peasants, begged,
implored, and called them "citizens" and "saviors of the nation." In a word, it
negotiated. And it also succeeded, at least in regard to the liberal caudillos this
book has dealt with.

The republican state's summoning of peasants as citizens was not always
sincere, and it was frequently double-dealing. All the same, the language of
nationhood deployed by national caudillos provided Andean peasants and
montonero leaders with rhetorical and political tools they made theirs and
used with profit. By appealing to the language of citizenship and statehood,
village peasants sought, and attained, tax exemptions and appropriated the

tithes; montonero leaders enhanced their local power, prestige, and legitimacy; and national caudillos found in the rural populations the military and political support they desperately needed to maintain their hold on the state. Even in cases in which village peasants were not granted what they demanded from the state, as was the case with the San Miguelinos who fought against the Huanta rebellion, their awareness of the political conflicts at stake during the Independence wars, monarchist rebellion, and caudillo wars is manifest.

That these negotiations occurred in the midst, and apropos, of civil wars does not diminish their importance. Rather, it highlights yet another feature of the republican state that was absent from its imperial predecessor. In the colonial period, obviously, but worth keeping in mind, no such struggles for control of the state occurred between rival factions. So-called anticolonial rebellions pursued reform rather than state takeover and had no legitimate place within the framework of the imperial polity. Conversely, early republican politics were marked by permanent strife over state control; this struggle, moreover, defined much of the state's political fabric throughout that period. Beyond all other claims, political factions seeking legitimacy first and foremost laid claim to the state. That these confrontations occurred not just at the level of the elites but incorporated entire rural societies has been widely acknowledged in the historiography of various Spanish American countries (Mexico and Argentina, in particular) but has not found a place in the national narratives of nineteenth-century Andean republics, notably Peru.[7] I have already suggested some of the reasons for this omission in the introduction. I would now add that the problem of peasant participation in early-republican caudillo conflicts might not have received the attention of Andeanists specializing in the early national period because of the prevailing historiographical tendency to portray Andean *ayllus* in terms antagonistic to "modern" state ideologies, namely, liberalism;[8] or, more broadly put, because of the ideological strength of paradigms that postulate the irreconcilability between an alleged "indigenous project" and the "creole state project." But it is precisely these widely held paradigms that the unfolding of events in early republican Huanta so forcefully challenges. Huanta was an Andean province with a dense ayllu population actively engaged with the state, not in "patrimonial" or "ancient-regime" terms, as the ayllus of northern Potosí, studied by Platt, did (that is, seeking to maintain "corporate privileges"), but rather in the unruly terms ushered in by the early caudillo politics and the language of possibilities that, more or less willingly, liberal politicians opened up in their desperate quest for constituents. In the Huanta of the early civil wars, national caudillos successfully mobilized rural civilians by resorting to the language of citizenship. Perhaps these wars were among the few instances in which citizenship (in its very restricted meaning of inclusion, even if momentary, in the negotiation of rights and obligations with the state) was carried out in the rural areas.[9] Thus, the saga of the Huanta peasants illustrates with notable clarity the political arrangements that ruling elites, personified in the national caudillos, had to make in order to assume and maintain state power and their own status as political elites.

All of these arguments cast doubt, in the first place, on the widespread assumption that Peru's Andean rural populations, traumatized by the brutal repression that followed the Túpac Amaru rebellion, were politically disarmed and remained aloof from and unconcerned with the issues at stake during the Independence wars and ensuing caudillista struggles.[10] Granted, the defeat of Túpac Amaru marked the end of Inca-nationalist projects promoted by native Andeans, but it did not so much efface their political perceptions as encourage a shift to hispanicization and royalism, attitudes which historians have too often equated with passivity or conservatism. Yet, as the Huanta case demonstrates, opting for the king did not necessarily entail taking a reactionary position. For Huantan villagers and montoneros, the defense of the king had little to do with the doctrinaire monarchism embraced by some of their Spanish military allies or with the attachment to things Spanish exhibited by large segments of Peru's creole aristocratic elites—let alone with the kind of redemptory messianism that other scholars have associated with the rural poor's defense of the king in other contexts.[11] Rather, Huantino "monarchism" was pragmatically driven and had a strong social dimension. Not only did the Huanta rebels subvert the ethnic hierarchies that both republican and colonial societies sanctioned and refuse to pay the *contribución de indígenas* (the most tangible marker of ethnic subordination in the early Republic), but by forcing the hacendados to pay a wage to their laborers through an original "revolution of the tithes," they instituted a de facto, modern "labor code." Given the widespread reality of unpaid indian labor in the Andes until recently, that system must be considered ahead of its time.

None of this denies the more authoritarian (and from our perspective, conservative) vein in the rebels' practices, exemplified in particular in their treatment of women and the accusations of *abigeato* (cattle rustling) that loomed over some rebel caudillos, including Huachaca. Indeed, in some ways,

Huachaca's social behavior is reminiscent of that of a *gamonal* (a strongman or political boss notorious for his use of arbitrary violence and exactions on peasants)[12]—though Huachaca, unlike typical gamonales and unlike some of his fellow montonero chiefs, did not own a hacienda or appear to live off community peasants' resources and labor, as did the gamonales. The scarce evidence indicates, rather, that Huachaca's livestock thefts targeted either those who were socioeconomically his equals or hacendados considered wealthy by local standards—at least some of this occurring in the context of guerrilla warfare.[13] Significantly, in this regard, Huachaca had virtually no possessions, as, ironically, his most ardent accuser informs us: "that he [Huachaca] leave the place for *he has no possessions and is a quiden* [that is, a *quídam*, a nobody or despicable being]."[14] The accuser argued that in addition to being a protector of rustlers and a rustler himself, Huachaca was notorious for "his bad behavior and excesses . . . being a private individual with no more authority *than his libertine temper* . . . and for not knowing how to read or write, this brutal man lacks reason . . . *and even so he thinks that he can give orders and be a Justice of the Peace.*"[15] These charges, laid by Huachaca's close associate and rival, Tadeo Choque, were meant to question the legitimacy of Huachaca's claim to the office of justice of the peace. Yet given the identity of the accuser, they succeed, if anything, in exposing, more than Huachaca's frailties, Choque's own anxiety about the increased popularity that the caudillo of Uchuraccay was enjoying in a territory that Choque claimed as his own jurisdiction: namely, the old district of Ccarhuahurán, whose identity as a place distinct from Iquicha was still apparently being contested. Nevertheless, as we know from other threads of evidence, Choque was not making everything up. Let us thus concede, to his credit, that there was something real about Huachaca's violent behavior and "excesses" in connection with his claim to the office of justice of the peace.

The anthropologist Deborah Poole has convincingly described the extent to which local authorities in places where the state could not afford them protection resorted to deliberate, theatrical forms of violence to legitimize their claims to state office. Such behavior, which Poole dubs "performative violence," includes abigeato but is not restricted to it: "Livestock thefts reported from this period [1830–70] occurred within the context of these other, more inclusive, crimes committed by appointed authorities of the state, such as governors, mayors, municipal council members, and sub-prefects. The criminal activities of these men were directed to the building of personal power in the form of a monopoly over claims to state office, and not necessarily to the accumulation of material goods."[16] Perhaps the only difference between Huachaca and the cases Poole describes is that not everyone in Huanta would have considered Huachaca's illegal activities to be crimes. For example, the popular revolution of the tithes and perhaps even the public decapitation of Commander Quintanilla (see chapter 7) would not have been regarded as such.

One may safely presume that the success of Huachaca's "illegal" methods was precisely what most exasperated Choque, who despite being literate was not able to compete with his illiterate fellow's "performative violence" skills and charisma. Choque clung instead to the powers of the central state, switching allegiances as he saw fit in his search of the legitimacy he himself desperately needed as a local authority. Interestingly in this regard, Choque, in his efforts to discredit Huachaca, referred to his illiteracy as ignorance (that is, "not knowing how to read or write"), implicitly contrasting it with his own literacy.

We may safely presume as well that Choque, though a legitimate broker in the eyes of the current authority may not always have been seen as a legitimate leader in the eyes of his own people. Ironically, once again, it was Choque's own fate that provides the historian with yet another piece of evidence that attests to the popularity of his hated onetime comrade-in-arms. Huachaca, claimed Choque, usurping the authority of the *juez fiscal apoderado*, "had taken it upon himself to distribute *mitayo* plots of land."[17] Such an initiative, compounded with his earlier revolution of the tithes, no doubt puts Huachaca in a category closer to that of "social bandit" than gamonal.

Unlike Eric Hobsbawm's paradigmatic "social bandit," however, Huachaca did not aspire to lead the life of an outcast. Much to his contentment (and Choque's dismay), Huachaca not only was not indicted for his illegal actions but received official state sanction. His appointment as justice of the peace at the time of the Peruvian-Bolivian Confederation legitimated the role of chief justice that he had arrogated to himself in the days of the monarchist rebellion. This means that insofar as Huachaca could count on the favor of the presidential palace in Lima, the court at Uchuraccay—or what I have here called the government at Uchuraccay—attained the status of a local branch of the state's judicial system. Similarly, by presenting Huachaca with a general's uniform, Marshal Santa Cruz was making the montonero's military power an extension of the state's military powers. Hence, in the final analysis, "social banditry" at the local level, if properly legitimized, was perfectly consistent with state building at the national level.

Perhaps what allowed Huachaca to achieve what he did was not unrelated to his plebeian origins. For a variety of (understandable) reasons, historians have long been fascinated by the *kurakas* who led the so-called anticolonial rebellions of the late eighteenth century and by the ultimately tragic fate of the Inca nobility in Peru. In being so allured, they have left unnoticed the rebel Andean caudillos who, while socially less salient, were politically more successful.[18] Tadeo Choque was born in a hacienda property belonging to the patrician Colonel Pedro Tadeo Lazón.[19] One can easily picture his childhood as a *peón*, striving to conform to his masters' will and at the same stand out above other "indians." His literacy, his ownership of a hacienda, and his political career all bear witness that, in a way, he did stand out. Huachaca's birthplace is not known for sure, but we are certain he was a self-made *arriero*, having emerged from the lowest echelons of the trade and risen to a respectable position. Neither of them claimed kuraka ancestry, and there is no evidence they formed part of an ayllu, but their work and lives were intricately connected with ayllu villagers whose communities lay interspersed among the haciendas and whom they claimed to represent politically. There is no reason to think that their political trajectories and social universes were exceptional.

The saga of the Iquichanos invalidates an argument that is concomitant with the one I contested above, namely, that the criollos, traumatized by the violence triggered by the "indian masses" during the Túpac Amaru rebellion, were thenceforth reluctant to mobilize indians for fear that they would turn against them, as had happened on that occasion. This idea, widely cited in the past to substantiate the argument that there was a lack of popular participation during the Independence struggles and in post-Independence politics, still dominates historiography today. But, as the events in Huanta in the 1830s make clear, in the aftermath of Independence, creole and mestizo national caudillos not only did not shy away from mustering the peasantry but in fact succeeded in their efforts to do just that.[20] It is up to future studies to determine whether this was a virtue specific to the liberal caudillos. By now, however, it does seem certain that all national caudillos, regardless of their political persuasions, at least tried to muster the peasantry.[21] I am, moreover, tempted to suggest that the fiercest political antagonisms of the early caudillo period occurred not between the national ruling elites and the peasants, but rather between the various political factions competing for control of the state. The absence of peasant rebellions in Peru for four decades after the suppression of the Huanta uprising and the legislation concerning the death penalty are telling indicators. Indeed, unlike highly industrialized countries in the early nineteenth century such as England, where the death penalty applied to even minor thefts and "primitive" forms of industrial rebellion (such as destruction of machinery), in Peru the death penalty rarely applied to offences against property but served, rather, strictly political purposes. "New regimes that wished to reaffirm their authority, or languishing regimes on the verge of demise applied the death penalty in the belief that this measure could prolong their existence," wrote Basadre.[22] Social differentiation and class confrontation, in other words, were not nearly as sharp in the early caudillo period as they were to become decades later, when Peru entered the world market with its guano exports, the state became more centralized, and national wealth became increasingly synonymous with exports and "progress" with the coast.

Insofar as the Peruvian state lacked a professional army and the regular army was insufficient, which was the case for most of the nineteenth century, it is plausible that the scenario I have described for Huanta applied elsewhere: national caudillos may have sought to court local powers with sway over the peasantry in order to enlarge their armies. "Local powers" in Huanta during the guerrillas of 1834 included a wide array of actors, from montonero leaders to municipal authorities, *notables*, and hacendados, all of whom rallied around Orbegoso. A similar set of alliances were seemingly at work at the time of the Peruvian-Bolivian Confederation. Though details are scarcer concerning these alliances, evidence that Santa Cruz courted Huanta hacendados who had influence among the peasantry, including, for example, Pascual Arancibia, himself once an "Iquichano" general, as well as leaders more directly connected to the villagers, such as Huachaca, attests to the importance of local brokers in the state's attempts to mobilize the peasantry. Finally, Santa Cruz's special deference toward Huachaca and Huanta's lengthy resistance to the rule of Gamarra after the fall of the Confederation speak of the strength of the bonds that Huanta peasantry, in particular, commanded by the unyielding Huachaca, had forged with the La Paz caudillo. Overall, the evidence suggests that peasant political mobilization, far from being taken for granted, was crucial to the statesmen of the early Republic and hence merits more attention than historians have given it.

Even if we consider the Iquichano saga from the perspective of the peasants who fought against them, particularly in the monarchist uprising—the Morochucos and Sanmiguelinos, for example—the question of peasant mobilization remains a crucial one. Who were the brokers here? Or was it a case (as it seems superficially) of direct peasant mobilization by the state? Informed answers require additional research. To judge from the moving, albeit unsuccessful, pleas of the Sanmiguelinos to the authorities in Lima (see chapter 7), their loyalty to the state was far from unconditional. On both sides of the conflict, documents show villagers to have been keenly aware of the national implications of the militarily struggles in which they participated; they were not the benighted cannon fodder that historiography has portrayed.

In other words, this book has argued that the problem that the Iquichano story poses pertains not so much to "peasant resistance" as to the very nature of peasant–state relations in the early republican era. To be sure, the saga of the Iquichanos includes elements of "resistance" and contestation: witness the practices of the government of Uchuraccay and Huachaca's own populist attitudes. There is no question that the monarchist rebellion had radical underpinnings. Nevertheless, insofar as these practices were ultimately instrumental in the national caudillos' consolidation of power, it is essential to analyze them in connection with the process of state making. I should therefore like to conclude by highlighting the importance of these practices.

The early republican state in Peru was institutionally weak and politically unstable. But it was precisely such fragility that led its rulers to forge alliances with sectors of society like the peasants of Huanta, who shortly before had been seen as deserving nothing but contempt. Peasant support, in other words, could not be taken for granted, as the theory of coercion surmises. It needed to be won over, as E. P. Thompson writes of other contexts and different actors, "by the constant exercise of skill, of theater and of concession."[23] And skill, theater, and concession are precisely what generals Orbegoso, Santa Cruz, Necochea, Miller, Cerdeña, and Tristán displayed in their relationship with the peasants of Huanta.

Conceiving peasant–state relations as bargained relations, rather than as resulting from coercion alone, leads us in turn to broaden our very notion of state, by forcing us to look beyond the military into the societies from which these armies drew their support. I am not denying that coercion existed. The bulk of the troops in the regular army was constituted of men drafted almost invariably against their will and by notoriously cruel methods from the Andean rural areas. The violence of conscription, or *leva*, which disproportionately targeted Andean peasant communities, was so extreme that it opened up themes for what presumably became the first novels with social content in republican Peru.[24] At the same time, however, there were also the guerrilla armies, like those formed in Huanta to support Orbegoso, which were made up of civilians and were led by civilians acting in concert with the regular army to defend simultaneously local, regional, and national political agendas.

When and where, then, was coerced support more prevalent or more decisive than support attained through negotiation? The question remains to be addressed. Were armies made of conscripts alone able to win very many battles? In all probability they were, judging from the fact that conservatives (who were less prone to attracting guerrillas and thus presumably relied more heavily on the leva) retained power for longer spans of time than liberals during the two first republican decades. Yet even Santa Cruz, whose army enjoyed a solid reputation, campaigned aggressively (and successfully) to acquire military support from civilian populations in rural Huanta and elsewhere. Conceivably, in the absence of such support and regardless of the prowess of his army, his confederation might not have materialized.

In the end and despite much initial outcry about the Huanta peasants' ostensible attachment to the king, when push came to shove their royalist backgrounds became irrelevant to the generals summoning them; after all, most of them could themselves boast of militant royalist backgrounds. And this fact—for which I have provided ample evidence—ought to be stressed to avoid falling into fictitious ideological debates. To pretend that what we now see as "patriots" and "royalists" or "monarchists" and "republicans" were sharply defined parties, when in fact the lines dividing them could be so volatile and their respective loyalties so recent, would be misleading, to say the least. This way of assessing Peru's birth into national life does not lead back to the old notion of an incomprehensible, irrational, and purely fractious *caudillismo*. Neither does it dispute that Peru's once loyalist military officers did truly convert to republicanism after the proclamation of Independence. But it does, on the one hand, confirm the widespread interpretation that Independence in Peru resulted more from external pressure than from internal will at least, with regard to the upper sectors of society; and, on the other, it suggests that monarchism as an ideology did not prove long-lasting. Whether glorified or vilified, the Republic ultimately succeeded. And so, rather than lamenting what would have been an "ideal" independence or the "ideal" republic, it seems to me of more historical interest to delve into the inner workings of this early republican state.

The historiographical advances in this terrain have been considerable, particularly the contributions of the historian Paul Gootenberg. Challenging interpretations that likened early republican instability to chaos, anarchy, and caudillo factionalism alone and that called into question the very existence of a Peruvian state, Gootenberg demonstrated that behind the appearance of chaos there were projects, policies, and—however fragile—laws and institutions. Or as he put it, following a line of inquiry opened by Jorge Basadre, "That 'Peru' existed in 1850 [rather than having disintegrated like Gran Colombia or "the countless federations of Central America"] was no accident."[25] "In spite of its endemic uncertainty," wrote Gootenberg, "Peru had a state in formation, molded after the Spanish model, whose political elites kept an obstinate sense of diplomatic sovereignty, sometimes derived from its anti-Anglo-Saxon formation."[26] The "Hispanic mold" he was referring to was the Hapsburg state, a corporatist state which had endowed the Lima viceregal elites with a privileged trade status on which they would rely in all their economic transactions. The merchants, industrialists, and caudillos that dominated Peru's political scene in the first two republican decades—with Gamarra taking the lead—claimed Gootenberg, were ideological heirs of the Hapsburgs in their sense of entitlement to a protected and privileged status. Their staunch economic protectionism translated politically into nationalism, which, the argument continues, was successful to the extent that it rendered fruitless for two full decades the free-trade crusades launched by the emerging imperial powers from the north—that is, until guano made all of them free-trade liberals.[27]

Gootenberg was right, I believe. More disputable, however, are his claims regarding liberalism. Gootenberg argued that economic protectionism was a popular ideology during the early caudillo period[28] and that liberals failed to counter protectionist hegemony, in part because of their elitism: "Early liberal elites showed nowhere near the talent or inclination to cater to restless popular groups . . . as protectionists could and did." Moreover, "the failure of liberalism was . . . a failure of antiseptic social reactionaries unwilling to consider the plight of Peru's popular classes."[29] Gootenberg reached these conclusions, first, because his study concentrated on urban settings and, second and more decisively, because it sought to provide a rationale for politics inasmuch as they were shaped by trade policies—his use of the terms *conservatives* and *liberals* being coterminous, respectively, with "protectionists" and advocates of "free trade." Yet when ones incorporates the rural society into the picture—and one ought to, given Peru's demographic makeup—and views both liberalism and conservatism in broader political terms, then what emerges, as the events in Huanta so eloquently demonstrate, is a very different picture. On the one hand, alleged "antiseptic social reactionaries" appear here enlisting peasants with astounding success, the reason being perhaps that liberals in social and political matters did not always embrace the dogmas of economic liberalism. But even if they did, "free trade" may not have meant the same thing to Huanta's rural inhabitants as it did to better-off Limeños or even Arequipeños (just as royalism did not mean the same thing for these various social groups either). The idea of opening trade routes to the eastern lowlands and the southeastern Altiplano and of lifting tariffs with Bolivia, as envisioned by Santa Cruz, had reason to be appealing in Huanta, particularly considering that this province had more trade than industry and, in this sense, little to "protect." On the other hand, the purportedly popular Gamarra was repudiated by Huanta civilians for reasons that appear to have had more direct bearing on their civil and political rights than on their commercial policy choices; the cross-class alliance forged in Huanta against Gamarra in 1834 responded, first and foremost, one may argue, to Gamarra's top-down militarism.[30] Moreover, Gamarra's failure to attract peasant support appears not to have been limited to Huanta; he had the same problem in his own backyard.[31]

There seems to be, in brief, something essentially correct in Gootenberg's claim that protectionists warranted state sovereignty vis-à-vis northern hemisphere imperialism, and, in this sense, they stand as Peru's most committed early nationalists. Yet there is no reason to think that *all* those who opposed them in trade matters were removed from popular causes or had a vocation for statelessness, particularly given the father of protectionism's own reliance on top-down methods. Early liberals' permissiveness with the "lower orders," their propensity to ally with bandits, montoneros, and peasants, attest to the degree of unruliness that liberal caudillos not only were able to tolerate but even foment in their efforts to enlarge their constituencies. But this does not mean that they rejected the idea of the state altogether, as I hope to have demonstrated. On the other hand, the fact that the Lima economic project that Gamarra (notwithstanding his Cuzcocentrism) served so well was imposed on the rest of the country through full-fledged militaristic methods and by fomenting internal (and external) war at will, needs to be integrated into the broader discussions of state formation. In other words, one ought to take war—that "continuation of politics by other means"—as seriously as one takes diplomacy and political economy. And war, which was rampant during the early caudillo era, had its place in the highlands, where the decisive battles for control of Lima were ultimately and literally waged. Which is to say, if the external boundaries of the state were drawn in Lima through diplomacy, its internal boundaries were drawn in the highlands through war.

And the idea of war, and violence generally, leads to yet another layer of complexity in the question of state making. Should one accept Max Weber's famous formula that the central defining feature of the state is the "monopolization of legitimate violence,"[32] then the place of the state in this turbulent time of Peruvian history may appear more blurry, but at the same time more inclusive, as one attempts to discern, through the fog created by the many parties claming to be the state, who recognized whose violence as legitimate. The question "What is the state?" could thus well be rephrased as "Who is the state?" or even, "Where is the state?" Viewed this way, the state need not be conceived as a stable network of institutions, but rather as a contested place in and of itself: a state in formation, in the most literal sense of the term.[33] Hence, the pregnant reply of the Huanta montoneros to the question of why they were appropriating the tithes in 1834—that they were acting to "uphold the laws" and "to defend the state"—echoes down to us as much more than a capricious statement. For they had indeed been summoned by the legally elected President Orbegoso to take up arms in order to "defend the state" (and its laws) from Gamarra's coup. Similar claims about the legitimacy of "his government" (and his violence) had been brandished years earlier by Huachaca from his "Royal Prefecture" in Uchuraccay. Huachaca would later draw on this experience to serve the state under the liberal caudillos, who in legitimizing his self-appointed position as a supreme magistrate in the punas enhanced his political power and prestige. The Plebeian Republic thus allowed for political arrangements that would have been inconceivable under Spanish imperial rule. Such arrangements fit the idea of an "unruly order," to borrow Poole's apt expression, better than that of an "ancient regime," that some scholars have used to characterize the political reality of the Andean republics in the nineteenth century.[34]

To conclude, our look at very provincial, local, peasant, and, ultimately, plebeian aspects of early republican politics in Peru, which began by narrating the story of a forgotten "monarchist" rebellion, has paradoxically led us to a broad notion of state. It has also allowed us to identify competing state claims. The idea of state favored by Huantinos did not conform to the notion of state favored by the traders in Lima and the north, who, according to Gootenberg, dominated the political scene from the late 1820s to the early 1840s. For, if we accept his interpretation, this state had Hapsburgian ideological legacies; and whereas the Hapsburgs encouraged corporatism, economic protectionism, and aristocratic values and privileges, Huanta tended toward liberalism, both economically and politically, while socially it could not have been further removed from any nobility. If Huanta serves to exemplify other Andean places, one could then say that the state favored by the Gamarristas and the traders in Lima and the northern coast, for all its economic nationalism—or perhaps, precisely *because* of it—evolved in contraposition to much of rural Andean Peru. Historiography ought to tackle this question. Perhaps the fact that Gamarra's political stronghold was Cuzco has muddled the fact that his most powerful allies were in Lima and obscured the extent to which his aggressive pursuit of the presidency was eventually instrumental to the imposition of Lima's state project on the rest of Peru (pace the Cuzqueños). His overarching association with the former Inca capital may have concealed as well the fact that his support there was not universal but rather limited to the urban spheres. Indeed, as a recent study suggests, Gamarra failed to cater to the Cuzco peasantry.[35] Could he have done otherwise? I would not wager a judgment, but such quandaries give us, at any rate, something to think about in the present.

I wonder, finally, in playing with Gootenberg's compelling "dynastic" analogies, if a parallel between Huantan liberals and the eighteenth-century Bourbon modernizers would make any sense. The temptation to answer yes is great, given that Huanta itself thrived under the Bourbons, precisely because of some of their "liberal" reforms. But here again caution must be exercised. For, as stated at the beginning of this epilogue, the republican state, particularly as it was experienced in Huanta, although it displayed some continuities in relation to its Bourbon imperial predecessor, also differed from it in substantial ways.

Having said that, I cannot go much further. The history of liberalism in Peru's Andean rural areas has not been written, mainly because it has been thought to be nonexistent; but also, and more significantly, I think, because the equation sierra $=$ "backward Peru" still dominates both politics and scholarship. I have written this book in an attempt to question this idea and in the hope that others may determine the extent to which the conclusions I have reached on the basis of the available evidence for Huanta serve to deepen our understanding of Peru in the nineteenth century and, most importantly, perhaps, in the present.

Notes

ABBREVIATIONS

ADAY   Archivo Departamental de Ayacucho
AGN   Archivo General de la Nación (Lima)
AGI   Archivo General de Indias (Seville)
BN   Biblioteca Nacional (Lima)
BNM   Biblioteca Nacional (Madrid)
BRAHM   Biblioteca de la Real Academia de la Historia de Madrid
Crim.   Causas Criminales (Criminal proceedings)
CBC   Centro de Estudios Regionales Andinos Bartolomé
          de las Casas (Cuzco)
CDIP   Colección Documental de la Independencia del Perú
CEHMP–AHM Centro de Estudios Histórico Militares del Perú–Archivo
          Histórico Militar (Lima)
CONUP   Consejo Nacional de la Universidad Peruana
CSIC   Consejo Superior de Investigaciones Aentificas (Madrid)
cuad.   cuaderno (notebook)
JPI   Juzgado de Primera Instancia
IEP   Instituto de Estudios Peruanos
IFEA   Instituto Francés de Estudios Andinos
leg.   legajo (bundle of papers)
PUCP   Pontificia Universidad Católica del Perú
UNSCH   Universidad Nacional de San Cristóbal de Huamanga

CHAPTER 1. Introduction

All translations are Renzo Llorente's and mine unless otherwise indicated.

1   This hypothesis was endorsed by the newspapers *La República* and *El Diario*.

2   Alberto Flores Galindo, *Buscando un Inca: identidad y utopía en los Andes* (Lima: Instituto de Apoyo Agrario, 1987), 325. For most Peruvians, Sendero appeared "like lightning out of a clear sky," as Flores Galindo put it. Sendero's insurgency began precisely when most on the left decided to choose the electoral path and when sociologists and economists were describing Peru as a modern country, one with a growing proletariat and a peasantry in the process of extinction.

3   Mario Vargas Llosa et al., *Informe de la Comisión Investigadora de los Sucesos de Uchuraccay* (Lima: Editora Perú, 1983) (hereafter, *Informe*).

4 Unpublished transcripts of recordings of Vargas Llosa's interrogation of the *comuneros* in Uchuraccay, February 12, 1983 (hereafter, "Unpublished Transcripts").

5 When summoned by Vargas Llosa in February 1983 to reveal the details of the journalists' murders, the Uchuraccay comuneros refused to do so and consistently claimed, "That's all; we, ignorant men, we don't know anything else." "Unpublished Transcripts."

6 For further discussion and thorough bibliographical references on the Uchuraccay case (newspaper, journal, and magazine articles), see "Peru in Deep Trouble: Mario Vargas Llosa's 'Inquest in the Andes' Reexamined," in *Rereading Cultural Anthropology*, ed. George E. Marcus (Durham and London: Duke University Press, 1992).

7 I owe this information to Orin Starn. In 1989, the other two indicted Uchuraccay villagers were released by a pardon granted by President Alan García.

8 Vargas Llosa et al., *Informe*, 36, 39. This argument is stronger in the final report prepared by Vargas Llosa himself—but see also the appendixes by the anthropologists Fernando Fuenzalida and Juan M. Ossio in *Informe*. For further discussion of these issues, see Cecilia Méndez-Gastelumendi, "The Power of Naming, or the Construction of Ethnic and National Identities in Peru: Myth, History and the Iquichanos," *Past and Present*, no. 171 (May 2001): 127–60.

9 See "Nota de Prensa 177," "Nuestro Homenaje a todas las Víctimas de Uchuraccay," *La República*, January 26, 2003; Ponciano del Pino, "Uchuraccay: Memoria y representación de la violencia política en los Andes," paper presented at the SSRC workshop "Memoria Colectiva y Violencia Política: Perspectivas Comparativas Sobre el Proceso de Democratización en América del Sur," New York, 2001; Kimberly Theidon and Enver Quinteros, "Uchuraccay: La Política de la Muerte en el Perú," *Ideele*, no. 152 (February 2003): 27–30.

10 I have elaborated further on the Iquichano identity in Méndez-Gastelumendi, "The Power of Naming."

11 Juan José del Pino, *Las Sublevaciones Indígenas de Huanta 1827–1896* (Ayacucho: n.p., 1955), 13.

12 José Agustín de la Puente y Candamo, *Notas sobre la causa de la independencia del Perú*, 2d ed. (Lima: Studium, 1970). Later, De la Puente updated some of these ideas in a self-critical tone, *La Independencia del Perú* (Madrid: Colección Editorial Mapfre 1492, 1992).

13 For example, Gustavo Vergara Arias, *Montoneras y Guerrillas en la etapa de la emancipación del Perú (1820–1825)* (Lima: Imprenta y Litografía Salesiana, 1974); Ezequiel Beltrán Gallardo, *Las guerrillas de Yauyos en la emancipación del Perú, 1820–1824* (Lima: Editores Técnicos Asociados, 1977). These works had important precedents in such works as Raúl Rivera Serna, *Los guerrilleros del Centro en la emancipación peruana* (Lima: P. L. Villanueva, 1958).

14 The publication of Boleslao Lewin, *La rebelión de Túpac Amaru y los orígenes de la*

emancipación Americana (Buenos Aires: Hachette S. A., 1957) and Carlos Daniel Valcárcel, *La rebelión de Túpac Amaru* (México: Fondo de Cultura Económica, 1947) had a great impact on the construction of Túpac Amaru as a national hero, particularly by singling him out as the initiator of the cycle of Independence struggles in South America. For a discussion of the historiographical "rehabilitation" of Túpac Amaru's image, see David Cahill, *Violencia, represión y rebelión en el sur andino: la sublevación de Túpac Amaru y sus consecuencias: Documento de Trabajo*; no. 105, *Serie Historia* (Lima: Instituto de Estudios Peruanos [hereafter IEP], 1999).

15 Another proof of this conciliatory spirit was the publication, under the official auspices of the government and on the same occasion, of more than a hundred volumes of documents relevant to the Independence process. The main goal of this project, which brought together historians of many different social and political backgrounds, was to instill patriotism, regardless of whether the heroic acts had been performed by creoles, mestizos, or indians. *Colección Documental de la Independencia del Perú* (hereafter CDIP; Lima: Comisión del Sesquicentenario del Independencia del Perú, 1971–78).

16 Heraclio Bonilla and Karen Spalding, "La independencia en el Perú: las palabras y los hechos," in *La Independencia en el Peru* (Lima: IEP, 1972).

17 A similar interpretation of the Independence process appears in Alberto Flores Galindo, *Aristocracia y Plebe: Lima 1760–1830* (Lima: Mosca Azul, 1984).

18 Bonilla and Spalding, "La independencia," 10.

19 By the mid–nineteenth century the Chilean historian Benjamín Vicuña Mackenna wrote a treatise on Peruvian Independence in which he qualified the interpretations that stressed the lack of nationalism among Peruvians and the "external" nature of the process, which was seemingly widespread at that time. See Benjamín Vicuña Mackenna, *La independencia en el Perú*, prologue by Luis Alberto Sánchez, 5th ed. (Buenos Aires: Editorial Francisco de Aguirre, 1971). For an early twentieth-century account of Independence that argues for Peru's unwillingness to become indepent, see Nemesio Vargas, *Historia del Perú Independiente* (Lima: Imp. de la Escuela de Ingenieros por Juio Mesinas, 1903), 1:18.

20 José Carlos Mariátegui, *Siete Ensayos de Interpretación de la Realidad Peruana* (Lima: Biblioteca Amauta, 1952).

21 A frequently quoted passage can be found in José de la Riva Agüero, "Paisajes Peruanos," in *Obras Completas* (Lima: Pontificia Universidad Católica, 1969), 11:159.

22 Ibid., 49. Or, as French historian Jean Piel put it, "At Junín and Ayacucho the Peruvian soldiers on the two sides, that of the Crown and that of Independence, killed each other without a thought. To the majority the idea of an independent Peru meant nothing." Jean Piel, "The Place of the Peasantry in the National Life of Peru in the Nineteenth Century," *Past and Present* no. 49 (February 1970): 116. The historical synthesis of the Independence in Latin America that best reproduces

these Marxist-*dependentista* paradigms is John Lynch, *The Spanish American Revolutions, 1808–1826*, 2d ed. (New York: Norton 1986). An interpretation of Independence that, notwithstanding its sympathy with the Marxist paradigm, presented a variant of the Bonilla-Spalding thesis is that of Florencia Mallon, *The Defense of Community in Peru's Central Highlands* (Princeton: Princeton University Press, 1983), 51. Mallon holds that the incipient bourgeoisie of the central sierra wanted to break with colonial domination, for, unlike the creoles of Lima, the bourgeoisie in this region saw their interests and class development restricted by colonialism. As regards the role of the popular sectors, however, Mallon endorses the Marxist theory discussed here: that of "no perception" and "no participation." Similarly, see Nelson Manrique, *Yawar Mayu: Sociedades Terratenientes Serranas 1789–1910* (Lima: Desco and Instituto Francés de Estudios Andinos, 1988), 27–28. Both Mallon and Manrique, however, have written extensively about peasant participation in the War of the Pacific (1879–83).

23   For an empirically rich and nonpatriotic approach that considers peasants as participants in the political debates that preceded Independence, see Christine Hünefeldt, *Lucha por la tierra y protesta indígena* (Bonn: Bonner Amerikanistische Studiens 9, 1982); and Núria Sala i Vila, *Y se armó el tole tole: tributo indígena y movimientos sociales en el Virreinato del Perú, 1790–1814* (Ayacucho: Instituto de Estudios Regionales José María Arguedas, 1996). In the seventies some works emerged in reaction to the article by Bonilla and Spalding that did not support de la Puente's hypothesis, for example, Jorge Basadre, *El Azar en la Historia y sus límites* (Lima: P. L. Villanueva, 1973). Scarlett O'Phelan also disputed Bonilla but did not discuss the role of the popular sectors. See O'Phelan, "Acerca del mito de la Independencia concedida," in *Independencia y Revolución*, comp., Alberto Flores Galindo (Lima: Instituto Nacional de Cultura, 1987). For Bonilla's response to some of these critiques, see his "Clases Populares y Estado en el contexto de la crisis colonial," in *La Independencia en el Perú*, 2d ed., ed. Heraclio Bonilla (Lima: IEP, 1981).

24   Notably, Paul Gootenberg, *Between Silver and Guano: Commercial Policy and the State in Postindependence Peru* (Princeton: Princeton University Press, 1989); and Paul Gootenberg, *Tejidos y harinas, corazones y mentes: el imperialismo norteamericano del libre comercio en el Perú 1825–1840* (Lima: IEP, Series Colección Mínima no. 17, 1989).

25   Interestingly, the Huanta peasants' monarchist ventures sparked the curiosity more of nineteenth-century than of twentieth-century historians. The first historiographical approach to the monarchist uprising in Peru is probably that of Mariano Felipe Paz Soldán (1821–86), *Historia del Perú Independiente (tercer periodo 1827–1833)* (Lima: Librería e Imprenta Gil, 1929), originally published in the 1860s. Paz Soldán's treatment of the Huanta rebellion is more subtle and extensive than Jorge Basadre's in *Historia de la República*, vol. 1, 7th ed. rev. (Lima: Editorial

Universitaria, 1983). This, of course, does not include diaries and chronicles from the early republican period, which provide brief though significant data on the so-called Iquichanos. These authors include one president of the Republic, Rufino Echenique, the chaplain of another president, Luis José Orbegoso, and some European travelers. See Peter Blanchard, *Markham in Peru: The Travels of Clements R. Markham, 1852–1853* (Austin: University of Texas Press, 1991); José María Blanco, *Diario del Presidente Orbegoso al Sur del Perú*, Félix Denegri Luna, ed. (Lima: Pontificia Universidad Católica del Perú, Instituto Riva Agüero, Lima: 1974); José Rufino Echenique, *Memorias para la Historia del Perú*, vol. 1 (Lima: Editorial Huascarán, 1952); Heinrich Witt, *Un Testimonio Personal Sobre el Peru del Siglo XIX, (1824–1842)*, vol. 1 (Lima: Banco Mercantil, 1992). On Iquichano participation in the *caudillista* strife of the 1830s, see Nemesio Vargas, *Historia*, vol. 1.

26 Patrick Husson, "Guerre indienne et révolte paysanne dans la province de Huanta (département d'Ayacucho-Pérou) au XIXème siècle," Université Paris IV, 1983, published, in Spanish unrevised, as *De la Guerra a la Rebelión (Huanta siglo XIX)* (Cuzco: Centro de Estudios Regionales Andinos Bartolomé de las Casas [hereafter CBC], 1992). The first thesis on the Huanta monarchist uprising is actually by Iván Pérez Aguirre, "Rebeldes Iquichanos: 1824–1828," (Tesis de Bachillerato, Universidad Nacional de San Cristóbal de Huamanga Ayacucho, 1982). This work unearths an important array of unpublished sources from which my own work has benefited. His interpretation is, unfortunately, marred by a dogmatic Maoist agenda that makes it difficult to discuss his arguments in broad historiographical terms.

27 "The main problem posed by the war of the Iquichanos seems to be the transference of a conflict involving the dominant strata toward the social strata which in principle have no stake in the conflict. The problem of the transference of a conflict from the national to the regional level and from an elite to the people could, from our point of view, be resolved in part through an examination of the fundamental role of the duality manipulation-alienation." Husson, *De la Guerra*, 123.

28 Ibid., 229.

29 Ibid., 22. By the same token, "The two . . . uprisings. . . . expressed the great fear of the indigenous peasant masses when confronted with imminent change," ibid., 236.

30 Ibid., 240. Although Husson does not quote many theoretical works, his interpretation is clearly informed by the Marxist / modernizing approaches represented by such works as Eric Wolf, *Peasant Wars of the Twentieth Century* (New York: Harper and Row, 1966); Barrington Moore's classic *Lord and Peasant in the Making of the Modern World* (Boston: Beacon Press, 1967); and possibly the non-Marxist work of George Foster, "Peasant Society and the Image of Limited Good," *American Anthropologist* 67 (1965): 293–315.

31 Vargas Llosa et al., *Informe*, 39 (emphasis added).

32 A footnote cannot do justice to the many studies which during the past twenty-five years have come to question the theoretical and political assumptions on which Husson based his analysis, but see the two well-known studies of James Scott, which delve into nonviolent "resistance": *The Moral Economy of the Peasant: Rebellion and Subsistence in Southeast Asia* (New Haven: Yale University Press, 1976); and *Weapons of the Weak: The Everyday Forms of Peasant Resistance* (New Haven: Yale University Press, 1985). For the Andes, see, for example, Steve Stern, ed., *Resistance, Rebellion and Consciousness in the Andean Peasant World: 18th to 20th Centuries* (Madison: University of Wisconsin Press, 1987). The "defensive" reaction of the peasants before the advance of "capitalism" has been questioned for the Andean reality by a series of investigations that address peasant participation in colonial markets. See Olivia Harris, Brooke Larson, and Enrique Tandeter, eds., *Participación Indígena en los Mercados Surandinos: estrategias y reproducción social, siglos XVI a XX*, 2 vols. (Cochabamba: CERES, 1987); and Brooke Larson and Olivia Harris, eds., *Ethnicity, Markets, and Migration in the Andes* (Durham: Duke University Press, 1995).

33 An example appears in Wilfredo Kapsoli, *Los Movimientos Campesinos en el Perú*, 3d ed. (Lima: Ediciones Atusparia, 1987).

34 Nelson Manrique, *Las guerrillas indígenas en la guerra con Chile* (Lima: Centro de Investigación y Capacitación / Ital Perú, 1981).

35 In particular, Heraclio Bonilla, "El Problema Nacional y Colonial del Perú en el Contexto de la Guerra del Pacífico," in *Un Siglo a la Deriva*, Heraclio Bonilla (Lima: IEP, 1980).

36 Heraclio Bonilla's response to Manrique's work is in Heraclio Bonilla, "El Campesinado Indígena y el Perú en el Contexto de la Guerra con Chile," in *Hisla* 4 (1984) (English version in Stern, ed., *Resistance*). For a continuation of the debate, see Nelson Manrique, "Campesinado, Guerra y Conciencia Nacional," *Revista Andina* no. 4 (1), (1986): 161–72. Along the lines of Manrique's work, see also Florencia Mallon, "National and Antistate Coalitions in the War of the Pacific: Junín and Cajamarca, 1879–1902," in *Resistance, Rebellion and Consciousness*, ed. Stern, 232–79, and Florencia Mallon, *Peasant and Nation: The Making of Postcolonial Mexico and Peru* (Berkeley: University of California Press, 1995).

37 María Isabel Remy, "La sociedad local al inicio de la república. Cusco 1824–1850," *Revista Andina* no. 12 (1988); Jaime Urrutia, "Comerciantes, Arrieros y Viajeros Huamanguinos: 1770–1870," *Tesis de Bachiller* (Ayacucho: Universidad Nacional de San Cristóbal de Huamanga, 1982); Carlos Contreras, "Estado Republicano y Tributo Indígena en la Sierra Central en la Post-independencia," *Histórica* 13, no. 1 (July 1989): 517–50; Víctor Peralta, *En Pos del Tributo en el Cusco Rural: 1826–1854* (Cuzco: CBC, 1991); Betford Betalleluz, "Fiscalidad, Tierras y Mercado: Las Comunidades Indígenas de Arequipa, 1825–1850," in *Tradición y Modernidad en los Andes*, ed. Henrique Urbano, 147–61 (Cuzco: CBC, 1992); Charles Walker, "Montoneros, ban-

doleros, malhechores: Criminalidad y política en las primeras décadas republicanas," in *Bandoleros, abigeos y montoneros: Criminalidad y violencia en el Perú, siglos XVIII–XX*, ed. Carlos Aguirre and Charles Walker, 107–33 (Lima: Instituto de Apoyo Agrario, 1990); Charles Walker, "Peasants, Caudillos and the State in Peru: Cusco in the Transition from Colony to Republic, 1780–1840" (Ph.D. diss., University of Chicago, 1992). Although in his dissertation Walker argues for peasant political participation in the caudillo state, his sources often betray his argument. In his book *Smoldering Ashes: Cuzco and the Creation of Republican Peru, 1780–1840* (Durham: Duke University Press, 1999), Walker is less optimistic about peasant participation in caudillo politics and ends up endorsing a more conservative stance, in tune with the historiography of the 1970s; thus he claims that "the indigenous peasants remained largely detached from the caudillo struggles" and insists on the "separation between caudillo politics and Indian society" (213). Walker comes to these generalizations even though he has examined only one caudillo and a single region (Agustín Gamarra in Cuzco). For a more elaborate argument on early nineteenth-century "peasant politics," see Mark Thurner " 'Republicanos' and 'la Comunidad de Peruanos'": Unimagined Political Communities in Postcolonial Andean Perú," *Journal of Latin American Studies* 27 (1995): 291–318; and Thurner, *From Two Republics to One Divided* (Durham: Duke University Press, 1997). Thurner is, however, less concerned with early-republican caudillo politics than he is with *indigenismo*, textual analysis, and "post-colonial" theories. See also Cecilia Méndez G., "Los Campesinos, La Independencia y la Iniciación de la República: el caso de los iquichanos realistas," in *Poder y Violencia en los Andes*, ed. Henrique Urbano, 165–88 (Cuzco: CBC, 1991), and Méndez G., "República Sin Indios: La Comunidad Imaginada del Peru," in *Tradición y Modernidad en los Andes*, ed. Henrique Urbano, 15–41 (Cuzco: CBC, 1992).

38 Gustavo Gorriti Ellenboghen, *Sendero, La Guerra Milenaria* (Lima: Apoyo, 1990), 15.

39 For two very distinct but similarly comprehensive studies on state formation and rural society in Latin America, see John Lynch, *Caudillos in Spanish America, 1800–1850* (Oxford: Clarendon Press, 1992), and Fernando López Alves, *State Formation and Democracy in Latin America* (Durham and London: Duke University Press, 2000). On the "ruralization of power," see Tulio Halperín Donghi, *Hispanoamérica Después de la Independencia* (Buenos Aires: Paidós, 1972). Argentina's historiography on the subject has important recent contributions, such as Ariel de la Fuente, *Children of Facundo* (Durham: Duke University Press, 2000), and Noemí Goldman and Ricardo Salvatore, eds., *Caudillismos Rioplatanses: Nuevas Miradas a Un Viejo Problema* (Buenos Aires: Eudeba / Facultad de Filosofía y Letras, Universidad de Buenos Aires, 1998).

40 This classification is only an approximation, but for the elevations and names of the ecological niches I am following relatively closely the classic classification of Javier

Pulgar Vidal in *Las Ocho Regiones Naturales del Perú* (Lima: Editorial Universo, 1972), as well as Richard Burger, *Chavín and the Origins of Andean Civilization* (London: Thames and Hudson, 1992). In other parts of the Andes (especially in Bolivia), *montaña* (or *ceja de selva*) is most commonly called *yunga,* and in Peru this classification may also apply, although it was most common in ealier times, where montañas were referred to as *"yungas* of the jungle" (as opposed to the *"coastal yungas,"* which one does not find in Huanta). See figure 3.

41 Most English dictionaries define *punas* as "high Andean plateaus." This definition is inaccurate because in many Andean regions (and not just in Huanta), punas are anything but tablelands.

42 See map 1, "Peru in 1827."

43 On colonial Huamanga, see Steve Stern, *Peru's Indian Peoples and the Challenge of Spanish Conquest: Huamanga to 1640* (Madison: University of Wisconsin Press, 1982); Jaime Urrutia, *Huamanga, Región e Historia* (Ayacucho: Universidad Nacional de San Cristóbal de Huamanga, 1985); Carlos Contreras, *La Ciudad del Mercurio, Huancavelica 1570–1700* (Lima: IEP, 1982); Miriam Salas de Coloma, *Estructura colonial del poder español en el Perú: Huamanga (Ayacucho) a través de sus obrajes: siglos XVI–XVIII,* 3 vols. (Lima: Pontificia Universidad Católica del Perú [hereafter cited as PUCP], 1998).

44 This was due partly to the decline of the market circuits that the once-prosperous Potosí had fostered and partly to Peru's loss of a great part of its south (or Upper Peru, that is, present-day Bolivia) to the newly created viceroyalty of Río de la Plata. See also Manuel Burga, "El Perú central 1770–1860: Disparidades regionales y la primera crisis agrícola," *Revista Peruana de Ciencias Sociales* 1 (1987): 5–69.

45 For a history of Ayacucho's montaña and selva, see Núria Sala i Vila, *Selva y Andes: Ayacucho (1780–1929), Historia de Una Región en la Encrucijada* (Madrid: Consejo Superior de Investigaciones Científicas, 2001).

46 AGN, Superior Gobierno. leg. 37, 1313, "Expediente Promovido ante el Señor Gobernador Intendente de Huanta por los vecinos de esa jurisdicción . . .," 1819, f. 3v.; Hipólito Unanue, *Guía Política, Eclesiástica y Militar del Virreynato del Perú para el año de 1795, Compuesta por orden del Superior Gobierno* (Lima: Imprenta Real de los Niños Huérfanos [herafter cited as *Guía 1795*], reprinted in *Colección Documental de la Independencia del Perú* (hereafter cited as CDIP), tomo 1, *Los Ideólogos,* comp. Jorge Arias Schreiber Pezet, 1:717–78.

47 Unanue, *Guía 1795.*

48 Blanco, *Diario,* 46.

49 For a discussion of the concept of the frontier in Spanish America, see Patricia Cerda-Hegerl, *Fronteras del Sur, La región del Bío Bío y la Araucanía Chilena, 1604–1883* (Temuco: Universidad de la Frontera / Instituto Latinoamericano de la Universidad Libre de Berlín, 1993).

50 Loyalty to the Crown was not something of which only the white elite boasted. In the colonial era, it was even more important for indians to prove their loyalty because it was a prerequisite for receiving the confirmation of their titles as *kurakas*, which allowed them to claim property titles, privileges such as tax exemptions, and, most importantly, the right to rule over a given community of indians and collect tribute from them. The celebrated chronicler Guamán Poma de Ayala, who was born in southern Ayacucho in the postconquest sixteenth century is the most renowned example of a native Andean who struggled to demonstrate not only his own loyalty to the king but also that of his ancestors, in the so-called "wars of the *encomenderos*"—although he was never granted the recognition of kuraka he so longed for. See his *Nueva Coronica y Buen Gobierno*, 3 vols., John Murra and Rolena Adorno, eds., Jorge Urioste, trans. (Lima: IEP / Siglo Veintiuno, 1980).

51 This feature is, however, apparent only in the provinces south of Huanta. The area that corresponds to current Huanta province remains a blank spot on the "ethnic maps" of sixteenth-century Huamanga—its fate under the Incas being less well known (see, for instance, maps in Jaime Urrutia, *Huamanga*, 20, 51). The presence of *mitmas* dating back to Inca times is, in other words, not evident in Huanta. The possibility that the Incas may not have completely subdued every corner of the current Huanta province cannot be ruled out. For a recent overview of the archeological work in Ayacucho, see Cirilo Vivanco Pomacanchari, "Arqueología de Ayacucho: Un Examen Necesario," *Afanes, Búsqueda desde Huamanga* I, no. I (1996): 85–95. On pre-Hispanic Ayacucho, see Enrique Gonzales Carré, *Historia Pre-Hispánica de Ayacucho* (Ayacucho: Universidad Nacional de Sán Cristóbal de Huamanga, 1982). For Chanka archaeology, see Lidio Valdés, Cirilo Vivanco, and Casimiro Chávez, "Asentamientos Chanka en la cuenca del Pamapas y Qaracha, Ayacucho," *Gaceta Arqueológica Andina* no. 17 (1990): 17–26. On pre-Hispanic Huanta, see Martha Anders, "Dual Organization and Calendars Inferred from the Planned Site of Azángaro-Wari Administrative Strategies," 3 vols. (PH.D. diss., Cornell University, 1986).

52 Gorriti, *Sendero*; Cecilia Méndez G., "La Tentación del Olvido: Guerra, Nacionalismo e Historiadores en el Perú," *Diálogos*, no. 2 (2000): 231–48.

53 The Huanta chieftains may bear more resemblance to the Aymara caudillo Julián Apasa, who, under the name Túpaj Katari, led the siege of La Paz in 1781. Unlike the members of the Túpac Amaru clan, he was humbly born and had little education, though he doubtless became a charismatic and effective leader and ended up, like Túpac Amaru, being executed by the Spanish. See Sinclair Thompson, "Colonial Crisis, Community, and Andean Self-Rule: Aymara Politics in the Age of Insurgency, Eighteenth-Century La Paz," (PH.D. diss., University of Wisconsin, 1996), and Thompson, *We Alone Will Rule: Native Andean Politics in the Age of Insurgency* (Madison: University of Wisconsin Press, 2002). Other researchers have

called attention to a non-kuraka kind of indian leadership, particularly in the late eighteenth century, to whom the Huantinos seem to bear some resemblance as well. For example, David Cahill and Scarlett O'Phelan Godoy, "Forging Their Own History: Indian Insurgency in the Southern Peruvian Sierra," *Bulletin of Latin American Research* 2, no. 2 (1992): 125–67; Sala i Vila, *Y se Armó*; and Alejandro Diez Hurtado, *Comunes y Haciendas: Procesos de Comunalización en la Sierra de Piura (siglos XVIII al XX)* (Cuzco: CIPCA / CBC, 1998).

54 Basadre, *Historia* (1983 ed.), 2:168. See also Lynch, *Caudillos*.

55 Scarlett O'Phelan, "El sur andino a fines del siglo XVIII: cacique o corregidor," *Allpanchis Phuturinqa*, no. 11 (1978): 17–32; Sala i Vila, *Y Se Armó*; Thurner, *From Two Republics*.

56 In their respective studies of the peasant communities of nineteenth-century Piura (in northern Peru) and Chumbivilcas (Cuzco), the anthropologists Alejandro Diez and Deborah Poole have noticed the existence of a peasant leadership that does not fit the "classic" definitions of kuraka and *varayoq*. Their contributions are especially important in that they pay close attention, as few anthropological works do when covering the nineteenth century, to the way in which the peasant community's authority system, material culture, and power relations were molded in their relationship with the state. Yet neither of them delves into the impact of caudillo politics in the peasant community authority system and power relations. See Diez Hurtado, *Comunes y Haciendas*; and Deborah Poole, "Qorilazos, abigeos y comunidades campesinas en la provincia de Chumbivilcas (Cusco)," in *Comunidades Campesinas, Cambios y Permanencias*, 2d ed., ed. Alberto Flores Galindo, 257–95 (Chiclayo: Centro de Estudios 'Solidaridad,' 1988); and Poole, "Landscapes of Power in a Cattle-Rustling Culture of Southern Andean Peru," *Dialectical Anthropology* no. 12 (1988): 367–98.

57 For thought-provoking reflections on this issue, see Alberto Flores Galindo, *La Tradición Autoritaria: Violencia y democracia en el Perú* (Lima: Sur / APRODEH, 1999), 26–27.

58 On Huanta liberals, see José Coronel Aguirre, "Don Manuel Jesús Urbina: creación del Colegio de Instrucción Media González Vigil y las pugnas por el Poder Local en Huanta (1910–1930)," in *Libro Jubilar 1933–1983, Comité Central Pro-Bodas de Oro del Colegio National González Vigil* (Huanta: Colegio Nacional González Vigil and Universidad Nacional de San Cristóbal de Huamanga, 1983), 217–46; Cecilia Méndez G., "Estado, Poder Local y Sociedad Rural: Una Visión desde Ayacucho," paper presented at the XII International Conference of the AHILA, Porto, September 21–25, 1999; Cesar Itier, *El Teatro Quechua en el Cuzco*, vol. 2, *Indigenismo, Lengua y literatura en el Perú moderno* (Cuzco: CBC / IFEA, 2000), 89–90; Sala i Vila, *Selva y Andes*, 198–202.

59 "They [the peasants] have lived isolated and forgotten since pre-Hispanic times." Vargas Llosa et al., *Informe*, 38.

CHAPTER 2. The Republic's First Peasant Uprising

1   Horacio Villanueva Urteaga, *Gamarra y la Iniciación Republicana en el Cuzco* (Lima: Fondo del Libro del Banco de los Andes, 1981), 20–22, 27.

2   Regarding the "Bolivarian frenzy," see Basadre, *Historia*, 1:96–97.

3   Regarding the anti-Bolivarian climate and "microfederalist" projects, see Basadre, *Historia*, 1983 ed. 1:121–26, and Rubén Vargas Ugarte, *Historia General del Perú* (Lima: Milla Batres, 1968), 7:40–45.

4   *El Depositario*, no. 121, December 25, 1824. *El Depositario* was the boldest and most passionate proroyalist newspaper of the time.

5   *El Depositario*, no.126, April 7, 1825.

6   CEHMP-AHM, leg. 1, doc. 14, 1825. "En Ica . . . abundan los godos de un modo escandaloso" (In Ica, the godos [Spaniards] are scandalously abundant), stated the southern military commander shortly before arresting the *capitulados* (office to the Minister of War, CEHMP-AHM, leg. 7, doc. 4, 1824).

7   Around April 1825, Ignacio Alvarado was tried for inciting rebellion among "the towns of the Huanta puna." ADAY JPI, Crim., leg. 26, "Juicio Criminal contra Ignacio Alvarado, cabecilla de Iquicha," f.1. I have found no other evidence of detentions of capitulados in Huanta around this date.

8   *Monografía Histórico-Geográfica del Departmento de Ayacucho*, 181, cited in Pérez Aguirre, "Rebeldes Iquichanos," 65 (emphasis added). *Villa* was an honorific title meant to elevate Huanta from the status of pueblo (town) to one closer to that of a city.

9   Reconstructed on the basis of ADAY, JPI, Crim. leg. 55, cuad. 1, ff. 13, 15, 28; and Echenique, *Memorias*, 1:16–17. I am borrowing the expression "War of the Punas" from Husson. The original of Garay's "Proclama" in this section's epigraph is in ADAY, JPI CC, leg. 31, cuad. 585, f. 19.

10   Cited in Pérez Aguirre, "Rebeldes Iquichanos," 137.

11   CEHMP-AHM, leg. 19, doc. 14, April 5, 1826.

12   ADAY, JPI, Crim., leg. 55, cuad. 1, f. 28

13   ADAY, JPI, Prefecturas, leg. 64, unnumbered file on the trial of Benito and José Ruiz.

14   For an account of coca haciendas controlled by the rebels, see ADAY, JPI, Crim., cuad. 582, ff. 14–15. Besides Acón, Choimacota, and Buenalerma (to the northeast of the current Iquicha peasant community), Viscatán and Sintihuaylas to the north and Chungui to the south had coca fields. The coca region that was ultimately controlled by the monarchist rebels comprised, therefore, a territory stretching between the present provinces of Huanta and La Mar (see maps 2 and 4).

15   On the various titles with which Huachaca signed his authorizations, see ADAY, JPI, Crim., leg. 30, cuad 582, ff. 11, 13; and leg. 30, cuad. 579, f. 36; leg. 55, cuad. 1, f. 24.

16 ADAY, JPI, Crim., leg. 30, cuads. 582 and 569.

17 ADAY, JPI, Crim., leg. 55, cuad. 1, f. 14.

18 Ibid., f. 28 r / v.

19 Ibid., f. 28v.

20 Other tithe collectors appointed by Huachaca were José Quintanilla and Rafael Aristizabal. For Quintanilla, see ADAY, JPI, Crim., leg. 55, cuad. 1, f. 25r; for José Pérez de Valle, ADAY, JPI, Crim., leg. 30, cuad. 572, f. 1r; and for Rafael Castro and Manuel Leandro, ADAY, JPI, Crim., leg. 30, cuad. 582, f. 13r.

21 "Given and signed by my hand and countersigned by my General Secretary, done in this Headquarters of San Luis, October 8 of 1827. José Antonio Huachaca. Rafael de Castro. Secretary General." ADAY, 1827, JPI, Crim., leg. 30, cuad. 572, f. 1.

22 CEHMP-AHM, leg. 19, doc. 62, August 10, 1826. From the Prefect Pardo de Zela to the Minister of War and the Navy.

23 Cavero, Monografía, 1:193. Vargas Ugarte, Historia General, 7:119. On Arancibia, see ADAY, JPI, leg. 30, cuad 566, f. 5r.

24 El Peruano, August 22, 1826, cited in Cavero, Monografía, 1:191.

25 CEHMP-AHM, leg. 19, doc. 51. From Prefect Pardo de Zela to the Minister of War and the Navy, August 3, 1826.

26 AGN, PL-6–176, 1826, f. 19r.

27 References to this alliance abound in the correspondence seized from the rebels. ADAY, JPI, Crim., leg. 31, cuad. 585, 1826., esp. ff. 2, 5, 7, 18.

28 ADAY, JPI, Crim., leg. 29, cuad 564, ff. 66, 67; Pérez Aguirre, "Rebeldes Iquichanos," 74–75.

29 ADAY, JPI, Crim., leg. 31, cuad. 585, "Cuaderno Tercero del Juicio a Soregui . . .," 1826, f. 4. From Pascual Arancibia to Francisco Garay, Secce, June 27, 1826.

30 ADAY, JPI, leg. 30, cuad. 582, ff. 18rv, "Papeles que tratan sobre comisiones recibidas por Manuel Leandro . . .," f. 18v; ADAY, JPI, Crim., leg. 30, cuad. 579, f. 23v, "Papeles pertenecientes al juicio a Soregui."

31 ADAY, JPI, Crim., leg. 27, cuad. 521, f. 112, "Cuaderno cuarto del juicio a Soregui y otros."

32 ADAY, JPI, Crim., leg. 30, cuad. 579, ff. 19r / v, "Exhortación del cura José Franco Coronado . . . a los señores alcaldes y demás comunidades . . . de Iquicha, Cano y Tircos"; El Mercurio Peruano, no. 105, Lima, December 5, 1827.

33 It is also said that many never saw the pardons because Soregui succeeded in intercepting some and burning others. See, for example, ADAY, 1826, JPI, Crim., leg. 31, cuad. 585, f. 30v (declarations of Gregorio Guijas).

34 Declarations from Juan Ramos (ADAY, JPI, Crim., leg. 29. cuad. 564, f. 63v, 64r), Basilio Navarro (ibid., f. 25r), and Juan Heredia (ibid., f. 46r).

35   ADAY, JPI, Crim., leg. 29, cuad. 564, f. 64v.

36   Ibid., Deposition from Juan Heredia, f. 49r.

37   Rumors of the arrival of a fleet sent from Spain, which would come to unite the Huanta rebels with other conspirators in Lima and Huancayo, began to circulate as early as 1825 and continued incessantly throughout the following years. See the proroyalist newspaper *El Depositario*; ADAY, 1825, JPI, Crim., leg. 29, cuad. 564, ff. 49, 64, 66, 67. See also correspondence between Huachaca and the conspirators in Huancayo in ADAY, JPI, Crim., leg. 31, cuad. 585; 1826, AGN, RJ, Prefecturas, Ayacucho, leg. 93. Priests played an important role in disseminating these news items. Nicolás Carrasco, the priest in Pacaysancos, was accused of "having said in conversations and even sermons from the pulpit that Spaniards were blocking the port of Callao, that they were coming through Trujillo with the army" (AGN, RJ, Ministerio de Justicia, leg. 93). On the specific content of the monarchist propaganda, see chapter 5.

38   Reconstructed on the basis of AGN, R-J, Prefecturas-Ayacucho, leg. 93; Del Pino, *Las Sublevaciones*, 196–200, and Cavero, *Monografía*, 1:109. As Arbizu explained at her trial somewhat euphemistically, "In her house she accommodated José Vílchez, Don Francisco Franco Torres, Don José Villar, Don Cayetano Bargas, and other persecuted patriots brought by Pascual Arancibia and Choque." ADAY, JPI, Crim., f. 11 (verso), "Expediente Contra el presbitero Mariano Meneses, Capellán de los Iquichanos enemigos de la Patria."

39   Cited in Del Pino, *Las Sublevaciones*, 19.

40   *El Telégrafo de Lima*, no. 199, November 29, 1827.

41   "Until the twentieth," Tristán declared, "I worked as hard as I could to inspire the Morochucos and save the armaments that I found stored in Huancavelica, entering the capital on said day with my arms and Morochucos, and giving further inspiration to the city." Ayacucho, December 20, 1827, *El Mercurio Peruano*, no. 110, December 12, 1827.

42   Prefectura del Departmento of Ayacucho, November 22, 1827, from Domingo Tristán to the Chiefs of the Iquichanos ("Los Jefes de los Iquichanos"), ADAY, 1827, JPI, Crim., leg. 31, cuad. 585, f. 37v.

43   AGN, R-J, Prefecturas, Ayacucho, leg. 93, 1827. As tends to happen, the figures vary in accordance with the interests of whoever is offering the testimony. Tristán claimed that the number of montoneros who descended from the hills for the attack totaled three thousand (*El Mercurio Peruano*, Lima, December 12, 1827), and there were some who said they numbered four thousand. Most of the witnesses captured in this action, however, report numbers ranging from nine hundred to fifteen hundred, though the figure of three thousand is widely quoted by various sources in the aftermath of the events.

44   *El Mercurio Peruano*, no. 110, Lima, December 12, 1827.

45   BN, D9847, 1828, "Expediente sobre . . . extralimitación de reclutamiento en Acobamba para hacer frente a los iquichanos."

46   Declarations of Juan Ramos, ADAY, JPI, Crim., leg. 29, cuad. 564.

47   BN, D9847, 1828.

48   Husson, *De La Guerra*, 40–41.

49   ADAY, JPI, Crim., leg. 30, cuad. 579, 1828, f. 3r, "Cuaderno de los papeles pertenecientes a Francisco Garay," from Francisco Garay to Nicolás Soregui, Marcaraccay,
January 22, 1828.

50   "I likewise commend the conduct of Arancibia, Barreda, and Choque, who before
were part of it [i.e., the rebellion] and the bravery and enthusiasm with which the
officials and soldiers of my command have conducted themselves on many occasions when we found ourselves with large groups of rebels." From Francisco Vidal
to the Prefect of Ayacucho, Headquarters on route to Huanta, May 4, 1828. Cited
in Del Pino, *Las Sublevaciones*, 23–24.

51   ADAY, JPI, Crim., leg. 30, cuad. 579, f. 36r.

52   Ibid., f. 35.

53   ADAY, JPI, Crim., leg. 30, cuad. 566, Trial of Esteban Meneses. Declarations of
Esteban Meneses, f. 32r.

54   ADAY, JPI, Crim., leg. 29, cuad. 564, f. 76r.

55   ADAY, JPI, Crim., leg. 30, cuad. 579, f. 13: from Pacheco to Nicolás Soregui, Aran-
huay, March 20, 1828; ADAY, JPI, Crim., leg. 30, cuad. 566, ff. 1, 2, from Commander
Quintanilla to the Prefect of Ayacucho, Military Commander's Headquarters of
Tambo, March 20, 1828.

56   ADAY, JPI, Crim., leg. 30, cuad. 579, declarations by Ylario Taype.

57   Ibid., cuad. 566, Trial of Esteban Meneses, f. 1r.

58   Ibid., f. 1v, from Commander Quintanilla to Domingo Tristán.

59   CEHMP-AH, leg. 34, doc. 97, from Father Haro to Prefect Tristán, Chaca, April 4,
1828.

60   Headquarters of the Military Command of Tambo, May 12, 1828, from Gabriel
Quintanilla to Domingo Tristán. Cited in Cavero, *Monografía*, 1:209.

61   ADAY, JPI, Crim., leg. 29, cuad. 564, f. 2r.

62   ADAY, JPI, Crim., leg. 29, cuad. 564.

63   Del Pino, *Las Sublevaciones*, 23.

64   AGN, R-J, Ayacucho-Prefecturas, leg. 94.

65   Cavero, *Monografía*, 1:112.

66   Gervasio Alvarez, *Guía Histórica Cronológica, Política y Eclesiástica del Departamento
de Ayacucho para el Año 1847* (Ayacucho: Imprenta Gonzales, 1944), 22.

67   Cavero, *Monografía*, 1:212–16; Alvarez, *Guía*, 56.

68   Cavero, *Monografía*, 1:213. Quintanilla was among neither the executed rebels nor

those who surrendered in Pultunchara. Cavero believes that the rebel officers of 1833 used Quintanilla's influence over the Iquichano caudillos to encourage the peasantry to fight against Gamarrra's troops, though with little success.

69 This is the interpretation of Nemesio Vargas, cited in Cavero, *Monografía*, 1:215.

70 Cited in Cavero, *Monografía*, 1:215.

71 On April 3, 1834, Tristán informed the minister of war that two hundred men from Chupamarca had formed a *partida* (guerrilla unit) to monitor the enemy army's steps, while another two hundred men from Víñac would stay on "continuous alert" and had formed two additional partidas. CEHM-AHMP, leg. 26, doc. 16, 1834. See also AGN, PL 15–437, 1835, cuad. 2, f. 12rv and f. 16r. See chapter 7 for further discussion of the civil war of 1834.

72 AGN, PL 15–437, 1835, cuad. 2, ff. 12r-16r.

73 Ibid., ff. 12rv, 16r.

74 See chapter 7.

75 ADAY, JPI, Crim., Diezmos, leg. 59, cuad. 7, f. 15.

76 José Urbina, cited in Pérez Aguirre, "Rebeldes Iquichanos," 140. See also chapter 7.

CHAPTER 3. Royalism in the Independence Crisis

1 This military rebellion is popularly known as the "mutiny of Balconcillo."

2 Basadre, *Historia* (1983 ed.), 1:15–37.

3 Anonymous, AGN, Superior Gobierno, leg. 38, cuad. 1394, 1822.

4 Ibid.

5 Ibid.

6 Basadre, *Historia* (1983 ed.), 1:50.

7 Ibid, 51.

8 Ibid.

9 Ibid., 15–40.

10 Ibid., 36.

11 Ibid., 65.

12 Ibid., 64–65.

13 The Tribunal del Consulado gave generous sums to the antirevolutionary struggle, as Viceroy Abascal himself reported to the king: "The [Tribunal] has opportunely provided Your Excellency with as much as it could collect to aid the public treasury in its present afflictions. Every month since February of the present year [possibly 1813] this laudable body has given sixteen-thousand pesos for the support of one-thousand soldiers in the army, [and] the venerable, exemplary and most illustrious Archbishop, one-thousand six-hundred pesos for [that of] one-hundred soldiers; the most excellent town council, the Royal Tribunal of Mining and several other

bodies, communities, and individuals of this city have since that date likewise been lending their help, as far as their capacities allow, to this same end, all of which up to the end of August has equaled a rate of 24,300 pesos per month. This generous assistance comes from the strength of the voluntary contributions that had previously been given, following the example Your Excellency set, to aid the Madre Patria." Viceroy Abascal, CDIP, tomo XXII, 1:285. On this issue, see also Rubén Vargas Ugarte, *Impresos Peruanos 1584–1825* (Lima, 1953–1957), 12:57, and Flores Galindo, *Aristocracia y Plebe*, 210–22.

14   Víctor Peralta Ruiz, "El Cabildo de Lima y la Política en el Perú, 1808–1814," in *La Independencia en el Perú, De los Borbones a Bolívar*, ed. Scarlett O'Phelan Godoy, 29–56 (Lima: PUCP, Instituto Riva Agüero, 2001). On the early generation of liberals in Peru, see also Jorge Basadre, *Perú: Problema y Posibilidad*, 3d ed. (Lima: Banco Internacional del Perú, 1979), and Pablo Macera, *Tres Etapas en el Desarrollo de la Conciencia Nacional* (Lima: Ediciones Fanal, 1955).

15   This interpretation is in Víctor Peralta, *En Defensa de la Autoridad: Política y Cultura Bajo el Gobierno del Virrey Abscal. Perú 1806–1816* (Madrid: CSIC, 2003).

16   On these ironies, see Basadre, *El Azar*.

17   AGI, Lima, leg. 1801.

18   CDIP, tomo XXII, 1:228; Brian Hamnett, *Revolución y contrarrevolución en México y el Perú: liberalismo, realeza y separatismo: 1800–1824* (México: Fondo de Cultura Económica, 1978), 45, 330.

19   CDIP, tomo XXII, 1:228; Manuel de Mendiburu, *Diccionario Histórico Biográfico del Perú*, vol. II (Lima: Imprenta Gil, 1935).

20   Alfonso Crespo, *Santa Cruz, el Cóndor Indio* (Mexico: Fondo de Cultura Económica, 1944).

21   Timothy Anna, *The Fall of the Royal Government in Peru* (Lincoln: University of Nebraska Press, 1979), 25. For a similar analysis regarding the political behavior of Lima's upper class, see José de la Riva Agüero y Osma, *La Historia en el Perú* (Lima: Imp. Nacional de Federico Barrionuevo, 1910); Flores Galindo, *Aristocracia y Plebe*; John Fisher, "La Formación del Estado Peruano y Simón Bolívar (1808–1824)," in *Problemas de la Formación del Estado y de la Nación en Hispanoamérica*, ed. Inge Buisson and Guenther Kahle, 479 (Cologne and Vienna: Boehlau Verlag, 1984); Hamnett, *Revolución*; Lynch, *Spanish American Revolutions*.

22   *El Depositario*, December 25, 1825.

23   "All the European powers have resolved to put an end to revolution and the revolutionaries: they have promulgated the maxim of neither recognizing nor tolerating any system of representative government formed by the people themselves; and they have ordered that the overseas dominions or territories be returned to their former, legitimate owners. Against a sentence like this . . . what will a burglar be able to do? Ships will soon arrive, our troops will come, and the

puppet whom a small congressional club . . . has filled with sermons and titles [i.e, Bolívar] will flee in a vile and cowardly fashion." Gaspar Rico, *El Depositario*, Callao, April 7, 1825.

24 From General Rodil to General Canterác, Encampment at Topará, February 20, 1824, in Gral. E. P. Felipe de la Barra, ed., CDIP, tomo VI, *Asuntos Militares, Reimpresos de Campañas, Acciones Militares y Cuestiones Conexas, Años 1823–1826* (Lima: Editorial Salesiana, 1974), 9:405.

25 ADAY, JPI, Crim., leg. 29, cuad. 564, f. 43v.

26 Ibid., declarations by Ramos, ff. 64v-67r; and declarations by Heredia, ff. 43v-45r.

27 Ibid., f. 49v. Declarations from the Spanish capitulado Juan Callejas, resident of Huanta and ex-lieutenant colonel of the Spanish army.

28 Ibid., ff. 66v-67r. (emphasis added).

29 Basadre, *Historia* (1983 ed.), 1:66.

30 Fisher, "La Formación," 479; Hamnett, *Revolución*, 338.

31 Fisher, "La Formación."

32 Vargas Ugarte, *Historia General*, 7:66.

33 AGI, Lima leg., 1801, Real Cédula of November 16, 1818.

34 Virgilio Roel, *La Independencia: Historia General del Perú* (Lima: Editorial Gráfica Labor S.A., 1988), 433; De la Barra, ed., CDIP, tomo VI, *Asuntos Militares*, 9:257.

35 Luis Antonio Eguiguren, *La Sedición de Huamanga en 1812, Ayacucho y la Independencia* (Lima: Librería e Imprenta Gil, 1935). The author would not have shared my interpretation here, for his study proposed rather to examine the existence of a patriotic current in Ayacucho. Nevertheless, his work succeeds only in conveying, in a suggestive and well-documented fashion, the weakness of this current. What happened in Huamanga in 1812, according to Eguiguren's own data, was not an uprising per se but the fear that a few openly threatening anti-Spanish lampoons might inspire one.

36 CEHMP-AHM, leg. 9, doc. 4, November 12, 1821.

37 *La Aurora Astral*, no. 1, October, 23, 1823. Cited by Pedro Mañaricúa, "Un siglo de Periodismo en Ayacucho," reprinted by Salomón Carrasco Apaico, *Ayacucho, dos Siglos de Periodismo en el Perú* (Lima: Editorial Gagó Hnos, 1988), 11.

38 Ibid., 102.

39 Ibid., 104.

40 Ibid.

41 From A. José de Sucre to the minister of war, Headquarters at Huamanga, December 15, 1824 (Ella Dunbar, ed., CDIP, tomo V, 6:131). The United Liberation Army had been occupying Huanta since September 22, and on the twenty-fourth entered Huamanga, according to Rubén Vargas Ugarte's introductory study in *Historia de las Batallas de Junín y Ayacucho*, ed. Carlos Milla Batres, 26 (Lima: Editorial Milla Batres, 1974).

42   John Miller, *Memorias del General Miller al Servicio de la República del Perú* (Santiago de Chile: Imprenta Universitaria, 1912), 3:11. The hostility of Huanta's peasants was also reported by Sucre to the minister of war: "All of the army's equipment has been lost, some of it taken by the enemies, some of it pillaged . . . and some of it stolen by the indians in revolt." United Liberation Army of Peru, Headquarters at Huamanga, December 16, 1824, CDIP, tomo VI, 8:188.

43   Echenique, *Memorias*, 1:16–17. The harassment the patriots suffered before and after the final battle in Ayacucho is not recorded in the most widely circulated historiographic surveys of Peruvian Independence. I must, therefore, single out for mention the study by Felipe de la Barra, which, despite its patriotic tones, acknowledges that "the patriot army . . . had to contend with crowds of indians [*indiadas*] from Huanta and Huancavelica, whose hostility had grown in the face of the royalist forces's presence," Felipe de la Barra, *La campaña de Junín y Ayacucho* (Lima: Comisión Nacional del Sesquicentenario de la Indpendencia, 1974), 184–87. See also Heraclio Bonilla, "Bolívar y las guerrillas indígenas en el Perú," *Cultura: Revista del Banco Central del Ecuador*, no. 16 (1983).

44   Narciso Gavilán, *Ensayos Históricos* (Ayacucho: n.p., 1941), 25; AGN, OL, 144–62, 1826.

45   BN, D6738, 1824, "Expediente Relativo a un motín que estalló en el pueblo de Acomayo," Acos, December 26, 1824.

46   In September 1824, the priest of Jauja, N. Galarza, was discharged from his office for being "a declared enemy of the system of Independence" (CDIP, tomo I, vol. X, 252). In Huancayo, the same thing occurred with the local parish priest, not only "for having preached . . . against the patria, but also for having fled, abandoning his doctrina of Hondores the moment in which he found out that the Spaniards were in Tarma, and soon after he returned with them and ordered the destruction of the population." Article signed by "El Aldeano de Junín" (The Villager of Junín), *El Telégrafo de Lima*, no. 69, July 26, 1827. In the town of Pampas, part of the doctrina of Huaribamba, where, in contrast to Jauja, the authorities remained loyal until the very end, a priest was accused for his lack of royalist zeal, though the accusation ultimately proved to be unfounded, B.N. D8510.

47   "The region of Huancavelica was profoundly royalist; between 1815 and 1824 most of the members of the upper strata of this society withdrew to the coast, and those who had the wherewithal set sail for Spain," Henri Favre, "Evolución y Situación de la hacienda tradicional en la región de Huancavelica," in *Hacienda, Comunidad y Campesinado en el Perú*, ed. José Matos Mar, 110 (Lima: IEP, 1976).

48   Most studies on montoneras that sided with the partisans of Independence from 1820 to 1824 remain overfocused on military action and take for granted peoples' "natural" adherence to the Patria, rather than explaining it. See Rivera Serna, *Los*

Guerrilleros del Centro; Vergara Arias, *Montoneras y Guerrillas*; Beltrán Gallardo, *Las guerrillas de Yauyos*; Víctor Villanueva, *Del Caudillaje Anárquico al Militarismo Reformista* (Lima: Librería-Editorial Juan Mejía Baca, 1973); and Roel, *La Independencia.*

49 On Morochucos, see AGI, Lima, leg. 1801.

50 Witt, *Un Testimonio*, 1:236. Witt actually refers to the army that fought in Ayacucho as the Peruvian and Colombian Army, which he claims numbered fifty-five hundred (fifteen hundred Peruvians and four thousand Colombians); however, it is widely known that prominent officers who fought in this battle came from Great Britain and present-day Argentina, thus my figure of fifty-eight hundred, which is based on various other sources, including the testimonies of De la Barra and Valdés cited in the following note.

51 Jerónimo Valdés, "Exposición que Dirige al rey Don Fernando VII el Mariscal de Campo don Jerónimo Valdés Sobre las Causas que Motivaron la Pérdida del Perú" (Vitoria, 1827), in Roel, *La Independencia*, 619–39; and De la Barra, ed., CDIP, tomo VI, *Asuntos Militares*, 9:222–52. Of the 308 individuals belonging to the United Liberation Army who were reported dead in the Battle of Ayacucho, according to the latter source, 85 belonged to the Peruvian Division, while the remaining 223 to the Colombian Division (an arithmetical error in the original source makes the total dead 309). This death toll is representative of the composition of the army as a whole by nationality. Regarding the number of combatants in the Spanish army, on the other hand, some give the figure of 11,000 and even 12,000, though this seems somehow inflated.

52 Valdés, "Exposición," 625.

53 Leon Campbell, *The Military and Society in Colonial Peru, 1750–1810* (Philadelphia: American Philosophical Society, 1978).

54 The army that fought against Túpac Amaru numbered 15,210 men, 14,000 of whom were indians, according to Leon Campbell, "The Army of Peru and the Túpac Amaru Revolt, 1780–1783," *Hispanic American Historical Review*, 56 (February 1976): 48. These indians were mobilized by Spaniards and creoles, but also by their own kurakas.

55 See chapter 1, first section.

56 Cavero, *Monografía*, 1:188.

57 Huancayo was, as we shall see, the primary market for the coca produced in Huanta. This economic connection evidently facilitated the political links between the two cities. An anonymous letter written in Huancayo on November 2, 1827, and addressed to the "Spanish Commander of the Iquichano army" Francisco Garay can be added to the above-quoted testimonies that single out Huancayo as an important contact for the rebels of Huanta. The anonymous writer informed the Huanta rebels about the political chaos reigning in Lima and Huancayo, which

to his mind favored the "beating of the patriots." ADAY, 1827, JPI, Crim., leg. 31, cuad. 585.

58   Basadre, *Historia* (1968 ed.), 1:269. The original sources of this section's epigraphs are in BN, D-6037, 1825, and AGN, PL-7, 407, 1827.

59   For Huamanga's economic situation toward the end of the eighteenth century and beginning of the nineteenth, see Jaime Urrutia, "Comerciantes, Arrieros y Viajeros," and Urrutia, *Huamanga*; Husson, *De la Guerra*; and Demetrio O'Higgins, "Informe del Intendente de Guamanga D. Demetrio O'Higgins al Ministro de Indias d. Miguel Cayetano Soler," in the appendix to Jorge Juan y Antonio de Ulloa, *Noticias Secretas de America* (Buenos Aires: Ediciones Mar Océano, 1953). For the decline of *obrajes* and mining, see BN, D6037, 1825; AGN, PL-7, 90, 1827; and AGN, OL 163–326, 1827. For the way the war quotas, euphemistically called voluntary contributions, affected the population, see ADAY, Intendencias, Pedimentos, "Libro de erogaciones voluntarias . . ., 1820." The priests likewise blamed the war on the poverty of their parishioners, AGN, PL-7, 407, 1827.

60   On the coca circuits, see declarations of Huanta's tithe collector, Tomás López Gerí, in ADAY, JPI, Diezmos, leg. 55, cuad. I, 1826, f. 14; AGN, R-J, Prefecturas-Ayacucho, leg. 93; and AGN, Aduanas, C16.

61   AGN, 1819, Superior Gobierno, leg. 7, cuad. 1313, unnumbered folio.

62   Declarations of Huanta's tithe collector, Tomás López Gerí, in 1826: ADAY, JPI, Crim., leg. 55, cuad. I, f. 14; Antonio Alcedo, *Diccionario Geográfico-Histórico de las Indias* (1787), cited in Cavero, *Monografía*, 1:33.

63   Husson, "Guerre indienne," 54–55, 70–77.

64   O'Higgins, "Informe," in appendix of Juan and De Ulloa, *Noticias*, 520.

65   ADAY, Intendencias, Asuntos Administrativos, leg. 40, cuads. 39, 40.

66   The subdelegates' main function at the economic level was, however, as we shall see later, the collection of indian tribute.

67   "Don Bernardino Estábanez [*sic*] was very determined not to let the residents [*vecinos*] of the district begin land settlement with Y[our] M[ajesty] for their coca lands, or pay the cost of the lands for which they had already executed deeds," declared Francisco Peña. Other witnesses made declarations to the same effect. For example, Pedro Lazón, who "[knew] that don Miguel Fariña, under the guidance and protection of the aforementioned subdelegate [Estébanez] went about in Guanta gathering signatures from the hacendados in the montañas in order to present an appeal to the superiority[,] objecting to the payment of land settlements to Y[our] M[ajesty]," AGN, Tributos-Informes, leg. 2, cuad. 47, unnumbered folio.

68   AGI, Lima, leg. 1801, "Real Cédula concediendo varias gracias para el fomento de la agricultura población y comercio en la Provincia de Guamanga y sus montañas," 1816.

69 According to John Fisher, it was not uncommon for subdelegates to flout the authority of the intendants, their immediate superiors, by addressing themselves directly to the viceroy. Many charges similar to those of O'Higgins to the subdelegates had no effect in other regions, despite having been made in defense of the Crown's pecuniary interests. See John Fisher, *Government and Society in Colonial Peru: The Intendant System, 1784–1814* (London: Athlone Press, 1970).

70 The Real Cédula of 1816 gave "power to the Intendant Governor of the Province of Guamanga, or to the territorial subdelegates, to transfer the rights to available lands in the montañas and Muyunmarca to all who request them, whether they be small or big plots, provided that they do not exceed a square league, and preferring, other circumstances being equal: First the indian" AGI, Lima, leg. 1801, "Real Cédula concediendo varias gracias," 1816.

71 From A. José de Sucre to the Minister of War, Headquarters at Huamanga, December 15, 1824, CDIP, tomo V, 6:131. The town of Guaychao (i.e., Huaychao) mentioned here is located in the province of Cangallo. A homonymic town which took the side of the monarchist rebels (see map 6) is in Huanta province.

72 Ibid., 132.

73 Ibid., 268.

74 Cited in Husson, "Guerre indienne," 77.

75 On Cantón, see ADAY, JPI, Crim., leg. 30, cuad. 575, 1828, "Autos contra Juan Cantón y M. Riveros"; ADAY, JPI, Crim., cuad. 564, ff. 72v, 73r; ADAY, Protocolos Notariales, leg. 178, f. 250; leg. 179 and leg. 180, f. 249; AGN, Aduanas C16, leg. 456, cuad. 626; leg. 457, cuad. 639; and leg. 458, cuads. 641, 653 (years 1819–22); and BN D4712.

76 Husson, "Guerre indienne," 78.

77 See Burga, "El Perú."

78 ADAY, JPI, Crim., leg. 31, cuad. 583, f. 18, pamphlet signed "El Iquichano Amante del Rey" (The Iquichano Lover of the King).

79 From Antonio Huachaca and Pablo Guamán to Prefect Juan Pardo de Zela, Ayacucho, March, 11, 1826, ADAY, JPI, Crim., leg. 27, cuad. 521, f. 7 (emphasis added).

80 Statements by Manuel Gato, AGN, R-J, Prefecturas, Ayacucho, leg. 93.

81 From J. M. Cano to Fermín Pando, Ayacucho, November, 17, 1827. Cited in Cavero, *Monografía*, 1:200.

82 Lorenzo Huertas, "La Rebelión en las punas de Iquicha," in *Levantamientos Campesinos, siglos XVIII–XX*, ed. Juan Solano Sáenz, 112 (Lima: Universidad Nacional del Centro del Perú, 1981).

83 AGN PL 6–176, 1826, from Prefect Juan Antonio Gonzales to the Minister of Hacienda, July 3, 1827, f. 68r; see also declarations by P. V. Gálvez, acting mayor of Luricocha, on f. 65r.

CHAPTER 4. Words and Images: People and King

1 Carlos Daniel Valcárcel, comp., *La Rebelión de Túpac Amaru*, CDIP, tomo II, 2:713.

2 Michel Foucault, *The History of Sexuality*, vol. 1, *An Introduction* (New York: Vintage Books, 1980), 17–29.

3 Clifford Geertz, *The Interpretation of Cultures* (New York: Basic Books, 1973), 220–21.

4 Christopher Hill, *The World Turned Upside Down: Radical Ideas During the English Revolution* (London: Penguin Books, 1988).

5 Newspapers flourished in Spanish America during the free-speech and hyper-politicized period between 1808 and 1814 and after 1820, and had an impact in Huamanga. The so-called sedition of Huamanga in 1812 was fostered by anonymous pamphlets. See Eguiguren, *La Sedición*. On the role of newspapers during the Independence period, see Ascención Martínez Riaza, *La Prensa Hispanoamericana en la Independencia* (Madrid: Mapfre, 1992); Luis Monguió, "La Poesía y la Independencia, Perú 1808–1825," in *Literatura de la Emancipación*, 7–15 (Lima: Universidad Nacional Mayor de San Marcos, 1971); Raúl Porras Barrenechea, *Los Ideólogos de la Emancipación* (Lima: Milla Batres, 1974); Alberto Flores Galindo, *Túpac Amaru II-1780: sociedad colonial y sublevaciones populares* (Lima: Retablo de Papel Ediciones, 1976). The use of pamphlets in the Great Rebellion of the southern Andes in 1780–81 is best illustrated in Boleslao Lewin's classic *La Rebelión*.

6 For an excellent example of an analysis of documents beyond their texts in an illiterate peasant context see Daniel Field, *Rebels in the Name of the Czar* (Boston: Houghton Mifflin Company, 1976).

7 ADAY, JPI, Crim., leg. 28, cuad. 543, f. 1.

8 Ibid. The original orthography, word separation, and capitalization have been followed here as well as in the subsequent Spanish citations.

9 Ibid.

10 Ibid.

11 On "imperialist nationalisms," see Benedict Anderson, *Imagined Communities: Reflections on the Origin and Spread of Nationalism* (London: Verso, 1983).

12 ADAY, JPI, Crim., leg. 28, cuad. 543, f. 1.

13 Ibid.

14 I thank Pedro Guibovich for this piece of information.

15 ADAY, JPI, Crim., leg. 28, cuad. 543, f. 14r.

16 Ibid., f. 16.

17 Ibid., f. 37v.

18 Ibid., f. 18v.

19 Ibid.

20   A witness declared that he had met Guerrero in Chacabamba, a hacienda that played a pivotal role in the monarchist uprising.

21   Notably, the newspaper *El Depositario*. See chapters 2 and 3.

22   See chapters 5 and 7.

23   I say "perhaps" because I am not sure that the phrase "sus hijitos se muera," in particular, has Quechua influence. The error of agreement in this phrase is a feature common to the proclamations of the Spaniard Francisco Garay. In this sense, the construction may well simply be reflecting a form of pronunciation whereby final consonants of words are omitted (in this case, "muera" instead of "mueran") and which is widespread in some regions of Spain (like Andalucía and Canarias), as well as in the Caribbean and northern sections of South America.

24   ADAY, JPI, Crim., leg. 28, cuad. 543, f. 1. I have not transcribed the end of this proclamation because part of the copy I have at my disposal is illegible. The original text reads, "Señores: no es libelo infumario [*sic*]; sino un discurso sierto y verdadero; por que Dios manda vestir al desnudo y darde comer al hambriento, tener mesericordia al proximo [*sic*]. V.V. han observado estas *cosas?* Mas bien con balor impio tean [*sic*] devorado los Corazones de los inocentes [illegible] . . . han quitado sus tristes pellejitos mantitas rotozas y fresaditas . . . y los demas alcaldes, y gobernadores Patriotas: si les ha quedado alguna pequeña compasion sera virtud de que [*sic*] de una vez les quitais la vida para que [no?] vean mas padecer asus tiernecitos hijos y mujeres de hombres desnudas y setenta mil meserias: o de no[,] dejadlos quietos en sus tristes ranchos en paz y quitud [*sic*] para que bayan buscando dineros para pagar los pechos injustos que poco importa que sus hijitos se muera [*sic*] de hambre, por quedarles el conçuelo de que ellos solos sufriran vuestro furror, yra rapiña y . . ."

25   ADAY, JPI, Crim., leg. 31, cuad. 585, ff. 18, 19.

26   Ibid. The original reads, "[Americanos:] . . . Decirme [*sic*] vosotros aquellos que con ansias deseabais reposar en los brazos de la Libertad [read Patria] que bentajas ós a propocionado? ¡No puedo explicarlo! Publiquenlos los miserable [*sic*] que Regando los suelos con lagrimas de sangre no tienen suficiente para el sosten de sus familias por los pesados tributos que los abruman. . . . Diganlos las calles y las plazas de todo el Perú, Regada con la sangre inocente de vuestros Padres. Diganlos, las Ynfelices viudas, que cargadas con sus pequeñuelos hijos al cielo claman por sus Padres, y ultimamente diganlos las casadas que aprecencia [*sic*] de sus maridos fueron bioladas." As with all other sources quoted, I have retained this proclamation's syntax, orthography, and capitalization, although not all "misspelled" words or "incorrect" grammar structures are followed by "*sic*." I reserve "*sic*" for spelling or grammatical oddities that may not look so obvious or necessarily archaic.

27   Ibid. The original text reads, "Americanos: Estad seguro [*sic*] de que ós hablo con el lenguaje de la verdad, y para prueva de ellos [*sic*], teneis el portentoso milagro, en

el Corto Rincon de estas Punas, que unos pocos de hombres, sin diciplina, ni armas, solo con Piedras, y palos han derrotado varias veses á los que se nombran imbencible [sic] dejandonos el campo cubiertos [sec] de armas, y cadaveres, con tan prodigioso portento nada teneis que temer. Valerosos americanos á las armas, un Enemigo Ereje quiere tiranizar la Religion, y el Trono Ereditario de Fernando. El Dios de Los Exercitos nos dice Guerra, Guerra, los Campos de Marte ós combidan á una gloriosa Lucha la que [sic] no deveis dudar. . . . Francisco Garay."

28 Declarations by Francisco Garay ADAY, JPI, Crim., leg. 31, cuad. 585, f. 21v.

29 ADAY, JPI, Crim., leg. 31, cuad. 585, f. 18. The original text reads, "A las Comunidades de los Pueblos de la Villa de Huancabelica: Amados Hermanos: Ya hemos hechos [sic] saber á Ustedes que no solo no nos hemos presentado á el infame Govierno de la Patria, sino que no lo hemos pensado, y suplicamos á Vs. no lo crean, aún quando los [sic] digan algunos Malvados. Haora [sic] preguntamos á Vs. que es lo que piensan, si estan Gustosos con ser esclavos de los viles Patriotas, de estos hombre [sic] bajos Ladrones que no piensan sino en robarnos de contribuciones, sera posible que solo trabajemos para ellos, mientras nuestras caras essposas ynuestros [sic] tiernos hijos perescan de hambre y los beamos desnudos? No creemos en vs. tanta Bajesas [sic] ni menos tengan unos corazones de fieras: aprender [sic] de nosotros, que sin esperanza de áusilio de nuestras tropas, hemos sacudido el yugo de la tirania, hoy que estan nuestro campeones, e inbencibles los señores Loriga, Rodil Ricafor y Morales, en nuestras costas, no lebantaran el grito de Viva el Rey y muera la Patria y sus satelites: armesen [sic] hermanos de valor, tengan un Lugar libre de esta vil casta de Ynsulgente [sic], que todo su [fidelidad ?], á nuestro amado Rey Fernando, asi hermanos hasi lo esperamos de su acentrado [sic] Realismo, y que lebantando el Grito de Viva el Rey aguardemos á nuestros Generales Españoles y tengamos la gloria de entregarle estos lugares, defendido con la [sic] una porsion de nuestra sangre, y asi lo esperamos de un amor á la Religion, y al mejor de los Reyes: El Yquichano Amante del Rey."

30 ADAY, JPI, Crim., leg. 31, cuad. 585, f. 21v.

31 ADAY, JPI, Crim., leg. 29, cuad. 564 (Cuaderno 2do. del Juicio a Soregui . . .), f. 18r. See also ADAY, JPI, Crim., leg. 29, cuad. 564, f. 53r, 87v.

32 ADAY, JPI, Crim., leg. 31, cuad. 585, f. 32v.

33 Ibid., f. 30r.

34 ADAY, JPI, Crim., leg. 30, cuad. 566, f. 40r.

35 Gregorio Guijas declared, "Don Juan Canton made him [Guijas] write more instructions for the first Chief of the King's troops that Guijas may find, of which [troops] it was said were around, and later on Belarde said that he had rewritten them [the instructions], and showed him [Guijas] other instructions bearing his [Belarde's] handwriting." ADAY, JPI, Crim., leg. 31, cuad. 585, f. 32v.

36 ADAY, JPI, Crim., leg. 30, cuad. 579, f. 1r / v. All subsequent references to this letter come from this source.

37 Ibid.

38 Ibid.

39 For a vivid example, see the letter that Prefect Domingo Tristán addressed to Nicolás Soregui on December 12, 1827, ADAY, leg. 30, cuad. 579, 1828, f. 39. See also chapter 7.

40 ADAY, JPI, Crim., leg. 31, cuad. 585.

41 Ibid.

42 See chapter 2.

43 ADAY, JPI, Crim., leg. 30, cuad. 579, f. 49. The letter was signed by Huachaca, Soregui, Juan Ramos, and Méndez, but seems to have been dictated by Huahaca because it is written in the first person: "cange [sic] por mi esposa que esta en poder de VV."

44 ADAY, 1828, JPI, Crim., leg. 29, cuad. 564, f. 76r. Comandancia Militar de Tambo, March 2, 1828: Gabriel Quintanilla to the prefect.

45 Commander Quintanilla to the judge. ADAY, JPI, Crim., leg. 29, cuad. 464, f. 79r.

46 ADAY, JPI, Crim., leg. 30, cuad. 579, "papeles 'E.' "

47 Ibid, "papeles 'E,' " f. 6r. Luis Pampa, January 26, 1828.

48 So declared Fray Francisco Pacheco: "From there they continued up to Molle-pata . . . where the Father dn. Mariano Mercedes preached to the troop, forced by Huachaca" (ADAY, JPI, Crim., leg. 29, cuad. 564, f. 33v). For his part, the priest Manuel Navarro said, "When they [the rebels] tried to enter Huanta on the past twelfth of November, he who speaks advised Huachaca that he should not do it, that they should not sacrifice that villa, and that with his advise Huachaca quit the day before" (ADAY, JPI, Crim., leg. 29, cuad. 564, f. 37v). On Huachaca's relationship with the Church, see also chapter 6.

49 Basadre, *Historia* (1983 ed.), 1:175.

50 The November 12, 1823, law considered as an abuse of freedom of press, among others, "the publication of maxims or doctrines to destroy the Religion and the Constitution." Basadre, *Historia* (1983 ed.), 1:45.

51 Ibid., 1:175

52 Ibid.

53 Ibid.

54 Ibid.

55 All of this can be found in ibid., 1:173–74.

56 See map published by Dionisio Ortiz, O.F.M., *Las Montañas del Apurímac, Mantaro y Ene* (Lima: Imprenta Editorial San Antonio, 1975), 1:144–45.

57 Dionisio Ortiz, O.F.M., *La Montaña de Ayacucho* (Lima: Ed. Gráfica, 1981), 97. As for

the Ocopa convent, it was reestablished by President Orbegoso's 1836 decree, which abolished the one given by Bolívar in 1824.

58 Ibid., 173–74.

59 See chapter 3.

60 Ortiz, *La Montaña*, 97. Around 1814, states Ortiz, the missionaries of Ocopa focused their attention deeper into the selva, to the route linking Andamarca-Pongoa-Perené-Tambo-Ucayali, thus abandoning the Huanta area.

61 See Charles Tilly's classic *La Vendée* (Cambridge: Harvard University Press, 1964).

62 A decree issued by Bolívar in Cuzco in July 1825 provided for the "intervention of the Intendant or governor in the agreement of the parish's duties with the indians" (Basadre, *Historia* [1983 ed.], 1:173). Whether this decree and some others that, according to Basadre, rectified it were implemented and whether they favored or were detrimental to the peasantry only future research will tell.

63 Ibid., 1:27.

64 On the rumors, see chapters 2 and 3. For further speculation on the links between the Holy Alliance and the Huanta uprising, see Patrick Husson, *De la Guerra*. On the Holy Alliance's pretensions in America, see Manfred Kossok, *Historia de la Santa Alianza y la Emancipación de América Latina* (Buenos Aires: Sílaba, 1968).

65 "Expresión Leal Y Afectuosa de Ayuntamiento de Lima; con Motivo de la Solemne Proclamación de Nuestro Católico Monarca el Señor D. Fernando VII," in Manuel de Odriozola, *Documentos Históricos del Perú* (Lima: Tipografía de Aurelio Alfaro, 1864), 2:359.

66 See José Antonio Rodríguez, "La Exaltación Religiosa del Monarca en el Cusco Colonial: Espinosa Medrano y el sermón fúnebre," in *La Venida del Reino: Religión, evangelización y cultura en América, siglos XVI–XX*, comp. Gabriela Ramos (Cuzco: CBC, 1994). According to Rodríguez, this sermon, which was delivered in Cuzco, exalted the king as the defender of the Eucharist in an attempt to link his devotion to the Corpus Christi, the Catholic feast of the Eucharist, which became in Cuzco "the symbol of the triumph of the Christian God over the Idolatry." This same feast nonetheless incorporated elements pertaining to the pre-Hispanic Inti Raimy, feast of the Sun, god of the Incas, a principal celebration in Cuzco.

67 See, among others, Sergio Serulnikov, *Su verdad y su Justicia: Tomás Katari y la insurrección aymara de Chayanta, 1777–1780* (Buenos Aires: Universidad de Buenos Aires, 1994); Charles Walker, "La Violencia y el sistema legal: Los Indios y el Estado en el Cuzco Después de la Rebelión de Túpac Amaru" in *Poder y Violencia en los Andes*, ed. Henrique Urbano, 125–47 (Cuzco: CBC, 1991); Stern, *Peru's Indian Peoples*.

68 ADAY, 1817, Intendencias, Pedimentos, leg. 42, cuad. 45. Real Cédula of January 24, 1817.

69 François-Xavier Guerra, *Modernidad e Independencias, Ensayos sobre las Revoluciones Hispánicas* (Mexico City: Fondo de Cultura Económica, 1992), chapter 5.

70 Ibid., 155.

71 Ibid., 156.

72 Ibid., 155.

73 Ibid., 156.

74 For the expressions of allegiance to the king in Peru, in the context of the French invasion of the Iberian peninsula, see Hamnett, *Revolución y Contrarrevolución*, 33–34; and Armando Nieto Vélez, *Contribución a la Historia del Fidelismo en el Perú, 1808–1810* (Lima: Instituto Riva Agüero, 1960).

75 BN 562434. Fray Calixto Cárdenas y Berrocal, "Panegírico en acción de Gracias. . . . Por la proclamación del Señor don Fernando Rey de España y Emperador de las Indias" (Lima: Casa Real de los Niños Expósitos [hereafter BN 562434].

76 Ibid., 23–24.

77 Ibid., 24–25.

78 Ibid., 25–26.

79 "Informe del subdelegado José de Larrea de la jura de la constitución en Angaraes," CDIP, *Documentación Oficial Española*, tomo XXII, 1:295 (emphasis added). *Baile* and *danza,* which in English would be rendered as "dance," are not always the same thing in Spanish. While *baile* suggests the idea of a social event, *danza* conveys the idea of an artistic representation, at least in the present-day meaning of the term. Thus I have translated *danza* as "dance" and left *"baile"* untranslated.

80 Ibid., 295.

81 Ibid., 275.

82 See, for example, AGI, Lima 1577, "Proclama a los Habitantes de Ultramar," a printed document written in Spanish and Quechua and calling for acceptance of the Constitution of 1812.

83 Ibid., 275.

84 Christine Hünefeldt, "Los Indios y la Constitución de 1812," *Allpanchis Phuturinqa,* no. 11 / 12 (1978): 33–52.

85 For example, Lorenzo Huertas, "Las Luchas por la Independencia en Ayacucho," in *Simposium sobre la Independencia en Ayacucho* (Ayacucho, 1974), 139 (mimeo).

86 The highly politicized period in Spain and the colonies after the French invasion of the Peninsula came to a halt in 1814, when Fernando recovered the throne of Spain and ruled as absolute monarch. In addition to annulling the 1812 Constitution, the king issued a decree in 1814 banning freedom of speech. He lifted the ban six years later, triggering a new wave of politicization that culminated in the proclamation of independence in the colonies of continental America. See Monguió, "La Poesía," 7–15.

87 See Waldemar Espinosa Soriano, *La destrucción del imperio de los incas: la rivalidad política y señorial de los kurakazgos andinos,* 3d ed. (Lima: Amaru Editores, 1981).

88 Teresa Gisbert, *Iconografía y Mitos Indígenas en el Arte* (La Paz: Gisbert, 1980), 117.

89   Juan Carlos Estenssoro, lecture given at the Instituto Riva Agüero, Lima, 1999;
Thierry Saignes, "Es posible una historia 'chola' del Perú?" *Allpanchis Phuturinqa* 2,
no. 35/36 (1990): 635–57; Saignes, "De la Borrachera al retrato: los caciques andinos entre dos legitimidades (Charcas)," *Revista Andina* no. 9 (1987): 139–70.

90   Gisbert, *Iconografía*, 165; Karen Spalding, *De Indio a Campesino* (Lima: IEP, 1974),
and Spalding, *Huarochiri, an Andean Society Under Inca and Spanish Rule* (Stanford:
Stanford University Press, 1984); Stern, *Peru's Indian Peoples*.

91   Seventeenth-century kurakas' garments displayed in an exhibit at the Brooklyn
Museum in 1994 included headdresses and *mantas* (blankets) the designs of which
display, symmetrically, on one side the coat-of-arms of the Hapsburgs, and on the
other that of the Inca. On eighteenth-century "neo-Inca" iconography and symbols of prestige, see John Howland Rowe, "El Movimiento Nacional Inca del siglo
XVIII," *Revista Universitaria*, no. 7 (1954), reprinted in Flores Galindo, *Túpac Amaru*,
13–53.

92   Gisbert, *Iconografía*, 117; Saignes, "De la Borrachera," 156.

93   AGN, Derecho Indígena, 1643, cuad. 109, f. 2.

94   David Cahill, "Conclusion" in Peter Bradley and David Cahill, *Habsburg Peru:
Images, Imagination and Memory* (Liverpool: Liverpool University Press, 2000), 149.

95   See the sentence passed on Túpac Amaru in Valcárcel, *La Rebelión*, tomo II, 2:765–
73; see also Cahill's discussion on Areche's sentence, in David Cahill, "The Inca
Politics of Nostalgia," in Bradley and Cahill, *Habsburg Peru*.

96   Juan Carlos Estenssoro, "Discurso, Música, y Poder en el Perú Colonial," Tesis de
Maestría (Lima: Pontificia Universidad Católica del Perú, 1990), 2:533; see also
Cecilia Méndez G., "Incas Sí, Indios No: Notes on Peruvian Creole Nationalism
and its Contemporary Crisis," *Journal of Latin American Studies* no. 28, part 1
(February, 1996): 197–225. For a sympathetic interpretation of creoles' political
resort to Inca symbolism in the early nineteenth century, see Flores-Galindo,
Buscando un Inca. For a revisionist approach to Flores-Galindo's "Andean Utopia,"
see Cahill "Inca Politics."

97   César Itier, "Quechua y Cultura en el Cuzco del Siglo XVIII," in *Del Siglo de Oro al
Siglo de las Luces*, comp. César Itier, 105 (Cuzco: CBC, 1995).

98   Ibid., 106.

99   Ibid.

100   On this issue, see Luis Monguió, "La Ilustración Peruana y el Indio," *América
Indígena* 45, no. 2 (1985), and Juan Carlos Estenssoro, "Modernismo, Estética,
Música y Fiesta," in *Tradición y Modernidad en los Andes*, ed. Enrique Urbano, 181–
95 (Cuzco: CBC, 1992).

101   Cahill, "Inca Politics," and "The Colonial Inca Nobility: Social Structure, Culture
and Politics in Late Colonial Cuzco," paper presented at the conference "New

World, First Nations: Native Peoples of Mesoamerica and the Andes Under Colonial Rule," University of New South Wales, Sydney, October 1–3, 2002.

102   The "peasantization" of Andean native elites was first described by Karen Spalding in her groundbreaking *De Indio a Campesino* and later on in her now-classic *Huarochirí*.

103   Walker, "Peasants, Caudillos," 101.

104   Vargas, *Historia*, 1:26.

105   Guillermo Durand Flórez, comp., *La Rebelión de Túpac Amaru*, CDIP, tomo II (Lima: Comisión del Sesquicentenario de la Independencia Nacional, 1971), 4:121–283; Carlos Daniel Valcárcel, comp., *La Rebelión de Túpac Amaru*, CDIP, tomo II, 2:580–91, 781. "Other *caciques* who remained faithful were Nicolás Rosas of Anata; Sucacuahua of Umachiri; Huaranca of Santa Rosa; Manco Turpos of Azángaro; Carlos Visa of Achalla; Chuquicallota of Samán; Sinan Inca of Coporaque; Huambo Tupa of Yauri; Callu of Sicuani; Antonio of Checacupi; Cotacallapa and Huaquisto of Caraballa; Game and Carpio of Paruro; Espinosa of Cotoca; Huamanchaco of Coporque; and Pacheco Callitupa of Quispicanchis." Lilian E. Fisher, *The Last Inca Revolt, 1780–1783* (Norman: University of Oklahoma Press, 1966), 106–07.

106   AGI, Lima, 1482, 1483.

107   Colección Matalinares, tomo 115, ff. 141v / 142r, Biblioteca de la Real Academia de la Historia de Madrid (hereafter BRAHM).

108   From privates to colonels and brigadiers, all members of the Army of Upper Peru who "spontaneously volunteered to come and subject [the province of Cuzco] to reason and to the obedience of the Sovereign" were awarded lands in proportion to their rank; they were also allowed to sell these lands or dispose of them as they wished "should they choose not to settle in the partido in which these lands had been assigned to them." Such land sales entailed no detriment to the promotions which members of the army were also awarded. These stipulations were given in Lima on April 13, 1815. For details, see Manuel Jesús Aparicio Vega, comp., *La Revolución del Cuzco de 1814*, CDIP, tomo III (Lima: Comisión Nacional del Sesquicentenario de la Independencia, 1974), 7:588–89.

109   ADAY, Intendencias, Pedimentos, leg. 47, cuad. 55.

110   ADAY, Protocolos Notariales, Registro de Indios, 1774–1792, leg. 96.

111   AGI, Lima 1482. For additional information on Huantino participation in the defeat of the Túpac Amaru uprising, see Valcárcel, *La Rebelión de Túpac Amaru*, CDIP, tomo II, 1:105, 631, 635, 637, 646, 654, 655.

112   Aparicio Vega, *La Revolución del Cusco de 1814*, CDIP, tomo III, 7:584–85. For Huanta's role in the uprising of 1814, also see "Memoria Militar del General Pezuela" and "Memoria Historica sobre la Revolución de 1814 of Manuel Pardo y Riva-

deneira," in Felix Denegri Luna, comp., *Memorias, Diarios y Crónicas*, CDPI, tomo XXVI (Lima: Comisión del Sesquicentenario de la Independencia, 1971), 1:335, 456.

113 Carlos García Rosel, "Históricas," in *El Tiempo*, Lima, November 16, 1928, cited in Cavero, *Monografía*, 1:179. According to this source, the battles in which Huachaca reportedly participated were fought by the Huantinos against the Cuzco forces commanded by D. J. Gabriel Béjar, Hurtado de Mendoza y Angulo, first in the city of Huanta and its outskirts on September 30 and October 1, 1814, and then in Matará on January 27, 1815.

114 Clause no. 5 of the Instructions to Subdelegates of 1784, AGI, Lima 1103.

115 Clause no. 4 of the Instructions to Subdelegates of 1784 provided that "it is the subdelegates' duty . . . not to allow the Indians to assemble on their own for the election and to actually choose the officials of their republic, and when it is time for these assemblies on the days, and in the towns that are accustomed to having them . . . the subdelegate shall always attend them, and preside over them" (AGI, Lima 1103). For a more extended quotation and analysis see chapter 6.

116 Other researchers have also noticed this process. See, for example, David Cahill, "Independencia, sociedad y fiscalidad: el Sur Andino (1780–1880)," *Revista Computense de Historia de América*, no. 19 (1993): 249–68; and Sala i Vila, *Y Se Armó*.

117 The decline of the prestige of the kurakas in the seventeenth century does not seem to have been a phenomenon exclusive to Huamanga; Spalding describes a similar process taking place in Huarochirí and other areas (see, for instance, Spalding, *Huarochirí*). For the situation of Huamanga's kurakas in the seventeenth century, see Leocadio Edgar Sulca Báez, "Curas y Kurakas Ayacuchanos. Tierra y poder en la sociedad colonial" (Título de Antropólogo Social, Ayacucho: UNSCH, 1986), and Stern, *Peru's Indian Peoples*.

CHAPTER 5. Landscapes and Networks

1 Tristan Platt, *Estado Boliviano y Ayllu Andino: Tierra y Tributo en el Norte de Potosí* (Lima: IEP, 1982); David Cahill, "Colour by Numbers: Racial and Ethnic Categories in the Viceroyalty of Peru," *Journal of Latin American Studies* 26, no. 2 (1994): 334.

2 An account of the major changes that the indian tribute underwent during the republican period can be found in Carlos Contreras, "Estado Republicano y Tributo Indígena en la Sierra Central en la post independencia," *Histórica* 13 (1989): 517–50, and Carlos Contreras, "Etnicidad y Contribuciones Directas en el Perú Después de la Independencia," paper presented at the 51st International Congress of Americanists, Santiago de Chile, 2003. One of the most dramatic changes in relation to the colonial period was the creation of the *contribución de castas*, a head tax for mixed-blood people.

3   AGN, 1801, Tributos-Huanta, leg. 5, cuad. 19.

4   Platt's notion that the Andean communities accepted and even demanded that the state collect the tribute in the belief it would guarantee them access to and protection of their communal lands (the so-called "pacto tributario," or tribute-for-land pact) has been too often taken as a widespread Andean pattern despite the fact that his study was describing only a regional phenomenon in an area of present-day Bolivia (Platt, *Estado*). A recent study confirms that the tributary pact was in effect in late colonial Arequipa (southern Peru): see Sarah Chambers, "Little Middle Ground: The Instability of Mestizo Identity in the Andes," in *Race and Nation in Modern Latin America*, ed. Nancy P. Appelbaum, Anne S. Macpherson, and Karin Alejandra Rosenblatt, 32–55 (Chapel Hill: University of North Carolina Press, 2003); other studies, however, suggest a much less uniform picture regarding tributary patterns in late colonial Peru. See, for instance, Hunefeldt, *Lucha por la Tierra*.

5   This does not include the *estancias* and haciendas, some of which also appear registered with their respective *ayllus*. AGN, Tributos–Huanta, 1801 leg. 5, cuad. 19.

6   ADAY, Intendencia, Pedimentos, leg. 47, cuad. 55.

7   AGN, Tributos–Huanta, 1801, leg. 5, cuad. 19, 1801.

8   The metamorphosis of ayllus in the province of Huarochirí throughout the colonial period is well accounted for in Spalding, *Huarochirí*, chapters 1 and 2. For a study that shows the process of atomization of ayllus over the course of five hundred years in an Aymara region, see Thomas Abercrombie, *Pathways of Memory and Power: Ethnography and History Among an Andean People* (Madison: University of Wisconsin Press, 1998).

9   A description of the capital of Huanta in 1834 suggests that it had "four Aillos or Parcialidades": Espíritu Santo, Mainai, Viro-viro, and Pata Sullo (Blanco, *Diario*, 46). The author was clearly alluding to settlements on the outskirts of the town. This toponymy is not consistent with the information about ayllus associated with the town of Huanta during the late colonial period, according to which the two ayllus associated with the town were Cocha and Mitma. For other examples of the use of ayllu as equivalent to "hamlet" (*estancia*, small cattle ranch), in a word, a minor settlement, see Mariano Felipe Paz Soldán, *Diccionario Geográfico Estadístico del Perú* (Lima: Imprenta del Estado, 1877), xix, xv.

10 Evidence for Andean noncontiguous patterns of settlement is abundant. The classic reference on this issue is John Murra's studies on "vertical ecological complementarity," John Murra, *Formaciones Económicas y Políticas del Mundo Andino* (Lima: IEP, 1975). Subsequently, other scholars have made important contributions to Murra's model, revising or complementing his findings. See, for, example, Poole, "Landscapes of Power," and Bruce Mannheim, *The Language of the Inka since the European Invasion* (Austin: University of Texas Press, 1991), chap. 2.

11 "From now on the aborigines shall not be called *Indians* or *Natives*; they are

children and citizens of Peru, and as Peruvians they shall be known. Given in Lima, on 18 August, 1821. José de San Martín, and Juan García del Río," cited in José la Puente Candamo, comp., CDIP. tomo XIII (Lima: Comisión del Sesquicentenario de la Independencia, circa 1971), 1:350. This famous "decree" was actually one of the clauses of a decree that abolished the indian tribute (which was soon after reestablished).

12   In the province of Huaylas, Ancash, the term *Peruvian* was claimed by the peasants themselves during the nineteenth century, according to the research of Mark Thurner, "Republicanos." I have not found the same phenomenon among Huanta's peasants in the documents I have examined (up to 1850–60, approximately). On the change from *indian* to *Peruvian*, see also Méndez, "La Tentación," 231–48.

13   On the shift from *indian* to *indígena*, see Thurner, "Republicanos."

14   An assessment of these issues that differs from mine can be found in Marisol de la Cadena, *Indigenous Mestizos: The Politics of Race and Culture in Cuzco* (Durham: Duke University Press, 2000).

15   ADAY, 1828, JPI, Crim., leg. 30, cuad. 581, f. 22r.

16   ADAY, JPI, Crim., leg. 27, cuad. 521, f. 65v, "Cuaderno Cuarto del juicio a Soregui y otros."

17   Ibid.

18   From Francisco Pacheco to Nicolás Soregui, Aranhuay, January 16, 1827. ADAY, JPI, Crim., leg. 30, cuad. 579, ff. 4/5, "Cuaderno primero del juicio a Soregui y otros . . . Papeles del padre Pacheco."

19   Izcuchaca, November 28, 1827, from José Merino to Manuel Patricio Fernández, ADAY, JPI, Crim., leg. 28, cuad. 545, f. 3v.

20   Declarations by José Merino to Superintendent Manuel Patricio Fernández. Izcuchaca, November 28, 1827, in ADAY, JPI, Crim., leg. 28, cuad. 545, f. 1. The "insurgents' possessions" and the "interests of the insurgents" were the tithes they expropriated from the hacendados.

21   For more precise altitudes and geographical information, see chapter 1.

22   *Montaña* refers to a very specific ecological niche in the Andes and should not be translated as "mountain." See chapter 1.

23   The towns of Huancavelica were successfully mobilized at the start of the rebellion, but it has not been possible for me to determine whether they participated in the armed actions of 1827 and thereafter. See AGN, 1825, RJ—Prefecturas, Ayacucho, leg. 93; ADAY, JPI, Crim., leg. 31, cuad. 583, f. 18; ADAY, JPI, cuad. 545, leg. 28, ff. 1–4.

24   There is another town by the name of Huaychao in present-day Huanta province (see maps 3 and 6).

25   This reconstruction is based on ADAY, 1828, JPI, Crim., leg. 30, cuad. 566, f. 12; AGN,

various documents from sections OL, PL, and Prefecturas-Ayacucho; and from CDIP tomo V, 6:268.

26 My reconstruction here is based on AGN, 1782–1801, Tributos-Huanta, leg. 3, cuads. 49, 67; leg. 4, cuad. 105; and leg. 5, cuad. 19. These *cuadernos* (notebooks) include the tributary rolls for the years 1782, 1787, 1796, and 1801. After this date one loses the trail of Huanta's tributary rolls on a settlement-by-settlement basis. In the figures presented I have taken into account the *alcaldes de indios* (indigenous mayors), village authorities who, along with the villagers who served in the Church, were exempted from paying tribute but formed part of the registered population. There was at least one indigenous mayor per town, and in the capitals of doctrina there were usually two.

27 Blanco, *Diario*, 46. The town of Huanta was elevated to the category of *villa* shortly before Independence.

28 Regarding Lucre, see AGN, Prefecturas, Ayacucho, leg. 93, 1825. For Marcarí: ADAY, JPI, Crim., leg. 29, cuad. 564, ff. 14r / v.

29 Other researchers have found more homogeneous patterns for *estancia*, based on tributary rolls in other areas of the Andes, for example, Nicolás Sánchez Albornoz, *Indios y Tributos en el Alto Perú* (Lima, 1978). The meticulous nineteenth-century geographer Mariano Felipe Paz Soldán, on the other hand, citing reasons similar to those I provide here, noted the enormous difficulty of classifying settlements in rural Peru, and the fact that nomenclature varied, too, from region to region. Ever mindful of nuances, he was at the same time sympathetic to the idea of taxonomic homogenization, which he deemed necessary for the sake of clarity, and "national unity." Thus he grouped entities such as *estancias, pagos, parcialidades, caseríos, barrios,* and *ayllos* [*sic*], under the category of "hamlets" (*aldeas*), under the rationale that they did not have "political authorities or church of their own— although, in some there exists a church of the estate [*fundo*] which bears the same name—and which depend on the town, villa or city in whose district they are located." Paz Soldán, *Diccionario Geográfico*. His definition of *pueblo*, which I am rendering here as "town" or "village" (ibid., xv), is particularly useful. See chapter 6.

30 The actual figures are as follows. In 1782, out of 1,362 individuals paying the indian tribute in the *repartimiento* of Huanta, 537 are listed as "landless," while 825 own land (AGN, Tributos, Huanta, leg. 3, cuad. 49, 1780–1782). In 1801, the figures are 1,184 landless and 1,345 with land, out of a total of 2,529 tribute payers (AGN, Tributos, Huanta, leg. 5, cuad. 19, 1801). The figures do not include the villagers exempt from tribute.

31 One capitulado, Manuel Gato, described the composition of the army that participated in the thwarted attack on Ayacucho in these terms: "about 1,500 men would come from them, 1,000 from the punas and the rest from Huanta," AGN, 1825, R-J,

Prefecturas, Ayacucho, leg. 93, unnumbered folio. Other witnesses declared higher numbers, which are consistent with the testimony provided by the traveler Heinrich Witt, who upon visiting Ayacucho in 1828 was told that the army that prepared to storm Ayacucho consisted of three thousand to four thousand men, thirty of whom were Spanish capitulados. Witt, *Un Testimonio*, 1:222.

32 The *alcaldes'* importance in the mobilization of the communities finds expression in several testimonies. When the priest José Franco Coronado sent a message to "Iquicha, Cano and Tricos" urging them to surrender, he addressed himself to the *"señores alcaldes* and other communities" (ADAY, JPI, Crim., leg. 30, cuad. 579: Cuaderno primero del juicio a Soregui, "Papeles del Cura Navarro," 1828, ff. 111r / v). In 1825, the Spaniard Miguel Fariña circulated an order directing the "pueblos, estancias and punas [*sic*] . . . to gather with their alcaldes in the place of Uchuraccay" (cited in Pérez Aguirre, "Rebeldes," 101). The call to the towns of Huancavelica—San Cristobal, Huando, Izcuchaca, and Caja—was likewise made through their alcaldes (AGN, RJ-Prefecturas, Ayacucho, leg. 93, unnumbered folios).

33 David Cahill called my attention to this change in nomenclature. Indeed, the first document in which I have found the word *varayoq* used in lieu of *alcalde indígena* dates from 1853 (see next footnote).

34 I have found several testimonies that shed light on the authority and representativity of the alcaldes indígenas in various towns of Huanta; these testimonies are consistent with the information anthropologists have provided for other regions in later periods. For example, in the trial of José Antonio de La Barreda, an early collaborator of the monarchists who was accused of having stolen livestock from peasants in several communities, the *regidor* (indigenous alderman) of the town of Marccaraccay said "that he had no knowledge of any harm done by [Barreda] despite being a vara official." Some decades after the rebellion, the alcaldes' authority persisted. "This occurred in the town's square in front of three *varayos* [*sic*] and a large number of inhabitants," said José Ramírez, plaintiff in a trial in Luricocha in September 1853.

35 The priest Manuel Navarro said "that [in Mayhuavilca] the mayors or indians had killed a witch" (ADAY, JPI, Crim., leg. 29, cuad. 564: Cuaderno segundo del juicio a Soregui, "Papeles del Cura Navarro," f. 40r.). The other witnesses refer to the same facts in similar terms, freely interchanging the terms *alcalde* and *indio*.

36 "I reward [Soregui], heeding the powers bestowed upon me in the name of the king and the communities and divisions" reads the appointment of Soregui as brigadier-general. ADAY, 1828, JPI, Crim., leg. 30, cuad. 579: Cuaderno primero del juicio a Soregui, "Papeles de Soregui," f. 36. See chapter 2 for full appointment.

37 "I request that all of the civilian and military vara officials give him [José Pérez del Valle] all the necessary assistance" (ADAY, 1828, JPI, Crim., leg. 30, cuad. 572, f. 1).

38 "And so we are, and so Belarde does not want you to be commander or me to be

captain or Staff, but he alone wants to assume all positions, and so seek to go forth, for accordingly keep in touch and put them in their places with the direct vote of the community." ADAY, JPI, Crim., leg. 31, cuad. 585, Cuaderno tercero del juicio a Soregui, f. 9v.

39 The missive was signed by Choque in Cancaíllo on December 13, 1826, that is, before the most dramatic actions of the rebellion had taken place. ADAY, JPI, Crim., leg. 31, cuad. 585, Cuaderno tercero del juicio Soregui y otros, f. 11v. We do not know whether Melchor Porras indeed came to assume the position of *alcalde mayor*, but he did serve as tithe collector for the rebels.

40 ADAY, 1828, JPI, leg. 30, cuad. 582, "Quaderno de los papeles que tratan sobre comiciones recividas por Manuel Leandro de los gefes de los rebeldes de Yquicha," f. 7.

41 There is little knowledge about the workings of *cabildos de indios* in the countryside of Peru during the early republican period, but their functioning has been reported for Peru's northern regions, in particular. See Diez Hurtado, *Comunes y Haciendas*. Diez suggests the importance of the cabildos de indios in the late colonial period, in particular, and contends that although they continued operating in the republican era, their authority was increasingly constrained by the emergence of the new republican authorities, among them, the *gobernador*. For the colonial segment of the nineteenth century, see Christine Hünefeldt, "Los indios y la constitución de 1812," *Allpanchis Phuturinqa*, no. 11 / 12, (1978): 37.

42 ADAY, 1828, JPI, leg. 30, cuad. 582, f. 11.

43 A document signed on February 12, 1828, by Pedro Porras and the mayor Félix Galindo was drawn up at the "Aranhuay Commander's Headquarters," and it was addressed to Soregui (ADAY, 1828, JPI, Crim., leg. 30, cuad. 579, "Primer cuaderno del juicio a Soregui," "Papeles A").

44 The reference to Huaillay as a headquarters is as follows: "Cuartel General de Huaillai," February 8, 1828, from Tiburcio Figueroa to Soregui, ADAY, 1828, JPI, Crim., leg. 30, cuad. 579, "Papeles A," f. 26.

45 A thorough description of Secce's placement is found in Cavero, *Monografía*, 1:168. I was able to confirm this description myself upon visiting Secce.

46 *Originario* and *forastero* are tribute-based categories of colonial origin, indicating "original" settlers and "outsiders," respectively. For a long-term study of these categories, see Sánchez Albornoz, *Indios y Tributos*.

47 The town with the largest tributary population was Tambo, with 350 tribute payers, followed by San Pedro de Huanta with 235, Huamanguilla with 219, and Luricocha with 153. AGN, Tributos, Huanta, leg. 5, cuad. 19, Primer Repartimiento: Huanta, July–December 1801.

48 A document signed by Huachaca on February 12, 1828, in San Luis (i.e., Luis Pampa) and addressed to Soregui states, "The other towns will receive notice that I

am at this moment doing business with that town's [Aranhuay's] Mayor of Spaniards" (ADAY, 1828, JPI, Crim., leg. 30, cuad. 679, "Papeles A," f. 30).

49   In the Sierra of Piura, in northern Peru, out of ten towns being ruled by cabildos indios (town councils of indians) at the end of the eighteenth century, two of them existed parallel to cabildos de españoles. Diez Hurtado, *Comunes y Haciendas*, 119. In 1811 and 1812, alcaldes de españoles were elected in several towns of the partidos of Tayacaja and Angaraes (in today's department of Huancavelica), alongside alcaldes de indios (BN, D10263, 1811).

50   Cahill, "Colour by Numbers," 342.

51   This is not a widely explored topic, but interesting insights can be found in Natalia Majluf, "The Creation of the Image of the Indian in 19th Century Peru: The Paintings of Francisco Laso" (PH.D. diss., University of Texas, 1994); and Chambers, "Little Middle Ground."

52   "Nicolás Cisneros *alcalde de españoles in the town of Seque*, district of Marcaraccay province of Huanta . . . united with the *alcalde de naturales* [i.e., natives or indians] Alejo Rivera and in the name of both communities as their representatives" can be read at the beginning of a request to the prefect of Ayacucho in 1831, AGN, PL 11–32, 1831, f. 3r (emphasis added).

53   ADAY, JPI, Crim., leg. 29, cuad. 564, Cuaderno segundo del juicio a Soregui, f. 87.

54   José Coronel, personal communication.

55   It is quite possible that the Huayanay hacienda, in the doctrina of Luricocha, was the site of another headquarters, yet I have found no documents which would allow us to confirm this fact.

56   "The Tucuvilca quarters (which is their [the Ruiz's] home), where they always lodged Huachaca, Mendes, Soregui and every ringleader," stated Francisco Ozaeta, governor of Tambo (Tambo, August 14, 1828, f. 2v.). There are other versions, such as that of Domingo García Quintas: "In the home of José Ruiz with Soregui were the meetings of those of Huanta" (AGN, 1828, R-J, Ayacucho Prefecturas, leg. 93, undated). The accused, José Ruiz, did not deny these charges: "Asked whether Guachaca, Mendes and other ringleaders were continually lodged in Tucuvilca, he said: as the declarant was in Huanta and also in the montaña, they used to lodge at Tucuvilca when they were going to invade Tambo, but the one who is speaking was not there when they were," ADAY, 1828, JPI, Prefecturas, leg. 64, ff. 3v / 4r.

57   Cited by Pérez Aguirre, "Rebeldes Iquichanos," 8.

58   ADAY, JPI, Crim., leg. 94, unnumbered cuad., f. 6IV. Pedro Cárdenas participated in the riot in Tambo in March 1826, killing, it was said, "seven *cívicos* [civilian policemen]." In Quintanilla's assault on Uchuraccay, Cárdenas is referred to as "sergeant major . . . mayordomo of Ascarza." ADAY, JPI, Crim., leg. 30, cuad. 566, Juicio a Meneses (in the Cuaderno Segundo del Juicio a Leandro), f. IV.

59   Ninaquiro also appears as "Cano y Ninaquiro" and was registered as a pueblo with

one alcalde in the indian tributary rolls from 1786 onward; its population that year included seventy tribute payers, and in 1801 some ninety. In 1801, Challhuamayo figures as an estancia, with only thirteen tribute payers, and its official registration does not begin until that year.

60 On February 8, 1827, in Ayahuanco, Huachaca issued an order to bring detractors "to the Iquicha headquarters." ADAY, 1827, JPI, Crim., leg. 27, cuad. 521, Cuaderno cuarto del juicio a Soregui y otros, f. 49r.

61 See, for example, Paz Soldán, *Diccionario*, and Méndez-Gastelumendi, "The Power of Naming," 127–60.

62 The Franciscans' map on which I am relying is in Ortiz, *Las Montañas*, 144–45. The map dates from 1782, and other very similar examples can be found in the Archivo de Indias. O'Higgins's map is also in the Archivo de Indias, in AGI, MP, Peru-Chile 158, "Mapa original de la Intendencia de Guamanga del Perú . . . [1803–1804]," and has been reprinted in Eleodoro Villazón, *Alegato de parte del Gobierno de Bolivia en el Juicio Arbitral de Fronteras con la República del Perú* (Buenos Aires, 1906), 164–65.

63 On the harassment of patriots by the peasants of Huanta and Huando during the Independence campaigns, see the following: CDIP, tomo V, 6:102, 132, 268, 533–34; AGN, Colección Santa María, 00611: 11 and 12; Miller, *Memorias*, 3:11–12. For Huantino participation in crushing the Cuzco rebellion of 1814–15, see CDIP, tomo III, 7:583–85; CDIP, tomo XXVI, 4:72; tomo XXVI, 1:335, 452, 453.

64 Huanta historian Luis E. Cavero states, "When the viceroy of Peru, Don Francisco de Toledo, made his visit to the city of Guamanga in 1571 . . . he found there the *encomienda* [i.e., indians granted to a conquistador] in Iquicha." *Monografía*, 1:178. However, I have found no evidence that a place by the name of Iquicha existed in the sixteenth century. See Méndez-Gastelumendi, "The Power of Naming," 134, 135.

65 See chapter 4.

66 Witt, *Un Testimonio*, 1:230. Most prominent among the twentieth-century myth-makers of Iquichanos is the Ayacuchan scholar Víctor Navarro del Aguila, who in his thesis *Las Tribus de Anku Wallokc* (Cuzco, 1939) identified the Iquichanos as "beheaders of cadavers," and warlike "tribes" that formed part of the "Chanka Confederation," allegedly a pre-Hispanic polity known by its staunch opposition to Inca rule. Most recently, the novelist Vargas Llosa unknowingly recreated Navarro's myths on Iquichanos in his efforts to come up with a "rational" explanation for the killings of eight journalists in the heights of Uchuraccay in 1983 (see chapter 1). Yet, as I have shown elsewhere, much of the mythology concerning the "Iquichanos" was prompted by the facts surrounding the monarchist rebellion and subsequent history rather than by an actual knowledge of Huantan pre-Hispanic past (Méndez-Gastelumendi, "The Power of Naming").

67 The records of land settlement (*composición de tierras*) on which I base my findings

correspond to the years 1800 and 1802 and are the following: ADAY, Intendencia, Asuntos Administrativos, leg. 41, cuad. 7, "Legajo de los expedientes de composiciones de las haciendas [sic] cocales de Guanta"; ADAY, Intendencia, Asuntos Administrativos, leg. 40, cuad. 39 (1800); ibid., leg. 40, cuad. 40 (1800); ibid., leg. 41, cuad. 5 (1802); and ibid., leg. 41, cuad. 7 (1802).

68 The Choimacota documents of May 1827 bear the signatures of Huachaca and Arancibia; see ADAY, 1828, JPI, Crim., leg. 30, cuad. 582, ff. 16–17. On Choimacota in the year 1828, see ADAY, JPI, Crim., leg. 30, cuad. 579, f. 70.

69 The priest of Choimacota, Acón and Sintiguailas, don Lucas Retamoso, defending himself from certain accusations, stated that "there is no one here to administer such an operation [the removal of garbage], . . . both the hacendados and farmhands and the foreigners in their stay will have to manage things *because their stay in these gorges are [sic] for very short spells*" (B.N. D9846, 1836, emphasis added). The testimony is from 1836, but I believe it can also serve to illustrate what was taking place a few years before.

70 ADAY, 1828, JPI, Crim., leg. 30, cuad. 579, "Papeles A," f. 70.

71 Reconstructed on the basis of ADAY, 1828, JPI, Crim., leg. 30, cuad. 582.

72 Although Eric Wolf's famous piece on the "closed corporate community" is out of date by all academic standards, the image of the Andean peasant communities as self-contained entities is so powerful that it still pervades the language of the very historians in search of connections between the peasants and the state. The allusions are no longer to the economic life of the community, but appear rather as binary constructs related to ethnicity, politics, or "ideology," as when historians define Andean "Indians" as intrinsically opposed to the "criollo society" (or criollo state project) or as steadily resisting powerful "outsiders" and remaining aloof from the early republican caudillo struggle. An example of these constructs can be found in Charles Walker, *Smoldering Ashes*. The binary construct that opposes *criollo* to *andino* is also embedded in Florencia Mallon's interpretation of the "Andean utopia" (a concept originally formulated by Peruvian historians Alberto Flores Galindo and Manuel Burga) as a "counter hegemonic" project (see Mallon, *Peasant and Nation*, conclusions). Flores Galindo himself did not conceive of "Andean Utopia" as a specifically indigenous political project, but rather as a national one.

73 Chacabamba had twenty-eight tribute payers in 1796 and nineteen in 1801 (AGN, Tributos, Huanta, leg. 3, cuad. 49, and leg. 5, cuad. 19). In 1834, it is referred to as a hacienda in which there are alcaldes indígenas (ADAY, 1834, JPI, Crim., leg. 37).

74 Of the twenty-four prisoners taken by Commander Quintanilla in the final raid on Uchuraccay in March 1828, only Meneses "handled Spanish." ADAY, 1828, JPI, Crim., leg. 30, cuad. 566, f. 7r.

75 Meneses declared that "he remained on his hacienda in the punas until indians from Ranra and Chacabamba, *on whose lands his estate* [finca] *stands*, took him away

from there by force." ADAY, 1828, JPI, Crim., leg. 30, cuad. 566, f. 32v. (emphasis added). The testimony is not clear enough for us to know whether the property in question was his own estate or land he occupied (perhaps) on lease from the community, as happened, for instance, in the partido of Tapacarí in Bolivia, where communities rented their lands to private individuals; see Sánchez Albornos, *Indios y Tributos*. Moreover, Meneses uttered that "while being in Ninaquiro, Antonio Santos Huachaca arrived before the surprise [i.e., the arrival of Quintanilla with his troops in Uchuraccay], with some others bearing as a prisoner the *indijena* [*sic*] Asebedo, who was saying that everyone from Ranra and Chacabamba had turned themselves over to Quintanilla at Tambo. That with this news they forced him to write to the caudillo Huachaca, who was in Chaca," ADAY, 1828, JPI, Crim., leg. 30, cuad. 566, ff. 31v, 32r.

76 All declarations on and by Meneses can be found in ADAY, 1828, JPI, Crim., leg. 30, cuad. 566, ff. 10r / v, 30–32.

77 Alejandro del Río, *Ninabamba, una Hacienda Jesuita del siglo XVIII* (Lima: Seminario de Historia Rural Andina, Universidad Nacional Mayor de San Marcos, 1987); Urrutia, *Huamanga*, 97–167, and "Comerciantes, Arrieros y Viajeros," 82–83; Stern, *Peru's Indian Peoples*, 162–63; Miriam Salas, *De los obrajes de Canaria y Chincheros a las comunidades indígenas de Vilcashuamán, siglo XVI* (Lima: n.p., 1979); Cavero, *Monografía*, 1:57–59; and Husson, "De la Guerra."

78 Leocadio Edgar Sulca Báez "Curas y Kurakas Ayacuchanos: Tierra y poder en la sociedad colonial" (Tesis, Título de Antropólogo Social, Ayacucho: UNSCH, 1986); Stern, *Peru's Indian Peoples*.

79 AGN, Tributos–Huanta, leg. 5, cuad. 19, July–December 1801; and leg. 3, cuad. 9, 1781–1782.

80 AGI, Lima 1801, "Real Cédula concediendo varias gracias para el fomento de la agricultura poblacion y comercio en la Provincia de Guamanga y sus montañas," 1816. See also chapter 3.

81 I have not come across such cases, but Núria Sala has located a couple of communities in Huanta above three thousand meters (Pampacoris and Secce) which as of the 1960s still had communal holdings in the selva of the Apurímac. Sala i Vila, *Selva y Andes*, 258.

82 The royal warrant of 1816 gave "power to the Intendant Governor of the Province of Guamanga, or to the territorial subdelegates, to transfer the rights to available lands in the montañas and Muyunmarca to all who request them, whether they be small garden patches [*huertas*] or large sections, provided that they do not exceed a square league, and giving preference, all other circumstances being equal: *First to the indian*: second, to whomever promises to take up residence punctually in these very montañas or valleys: third, to those who are natives of the town or doctrina which the montañas in question have bordered up to now: fourth, to neighbors of

the same town or doctrina: fifth, to natives of the corresponding district: sixth, to those of the province; and seventh, to any outsiders, and between any two with an identical request, to the first who turns up" (emphasis added). AGI, Lima, 1801 "Real Cédula concediendo varias Gracias," 1816.

83   ADAY, 1828, JPI, Crim., leg. 30, cuad. 582, f. 12r. The documents do not specify whether Belarde belonged to one of the ayllus comprising the town of Marccaraccay.

84   See the section "Choimacota and Paraíso: The Coca Montañas" above.

85   ADAY, 1828, JPI, Crim., leg. 30, cuad. 581, f. 7.

86   "Ysidora Urbano, legitimate wife of Leonardo Quispe, with his permission and in the name of Carlos Lima Quispe, my son-in-law, my brother-in-law Buenaventura Chávez, and my cousin Melchora Huamán, widow of Andrés Guillén, residents of the district of Chupas, in the doctrina of Carhuahuran . . .," ibid., f. 21r.

87   Ibid., ff. 7, 21r.

88   Ayahuanco more than doubled its tribute-paying population in twenty years: in 1780 there were thirty-seven tributaries (thirty-two with lands and five without lands); in 1801 the tributaries numbered eighty: fifty with lands and thirty without lands. Chagua was a district belonging to the doctrina of Ccarhuahurán; in 1801 the tributaries of Ccarhuahurán numbered fifty-seven without lands. AGN, 1801, Tributos, Huanta, leg. 3, cuad. 49, and leg. 5, cuad. 19.

89   ADAY, JPI, Crim., leg. 30, cuad. 581.

90   Having one to eight head of cattle is a privilege of "middling" and well-to-do peasants, "since the poor have none," according to a 1980 study of the community of Culluchaca, in the province of Huanta. Abilio Vergara, Juan Arguedas, and Genaro Zaga, *Reciprocidad y Ciclos Productivos en la Comunidad de Culluchaca* (Ayacucho: Instituto de Estudios Regionales José María Arguedas, n.d.), 39. At the time of the monarchist rebellion, Culluchaca was a hacienda, the property of Juan Cantón, and on more than one occasion it gave shelter to the rebels (see chapters 2 and 5).

91   ADAY, JPI, Crim., leg. 30, cuad. 581, 1828, 21r.

92   Declarations of Ignacio Alvarado, a Huanta civilian police cavalry captain, ADAY, JPI, Crim., leg. 30, cuad. 581, 1828, ff. 14r / v.

93   The accusation made by Mayor Fernando Curiñaupa, Elifonso Chagua, and Ysidora Urbano, who identified themselves as "indians of the town of Ayahuanco," deserves to be cited at length: "Don Antonio de la Barreda looked at us cruelly, not wanting to hand over any of the livestock that he had rustled from our town, so that on that day we found one hundred and some sheep, in the possession of Melchor Gente of Marcaraccay and put out to graze by said Barreda, which belonged to the mayor and the second petitioner, that are the only ones that appear out of the three hundred we had; for he has sold the rest at an equitable price; said

Gente fully confesses he got the livestock from Barreda and in the end we know our own. And of the third [petitioner] they are in his power and in Seque three mother cows loyal to take possession" (ADAY, 1828, JPI, Crim., leg. 30, cuad. 581, ff. 21rv). The testimony was partially corroborated by Barreda himself and other witnesses at the trial.

94 Poole, "Landscapes of Power"; Poole, "Qorilazos, abigeos y comunidades"; Deborah Poole, ed., *Unruly Order: Violence, Power, and Cultural Identity in the High Provinces of Southern Peru* (Boulder: Westview Press, 1994). For an example outside the Andes, see James Brooks, "Served Well by Plunder: *La Gran Ladronería*, and Producers of History Astride the Río Grande," *American Quarterly* 54, no. 1 (March 2000): 23–75.

95 ADAY, JPI, Crim., leg. 30, cuad. 582, 1828, f. 36.

96 In the 1830s Huachaca himself was accused of *abigeato*. See ADAY, JPI, Crim., leg. 37, 1834, "Expediente Criminal seguido de oficio contra los indígenas Paula Ramos, Julián Piña, Ygnacio Ccasani por resistirse a la justicia." The charges were never proved, however, and it seems that the alleged "cattle theft" was no ordinary rustling, but rather occurred as part of a larger politico-military mobilization in the province, which was encouraged by the national caudillos themselves, and whose details I will explore in chapter 7.

97 On Cantón, see ADAY, JPI, Crim., leg. 30, cuad. 575, 1828, "Autos contra Juan Canton y M. Riveros"; AGN, Aduanas C16, leg. 456, cuad. 626; leg. 457, cuad. 639, and leg. 458, cuads. 641, 653 (1819–1822); ADAY, Protocolos Notariales, leg. 178, f. 250; leg. 179; leg. 180, f. 249; and ADAY, JPI, Crim., cuad. 564, ff. 72v, 73r.

98 On Soregui, see ADAY, Protocolos Notariales, leg. 91, Escribano Gerónimo García y Aramburú, ff. 399r–405, 167r, 168v, 481r–482r, and 500r–501v; ADAY, JPI, Crim., leg. 29, cuad. 564, ff. 67v, 84r; ADAY, JPI, Crim., leg. 29, cuad. 264, f. 87r; ADAY, 1828, JPI, Crim., leg. 30, cuad. 575, f. 18v.

99 ADAY, 1828, JPI, Crim., leg. 30, cuad. 579, "Papeles A," ff. 13f.

100 ADAY, JPI, Prefecturas, leg. 64, f. 3r.

101 Ibid., f. 49v. Other villagers made similar declarations. "The [Ruiz] family," said Tambo's governor, Francisco Ozaeta, "openly trades with them [the caudillos] and also supplied food to the rebels." ADAY, JPI, Prefecturas, leg. 64, f. 9r.

102 It was said that Huachaca sought out Benito and José Ruiz "in order to take their lives, the two of them having contributed to the surrender of Chacabamba." Declarations by Martín Qquente (or Ccente), *"residente indígena"* in this hacienda, ADAY, 128, JPI, Crim., Prefecturas, leg. 64, f. 49v. Villagers from districts bordering Tucuvilca made declarations to the same effect.

103 ADAY, JPI, Crim., Prefecturas, leg. 64, f. 49v.

104 Félix Galindo, mayor of Ayahuanco, declared that "having neared the town of Marcaraccay upon returning from the montaña, Don Pascual Arancibia sum-

moned him for his private business in the montaña, where [sic] he told the deponent [Félix Galindo], the vara official of the town of Marcaray [sic] José Quispe, alderman Norverto Sulca, and don Mariano Osorio that the purpose of having come from the Montaña was for him to meet with the Prefect General to inform him that the mayor of the infidels was being held prisoner." ADAY, 1828, JPI, Crim., leg. 30, cuad. 581, ff. 91v., 10r.

105 Huanta historians assert that his home town was San José de Iquicha, but no town by that name appears in written records until much later.

106 ADAY, JPI, Crim., leg. 27, cuad. 521, f. 18v.; ADAY, JPI, Crim., leg. 29, cuad. 564, ff. 96v–99r.

107 In the town of Mayhuavilca a woman was executed on the accusation of being a witch—on Huachaca's orders, according to several witnesses' accounts—and with massive support from the towns' mayors (who claimed to be obeying Huachaca's orders) and the rest of the villagers of this and other towns in the punas. Cf. ADAY, JPI, Crim., leg. 29, ff. 23r, 27rv, 29r, 35rv, 40r, 46v, 47r; 53v, 54r. More references to this case will be discussed in the next chapter.

108 Sebastián Cahuana (or Cabana), a villager from Challhuamayo, declared that "coming to Huanta driving his cattle, [he] slept in Uchuraccay the night they were surprised [by Commander Quintanilla]." ADAY, 1828, JPI, Crim., leg. 30, cuad. 566, f. 7v.

109 See Cavero, Monografía, 1:57, 67; del Río, Ninabamba, 19; Urrutia, "Comerciantes, arrireros y viajeros," 23–24; Stern, Peru's Indian Peoples; Stefano Varese, La Sal de los Cerros, 2d ed. (Lima: Retablo Papel, 1973), 72, and Ortiz, Las Montañas.

110 Karen Spalding, "The Colonial Indian Past and Future Research Perspectives," Latin American Research Review 2 (spring 1972): 49.

111 From Francisco de Ozaeta to the prefect, Tambo, May 21, 1826; ADAY, JPI, Prefecturas, leg. 64, unnumbered file (from the trial of Benito and José Ruiz), f. 9r.

112 Blanchard, ed., Markham in Peru, 70.

113 On Huamanga's trading circuits at the end of the eighteenth century, see Urrutia, Huamanga. For the mining circuits in the southern Andes in the colonial period, see Carlos Sempat Assadourian, El Sistema Económico Colonial (Lima: IEP, 1982); Contreras, La Ciudad; and Magdalena Chocano, Comercio en Cerro de Pasco a fines de la época colonial (Lima: UNMSM, Seminario de Historia Rural Andina, 1982).

114 According to the historian Miriam Salas, muleteers in Huamanga were far from being racially homogeneous (personal communication).

115 Here is a vivid testimony of the empowering positioning of the high-altitude communities: "For a long time I had noticed they were freely conveying coca from the montañas to the towns of Huanta, Tambo, and Ayacucho in the midst of the rebellion of the Yquichanos, whose vigilance the traffickers could not escape,

it being that much more difficult inasmuch as they [the Iquichanos] were positioned in a precise and essential spot." From Prefect Manuel Lopera to the Minister, October 19, 1839. AGN, PL, 19–118.

116   Vargas Llosa et al., *Informe*, 7, 36, 73.

CHAPTER 6. Government in Uchuraccay

1   Huachaca and Arancibia ordered the subdelegate Manuel Ynga: "Tomorrow . . . you will make available all the assistance at your disposal, food for both the troops and staff officers and pack animals, because sixteen of them are needed, soon, *without harming the traginantes* [peddlers and traveling merchants], *but only the hacendados, with no omissions or leniency.*" Signed by Huachaca and Arancibia, Choimacota headquarters, May 18, 1827. ADAY, 1827, JPI, leg. 30, cuad. 582, f. 17 (emphasis added).

2   The Spaniard Juan Callejas, a capitulado lieutenant colonel, said that he "heard from Zoregui [*sic*] that he . . . was the one who ran everything because Huachaca was inept and a drunk." ADAY, JPI, Crim., leg. 29, cuad. 564, f. 49r. Another Spaniard, Juan Fernández, in turn wrote to Soregui, "The General [Huachaca] had me detained until the departure of said officer . . . although I am much displeased here since I am happy only in your company and that of all my friends," San Luis (i.e., Luis Pampa), January 22, 1828. ADAY, JPI, Crim., leg. 30, cuad. 579, "Papeles de Juan Fernández," f. 1.

3   Confession of Francisco Pacheco, ADAY, JPI, Crim., leg. 29, cuad. 564, f. 100v. This allusion certainly allows for more than one interpretation. Pacheco was making this deposition before a tribunal that was trying him for his participation in a pro-Spanish rebellion—he may well have been seeking to disassociate himself from the Spaniards, "enemies of the Patria" and, if this was the case, the allusion to the Spanish would be political rather than ethnic.

4   ADAY, JPI, Crim., leg. 29, cuad. 564, f. 64, testimony of Juan Ramos. Another version of the facts was given by the priest Manuel Navarro: "When they tried to enter Huanta on the past 12 November [I] advised Huachaca not to do so, nor to sacrifice that town, and with [my] advice Huachaca withdrew the day before[,] or the preceding day[,] from Artiaga to half a league from the town[,] until reaching the heights of Culluchuca two and a half leagues away[,] when Zoregui [*sic*], Arancibia [and] Pineda, who were leaders of the capitulados[,] made him return." ADAY, JPI, Crim., leg. 29, cuad. 546, f. 37v.

5   Choque and Bernardino Galindo to Francisco Garay, Cancaíllo, December 13, 1826. ADAY, JPI, Crim., leg. 31, cuad. 585, f. 12r / v.

292 NOTES TO CHAPTER 6

6 Signed by Tadeo Choque and Bernardino Galindo in Cancaíllo, December 29, 1826. ADAY, 1826, JPI, Crim., leg. 31, cuad. 585, f. 9v.

7 "[Feliciano Guillén says] . . . that he has orders from Señor General Huachaca not to obey anyone [else]." From Juan Cantón to Tadeo Choque and Pascual Arancibia, Santa Gertrudis, ADAY, 1827, JPI, Crim., leg. 30, cuad. 575, f. 6v. This rivalry between the leaders was an important factor in the defeat of the rebellion. After the unsuccessful invasion of Ayacucho, Choque and Arancibia, along with Antonio Barreda, went over to the government's ranks. "Don Pascual Arancibia and Tadeo Choque are not only pardoned but also commended for their subsequent service to the Peruvian cause," wrote Domingo Tristán to Judge Luciano María Cano. Ayacucho, July 16, 1828. ADAY, 1828, JPI, Crim., f. 77r. Francisco Vidal, in turn, had previously written to Tristán: "For me it is only too plausible to give you the news that the pacification of these punas, as an end to the misfortunes that over a four-year period have upset the entire department; to commend likewise the noble conduct of Arancibia, Barrera and Choque[,] who were previously on Guachaca's side." Huanta, May 14, 1828, cited in Cavero, *Monografía*, 1:208–09.

8 "Soregui was the most enthusiastic about attacking the city [of Huanta] and seizing it, and his influence was the reason they came since the indians did not want to." Deposition of Domingo García Quintas, AGN, RJ, Prefecturas, Ayacucho, leg. 93, unnumbered page.

9 ADAY, JPI, Crim., leg. 27, cuad. 521, f. 49. Signed by Huachaca, Ayacucho, February 8, 1827.

10 Witt, *Un Testimonio*, 1:231–32.

11 Upon arriving in Marcarí with coca for Francisco Garay, a man was ordered to return with lead "and although the *yaya* [Father] Urribarren told him that he had to take the lead[,] he absolutely refused to do so." Garay to Soregui, ADAY, JPI, Crim., leg. 30, cuad. 579, "B," f. 9.

12 See the entry for "diezmos" in Francisco García Calderón, *Diccionario de la Legislación Peruana*, vol. 1 (Lima and Paris: Laroque, 1979). The original sources of this section's epigraphs can be found in ADAY, JPI, CC, leg. 30, cuad. 572, f. 1r, and ADAY, JPI, Crim., leg. 29, f. 105r.

13 A quantity known as two half-ninths (*dos medios novenos*, approximately 9 percent, in terms of the amounts actually paid), added to another known as the "caroline tax" (the *pensión carolina*, 2 percent), was what the state retained from the tithe auctions during the last period of the colonial era. This represented, approximately, 11 percent. During the Republic, the percentage retained by the state doubled. A decree issued on September 22, 1826, created the *noveno general* (i.e., "general ninth-part tithe"), equivalent to 11 percent of the total auction, which increased the percentage from tithe auctions kept by the state to 22 percent. This noveno general

was also called the *noveno de consolidación* (consolidation tithe), in accordance with a document from 1854: *"Noveno de Consolidación*: to the consolidation of the state debt shall belong in its entirety one-ninth deducted from the total gross value . . . which deduction is ordered by the supreme decree of 22 September, 1826." AGN, OL 385–201, 1854. In addition to this last source, this reconstruction of the changes in the tithe is based on AGN, PL 12–135, 1832, and AGN, OL 325–726, 1846.

14 Antolín Cárdenas, reportedly Huachaca's "brother-in-law" (the term does not suggest the same thing it does now in Peru and elsewhere; rather, it then indicated a more complex relationship, including friendship and various forms of ritual kinship), said that "the tithes were the responsibility of Don Antonio Bellido, who got them from the chapter board's auctioning, and who at the time was Valle's *mayordomo*." ADAY, JPI, Crim., leg. 29, cuad. 564, f. 97v.

15 The list included José Franco (*subdelegado* and mayor), Bernardino Galindo and José Girón (Huachaca's secretaries), Feliciano Guillén, another collaborator; Justo Paredes, a hacendado who served as a commander, leading the Luricochinos in Macachacra (ADAY, JPI, Crim., leg. 29, cuad. 564, f. 34r); and José Ruiz and Juan Cantón, likewise hacendado collaborators (ADAY, JPI, Crim., leg. 30, cuad. 128, ff. 14, 15). On the other hand, Tadeo Choque himself, who held the rank of general, wrote to Francisco Garay, "For this reason I have to tell you that as for the tithe[,] you should collect it from all people without exception[,] myself included" (ADAY, JPI, Crim., leg. 31, cuad. 585, f. 9r.). Lastly, Franciso Garay, who held equally important military posts, testified that he "did not take charge of this tithe, and [he] added that he himself paid it like anyone else because it was collected from him," ibid., f. 23r.

16 Several witnesses who testified at the trial of Manuel Leandro complained. For example, Don Mariano Mancilla claimed that Leandro "wanted to seize [his properties] at every turn"; Manuel Urrivarre complained likewise, "when the hacendados did not want to pay him [Leandro] the tithe, he [Leandro] had their *arrobas* seized" (ADAY, JPI, Crim., leg. 30, cuad. 569, ff. 14v, 15v). For his part, the captain of the Huanta Civilian Cavalry (*Caballería Cívica de Huanta*) wrote to the prefect, "Have no doubt that his [José Murrieta's] hacienda has been seized and mine also on the orders of the caudillo Huachaca[,] and some arrobas sent to this town for the sustenance of the wife . . . have been taken by the rebels" (ADAY, JPI, "Sobre indagar la conducta que observaron don José y don Manuel Murrieta en el tiempo y lugares de la Revolucion de Yquicha," undated). Finally, on December 28, 1827, Huachaca wrote to Soregui, in Acopita, that "[it is] odd that so far you have given me no news about my *paysano* Arancibia, and whether he has turned over all the arms and munitions. . . . should he not do so [we shall] attack with a company of cavalry and then confiscate his goods until he hands everything over, should he

persist I will not stop until every last bit of the tithe has been accounted for." ADAY, 1827, JPI, Crim., leg. 30, cuad. 579, Papeles "A," f. 3r.

17 ADAY, 1828, JPI, Diezmos, leg. 55, cuad. 6, f. 17. José Ramires to Rafael Quisoruco, Palma Pampa, September 2, 1828.

18 "For Guachaca has caused many disturbances on the coca haciendas, because after a long period of armed revolution crimes of every sort continue to take place and because men no longer under the military's charge cannot but devote themselves to think on and protect their own interests." Prefect Tristán to the Minister of State in the Office of Government, Huanta, February 16, 1828. AGN-RJ Ministerio de Justicia, leg. 93, unnumbered folio.

19 "What they call *avío* is the wage in coca that the coca plantations' owners usually pay to their farmhands, either because they have no money or because the laborers stipulated that they be paid in coca and not money. Whence the origin of the corruption of the hacendados in wanting to pay the tithe on the cash that remains after deducting the avíos." ADAY, JPI, Crim., leg. 57, cuad. 37, 1844, f. 9v. (emphasis added).

20 ADAY, JPI, leg. 30, cuad. 569, f. 16r.

21 Several witnesses brought accusations against the hacendado José Antonio de la Barreda. The captain of Huanta's Civilian Cavalry, Ignacio Alvarado, stated, "From time immemorial . . . Barrera [*sic*] . . . has acted oppressively toward the miserable inhabitants of the montaña, taking advantage of a thousand wicked pretexts not to pay them for their work." ADAY, JPI, Crim., leg. 30, cuad. 581, ff. 14rv, 21r. The irony is that Barreda had at one time collaborated with the monarchist rebellion. For more on Barreda, see chapter 5.

22 Following is some evidence as to the origins of the labor on the coca plantations: "The indians, who with the aim of working on the coca plantations that are in those [places], go there for a set period of time, return after the harvests come to an end, the owners of the haciendas being the residents of Huanta" (AGN, Superior Gobierno, leg. 37, cuad. 1313, 1819, "Expediente promovido ante el Señor Gobernador de Huanta por los vecinos de esa jurisdicción solicitando la creación de la plaza de Alcalde Ordinario," f. 3v., signed by the subdelegate of Huanta, Pedro José Lazón, Huanta, January 20, 1820). The term *indian* was generally reserved for peasants from the highlands; those from the selva and sections of the montañas were usually called "infidels" or *chunchos* or, less frequently, *selváticos*. Thus one may deduce that the "indians" mentioned in the citation came from Huanta's punas and high-altitude valleys, not from the selva, even though the latter also went to work in the coca fields, as is indicated in other documents, for example, ADAY, JPI, Diezmos, leg. 57, cuad. 37, 1848.

23 ADAY, JPI, Crim., "Sobre Indagar la Conducta que Observaron Dn. José y Don Manuel Murrieta en el Tiempo y Lugares de la Revolución de Yquicha" (no date).

24 The name of the dossier in which the tithe collectors José Ramírez and Rafael
    Quisoruco presented their complaints provides a telling illustration of this aspect:
    "Expediente Sobre que las Arrobas de Coca Extraídas de Viscatán por los Rebeldes
    que Ocuparon aquellos Países pertenecen al Estado, año de 1828." ADAY, 1828, JPI,
    Crim., Diezmos, leg. 55, cuad. 6, f. 18.

25 Ibid.

26 Ibid.

27 Platt, *Estado Boliviano*.

28 This interpretation is in Husson, "Guerre Indienne," 135.

29 This contrast is posited by Nelson Manrique. See *Yawar Mayu* and, above all,
    Mercado Interno y Región: Sierra Central, 1820–1930 (Lima: Desco, 1987), 18–19.

30 ADAY, JPI, Crim., leg. 30, cuad. 582, "Cuaderno de los Papeles que tratan sobre
    comiciones resividas por Manuel Leandro de los Gefes de los Rebeldes de Yqui-
    cha," 1828.

31 Ibid., f. 11r. (emphasis added).

32 Ibid., f. 1r.

33 Ibid.

34 Ibid. (at the margin).

35 García Calderón, *Diccionario*, vol. 2, entries for *intendente*, *prefecto*, and *subdelegado*.

36 The original reads, "terreno de monte en donde tienen emprendidos plantada de
    coca. . . . Y como estos sequierian [*sic*] quitarle de tal tereyno [*sic*] el uno quería mas
    como el otro." ADAY, JPI, Crim., leg. 30, cuad. 582, f. 5. The source of this section's
    epigraph is f. 10v.

37 "Thus to don Gregorio Chinga corresponds [the land] from his house on down[;]
    no one has the right to intrude, and both sides of his land belong to another
    owner." Ibid.

38 Ibid., f. 6.

39 Ibid. (emphasis added).

40 Ibid., f. 12r / v.

41 Ibid., f. 8rv.

42 Ibid.

43 Ibid.

44 This cannot fail to draw our attention, since Leandro had yet to be appointed
    governor.

45 ADAY, JPI, Crim., leg. 30, cuad. 582, f. 9.

46 Ibid., f. 10r / v.

47 Ibid., f. 10v.

48 Ibid.

49 Ibid.

50 In juridical terminology, the expression *a costa delincuentes* (that I have translated as

"at the delinquents' expense") means that the expense of transporting a defendant to the courts was the responsibility of the defendant himself or herself. I thank Armando Guevara for this clarification.

51 "Huachaca [signature and mark] By gen. Ezcurra, De Barv [illegible . . .] ensa General Secretary." ADAY, JPI, Crim., leg. 30, cuad. 582, f. 10v. (emphasis added).

52 Signed by Military Political Judge and Colonel of the Royal Army José Perez del Valle. Huachaca signed in the margin of the document. Ibid., f. 8r.

53 ADAY, JPI, Crim., leg. 29, f. 46v, 47r. (emphasis added). Other accounts of these events appear in the same file: ff. 23r, 27rv, 29r, 35rv, 40r, 53v, 54r.

54 Irene Silverblatt, *Moon, Sun, and Witches: Gender Ideologies and Class in Inca and Colonial Peru* (Princeton: Princeton University Press, 1987).

55 ADAY, JPI, Crim., leg. 27, cuad. 521, f. 37r.

56 Ibid., cuad. 521.

57 However, the circumstances of this episode hint that the woman's "betrayal" may not have been altogether voluntary. In relating the facts, Quintanilla referred to "an indian woman who according to testimony confesses. . . ." ADAY, JPI, Prefecturas, leg. 64, ff. 8v., 9r.

58 Dunbar, ed., *La Acción Patriótica*, CDIP, tomo V, 1975, 6:231.

59 Ibid., 133.

60 Women guerrillas like María Parado de Bellido, glorified in Peruvian historiography for having been executed by a Spanish firing squad, made up the armies of Morochucos, renowned for their commitment to the cause of Independence.

61 On the *rabonas*, see "Apéndice Documental," in *Juan Mauricio Rugendas: El Perú Romántico del siglo XIX*, ed. Carlos Milla Batres, 260 (Lima: Milla Batres, 1975), and Jorge Basadre, *La Iniciación de la República*, vol. 1 (Lima: Editorial F. & E. Rosay, 1929), 99–100. See also our discussion in chapter 7.

62 ADAY, JPI, leg. 30, cuad. 582, f. 16r.

63 The first of these orders was actually addressed by Huachaca and Arancibia to Manuel Ynga, who was evidently Leandro's successor in the position. It was dated at the Choimacota headquarters May 18, 1827, and it commanded him to make available "all the assistance at your disposal, food for both the troops and staff officers and pack animals, because sixteen of them are needed, soon" as well as "some arrobas of coca to aid each and every one of our men." It also included a warning against "harming the *traginantes*" (ADAY, 1827, JPI, leg. 30, cuad. 582, f. 17r / v). See n.1 above. A second letter came from Pucará and ordered Leandro to gather the people from the haciendas in that spot, "[by tomorrow at two in the afternoon] each hacienda with its overseers [,] and for [that] they shall take all the spears in the possession of don José Franco since by this means it will be apparent that they are loyal to the King . . . with the penalty of execution for whoever withdraws." ADAY, 1827, JPI, Crim., leg. 30, cuad. 582, f. 18r.

64 ADAY, JPI, leg. 30, cuad. 582, f. 10v.

65 Letter from José Caceda to the Intendant of Cañete, Huangazca, November 28, 1824. Dunbar, ed., *La Acción Patriótica*, CDIP, tomo V, 6:109.

66 Juan de Dios Castilla, Chungui, December 16, 1824. Dunbar, ed., *La Acción Patriótica*, CDIP, tomo V, 6:135.

67 Letter from Manuel Santiago de los Ríos, Intendant Governor of the Province of Castrovirreyna, to the Prefect of the Department, Huancavelica, January 3, 1825. Ibid., 587.

68 AGI, Lima, 1103, doc. 462, Lima, April 20, 1785.

69 Fisher, *Government and Society*, 39.

70 Francisco López Sánchez was the bishop at the time. Cited in Vargas Ugarte, *Impresos Peruanos*, 2:317.

71 As one of the symptoms of neglect he pointed to the fact that the church in the town of Huanta had been under construction for more than thirty years and was still not finished at the time of his last visit (490). He also noted the scant results of the Church's work on the selva's borderland: "Since the conversions on Guanta's borders began many years ago until today [approximately 1804] hardly the slightest number of infidels have been instructed in the Christian doctrine, this being the most telling proof of the nil effect that has been obtained." O'Higgins, "Visita," in "Appendix" to Jorge Juan and Antonio Ulloa, *Noticias Secretas*, 518–19.

72 O'Higgins's authority was flouted not only by his subordinates; even the Crown itself remained unresponsive to his lawsuits, when not in fact favoring the defendants. This was quite ironic, given that O'Higgins represented, in theory, the interests of the Crown, but there is ample documentation proving that this was the case, and John Fisher also demonstrates it. See Fisher, *Government and Society*.

73 The first quotation from Hidalgo is taken from an official letter to the subdelegate, the second from a letter to the intendant of Huamanga. AGN, Superior Gobierno, 1819, leg. 1313, cuad. 1212, "Expediente promovido . . . por . . . los vecinos de Huanta."

74 AGN, Superior Gobierno, 1819, leg. 37, cuad. 1313, f. 12r.

75 Ibid., f. 12v.

76 From Gregorio Hidalgo to the intendant of Huamanga, ibid., f. 10r.

77 Ibid.

78 In his charges against Melchor Porras, Gregorio Hidalgo proposed that Toribio Benegas, "a vecino español and hacendado," be named mayor of Viscatán, given that he had been elected "unanimously by [vote of] all of the hacendado vecinos and adult men" of the Viscatán gorge. Ibid.

79 ADAY, JPI, leg. 29, cuad. 564, f. 60r, testimony of Juan Ramos. Cabrera, however, would not succeed in holding the intendant's position for long.

80 ADAY, JPI, Crim., leg. 27, cuad. 521, f. 7. From Antonio Navala Huachaca and Pablo Guamán to Prefect Juan Pardo de Zela, Ayacucho, March 11, 1826 (emphasis added).

81   ADAY, Intendencia, Asuntos Administrativos, leg. 41, cuad. 7, 1802; AGN Tributos-Informes, leg. 2, cuad. 47, 1809; and ADAY, Intendencia, Asuntos Administrativos, leg. 42, cuad. 55.

82   I shall elaborate on this point below. For introductory information, see Fisher, *Government and Society*, 79–80; García Calderón, *Diccionario*, vol. 2, entries for *intendente* and *subdelegado*; and Gisela Morazzini de Pérez Enciso, *Las Ordenanzas de Intendentes de Indias* (Caracas: Universidad Central de Venezuela, 1972), 134, 136–38, 144–45.

83   Mark Thurner, *"Republicanos,"* 295–97.

84   However, not all of the hacendados had arrived in Huanta that recently. Some, like the Spaniard Miguel Fariña, had successfully established themselves in the region at least as early as 1809 (AGN, Tributos, Informes, leg. 2, cuad. 47, 1809, f. 2). It is quite possible that Fariña, whose conduct was hardly beyond reproach (he had been the accomplice of a previous subdelegate accused of extorting indians in the payment of their tributes and the illegal usufruct of their labor), joined with the 1819 plaintiffs owing to a similar antipathy toward the Lazóns.

85   Nevertheless, it is important to clarify that not all hacendados who signed the 1819 petition in Huanta joined the monarchist rebellion. One of them, José Jorge Aguilar y Vílchez (who is mentioned, along with Lazón, in the letter by Huachaca cited above), was an open opponent of Huachaca in the 1820s and throughout the rebellion, which leads one to believe he had made some sort of deal with Lazón. The case of Melchor Porras was exactly the opposite. Porras, who was Lazón's loyal mayor in 1819, would subsequently go over to the rebels' side (in December 1826, Choque gave Garay instructions to make Porras "Magistrate of that gorge," ADAY, 1826, JPI, Crim., leg. 31, cuad. 585, f. 12r / v), and soon thereafter he would serve as their tithe collector (Autos Seguidos por T. López Gerí, cited in Pérez Aguirre, "Rebeldes Iquichanos," 115). This means the power struggles between Lazón and the hacendados demanding "mayors of Spaniards" in 1819 expressed contrary tendencies, though not always irreconcilable ones.

86   For Soregui's commission, see ADAY, JPI, Crim., leg. 30, cuad. 579, f. 36, which is extracted in chapter 2.

87   José Antonio de la Barreda testified that "[he] also saw Guijas in Seque and found out that he was Choque's secretary." ADAY, JPI, Crim., leg. 31, cuad. 582, f. 24r.

88   "To answer the correspondence that he had with . . . Mr. Prefect General, the deponent [Qqente] being one of the Commanders who served the rebels in Chacabamba." In his zeal to defend the Ruizes from the charges that had likewise been brought against him, Qqente declared, "The Ruizes had only served with the rebels in order to obey the orders that the deponent and *the others who were in command gave them*, and it was known that this obedience was given in order to avoid the harm that could be caused to their livestock that was nearby." AGN, JPI, Prefecturas, leg. 64, f. 49v (emphasis added).

89 Scarlett O'Phelan Godoy, *Un siglo de Rebeliones Anticoloniales* (Cuzco: CBC, 1988), 243–44.

90 All this was, in a way, to be expected, given that the power, prestige, and legitimacy of kurakas, particularly those belonging to the highest ranks, had begun to erode in Huamanga, as elsewhere, as early as the late seventeenth century. By then, writes Jaime Urrutia, in Huamanga "the ethnic groups functioned only as fragmentary units and with local representatives; the great chief ['el gran señor de la etnía'] hardly existed any longer and the route of access to the *kurakazgo* was increasingly dependent on the colonial authority." Urrutia, *Huamanga*. See also Spalding, *Huaro-chirí*; Sulca Báez, "Curas y Kurakas Ayacuchanos"; and the analysis in the final section of chapter 5.

91 Foucault, *The History of Sexuality*, 1:27

92 Ibid.

93 For some examples, see Spalding, *De Indio a Campesino*, 47, and Urrutia, *Huamanga*, 118.

94 Francisco García Calderón, *Diccionario*, vol. 2, entries for *intendente* and *subdelegado*.

95 "The first obligation, to which they must continuously dedicate themselves[,] is the administration of justice." AGI, Lima 1103, "Instrucción y capitulos, que deveran cumplir como se previene, mis subdelegados en los respectivos partidos sugetos a la Intendencia de esta capital de Lima" (hereafter "Instrucción, 1784"). See also Fisher, *Government and Society*, thanks to whose references I was led to these directions for subdelegates in the Archivo de Indias. The *Instrucción* that I am using as a reference here corresponds to that of the Intendancy of Lima, and I am proceeding on the premise that the general clauses are valid for the other intendancies as well. Still, I am aware that the discovery of the specific "Directions for Subdelegates" of Huamanga might modify my conclusions.

96 The hacendado plaintiffs of 1819 referred to Pedro José Lazón as a "subdelegate-judge."

97 AGI, Lima 1103, "Instrucción, 1784" (emphasis added). The subdelegates were supposed to rectify the vices of the *corregidores*, the officials they replaced, who were notorious for their extortion of indians through *repartimientos* (the compulsory selling of goods). For this reason, the 1784 Directions for Subdelegates stipulated, in the second clause, that "in the partidos under their rule they [the subdelegates] are prohibited from any kind of business, [or] trade, and may not do so, either with titles of repartimiento, or the financing of indians, and residents of their territory, even should they make use of intermediaries." AGI, Lima 1103, "Instrucción, 1784." However, there is abundant evidence to the effect that this was the clause most systematically violated by the subdelegates.

98 Ibid., clause 4 (emphasis added).

99 The historiography has repeatedly drawn attention to the traumatic effects of the

repression that followed Túpac Amaru's defeat, laying particular emphasis on its repercussions among the indigenous elites and Peru's broader social and political history. Our knowledge of the way in which the post–Túpac Amaru reforms, including the establishment of the intendancies, affected the political life of indian communities at the local level is, however, less extensive; but what we do know suggests that the 1784 directions for subdelegates, at least the clauses cited above, were indeed put into practice. Several studies confirm the growing intervention of Spanish and creole functionaries in the governance of indian towns in the period following the Túpac Amaru rebellion, in particular, Cahill and O'Phelan Godoy, "Forging," 125–67. This was true even in places not touched by the rebellion (see Sala i Vila, *Y Se Armó*, and Diez Hurtado, *Comunes y Haciendas*). For an opposing and, to my view, less persuasive interpretation, see Walker, *Smoldering Ashes*. Mark Thurner, in turn, suggests that the interference of local authorities ("whites," or mixed-blood *mistis*) in the indian communities did not crystallize in the province of Huaylas until the early years of the Republic ("*Republicanos*," esp. 296–97).

100 AGI, Lima 1103, "Instrucción, 1784," clause 7: "It shall be guarded in a chest with three keys, of which the Subdelegate shall have one, the Governor, or Indian Mayor another, and the oldest alderman the other."

101 "After the proclamation of our Independence, the name of governor was given to those who had previously been called subdelegates and the same powers were granted to them (Reg. Prov. 12 February, 1821). They were later called intendants; and finally they were given the name of Sub-prefects, which remains their name today, and the territory over which they ruled was called province instead of *partido*, which was the designation given by the laws of Spain" Francisco García Calderón, *Diccionario*, vol. 2, entry for *gobernadores* (italics added).

102 See Morazzini de Pérez Enciso, *Las Ordenanzas de Intendentes de Indias*, 137–38.

103 The position of subdelegate was, however, usually held by "native sons" of the region, that is, by Huantinos of Spanish descent, or creoles, who at the time fell under the category of españoles.

104 For example, "Royal Prefecture of Luis Pampa, 2 March 1827," ADAY, JPI, Crim., leg. 30, cuad. 582, f. 8r; and "Royal General Prefecture of Luis Pampa, 22 February, 1827," ibid., f. 10v.

105 ADAY, JPI, leg. 30, cuad. 582, f. 6.

106 AGI, Lima, 1103, "Instrucción, 1784," clauses 11–15. For the appointment of Leandro in 1827, see the citation earlier in this chapter and ADAY, JPI, leg. 30, cuad. 582, f. 11r.

107 "It being advisable to appoint a *Governor and Subdelegate*," Huachaca declared in appointing Leandro, "on my order and command . . . all those individuals [shall] consider him and view him as . . . *Subdelegate*." And then in another document: "The *mayor* of the Acón gorge with sufficient mandate, *Don* Manuel Leandro,

shall with justice attend to the petitioner. Prefecture of Luis Pampa, 26 March, 1827"; the document is signed by Huachaca. ADAY, 1827, JPI, leg. 30, cuad. 582, f. 6 (emphasis added).

108 ADAY, JPI, Crim., leg. 30, cuad. 582 (emphasis added). Núria Sala cites an interesting case from 1803 in which a cacique in Puno is entrusted by the colonial administration with duties similar to those Huachaca conferred upon Leandro: "that he [Mariano Hinojosa y Cutimbo], for being cacique *propietario*, shall rule not just over tributary Yndians, but also the Spanish *vecinos* and the *castas*" (cited in Sala i Vila, *Y Se Armó*, 92). Sala admits this was a rare case, yet the very fact that it existed suggests that the juridical criteria and bureaucratic rationale of the Uchuraccay government may have had some antecedents in either legally established or de facto forms of local and regional government at work during the final stages of colonial rule. These are yet to be revealed by historians. At any rate, the influence of the Consitution of 1812, which abolished ethnically separated town councils (cabildos) should be considered. The range of powers attained by Huachaca, on the other hand, and particularly their legal (and regal) justification, bear some resemblance to those of the *alcalde mayor indígena*, the only type of kuraka endowed by the Spanish administration with the power to exercise justice in the name of the king—their jurisdiction covering criminal and civilian matters. The alcaldes mayores were usually entrusted with several provinces, and the range of their powers surpassed that of the provincial kurakas and the village alcaldes, both of whom were subordinate to them. Still, unlike the judges at Uchuraccay, the alcaldes mayores' jurisdiction was limited to the "republics of indians." Just as happened with other types of kurakas, the position of alcalde mayor indígena began to lose prestige by the mid-eighteenth century; after the Túpac Amaru rebellion it was granted even to individuals identified as españoles, as happened with the position of cacique more generally (as pointed out in chapter 5). See Waldemar Espinoza Soriano, "El Alcalde Mayor Indígena en el Vierreinato del Perú," *Anuario de Estudios Americanos* 17 (1960): 183–300.

109 The subdelegate was replaced by the subprefect through the Provisional Regulation of 1821. García Calderón, *Diccionario*, vol. 2, entry for *subprefecto*. The real change, however, would take some time. Apparently, many subdelegates (at least in Huanta) remained in their posts, while subprefects were appointed for the same jurisdictions. In the case of the monarchist rebels, the matter is quite complex: they continued to appoint subdelegates, but not subprefects. Even so, it was not unusual for them to call the Uchuraccay headquarters the Prefecture of Luis Pampa, as we have noticed.

110 It seems that at certain times the word *alcalde* (mayor) was simply used in lieu of "leader" or "chief" ("headmen" [*mandón*] in the terminology of the era). For example, when Tadeo Choque appeared at a trial, he was introduced as "mayor

of the Carhuahurán punas," the term *punas* suggesting a geographical region (which, in this case, was also referred to as Iquicha) and not precisely a formally delimited territory or political jurisdiction. Choque, therefore, could not have been a mayor of indians, because they were necessarily village authorities. Being an indígena (the authorities referred to him thus) and his jurisdiction not being limited to a district or province or specific town, he could not have been a mayor of Spaniards either.

111 Among the several individuals who worked as subdelegates for the Uchuraccay government, another whose status was also presumably indígena stands out: Manuel Ynga, who eluded capture and, years after the defeat of the rebellion, was accused of being one of the "generals" who escorted Huachaca.

112 The supervision of indians by "Spanish" functionaries was another point reiterated in the 1784 Directions of Subdelegates, especially in clauses 3, 4, 5.

113 One cannot apply here the schema that seems to be valid for Ancash, according to the analysis furnished by Thurner, in which the peasants of Huaylas communities appear to recreate, throughout the nineteenth century, the colonial concept of republic. Thurner, " 'Republicanos.' "

114 Especially Eric Van Young, "Quetzalcóatl, King Fernando and Ignacio Allende Go to the Seashore; or Messianism and Mystical Kingship in Mexico 1800–1820," in *The Independence of Mexico and the Creation of the New Nation*, ed. Jaime Rodríguez O., 109–27 (Los Angeles: UCLA Latin American Center Publications, and Irvine: Mexico / Chicano Program, University of California, Irvine, 1989); and "The Raw and the Cooked: Elite and Popular Ideology in Mexico, 1800–1821," in *The Middle Period in Latin American History: Values and Attitudes in the 17th–19th Centuries*, ed. Mark D. Szchuman, 75–102 (Boulder: Lynn Reinner, 1989). For a reading of "naive monarchism" much more in agreement with the views I suggest, see Field, *Rebels*.

115 Jan Szeminski, "Why Kill the Spaniard? New Perspectives on Andean Insurrectionary Ideology in the 18th Century," in *Resistance, Rebellion, and Consciousness in the Andean Peasant World, 18th to 20th Centuries*, ed. Steve Stern, 166–92 (Madison: University of Wisconsin Press, 1987).

CHAPTER 7. The Plebeian Republic

1 ADAY, JPI, Crim., leg. 30, cuad. 569, "Cuaderno Primero del Juicio a Leandro," f. 15v, 34r.

2 On Cantón and the sources I rely on, see chapter 5, last section.

3 AGN, R-J, Prefecturas, Ayacucho, leg. 94. From Prefect J. A. Gonzales to Subprefect of Huanta J. G. Quintanilla, April 15, 1830, unnumbered folio.

4 Ibid.

5 For details on this mutiny, see chapter 2, last section, and Basadre, *La Iniciación*, 1:247–49.

6 Basadre, *Historia* (1983 ed.), 1:278–79.

7 The National Convention was an entity created to draft a new constitution, but it was endowed by Gamarra himself with the power to name a provisional president until popular elections could be held.

8 On the first generation of conservatives and liberals, see Basadre, *Perú: Problema y Posibilidad*.

9 Basadre, *Historia* (1983 ed.), 1:276.

10 Ibid., 2:7.

11 Ibid. See also Basadre, *La Multitud, la Ciudad y El Campo en la Historia del Peru* (Lima: Mosca Azul, 1980 [1929]), 176–78, 196–97.

12 Basadre, *La Iniciación*, 1:308–14; Basadre, *Historia* (1983 ed.), 2:1–9.

13 Basadre, *Historia* (1983 ed.), 2:1–9.

14 On Huaylacucho, see Álvarez, *Guía*, 58–59. On Tristán's letter, see chapter 2 and CEHM-AHMP, leg. 26, doc. 16, 1834. See also AGN, PL 15–437, 1835, cuad. 2, ff.12rv, 16r.

15 AGN. PL 15–437, 1835, f. 12r / v. The letter was dated "Guancayo General Headquarters, April 20, 1834" (emphasis added).

16 Ibid., f. 7v.

17 Ibid., f. 16r (emphasis added).

18 Ibid., f. 7r / v. Letter signed in "Luna Huana [i.e., Lunahuaná] March 4, 1834." Note the contrast between the words Tristán used with Huachaca now and those he had resorted to a few years before, when as prefect of Ayacucho he was trying to persuade the ex-officer of French-Basque origin, Nicolás Soregui, who was fighting on the side of the rebels, to lay down his arms. "Born . . . in the most enlightened country in the world," wrote Tristán to Soregui, "you should not mix with that mob of sheep . . . that mob of drunks, thieves, and beasts who have only the shape of men: be ashamed of company so unworthy of a well-bred Frenchman, accept my fatherly invitation before I begin to punish inexorably those rabid, impotent beasts who plan to devour their very Mother [i.e., the Patria]." ADAY, JPI, Crim., leg. 30, cuad. 573, ff. 39v, 40r. Using similar arguments Tristán had sought to dissuade father Manuel Navarro, also accused of complicity with the Iquichanos: "[Here] no one is free . . . from a barbarous people." ADAY, JPI, Crim., leg. 30, cuad. 579, "Papeles pertenecientes al Cura Navarro," f. 18.

19 AGN, PL 15–437, 1835, f. 17r. The secretary endorsing this act, which was a copy of its original, was José Girón, a man who was involved in the monarchist convulsions as a secretary of Huachaca and was pardoned after having surrendered following the failed assault on Ayacucho. Girón was fifty years old at the time of the uprising and his son Ygancio Girón worked for a while as tithe collector for the rebels. ADAY,

JPI, Crim. (Cuaderno Cuarto del juicio a Soregui), ff. 31, 40r; ADAY, JPI, Crim., leg. 30, cuad. 566 (Cuaderno Segundo del Juicio a Leandro), ff. 6r, 40v.

20 AGN, PL 15–437, f. 19r.

21 Ibid., f. 19r.

22 There were two exceptions: the secretary endorsing this act, Rafael de Castro, who had been a tithe collector during the monarchist rebellion; and Governor Pedro Cárdenas, who had worked with the rebels as the administrator of the Uchuraccay hacienda (unless our records are identifying a homonym, which is plausible since one Pedro Cárdenas was reported dead during the government's final assault on Uchuraccay in 1827).

23 BN, D47, 1828; ADAY, JPI, Crim., leg. 30, cuad. 581, f. 15r / v.

24 AGN, PL 15–437, 1835, "Cuaderno Primero del Documentos y Cuentas que Presenta Don Juan Urbina," and "Don Juan Urbina. Segundo Cuaderno sobre los Gastos de las Guerrillas de Huanta."

25 CEHMP-AHM, 1834, leg. 3, doc. 16, From Domingo Tristán to the Minister of War, Lima, April 3, 1834.

26 CEHMP-AHM, leg. 26, doc. 32, 1834 (emphasis added).

27 Blanco, Diario, 44.

28 Ibid., 47.

29 Ibid., 46.

30 This happened in October 1834. See AGN, Tributos, Informes, leg. 3, cuad. 62, 1840.

31 Walker, "Montoneros, bandoleros, malhechores"; Méndez G., "Incas Sí, Indios No."

32 Basadre speaks of "feudal despotism" in connection with Gamarrista rule in Ayacucho, La Iniciación, 1:236

33 ADAY, JPI, Crim., leg. 34, "Criminales Contra los Alcaldes y Demás municipales de Huanta sobre [el] desacato con que trataron al primer Gefe de la Republica sin haber salido á recibirle en su ingreso á aquel pueblo ni aun presentandolese siquiera en la puerta de su alojamiento,"1834.

34 See chapter 2.

35 CEHMP-AHM, leg. 27, doc. 17, 1834.

36 AGN, OL. 232–391, Prefecturas, Ayacucho.

37 AGN, PL 14–460, 1834. Cabrera's letter is dated June 14, 1834.

38 AGN, OL 240–265, Prefecturas, Ayacucho.

39 AGN, OL 247–42, November 28, 1835.

40 ADAY, JPI, Diezmos, leg. 56, cuad. 7, f. 15 r / v (emphasis added).

41 Ibid., f. 15v (emphasis added).

42 Cited in Pérez Aguirre, "Rebeldes Iquichanos," 140 (emphasis added).

43 The original reads, "Don José Antonio Huachaca, Brigadier y General en Jefe de los Reales Exercitos de Voluntarios defensores de la ley del Campo de Yquicha" (ADAY,

JPI, Crim., leg. 30, cuad. 582, f. 13r). Another version was "José Antonio Abad Guachaca, Brigadier y Comandante General de los Reales Ejercitos de la División de Reserva Defensoras [*sic*] de la ley" (ADAY, JPI, Crim., leg. 30, cuad. 582, f. 11r).

44   "El Ciudadano J. Antonio Nav. Huachaca, General en Jefe de la Division Ristaurador de la Ley de los Balientes y Bravos Equichanos defensores de la justa causa." Quoted in del Pino, *Las Sublevaciones*, 29.

45   Basadre, *Historia* (1983 ed.), 11:43.

46   Ibid., 37.

47   See Méndez G., "Incas Sí, Indios No."

48   Basadre, *La Iniciación*, 2:116.

49   President José de La Mar, who ruled Peru in the late 1820s, was born in Cuenca, in present-day Ecuador, then a part of Gran Colombia; Guillermo Miller was British; Mariano Necochea and San Martín were from the former viceroyalty of Río de La Plata, today Argentina; Bolivar was from Venezuela. On the other hand, as Charles Walker points out in *Smoldering Ashes*, many of Gamarra's political aides were Spanish capitulados. This was also the case of the Orbegosista Blas Cerdeña.

50   The opposition to Santa Cruz in Peru was far from monolithic. Gamarra's Cuzco and the Lima of Felipe Pardo y Aliaga, which opposed the Confederation with equal vigor, had less in common than Cuzco and La Paz did. Socially, "ethnically," and even politically (given his ambition of integrating Peru and Bolivia), Santa Cruz had more in common with Gamarra, himself a mestizo, than with creole aristocrats like Salaverry and Pardo. Yet if I choose to emphasize the Lima creole opposition to Santa Cruz it is because it has been the dominant interpretation in the historiography and the "official" version in Peruvian museums and high school textbooks.

51   Bolívar's contempt for indians has been analyzed in Henri Favre, "Bolívar y los Indios," *Histórica* 10, no. 1 (1986): 1–18, and in Méndez, "República sin Indios."

52   Basadre, *Historia*, 2:37.

53   From Juan Espinosa to Juan Mauricio Rugendas, Arequipa, July 1, 1838, cited in Rugendas, *El Perú Romántico*, 260. More evidence on Santa Cruz's army is found above, in the epigraph at the opening of the section on the Peruvian-Bolivian Confederation.

54   Cavero, *Monografía*, vol. 1.

55   AGN, 1831, PL 11–32,. ff. 15r / v.–16r, correspondence between the *apoderado fiscal* of Huanta, Cayetano Palomino, and Subprefect and Military Commander José Gabriel Quintanilla (August 26, 1831) and from Quintanilla to the Prefect of the Department (September 5, 1831).

56   Private archive of the Santa Cruz family in La Paz. Letter from Santa Cruz to General Trinidad Morán, Lampa, September 22, 1835.

57   Ibid. Letter from Santa Cruz to Trinidad Morán, Arequipa, October 1, 1835.

58 ADAY, 1840, JPI, Crim., leg. 57, cuad. 12, f. 1, "Reclamo dirigido por Cesilio Escobar y Domingo Cáseres, vecinos del pueblo de Huamanguilla, al Juez de Primera Instancia."

59 ADAY, 1840, JPI, Diezmos, leg. 57, cuad. 12, f. 3, Ayacucho, November 18, 1840.

60 Cavero, *Monografía*, 1:217.

61 Ibid., 219–20; Vargas, *Historia*, 9:155–56.

62 Cavero, *Monografía*, 1:219–20; Vargas, *Historia*, 9:156. In describing the events recounted above, historian Nemesio Vargas refers to Choque as "Captain Choque." Though I have found no proof that he was ever conferred this title, the hypothesis is not unlikely, particularly given Choque's antecedents. Not only was Choque in the habit of switching sides with great ease; he also explicitly served Gamarrista authorities. Indeed, the bureaucratic records of Gamarra's first term show Choque acting as governor in Ccarhauhurán, doing his best to serve the Gamarra-appointed politico-military authorities in the province as of 1831, though only a few years later he was to join the guerrillas that fought Gamarra in Ayacucho (ADAY, 1831, JPI, Crim., leg. 34, ff. 12–17).

63 Vargas, *Historia*, 9:156; García Calderón, *Diccionario*, entry for *Yanallay*.

64 From Fernando Lopera to the Colonel Acting Prefect of Ayacucho, Secce, November 15, 1839, cited in Cavero, *Monografía*, 1:220.

65 Ibid., 224.

66 Ibid. (emphasis added).

67 On how violence produces, rather than reflects, social relations, see Brooks, *Captives and Cousins* (Chapel Hill: University of North Carolina Press, 2002).

68 The reader may recall how the government boasted of having decapitated the rebel caudillo Jose del Valle at the time of the monarchist uprising (see chapter 2). On the Independence wars, see Echenique, *Memorias*.

69 An example is found in De la Fuente, *Childern of Facundo*.

70 See, for example, *La Aurora Peruana*, Cuzco, October 31, 1835; *La Estrella Federal*, Cuzco, December 21, 1836 (BN, D10206).

71 From Juan Espinosa to Juan Mauricio Rugendas, Arequipa, July 1, 1838, in Milla Batres, ed., *El Perú Romántico del Siglo XIX*, 259–60.

72 *El Debate*, Ayacucho, November 6, 1896, cited in Juan José del Pino, *Las Sublevaciones*, 29.

73 ADAY, JPI, Crim., leg. 44, cuad. 874, 1838, unnumbered folio.

74 That Santa Cruz's recognition of Huachaca's authority was more than symbolic is attested by several testimonies. One that stands out is a denunciation made by Tadeo Choque, Huachaca's lifelong rival, in 1838. Choque sued Huachaca, accusing him of usurping the position of justice of the peace after his term had expired, in addition to committing other abuses against the populations of the area, including abigeato. But his suit was to no avail. The attorney refrained from opening

process, adducing that the government condoned and even legitimated Huachaca's powers. See the opening epigraph of this book (ADAY, leg. 44, cuad. 874, "Proceso criminal que se sigue de oficio contra el Juez de Paz del Distrito de Carhuahurán don Antonio Abad Huachaca por los excesos y Abusos que comete con los pobladores," 1838, unnumbered folio).

75 AGN, PL 6–176, 1826.

76 Ibid., f. 80r.

77 AGN, 1831, PL 11–96, f. 4r / v (emphasis added).

78 Ibid., f. 5r (emphasis added).

79 Ibid.

80 "This ministry does not find, among the services rendered by this district for the pacification of Iquicha, anything beyond the natural obligation which every citizen bears to defend the Patria in critical junctures and times of distress; for in defending it one is defending oneself and one's own interests." Ibid., f. 8r.

81 ADAY, PL 11–82, 1831, f. 2r.

82 ADAY, JPI, Crim., leg. 30, cuad. 596, 1827, f. 37v, From Francisco Javier Mariátegui, Minister of Government, to the Prefect of Ayacucho, November 27, 1827 (emphasis added).

83 Ibid., f. 35r, From Tristán to Manuel Navarro, Huanta, December 26, 1827.

84 Unpublished transcripts of the recordings corresponding to Vargas Llosa's interrogation of the peasants of Uchuraccay in 1983. Russian peasants similarly claimed devotion to the tzar and conveyed naiveté before the authorities while trying to obtain further benefits from the laws regarding the abolition of servitude in mid-nineteenth-century Russia. See Field, *Rebels*.

85 AGN, PL 27–51, 1847, f. 10r.

86 Ibid. (emphasis added).

87 Ibid., From the governor of Tambo, Anselmo Cordero to the subprefect of Huanta, Tambo, August 16, 1841, f. 8 (emphasis added).

88 Ibid., From the governor of the district of Tambo to the subprefect of Huanta Tambo, April 12, 1841, f. 12r.

89 Mannheim, *The Language of the Inka*, chap. 2.

90 AGN, 1847, PL, 27–51, Declarations of José Manuel Cárdenas, agricultural worker [*labrador*] from Vicos, Tambo, May 12, 1843, f. 24v.

91 The expression "present their offerings in Huamanguilla" ("llevando sus obsequios") may simply be alluding to the rituals that usually accompanied (and still accompany) agricultural life in the Andes, but it could be more audaciously interpreted as referring to practices that were meant to delimit territorial boundaries. Insofar as Andean community patterns of settlement followed a noncontiguous territorial logic, it is understandable that boundaries need be constantly "reenacted." As Deborah Poole put it, "[In the Andes] territory is an actively constructed

concept, whose boundaries must be constantly recreated through daily exchanges of offerings and formalized salutation between neighbors." Poole, "Landscapes of Power," 384.

92   AGN, 1847, PL, 27–51, Declarations of José Manuel Cárdenas, Tambo, May 12, 1843, f. 24v.

93   Paz Soldán, *Diccionario*, xv. In the early twentieth century, geographers' categorizations of places were less sensible to nuances and endowed with markedly fixed hierarchies in which the variable "race" intervened (i.e., "lesser" places were defined as "dwellings of Indians"); see, for example, Germán Stiglich, *Diccionario Geográfico del Perú* (Lima, 1922), v.

94   Although I have not been able to determine when the church of the current town of Iquicha was built, it stands in stark contrast to those of the neighboring villages, both in style and size. It is much taller than the churches of Huaychao and Uchuraccay, which until not long ago formed part of haciendas, appearing rather disproportionate to the small population (perhaps a sign of Iquicha's major importance in another era). The construction is made of stone, using techniques that resemble those of the Wari epoch (sixth through eleventh century of our era) but which could well have been employed a mere few decades ago (see figure on p. 230). It differs, too, from the church of Secce, which can be easily identified as Spanish (see figure on p. 133). This description applies to the remains of the church, as the greater part of it has been burned (as has that at Uchuraccay), a consequence of the recent war. I am thankful to José Coronel, who provided me with photographs of both the Uchuraccay and Iquicha churches as they were in 1994, which I was later able to see in person. Archaeological work in this area could shed invaluable light to complement my findings (and nonfindings).

95   Andean noncontiguous patterns of territoriality have been widely acknowledged in the historical and anthropological literature, particularly following John Murra's seminal studies of the 1960s and 1970s. Although the persistence of noncontiguous patterns of settlement is apparent in many regions of the Andes throughout the centuries, few investigators have traced their evolution with reference to the expansion of the state during the republican period. On how pre-Hispanic notions of territoriality and community were recreated within the framework of Spanish institutions, see Spalding, *Huarochirí*; Abercrombie, *Pathways*; Carlos Sempat Assadourian, *Transiciones Hacia el Sistema Colonial Andino* (Lima: IEP, 1994); and Luis Miguel Glave, "Sociedad, Poder y Organización Andinas, El Sur peruano Hacia el Siglo XVII," in *Comunidades Campesinas*, ed. Flores Galindo, 61–94. The notion of community as molded by the community's interaction with the state is discussed in Poole, "Qorilazos, abigeos y comunidades," and in Diez Hurtado, *Comunes y Haciendas*.

96   CEHMP-AHM. leg. 8, doc. 27, 1848, from the Prefect of Ayacucho to the Ministry of Government, August 5, 1848.

97   *Guía Política, Eclesiástica y Militar del Perú de 1849,* cited in Cavero, *Monografía,* 1:70.

98   *El Comercio,* July 12, 1853. The census shows the following information: "Born: 89 men, 101 women. Married: 30. Dead: 60 men, and 87 women."

99   Paz Soldán, *Diccionario,* 465. Luis E. Cavero states that the district of Iquicha was created by the law of January 2, 1857, and subsisted in this capacity in the political demarcations of 1867 (Cavero, *Monografía,* 1:178).The first map on which I have located a place called Iquicha appears in Mariano Felipe Paz Soldán, *Atlas Geográfico del Perú* (Paris, 1865).

100 This unique repository is kept in the notary of Leoncio Cárdenas in Huanta and remains unclassified.

101 Uchuraccay is said to belong to the "district of Cercado" in the "Querella por Robo de ganado en campo a Abierto," Huanta, 1915. Notaría Cárdenas, Huanta, unclassified. In 1922, Germán Stiglich lists Iquiche [*sic*] as a settlement ("*Pobl.*") in the province of Huanta with 422 inhabitants, but mentions no district with that name. Stiglich, *Diccionario Geográfico,* 563.

102 ADAY, JPI, Crim., leg. 44, cuad. 874, 1838.

103 Blanchard, *Markham in Peru,* 70.

104 Antonio Raimondi, *Mapa del Perú* (1888 ed.), 21, 25, 26. I thank Nicanor Domínguez for providing me with a copy of this map.

105 The so-called Morochucos are among the fairest-skinned inhabitants of Ayacucho, and culturally they have been perhaps the most hispanicized and mestizo. There are reasons to doubt that they would have agreed to be portrayed as "indians."

106 The celebrated Ayacuchan physician and geographer Luis Carranza wrote in 1883, "All of this region was originally inhabited by the Pokras and Huamanes, tribes of the Chanka race; and *perhaps* the Iquichano Indians, who form a special community between Huanta and La Mar, are today's representatives of the ancient Pokras." Luis Carranza, *La Ciencia en El Perú en el silgo XIX* (Lima: Editorial Edili, 1988), 1:267 (emphasis added). A diligent scholar, Carranza was careful enough to write "perhaps," but writers who followed were not nearly as cautious. The idea of the Iquichanos as both archaic and barbarous took more elaborate expression in the twentieth century, particularly in the dissertation of the Ayacuchan *indigenista* writer Victor Navarro del Águila, *Las Tribus de AnkuWallokc* (Tesis, Universidad del Cusco, 1939). More recently, Jaime Urrutia has disputed the existence of an ethnic group called Pokras; see Jaime Urrutia Ceruti, "Los Pokras o el mito de los Huamanguinos," *Revista del Archivo Departamental de Ayacucho,* no. 13 (1984). For further discussion of these issues, see Méndez-Gastelumendi, "The Power of Naming."

107 Particularly, see Vargas Llosa et al., *Informe,* whose text, along with the anthropological appendixes by Ossio and Fuenzalida, reproduce (perhaps unknowingly)
the conceptualizations of the Iquichanos as rude, archaic, and violent created
by Navarro del Aguila in 1939. For further discussion on these issues, see Méndez-
Gastelumendi, "The Power of Naming." An interesting exception among early
twentieth-century scholars was Nemesio Vargas, who commended Huanta's peasants' bravery and military skills on practical (rather than "mythical") grounds.
Wrote Vargas, "Doubtless, the Huantinos and the Iquichanos are the bravest men
of Peru. Many old veterans who had fought with them have told me of portentous
feats bordering on temerity. I think that a full-regimentals battalion in the army,
called Ayacucho, should comprise them, to which only those with proved courage
should be admitted. They alone could defend Peru's autonomy against any foreign
nation," Nemesio Vargas, *Historia del Perú Independiente* (Lima: author's edition,
1942), 9:156. It must be clear, however, that Vargas's views on the Iquichanos did not
reflect his views of indians in general, which otherwise conformed to the classical
stereotype of the "backward race." See Nemesio Vargas, *Historia del Perú Independiente* (Lima: Imp. de la Escuela de Ingenieros por Juio Mesinas, 1903), vol. 1.

108 Méndez-Gastelumendi, "The Power of Naming"; Mayer, "Peru in Deep Trouble."

109 I am using the term *myth* here in the Barthian sense of "a form of speech." Roland
Barthes, *Mythologies*, trans. Annette Lavers (New York: Hill and Wang, 1972).

110 Resolution no. 019–91-GRLW / SRAS-DRT, of June 13, 1991. *Directorio de Comunidades
Campesinas* (Lima: Ministerio de Trabajo y Promoción Social, Instituto Nacional
de Desarrollo de Comunidades Campesinas [INDEC], December 1991), 195.

EPILOGUE

1 On Choque as governor of Luricocha, see ADAY, JPI, Crim., leg. 34, 1831 ff. 12–17;
as governor of Ccarhuahurán, AGN, PL, 16–407, 1836, f. 7r; and as "governor of all
the punas," Cavero, *Monografía*, 1:219, 220.

2 Unlike the justice of the peace, the governor had to report directly to the subprefect, the supreme political authority in a province. The position of justice of the
peace seemed to have allowed, in the long run, greater autonomy. The political
importance of justices of the peace in local power structures of the caudillista state
has been underscored by John Lynch for the case of Argentina. Lynch, *Caudillos.*

3 On defeatism in Peruvian historiography, see Magdalena Chocano, "Ucronía y
Frustración en la Conciencia Histórica Peruana," *Márgenes* 1, no. 2 (1987): 43–60.

4 Gootenberg, *Between Silver.*

5 Estenssoro, "Discurso, Música y Poder," 533.

6 Itier, "Quechua y Cultura"; Méndez G., "Incas Sí"; and Méndez, "Guerra, Nacionalismo."

7 Bolivia may be the best studied Andean country in this regard, but the emphasis is, as usual, on the second part of the nineteenth century. For a recent study, see Marta Irurozqui, "A Bala, Piedra y Palo," La Construcción de la Ciudadanía Política en Bolivia, 1826–1952 (Sevilla: Diputación de Sevilla, 2000). For a discussion of Peru, see my introduction. For a compelling comparative study on state formation and rural mobilization in Latin America, see López-Alves, State Formation. For Argentina, De la Fuente, Children, and Goldman and Salvatore, Caudillismos Rioplatenses. Mexico's literature on rural mobilization in the nineteenth century is too vast to be cited here, but for a useful overview, see John Tutino, From Insurrection to Revolution in Mexico: Social Bases of Agrarian Violence (Princeton: Princeton University Press, 1986), Mallon, Peasant and Nation, and Leticia Reina, La reindianización de América; for a recent approach more connected to our own discussion, see Guy P. C. Thomson with David G. LaFrance, Patriotism, Politics, and Popular Liberals in Nineteenth-Century Mexico (Wilmington: Scholarly Resources, 1999); for Central America, Aldo A. Lauria-Santiago, An Agrarian Republic (Pittsburgh: University of Pittsburgh Press, 1999), chap. 5.

8 Scholars tend to generalize an interpretative model that Tristan Platt furnished specifically for northern Potosí, and which he substantiates more persuasively for the later rather than the earlier part of the nineteenth century; see Platt, Estado Boliviano. See also chapter 5.

9 Particularly since the right to vote was restricted to a minority of property owners and professionals with a given income, and it excluded servants. For a different approach in the case of Bolivia, see Irurozqui, A Bala.

10 Peasants' "aloofness" from caudillo politics continues to be endorsed even by more recent studies concerned with the indigenous peasantry in the early republican period. For example, Charles Walker, citing the "irreconcilable" nature of "Indian society" and "caudillo" politics, writes, "Peruvian caudillos failed to create a mass fighting force from the majority of the region's population, Indians. The indigenous peasantry of the Southern Andes resisted fighting in the wars that decided the caudillo struggle." Moreover, "the indigenous peasantry remained largely detached from the caudillo struggles." Walker, Smoldering Ashes, 212–13. As already mentioned, Walker reaches these conclusions although his study deals only with one caudillo: Gamarra. Similarly, see Paul Gootenberg, "Population and Ethnicity in Early Republican Peru: Some Revisions," Latin American Research Review 26 (fall 1991): 145; and John Lynch, The Spanish American Revolutions.

11 For example, Eric Van Young, The Other Rebellion: Popular Violence, Ideology, and the Mexican Struggle for Independence, 1810–1821 (Stanford: Stanford University Press, 2001). See also our discussion at the end of chapter 6.

12 The word *gamonal* was coined in the 1860s. See Poole, "Landscapes of Power," 372.

13 See chapter 7.

14 ADAY, leg. 44, cuad. 874, 1838, from Tadeo Choque to the *Juez de Letras* Don Pedro Flores, January 18, 1838, unnumbered folio (emphasis added). Note that at this time having no property amounted to being a "nobody," for citizenship's formal requirements entailed property ownership; see Irurozqui, *A Bala.*

15 Ibid., unnumbered folio (emphasis added).

16 Deborah Poole, "Performance, Domination, and Identity in the *Tierras Bravas* of Chumbivilcas (Cusco)," in *Unruly Order*, Poole, ed., 103.

17 ADAY, leg. 44, cuad. 874, 1838, from Tadeo Choque to the *Juez de Letras* Don Pedro Flores, January 18, 1838, unnumbered folio. *Mitayo* lands, or *tierras de mita,* refers to state-owned lands which were usufructed by private individuals. I thank Carlos Contreras for this information.

18 Recent historiography on Bolivia, however, has reassessed the role of the Aymara rebel leader Julián Apasa, best known as Túpaj Katari, who commanded the siege of La Paz in 1781. Apasa, who was no kuraka and had no ties with the native nobility but was an effective and charismatic peasant leader, may provide a better parallel with Huachaca than Túpac Amaru and other kurakas who rebelled against Spanish rule. For a recent study, see Thomson, *We Alone Will Rule.*

19 Cavero, *Monografía,* 1:182.

20 Since the argument that criollos in the Independence and post-Independence periods were reluctant to mobilize indians for fear and distrust of them is not supported by historical evidence, one may surmise it has ideological roots. Such a hypothesis may well have derived from the widespread idea that postulates the "irreconcilability" between "Indian" and "criollo" worlds. These kinds of binary constructs, of course, are not exclusive to the Andes. They may be in turn rooted in the idea that ethnic difference in itself provides a source of antagonism and violence. Marisol de la Cadena has convincingly argued that ethnic difference does not, in itself, ignite mutual rejection, let alone violence, although it is commonly portrayed this way. De la Cadena, *Indigenous Mestizos* (see introduction in particular).

21 Charles Walker argues in *Smoldering Ashes* that the conservative Gamarra failed to attract peasant support in his native Cuzco. This may well have been the case; nonetheless, Gamarra skillfully used the chasm between Choque and Huachaca to negotiate the surrender of the Huanta peasantry in 1839 and, once that was achieved, rewarded the peasants monetarily in Lima. By 1840, Gamarra's government still expected Choque to turn Huachaca and his children in to the government (*El Peruano*, Lima, September 2, 1840, and AHMP-CEHM, leg. 20, doc. 376, 1840). This means that Gamarra's policies with the peasantry deserve a more detailed study. Nevertheless, it does seem true that liberals, and not only in Peru, were the champions in mobilizing the peasantry in the nineteenth century. See

Lauria-Santiago, *An Agrarian*, chapter 5; Thomson and LaFrance, *Patriotism*; Mallon, *Peasant and Nation* (sections on Mexico). In Argentina, the label "federal" may be more appropriate than "liberal"; see De la Fuente, *Children*. For a broad Latin American comparative approach, see López-Alves, *State Formation*.

22 Cited in Cecilia Méndez G., "Una Vez Más La Pena de Muerte," *Crónicas de la Historia del Derecho*, no. 1 (1994): 56; E. P. Thompson, *La Formación Histórica de la Clase Obrera* (Barcelona: Laia, 1977), 1:77.

23 E. P. Thompson, "The Patricians and the Plebs," in *Customs in Common: Studies in Traditional Popular Culture* (New York: The New Press, 1993), 86.

24 See Basadre, *La Iniciación*, 1:96–97.

25 Gootenberg, *Between Silver*, 153.

26 Gootenberg, *Tejidos y Harinas*, 98.

27 Gootenberg, *Between Silver*.

28 "Protectionism was a decidedly 'popular' cause, if any existed." Gootenberg, *Between Silver*, 76.

29 Ibid., 27.

30 The question of whether Huantans' antimilitaristic, anti-Gamarrista stance connected with their trade policy options, and if so, how, remains open to investigation.

31 Walker, *Smoldering Ashes*.

32 Max Weber, *Economy and Society* (Berkeley: University of California Press, 1978), 2:909.

33 The idea of the state as claim has also been suggested in Mary Roldán's introduction to *Blood and Fire: La Violencia in Antioquia, Colombia, 1946–1953* (Durham: Duke University Press, 2002), which in turn finds inspiration in Derek Sayer, "Everyday Forms of State Formation: Some Dissident Remarks on 'Hegemony,'" in *Everyday Forms of State Formation: Revolution and the Negotiation of Rule in Modern Mexico*, ed. Gilbert M. Joseph and Daniel Nugent, 367–77 (Durham: Duke University Press, 1994).

34 Particularly, Marie Danielle Demelás, *L'Invention Politique: Bolivie, Equateur, Pérou au xixe siècle* (Paris: Editions Recherche sur les Civilisations, 1992); and François-Xavier Guerra, "The Spanish-American Tradition of Representation and its European Roots," *Journal of Latin American Studies* 26 (1994): 1–35. Platt writes in a similar vein, though without pretending to generalize outside northern Potosí and without resorting to the term *ancient regime*, but rather emphasizing the centrality of the "tributary pact" between the state and the ayllus; see Platt, *Estado Bolviano y Ayllu Andino* (notice the dichotomy implicit in the title).

35 Walker, *Smoldering Ashes*, but see n. 21 above.

Bibliography

BOOKS AND ARTICLES

Abercrombie, Thomas. 1998. *Pathways of Memory and Power: Ethnography and History Among an Andean People*. Madison: University of Wisconsin Press.

Aguirre, Carlos. 1993. *Agentes de Su Propia Libertad: Los esclavos de Lima y la desintegración de la esclavitud, 1821–1854*. Lima: Pontificia Universidad Católica.

Álvarez, Gervasio. 1944. *Guía Histórica, Cronológica, Política y Eclesiástica del Departamento de Ayacucho para el año 1847*. Ayacucho: Imprenta Gonzales.

Anders, Martha. 1986. "Dual Organization and Calendars Inferred from the Planned Site of Azángaro-Wari Administrative Strategies," 3 vols. PH.D. dissertation, University of Cornell.

Anderson, Benedict. 1983. *Imagined Communities: Reflections on the Origin and Spread of Nationalism*. London: Verso.

Anna, Timothy. 1979. *The Fall of the Royal Government in Peru*. Lincoln and London: University of Nebraska Press.

Aparicio Vega, Manuel Jesús, comp. 1974. *La Revolución del Cuzco de 1814*. Lima: CDIP, tomo III, volume 7.

Assadourian, Carlos Sempat. 1982. *El Sistema Económico Colonial*. Lima: IEP.

———. 1994. *Transiciones Hacia el Sistema Colonial Andino*. Lima: IEP.

Barthes, Roland. 1972 [1957]. *Mythologies*. London: Trinity Press.

Basadre, Jorge. 1929. *La Iniciación de la República*, tomos I and II. Lima: Ed. F. & E. Rosay.

———. 1968. *Historia de la República del Perú*, 6th ed., tomo I. Lima: Editorial Universitaria.

———. 1983. *Historia de la República del Perú*, 7th ed., tomos I and II. Lima: Editorial Universitaria.

———. 1973. *El Azar en la Historia y sus Límites*. Lima: PL Villanueva.

———. 1979. *Perú: Problema y Posibilidad*, 3d ed. Lima: Banco Internacional del Perú.

———. 1980. *La Multitud, la Ciudad y El Campo en la Historia del Perú*, 3d ed. Lima: Ediciones Treintaitrés y Mosca Azul Editores.

Beltrán Gallardo, Ezequiel. 1977. *Las guerrillas de Yauyos en la emancipación del Perú, 1820–1824*. Lima: Editores Técnicos Asociados.

Betalleluz, Betford. 1992. "Fiscalidad, Tierras y Mercado: las comunidades indígenas de Arequipa, 1825–1850." In *Tradición y Modernidad en los Andes*, comp. Henrique Urbano. Cuzco: CBC.

Blanco, José María. 1974. *Diaro del Viaje del Presidente Orbegoso al Sur del Perú*. 2 vols. Edited by Felix Denegri Luna. Lima: Pontificia Universidad Católica del Perú, Instituto Riva Agüero.

Bonilla, Heraclio. 1980. "El Problema Nacional y Colonial del Perú en el Contexto de la Guerra del Pacífico." In Bonilla, *Un Siglo a la Deriva*. Lima: IEP.

———. 1981. "Clases Populares y Estado en el contexto de la crisis colonial." In *La Independencia en el Perú*, 2d ed., edited by Heraclio Bonilla. Lima: Instituto de Estudios Peruano.

———. 1983. "Bolívar y las guerrillas indígenas en el Perú." *Cultura: Revista del Banco Central del Ecuador*, Vol. VI, No. 16: 81–95.

———. 1984. "El campesinado indígena y el Perú en el contexto de la guerra con Chile." *Hisla* 4: 135–44.

Bonilla, Heraclio, and Karen Spalding. 1972. "La independencia en el Perú: las palabras y los hechos." In *La Independencia en el Perú*, edited by Heraclio Bonilla. Lima: IEP.

Bradley, Peter, and David Cahill. 2000. *Habsburg Peru, Images, Imagination and Memory*. Liverpool: Liverpool University Press.

Brooks, James F. 2000. "Served Well by Plunder: *La Gran Ladronería*, and Producers of History Astride the Río Grande." *American Quarterly* 54 (1): 23–75.

———. 2002. *Captives and Cousins: Slavery, Kinship, and Community in the Southwest Borderlands*. Chapel Hill: University of North Carolina Press.

Buisson, Inge, and Guenther Kahle, eds. 1984. *Problemas de la Formación del Estado y de la Nación en Hispanoamérica*. Cologne and Vienna: Boehlau Verlag.

Burga, Manuel. 1987. "El Perú Central 1770–1860: Disparidades regionales y la primera crisis agrícola." *Revista Peruana de Ciencias Sociales* 1: 5–69.

Burger, Richard L. 1992. *Chavín and the Origins of Andean Civilization*. London: Thames and Hudson.

Cahill, David. 1993. "Independencia, sociedad y fiscalidad: el Sur Andino (1780–1880)." *Revista Complutense de Historia de América* 19: 249–68.

———. 1994. " 'Colour by Numbers': Racial and Ethnic Categories in the Viceroyalty of Peru." *Journal of Latin American Studies* 26 (2): 325–46.

———. 1999. *Violencia, represión y rebelión en el sur andino: la sublevación de Túpac Amaru y sus consecuencias*. Documento de Trabajo; no 105, Serie Historia. Lima: IEP.

———. 2000. "Conclusion." In *Habsburg Peru, Images, Imagination and Memory*. Peter Bradley and David Cahill. Liverpool: Liverpool University Press.

———. 2000. "The Inca Politics of Nostalgia." In *Habsburg Peru, Images, Imagination and Memory*. Peter Bradley and David Cahill. Liverpool: Liverpool University Press.

———. 2002. "The Colonial Inca Nobility: Social Structure, Culture and Politics in Late Colonial Cuzco." Paper presented at the conference "New World, First Nations: Native Peoples of Mesoamerica and the Andes Under Colonial Rule," University of New South Wales, Sydney, October 1–3.

Cahill, David, and Scarlett O'Phelan Godoy. 1992. "Forging Their Own History: Indian Insurgency in the Southern Peruvian Sierra." *Bulletin of Latin American Research* 2 (2): 125–67.

Campbell, Leon G. 1976. "The Army of Peru and the Túpac Amaru Revolt, 1780–1783." *Hispanic American Historical Review* 56 (1): 31–57.

———. 1978. *The Military and Society in Colonial Peru 1750–1810*. Philadelphia: American Philosophical Society.

Carranza, Luis. 1988. *La Ciencia en el Perú en el siglo XIX*, tomo 1. "Selección de Artículos publicados por el Dr. Luis Carranza. . . ." Sociedad Geográfica de Lima, Lima: Editorial Edili.

Carrasco Apaico, Salomón. 1988. *Ayacucho, dos siglos de Periodismo en el Perú*. Lima: author's edition.

Cavero, Luis E. 1953. *Monografía de la Provincia de Huanta*, Vol. 1. Lima: n.p.

Cerda-Hegerl, Patricia. (undated, c. 1993). *Fronteras del Sur, La región del Bio Bio y la Araucanía Chilena, 1604–1883*. Temuco: Universidad de la Frontera / Instituto Latino-americano de la Universidad Libre de Berlín.

Chambers, Sarah. 2003. "Little Middle Ground: The Instability of Mestizo Identity in the Andes." In *Race and Nation in Modern Latin America*, edited by Nancy P. Appelbaum, Anne S. Macpherson, and Karin Alejandra Rosenblatt, 32–55. Chapel Hill and London: University of North Carolina Press.

Chocano, Magdalena. 1982. *Comercio en Cerro de Pasco a fines de la época colonial*. Lima: Seminario de Historia Rural Andina, Universidad Nacional Mayor de San Marcos.

———. 1987. "Ucronía y Frustración en la Conciencia Histórica Peruana." *Márgenes: encuentro y debate* 1 (2): 43–60.

Contreras, Carlos. 1982. *La Ciudad del Mercurio, Huancavelica 1570–1700*. Lima: IEP.

———. 1989. "Estado Republicano y Tributo Indígena en la Sierra Central en la post independencia." *Histórica* 13: 517–50.

———. 2003. "Etnicidad y Contribuciones Directas en el Perú Después de la Independencia." Paper presented at the 51st International Congress of Americanists. Santiago de Chile.

Coronel Aguirre, José. 1983. "Don Manuel Jesús Urbina: creación del Colegio de Instrucción Media González Vigil y las pugnas por el Poder Local en Huanta (1910–1930)." In *Libro Jubilar, 1933–1983, Comité Central Pro-Bodas de Oro del Colegio National González Vigil*. Huanta: Colegio National González Vigil and Universidad Nacional de San Cristóbal de Huamanga.

Crespo, Alfonso. 1944. *Santa Cruz, el cóndor indio*. Mexico City: Fondo de Cultura Económica.

De la Barra, Felipe. 1974. *La campaña de Junín y Ayacucho*. Lima: Comisión Nacional del Sesquicentenario de la Independencia.

De la Barra, Felipe, Gral. E.P., ed. 1974. *Asuntos Militares, Reimpresos de Campañas,*

Acciones Militares y Cuestiones Conexas, Años 1823–1826, CDIP, tomo VI, vol. 9. Lima: Editorial Salesiana.

De la Cadena, Marisol. 2000. *Indigenous Mestizos: The Politics of Race and Culture in Cuzco*. Durham: Duke University Press.

De la Fuente, Ariel. 2000. *Children of Facundo*. Durham: Duke University Press.

De la Puente y Candamo, José Agustín. 1970. *Notas Sobre la Causa de la Independencia del Perú*, 2d ed. Lima: Librería Studium.

——. 1992. *La Independencia del Perú*, Colección 1492. Madrid: Ed. Mapfre.

Del Pino, Juan José. 1955. *Las Sublevaciones Indígenas de Huanta 1827–1896*. Ayacucho: author's edition.

Del Pino H., Ponciano. 2001. "Uchuraccay: Memoria y representación de la violencia política en los Andes." Paper presented at the SSCR workshop "Memoria Colectiva y Violencia Política: Perspectivas Comparativas Sobre el Proceso de Democratización en América del Sur," New York.

Del Río, Alejandro. 1987. *Ninabamba, una Hacienda Jesuita del siglo XVIII*. Lima: Universidad Nacional Mayor de San Marcos.

Demelás, Marie Danielle. 1992. *L'Invention Politique: Bolivie, Equateur, Pérou au XIXe siècle*. Paris: Editions Recherche sur les Civilisations.

Denegri Luna, Félix, comp. 1971. *Memorias, Diarios y Crónicas*. Lima: CDIP, tomo XXVI, vol. 1.

Diez Hurtado, Alejandro. 1998. *Comunes y Haciendas: Procesos de Comunalización en la Sierra de Piura (siglos XVIII al XX)*. Cuzco: CIPCA / CBC.

Dunbar, Ella, comp. 1975. *La Acción Patriótica*, Lima: CDIP, tomo V, vol. 6.

Durand Flórez, Guillermo, comp. 1971. *La Rebelión de Túpac Amaru*. Lima: CDIP, tomo II, vol. 4.

Echenique, José Rufino. 1952. *Memorias para la Historia del Perú*. Lima: Editorial Huascarán, tomo I.

Eguiguren, Luis Antonio. 1935. *La Sedición de Huamanga en 1812, Ayacucho y la Independencia*. Lima: Librería e Imprenta Gil.

Espinoza Soriano, Waldemar. 1960. "El alcalde mayor indígena en el virreinato del Perú." *Anuario de Estudios Americanos* 17: 183–300.

——. 1981. *La destrucción del imperio de los incas: la rivalidad política y señorial de los kurakazgos andinos*, 3d ed. Lima: Amaru Editores.

Estenssoro, Juan Carlos. 1990. "Discurso, música y poder en el Perú Colonial." Tesis de Maestría, 3 vols. Lima: Pontificia Universidad Católica del Perú.

——. 1992. "Modernismo, Estética, Música y Fiesta." In *Tradición y Modernidad en los Andes*, edited by Enrique Urbano. Cuzco: CBC.

Favre, Henri. 1976. "Evolución y situación de la hacienda tradicional de la región de Huancavelica." In *La Hacienda, la Comunidad y el Campesinado en el Perú*, edited by José Matos Mar. Lima: IEP.

——. 1986. "Bolívar y los Indios." *Histórica* 10 (1): 1–18.

Field, Daniel. 1976. *Rebels in the Name of the Czar*. Boston: Houghton Mifflin.

Fisher, John. 1970. *Government and Society in Colonial Peru: The Intendant System, 1784–1814*. London: Athlone Press.

——. 1984. "La Formación del Estado Peruano y Simón Bolívar (1808–1824)." In *Problemas de La Formación del Estado y de La Nación en Hispanoamérica*, edited by Inge Buisson, Günter Kahle, et al. Cologne-Vienna: Böhlau Verlag.

Fisher, Lilian E. 1966. *The Last Inca Revolt, 1780–1783*. Norman: University of Oklahoma Press.

Flores Galindo, Alberto, comp. 1976. *Túpac Amaru II—1780: sociedad colonial y sublevaciones populares*. Lima: Retablo de Papel Ediciones.

——. 1984. *Aristocracia y Plebe: Lima 1760–1830*. Lima: Mosca Azul.

——. 1987. *Buscando un Inca: identidad y utopía en los Andes*. Lima: Instituto de Apoyo Agrario.

——. 1987. *Independencia y Revolución*, 2 vols. Lima: Instituto Nacional de Cultura.

——. 1999. *La Tradición Autoritaria: Violencia y democracia en el Perú*. Lima: Sur / APRODEH.

Foster, George. 1965. "Peasant Society in the Image of Limited Good." *American Anthropologist* 67: 293–315.

Foucault, Michel. 1980. *The History of Sexuality*. Volume 1: *An Introduction*. New York: Vintage Books.

García Calderón, Francisco. 1879. *Diccionario de la Legislación Peruana*. Paris: Laroque.

Gavilán, Narciso. 1941. *Ensayos Históricos*. Ayacucho: author's edition.

Geertz, Clifford. 1973. *The Interpretation of Cultures*. New York: Basic Books.

Gisbert, Teresa. 1980. *Iconografia y Mitos Indígenas en el Arte*. La Paz: Gisbert y Cía Ed.

Glave, Luis Miguel. 1987. "Sociedad, Poder y Organización Andinas, El Sur peruano hacia el Siglo XVII." In *Comunidades Campesinas, Cambios y Permanencias*, 2d ed., edited by Alberto Flores Galindo. Chiclayo y Lima: Centro de Estudios 'Solidaridad,' and CONCYTEC.

Goldman, Noemí, and Ricardo Salvatore, eds. 1998. *Caudillismos Rioplatenses: Nuevas Miradas a Un Viejo Problema*. Buenos Aires: Eudeba / Facultad de Filosofía y Letras, Universidad de Buenos Aires.

Gootenberg, Paul. 1989. *Between Silver and Guano*. Princeton: Princeton University Press.

——. 1989. *Tejidos y harinas, corazones y mentes: el imperialismo norteamericano del libre comercio en el Perú 1825–1840*, Series Colección Mínima no. 17. Lima: IEP.

——. 1991. "Population and Ethnicity in Early Republican Peru: Some Revisions." *Latin American Research Review* 26: 109–58.

Gorriti Ellenboghen, Gustavo. 1990. *Sendero, La Guerra Milenaria*. Lima: Apoyo.

Guamán Poma de Ayala, Felipe. 1980 [1583–1615]. *Nueva Corónica y Buen Gobierno*,

3 vols., edited by John Murra and Rolena Adorno, translated by Jorge Urioste. Lima: IEP / Siglo Veintiuno.

Guerra, François-Xavier. 1992. *Modernidad e Independencias, Ensayos sobre las revoluciones hispánicas*. Mexico City: Fondo de Cultura Económica.

———. 1994. "The Spanish-American Tradition of Representation and its European Roots." *Journal of Latin American Studies* 26: 1–35.

Halperín Donghi, Tulio. 1972. *Hispanoamérica Después de la Independencia*. Buenos Aires: Paidós.

Hamnett, Brian R. 1978. *Revolución y contrarrevolución en México y el Perú: Liberalismo, realeza y separatismo: 1800–1824*. Mexico City: Fondo de Cultura Económica.

Harris, Olivia, Brooke Larson, and Enrique Tandeter. 1987. *La Participación indígena en los mercados surandinos, estrategias y reproducción social, Siglos XVI a XX*. Cochabamba: CERES.

Hill, Christopher. 1988. *The World Turned Upside Down: Radical Ideas in the English Revolution*. London: Penguin Books.

Huertas, Lorenzo. 1974. "Las Luchas por la Independencia en Ayacucho." In *Primer Simposio sobre la Independencia en Ayacucho*. Ayacucho: UNSCH, Departamento de ciencias histórico-sociales.

———. 1981. "La Rebelión en las Punas de Iquicha." In *Levantamientos campesinos, siglos XVIII–XIX*, edited by Juan Solano Sáenz. Lima: Universidad Nacional del Centro del Perú.

Hünefeldt, Christine. 1978. "Los indios y la constitución de 1812." *Allpanchis Phuturinqa* 11 / 12: 33–52.

———. 1982. *Lucha por la Tierra y Protesta Indígena*. Bonn: Bonner Ammerikanistische Studiens.

Husson, Patrick. 1983. "Guerre indienne et revolte paysanne dans la province de Huanta (départament d'Ayacucho-Pérou) au xixéme siecle." Ph.D. dissertation, Université Paris IV, Sorbonne.

———. 1992. *De la Guerra a la Rebelión: Huanta siglo XIX*. Cuzco: CBC.

Irurozqui Victoriano, Marta. 2000. " 'A Bala, Piedra y Palo,' La Construcción de la Ciudadanía Política en Bolivia, 1826–1952." Seville: Diputación de Sevilla.

Itier, César. 1995. "Quechua y Cultura en el Cuzco del Siglo XVIII: De la 'lengua general' al 'idioma del imperio de los Incas.' " In *Del Siglo de Oro al Siglo de las Luces*, compiled by César Itier, 89–111. Cuzco: CBC.

———. 2000. *El Teatro Quechua en el Cuzco, Tomo II, Indigenismo, Lengua y literatura en el Perú moderno*. Cuzco: CBC / IFEA.

Juan, Jorge, and Antonio de Ulloa. 1953. *Noticias Secretas de América*. Buenos Aires: Ediciones Mar Océano.

Kapsoli, Wilfredo. 1987. *Los Movimientos Campesinos en el Peru*, 3d. ed. Lima: Ediciones Atusparia.

Kossok, Manfred. 1968. *Historia de la Santa Alianza y la Emancipación de América Latina*. Buenos Aires: Sílaba.

Larson, Brooke, and Olivia Harris. 1995. *Ethnicity, Markets, and Migration in the Andes*. Durham: Duke University Press.

Lauria-Santiago, Aldo. 1999. *An Agrarian Republic: Commercial Agriculture and the Politics of Peasant Communities in El Salvador, 1823–1914*. Pittsburgh: University of Pittsburgh Press.

Lévi-Strauss, Claude. 1992 [1955]. *Tristes Tropiques*. New York: Penguin Books.

Lewin, Boleslao. 1957. *La rebelion de Túpac Amaru y los orígenes de la emancipación Americana*. Buenos Aires: Hachette S. A.

López-Alves, Fernando. 2000. *State Formation and Democracy in Latin America 1810–1900*. Durham: Duke University Press.

Lynch, John. 1976. *The Spanish American Revolutions: 1806–1826*. New York: W. W. Norton.

———. 1992. *Caudillos in Spanish America, 1800–1850*. Oxford: Clarendon Press.

Macera, Pablo. 1955. *Tres Etapas en el Desarrollo de la Conciencia Nacional*. Lima: Ediciones Fanal.

———. 1972. *Tierras y Población en el Perú, siglos XVIII–XIX*. Lima: Universidad Nacional Mayor de San Marcos, Seminario de Historia Rural Andina.

Majluf, Natalia. 1995. "The Creation of the Image of the Indian in 19th Century Peru. The Paintings of Francisco Laso." PH.D. dissertation. University of Texas, Austin.

Mallon, Florencia. 1983. *The Defense of Community in Peru's Central Highlands*. Princeton: Princeton University Press.

———. 1987. "National and Antistate Coalitions in the War of the Pacific; Junín and Cajamarca, 1879–1902." In *Resistance, Rebellion and Consciousness in the Andean Peasant World, 18th–20th Centuries*, edited by Steve J. Stern. Madison: University of Wisconsin.

———. 1995. *Peasant and Nation: The Making of Post Colonial México and Peru*. Berkeley: University of California Press.

Mannheim, Bruce. 1991. *The Language of the Inka since the European Invasion*. Austin: University of Texas Press.

Manrique, Nelson. 1981. *Las Guerrillas indígenas en la guerra con Chile*. Lima: Centro de Investigación y Capacitación / Ital Perú.

———. 1986. "Campesinado, Guerra y Conciencia Nacional." *Revista Andina* 4 (1): 161–72.

———. 1987. *Mercado Interno y Región: Sierra Central, 1820–1930*. Lima: Desco.

———. 1988. *Yawar Mayu: Sociedades Terratenientes Serranas, 1789–1910*. Lima: Desco / IFEA.

Mariátegui, José Carlos. 1971. *Siete Ensayos, Interpretación de la Realidad Peruana*. Lima: Biblioteca Amauta.

Markham, Sir Clements R. 1991. *Markham in Peru: The Travels of Clements R. Markham, 1852–1853*. Edited by Peter Blanchard. Austin: University of Texas Press.

Martínez Riaza, Ascención. 1992. *La Prensa Hispanoamericana en la Independencia*. Madrid: Mapfre.

Matos Mar, José, ed. 1976. *Hacienda, Comunidad y Campesinado en el Perú*. Lima: IEP.

Mayer, Enrique. 1992. "Peru in Deep Trouble: Mario Vargas Llosa's 'Inquest in the Andes' Reexamined." In *Rereading Cultural Anthropology*, edited by George E. Marcus. Durham: Duke University Press.

Méndez G., Cecilia. 1991. "Los Campesinos, La Independencia y la Iniciación de la República: el caso de los iquichanos realistas." In *Poder y Violencia en los Andes*, edited by Henrique Urbano. Cuzco: CBC.

——. 1992. "República sin Indios: La Comunidad Imaginada del Perú." In *Tradición y Modernidad en los Andes*, edited by Henrique Urbano. Cuzco: CBC.

——. 1994. "Una Vez Más La Pena de Muerte." *Crónicas de la Historia del Derecho* 1: 51–61.

——. 1996. "Incas Sí, Indios No: Notes on Peruvian Creole Nationalism and Its Contemporary Crisis." *Journal of Latin American Studies* 28 (1): 197–225.

——. 1999. "Estado, Poder Local y Sociedad Rural: Una Visión desde Ayacucho." Paper presented at the XII International Conference of the AHILA, Porto, Portugal, September 21–25.

——. 2000. "La Tentación del Olvido: Guerra, Nacionalismo e Historiadores en el Perú." *Diálogos* (Universidad Nacional de San Marcos, Lima) 2: 231–48.

——. 2001. "The Power of Naming, or the Construction of Ethnic and National Identities in Peru: Myth, History and the Iquichanos." *Past and Present* 171: 127–60.

Mendiburu, Manuel de. 1931–35. *Diccionario Histórico Biográfico del Perú*, vol. 9. Lima: Imprenta Gil, 1935.

Milla Batres, Carlos, ed. 1975. *Historia de las Batallas de Junín y Ayacucho*. Lima: Editorial Milla Batres.

——. 1975. *Juan Mauricio Rugendas: El Perú Romántico del siglo XIX*. Lima: Milla Batres.

Miller, John. 1912. *Memorias del General Miller al servicio de la república del Perú escritas en inglés por Mr. John Miller y traducidas al castellano por el General Torrijos*, tomo III. Santiago de Chile: Imprenta Universitaria.

Monguió, Luis. 1971. "La Poesía y la Independencia, Perú 1808–1825." In *Literatura de la Emancipación*. Lima: Universidad Nacional Mayor de San Marcos.

——. 1985. "La Ilustración Peruana y el Indio." *América Indígena* 45 (2).

Moore, Barrington. 1967. *Lord and Peasant in the Making of the Modern World*. Boston: Beacon.

Morazzini de Pérez Enciso, Gisella. 1972. *Las Ordenanzas de Intendentes de Indias*. Caracas: Universidad Central de Venezuela.

Morote Best, Efraín, comp. 1974. *Huamanga, una larga Historia*. Lima: CONUP.

Murra, John. 1975. *Formaciones Económicas y Políticas del Mundo Andino*. Lima: IEP.

Navarro del Aguila, Víctor. 1939. *Las Tribus de AnkuWallokc*. Tesis, Cuzco: Universidad del Cuzco.

Nieto Vélez, Armando. 1960. *Contribución a la Historia del Fidelismo en el Perú (1808–1810)*. Lima: Instituto Riva Agüero.

Odriozola, Manuel de. 1864. *Documentos Históricos del Perú*, vol. 2. Lima: Tipografía de Aurelio Alfaro.

O'Higgins, Demetrio. 1953. "Informe del Intendente de Guamanga d. Demetrio O'Higgins al Ministro de Indias d. Miguel Cayetano Soler." In the appendix to Jorge Juan y Antonio de Ulloa, *Noticias Secretas de América*. Buenos Aires: Ediciones Mar Océano.

O'Phelan Godoy, Scarlett. 1978. "El sur andino a fines del siglo XVIII: cacique o corregidor," *Allpanchis Phuturinqa*, no. 11: 17–32.

———. 1987. "Acerca del mito de la Independencia concedida." In *Independencia y Revolución*, compiled by Alberto Flores Galindo. Lima: Instituto Nacional de Cultura.

———. 1988. *Un Siglo de Rebeliones Anticoloniales*. Cuzco: CBC.

———, comp. 2001. *La Independencia en el Perú, De los Borbones a Bolívar*. Lima: PUCP, Instituto Riva Agüero.

Ortiz, Dionisio, O.F.M. 1975. *Las Montañas del Apurímac, Mantaro y Ene*, tomo 1. Lima: Imprenta Editorial San Antonio.

———. 1981. *La Montaña de Ayacucho*. Lima: Ed. Gráfica.

Paz Soldán, Mariano Felipe. 1865. *Atlas Geográfico del Perú*. Paris: Fermín Didot Hermanos, hijos y ca.

———. 1877. *Diccionario Geográfico Estadístico del Perú*. Lima: Imp. del Estado.

———. 1929. *Historia del Perú Independiente (tercer periodo 1827–1833)*. Lima: Lib. e Imprenta Gil.

Peralta Ruiz, Víctor. 1991. *En Pos del Tributo en el Cusco Rural: 1826–1854*. Cuzco: CBC.

———. 2001. "El Cabildo de Lima y la Política en el Perú, 1808–1814." In *La Independencia en el Perú, De los Borbones a Bolívar*, compiled by Scarlett O'Phelan Godoy, 29–56. Lima: PUCP, Instituto Riva Agüero.

———. 2003. *En Defensa de la Autoridad: Política y Cultura Bajo el Gobierno del Virrey Abscal. Perú 1806–1816*. Madrid: CSIC.

Pérez Aguirre, Iván. 1982. "Rebeldes Iquichanos 1824–1828." Tesis de Bachiller, Universidad Nacional de San Cristóbal de Huamanga.

Piel, Jean. 1970. "The Place of the Peasantry in the National Life of Perú in the Nineteenth Century." *Past and Present* 46: 109–33.

Platt, Tristan. 1982. *Estado Boliviano y Ayllu Andino: Tierra y Tributo en el Norte de Potosí*. Lima: IEP.

Poole, Deborah. 1988. "Landscapes of Power in a Cattle-Rustling Culture of Southern Andean Peru." *Dialectical Anthropology* 12: 367–98.

———. 1988. "Qorilazos, abigeos y comunidades campesinas en la provincia de Chumbivilcas (Cusco)." In *Comunidades Campesinas, Cambios y Permanencias*, 2d ed., edited by Alberto Flores Galindo. Chiclayo, Peru: Centro de Estudios 'Solidaridad.'

———, ed. 1994. *Unruly Order: Violence, Power, and Cultural Identity in the High Provinces of Southern Peru*. Boulder: Westview Press.

———. 1994. "Performance, Domination, and Identity in the *Tierras Bravas* of Chumbivilcas (Cusco)." In *Unruly Order: Violence, Power and Cultural Identity in the High Provinces of Southern Peru*, edited by Deborah Poole. Boulder: Westview Press.

Porras Barrenechea, Raúl. 1974. *Los Ideólogos de la Emancipación*. Lima: Milla Batres.

Pulgar Vidal, Javier. 1972. *Las Ocho Regiones Naturales del Perú*. Lima: Editorial Universo.

Raimondi, Antonio. [ca. 1880]. *Mapa del Perú*. Paris: Grabado eimp. por Erhard Fres.

Reina, Leticia, coordinadora. 1977. *La Reindianización de América*. Mexico City: Siglo Veintiuno, Nuestra America / Ciesas.

Remy, Maria Isabel. 1988. "La sociedad local al inicio de la república. Cusco 1824–1850." *Revista Andina* 12: 451–84.

Riva Agüero, José de la. 1910. *La Historia en el Perú*. Lima: Imp. Nacional de Federico Barrionuevo.

———. 1969. "Paisajes Peruanos." In *Obras Completas*, tomo xi. Lima: Pontificia Universidad Católica.

Rivera Serna, Raúl. 1958. *Los Guerrilleros del Centro en la Emancipación Peruana*. Lima: PL Villanueva.

Rodríguez, José Antonio. 1994. "La Exaltación Religiosa del Monarca en el Cusco Colonial: Espinosa Medrano y el sermón fúnebre." In *La Venida del Reino: Religión, evangelización y cultura en América, Siglos xvi–xx*, edited by Gabriela Ramos. Cuzco: CBC.

Rodríguez O., Jaime. 1998. *The Independence of Spanish America*. Cambridge: Cambridge University Press.

Roel, Virgilio. 1988. *La Independencia, Historia Genral del Perú*. Lima: Editorial Gráfica Labor S.A.

Roldán, Mary. 2002. *Blood and Fire: La Violencia in Antioquia, Colombia, 1946–1953*. Durham: Duke University Press.

Rowe, John Howland. 1976. "El Movimiento Nacional Inca del siglo xviii." *Revista Universitaria* 7. Reprinted in *Túpac Amaru ii, 1780, Antología*, edited by Alberto Flores Galindo. Lima: Eds. Retablo Papel.

Saignes, Thierry. 1987. "De la Borrachera al retrato: los caciques andinos entre dos legitimidades (Charcas)." *Revista Andina* 9: 139–70.

———. 1990. "Es Posible una historia 'chola' del Perú?" *Allpanchis Phuturinqa* 2 (35 / 36): 635–57.

Sala i Vila, Núria. 1996. *Y se armó el tole tole: tributo indígena y movimientos sociales en el*

Virreinato del Perú, 1790–1814. Ayacucho: Instituto de Estudios Regionales José María Arguedas.

——. 2001. *Selva y Andes: Ayacucho (1780–1929), Historia de Una Región en la Encrucijada*. Madrid: Consejo Superior de Investigaciones Científicas.

Salas de Coloma, Miriam. 1979. *De los obrajes de Canaria y Chincheros a las comunidades indígenas de Vilcashuamán, siglo XVI*. Lima [n.p.].

——. 1998. *Estructura colonial del poder español en el Perú: Huamanga (Ayacucho) a través de sus obrajes: siglos XVI–XVIII*. 3 vols. Lima: Pontificia Universidad Católica del Perú, Fondo Editorial.

Sánchez Albornoz, Nicolás. 1978. *Indios y Tributos en el Alto Perú*. Lima: IEP.

Sayer, Derek. 1994. "Everyday Forms of State Formation: Some Dissident Remarks on 'Hegemony.' " In *Everyday Forms of State Formation: Revolution and the Negotiation of Rule in Modern Mexico*, edited by Gilbert M. Joseph and Daniel Nugent. Durham: Duke University Press.

Scott, James. 1976. *The Moral Economy of the Peasant*. New Haven: Yale University Press.

——. 1985. *The Weapons of the Weak: The Everyday Forms of Peasant Resistance*. New Haven: Yale University Press.

Serulnikov, Sergio. 1994. *Su verdad y su justicia : Tomás Katari y la insurrección aymara de Chayanta, 1777–1780*. Buenos Aires: Instituto de Historia Argentina y Americana Dr. Emilio Ravignani (Series Cuadernos del Instituto Ravignani), Universidad de Buenos Aires.

Silverblatt, Irene. 1987. *Moon, Sun, and Witches: Gender Ideologies and Class in Inca and Colonial Peru*. Princeton: Princeton University Press.

Spalding, Karen. 1972. "The Colonial Indian Past and Future Research Perspectives." *Latin American Research Review* 2: 47–76.

——. 1974. *De Indio a Campesino*. Lima: IEP.

——. 1984. *Huarochirí, an Andean Society Under Inca and Spanish Rule*. Stanford: Stanford University Press.

Stern, Steve J. 1982. *Perú's Indian Peoples and the Challenge of the Spanish Conquest, Huamanga to 1640*. Madison: University of Wisconsin.

——, ed. 1987. *Resistance, Rebellion and Consciousness in the Andean Peasant World, 18th to 20th Centuries*. Madison: University of Wisconsin.

Stiglich, Germán. 1922. *Diccionario Geográfico del Perú*. Lima: Torres Aguirre.

Sulca Báez, Leocadio Edgar. 1986. "Curas y Kurakas Ayacuchanos. Tierra y poder en la sociedad colonial." Tesis, Título de Antropólogo Social, Ayacucho, UNSCH.

Szeminski, Jan. 1987. "Why Kill the Spaniard? New Perspectives on Andean Insurrectionary Ideology in the 18th Century." In *Resistance, Rebellion, and Consciousness in the Andean Peasant World, 18th to 20th Centuries*, edited by Steve J. Stern. Madison: University of Wisconsin.

Theidon, Kimberly, and Enver Quinteros. 2003. "Uchuraccay, La Política de la Muerte en el Perú." *Ideele* 152: 27–30.

Thompson, E. P. 1971. "The Moral Economy of the English Crowd in the Eighteenth Century." *Past and Present* 50: 76–136.

———. 1974. "Patrician Society, Plebeian Culture." *Journal of Social History* 7: 382–405.

———. 1977. *La Formación Histórica de la Clase Obrera*, vol. 1. Barcelona: Laia.

———. 1993. "The Patricians and the Plebs." In *Customs in Common: Studies in Traditional Popular Culture*. New York: New Press.

Thomson, Guy P. C., with David LaFrance. 1999. *Patriotism, Politics, and Popular Liberalism in Nineteenth-Century Mexico: Juan Francisco Lucas and the Puebla Sierra*. Wilmington, Del.: Scholarly Resources.

Thomson, Sinclair. 1996. "Colonial Crisis, Community, and Andean Self-Rule: Aymara Politics in the Age of Insurgency (Eighteenth Century La Paz)." PH.D. dissertation, University of Wisconsin.

———. 2002. *We Alone Will Rule: Native Andean Politics in the Age of Insurgency*. Madison: University of Wisconsin Press.

Thurner, Mark. 1995. " 'Republicanos' and 'la Comunidad de Peruanos': Unimagined Political Communities in Postcolonial Andean Perú." *Journal of Latin American Studies* 27: 291–318.

———. 1997. *From Two Republics to One Divided*. Durham: Duke University Press.

Tilly, Charles. 1964. *The Vendée*. Cambridge, Mass.: Harvard University Press.

Tutino, John. 1986. *From Insurrection to Revolution in Mexico: Social Bases of Agrarian Violence*. Princeton: Princeton University Press.

Unanue, Hipólito. 1968. "Guía Política, Eclesiástica y Militar del Virreynato del Perú para el año de 1795, Compuesta por orden del Superior Gobierno." Lima: Imprenta Real de los Niños Huérfanos. Reprinted in Colección Documental de la Independencia del Peru, compiled by Jorge Arias Schreiber Pezet. *Los Ideólogos* 8 (1): 717–78.

Urrutia Ceruti, Jaime. 1982. "Comerciantes, Arieros y Viajeros Huamanguinos: 1770–1870." Tesis de Bachiller. Ayacucho: UNSCH.

———. 1984. "Los Pokras o el mito de los Huamanguinos." *Revista del Archivo Departamental de Ayacucho*, no. 13.

———. 1985. *Huamanga, Región e Historia*. Ayacucho: UNSCH.

Valcárcel, Carlos Daniel, comp. n.d. *La Rebelión de Túpac Amaru*. Lima: CDIP, tomo II, vols. 2 and 3.

———. 1947. *La rebelión de Túpac Amaru*. Mexico City: Fondo de Cultura Económica.

Valdés, Jerónimo. 1827. "Exposición que Dirige al rey Don Fernando VII el Mariscal de Campo don Jerónimo Valdés Sobre las Causas que Motivaron la Pérdida del Perú." In *La Independencia*, Virgilio Roel, 619–39.

Valdés, Lidio, Cirilo Vivanco, and Casimiro Chávez. 1990. "Asentamientos Chanka en la cuenca del Pamapas y Qaracha, Ayacucho." *Gaceta Arqueológica Andina* 17: 17–26.

Van Young, Eric. 1989. "Quetzalcóatl, King Ferndinand and Ignacio Allende Go to the Seashore; or Messianism and Mystical Kingship in Mexico 1800–1820." In *The Independence of Mexico and the Creation of the New Nation*, edited by Jaime Rodríguez O. Los Angeles : UCLA Latin American Center Publications; Irvine: Mexico / Chicano Program, University of California Irvine.

———. 2001. *The Other Rebellion: Popular Violence, Ideology and the Mexican Struggle for Independence, 1810–1821*. Stanford: Stanford University Press.

Varese, Stefano. 1973. *La Sal de los Cerros*, 2d ed. Lima: Retablo de Papel Ediciones.

Vargas Llosa, Mario, et al. 1983. *Informe de la Comisión Investigadora de Los Sucesos de Uchuraccay*. Lima: Editora Perú.

Vargas Ugarte, Rubén. 1957. *Impresos Peruanos, 1809–1825*, tomo XII. Lima.

———. 1968. *Historia General del Perú*, vol. 7. Lima: Editorial Milla Batres.

———. 1974. "Introductory study." In *Historia de las Batallas de Junín y Ayacucho*, edited by Carlos Milla Batres. Lima: Editorial Milla Batres.

Vargas, Nemesio. 1903. *Historia del Perú Independiente*, tomo I. Lima: Imp. de la Escuela de Ingenieros por Juio Mesinas.

———. 1942. *Historia del Perú Independiente*, tomo IX. Lima, author's edition.

Vergara, Abilio, Juan Arguedas, and Genaro Zaga. n. d. "Reciprocidad y ciclos Productivos en la comunidad de Culluchaca" (mimeograph). Ayacucho: Instituto de Estudios Regionales José María Arguedas.

Vergara Arias, Gustavo. 1973. *Montoneras y Guerrillas en la Etapa de la Emancipación del Perú, 1820–1825*. Lima: Imprenta y Litografía Salesiana.

Vicuña Mackenna, Benjamín. 1971. *La independencia en el Perú*, 5th ed. Prologue by Luis Alberto Sánchez. Buenos Aires: Editorial Francisco de Aguirre.

Villanueva Urteaga, Horacio. 1981. *Gamarra y la Iniciación Republicana en el Cuzco*. Lima: Fondo del Libro del Banco de los Andes.

Villanueva, Víctor. 1973. *Del Caudillaje Anárquico al Militarismo Reformista*. Lima: Librería-Editorial Juan Mejía Baca.

Villazón, Eleodoro. 1906. *Alegato de parte del Gobierno de Bolivia en el Juicio Arbitral de Fronteras con la República del Perú*. Buenos Aires.

Vivanco Pomacanchari, Cirilo. 1996. "Arqueología de Ayacucho: Un Examen Necesario." *Afanes, Búsqueda desde Huamanga* (Ayacucho) 1 (1): 85–95.

Walker, Charles. 1990. "Montoneros, Bandoleros, Malhechores: Criminalidad y política en las primeras décadas republicanas." In *Bandoleros, abigeos y montoneros*, edited by Carlos Aguirre and Charles Walker. Lima: Instituto de Apoyo Agrario.

———. 1991. "La Violencia y el sistema legal: Los Indios y el Estado en el Cusco Después de la Rebelión de Túpac Amaru." In *Poder y Violencia en los Andes*, edited by Henrique Urbano. Cuzco: CBC.

———. 1992. "Peasants, Caudillos and the State in Perú: Cusco in the Transition from Colony to Republic, 1780–1840." ph.d. dissertation, University of Chicago.

———. 1999. *Smoldering Ashes: Cuzco and the Creation of Republican Peru, 1780–1840.* Durham: Duke University Press.

Weber, Max. 1978. *Economy and Society,* 2 vols. Berkeley: University of California Press.

Witt, Heinrich. 1992. *Un Testimonio Personal Sobre el Peru del Siglo xix,* vol. 1 (1824–1842). Lima: Banco Mercantil.

Wolf, Eric. 1966. *Peasant Wars of the Twentieth Century.* New York: Harper and Row.

DOCUMENT COLLECTIONS

Colección Documental del Sesquicentenario de la Independencia del Perú (cdip), Lima, 1971–79. Edited by Comisión del Sesquicentanario de la Independencia del Perú, 100 vols. Volumes consulted:

cdip, tomo i, vol. 10.

cdip, tomo ii, vols. 2, 3, 4, 7.

cdip, tomo iii, vols. 4, 7.

cdip, tomo v, vol. 6.

cdip, tomo vi, vols. 6, 8, 9.

cdip, tomo xxii, vol. 1.

cdip, tomo xxiii, vol 1.

cdip, tomo xxvi, vols. 1, 4.

ARCHIVES

Archivo General de la Nación (Lima)

Archivo General de Indias (Seville)

Archivo Histórico Militar del Perú (Lima)

Archivo Departamental de Ayacucho (Ayacucho)

Archivo Notarial of Mr. Leoncio Cárdenas (Huanta)

Private Archive of the Santa Cruz Family (La Paz)

Private Library of Mr. Félix Denegri Luna (Lima)

Private archive of Mr. Arturo Tineo (Ayacucho)

Biblioteca Nacional del Perú (Lima)

Biblioteca Nacional de Madrid (Madrid)

Biblioteca de la Real Academia de la Historia (Madrid)

Ministry of Agriculture records on comunidades campesinas (Lima)

Index

CECILIA MÉNDEZ is an

associate professor in the Department

of History at the University of California,

Santa Barbara.

Library of Congress Cataloging-in-Publication Data

Méndez G., Cecilia.
The plebeian republic : the Huanta rebellion and
the making of the Peruvian state, 1820–1850 /
Cecilia Méndez.
p. cm.
Includes bibliographical references and index.
ISBN 0-8223-3430-5 (cloth : alk. paper)
ISBN 0-8223-3441-0 (pbk. : alk. paper)
1. Huanta (Peru : Province)—Politics and
government. 2. Peasant uprisings—Peru—Huanta
(Province)—History—19th century. 3. Indians of
South America—Peru—Huanta (Province)—
Government relations. 4. Peru—Politics and
government. I. Title.
F3451.H79M46 2005
985'.05—dc22   2004022944